C0046 4325

C000071736

Jeanne Sutherland first went to Moscow in 1952 to work on Soviet internal affairs in the British Embassy at the height of the cold war. In Moscow she met her husband, Iain Sutherland, and later accompanied him on his diplomatic assignments, often working herself and always taking the opportunity to explore the countries in which they lived. In 1977 she completed an MA in Soviet Studies and began her research into Soviet (afterwards Russian) education. She is the author of *Schooling in the New Russia, Innovation and Change, 1984–95*.

For my children and grandchildren

FROM MOSCOW TO CUBA AND BEYOND

A Diplomatic Memoir of the Cold War

Jeanne Sutherland

The Radcliffe Press
LONDON • NEW YORK

Published in 2010 by I.B.Tauris & Co. Ltd
6 Salem Road, London W2 4BU
175 Fifth Avenue, New York NY 10010
www.ibtauris.com

Distributed in the United States and Canada Exclusively by Palgrave Macmillan,
175 Fifth Avenue, New York NY 10010

ISBN 978 1 84885 474 1

A full CIP record for this book is available from the British Library
A full CIP record for this book is available from the Library of Congress
Library of Congress catalog card: available

Typeset in Sabon by Dexter Haven Associates Ltd, London
Printed and bound in India by Replika Press Pvt Ltd

CONTENTS

LIST OF ILLUSTRATIONS

LIST OF ILLUSTRATIONS

.

ACKNOWLEDGEMENTS

I was prompted to write this book because of all the letters which Iain's parents had kept over more than thirty years. So perhaps I should begin by thanking David and Dorothy Sutherland, posthumously, for never throwing anything away. It was intended as something to leave for my children and grandchildren who might be interested in reading about their parents' and grandparents' peripatetic life. But as I continued writing I began to show it to family and friends, some of whom encouraged me to consider offering it for publication and gave criticism and advice.

Some, who had either written or edited books themselves, such as my American friends Roz and Eric Schneider, patiently read the text from the very early stages, made innumerable helpful suggestions about the format and corrected some of my early errors. My sister-in-law, Anne Sutherland, dug out letters that I had not discovered, read and criticised my writing and tried to make me keep it clear and correct. Sandra and Rodney Shields (author of *Margarita's Olive Press*) also read the text from the beginning and encouraged me to continue. Geoffrey and Kathy Murrell, former colleagues in Moscow and specialists on the area, read the chapter on the former Yugoslavia and gave me advice and help. Jane Grayson, a former lecturer in Russian literature at London University, and one of the supervisors for my MA, constantly encouraged me and urged me to go on looking for a publisher. My neighbour, Hilary Laurie, took time to give me a long list of those whom she thought might be interested. The Radcliffe Press was one of them.

To these, and all the others who have helped and encouraged me during the six or seven year long struggle, I am immensely grateful.

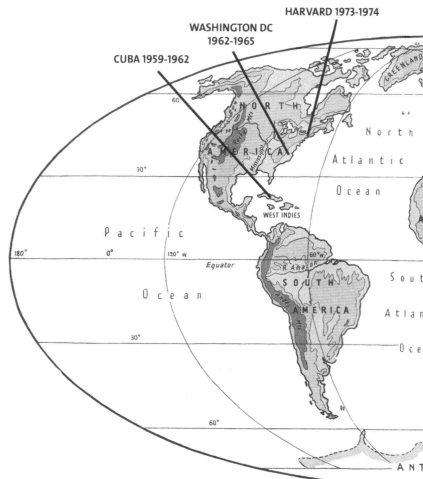

FORE

HARVARD 1973-1974

WASHINGTON DC
1962-1965

CUBA 1959-1962

GREENLAND

60

N O R T H

North

A M E R I C A

Atlantic

30°

Ocean

WEST INDIES

P a c i f i c

180°   0°   120° w

60°w

Equator   R. Amazon

S O U T H

Sout

O c e a n

A M E R I C A

Atlan

30°

Oce

60°

90

A N T

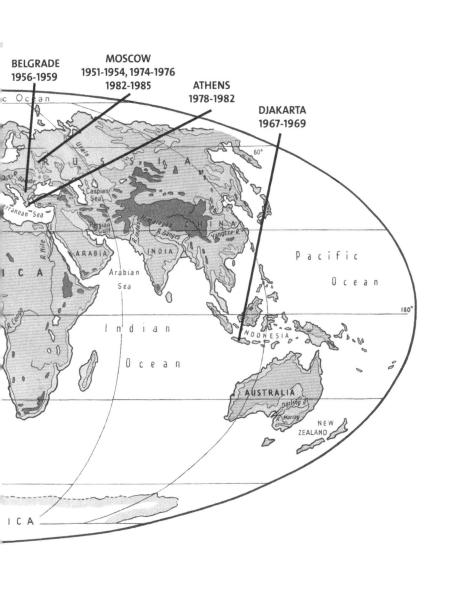

BELGRADE
1956-1959

MOSCOW
1951-1954, 1974-1976
1982-1985

ATHENS
1978-1982

DJAKARTA
1967-1969

INTRODUCTION

This is a book about letters, about a diplomatic family who served in many varied posts for over 30 years, about the history of the countries they lived in and how it affected their lives. The letters are written by my late husband, Iain, and myself, and occasionally by someone else connected with the family, to my husband's parents. The diary entries in the last chapters are mine.

My husband and I spent over thirty years in the diplomatic service, in the Soviet Union three times, in America twice, in the former Yugoslavia, Cuba, Indonesia and Greece, being uprooted and packing up every two, three or four years and moving on to the next place, sometimes with intervening postings in London. For both of us Moscow was our first posting in the Foreign Service and it is there that we met in the 1950s. We were married later in London, in the Crown Court Church of Scotland, originally the Church of the Scottish Embassy in London. And perhaps appropriately our wedding reception was held in the Ambassadors' waiting room in the Foreign Office.

As we served three times in the former Soviet Union (seven years in all) Russia is the country which most influenced our lives. I went there first at a young and impressionable age, after three years at university reading modern languages (French, Spanish and Russian), a few years dabbling in the banking world in London and working for the Air Ministry in the Embassy in Paris. Iain went after an English degree at the University of Aberdeen, serving in the army (part of the time in India) and doing PPE at Balliol College, Oxford, post demobilisation in 1947. He was given a year's Russian language tuition by the Foreign Office, part of which was spent at London University and part with a Russian émigré family in Paris. He came from a family of Scottish artists, was born in Edinburgh but spent most of his school life in Aberdeen.

1

Iain left Moscow in autumn 1953 and I in August 1954. We were not to return until 1974, twenty years later. By this time we were married with a family of three children, Iain was Minister in the Embassy, Deputy Chief of Mission, as it is now called. Being number two in the embassy meant that, in the absence of the Ambassador, Iain had to take charge. He took this very seriously and often did not come home for meals, hence the Sandwiches for the Chargé.

1

ARRIVAL IN MOSCOW 1951–52

M oscow in the 1950s was a strange, unknown and mysterious, if not sinister, place. It went a long way to fulfilling the Churchillian definition of Russia, 'a riddle wrapped in a mystery, inside an enigma'. It was only the specialists, the Kremlinologists, who were aware, or only partly aware as the case may be, of what was going on. Diplomats and journalists working in the Soviet Union tried to make sense of the little information that was available to the west but they had difficulty in finding out what was really happening. In fact they probably knew less than those in London or Washington.

Stalin was elderly and lacked the strength to control the country as he had in the past. He feared the exposure of his weaknesses by the colleagues who surrounded him and those who had witnessed, for example, the near panic he had shown in the early stages of the war. In the Politburo he was surrounded, among others, by such well-known old Soviet hands as Beria, Bulganin, Voroshilov, Molotov, Mikoyan and Malenkov. Others such as Khrushchev and Brezhnev were to become better known later. Stalin still wielded the power but there was already rivalry among the other leaders for the inheritance although this could only be guessed at by foreigners living in Moscow at that time. It was only later that the world began to learn more about his erratic, not to say manic behaviour in the last years of his life, and of the terror and trickery with which he managed to keep his supreme control.

This restricted and threatening political situation obviously had strong bearing on the life of foreigners living in the Soviet Union, particularly on diplomats from western embassies, as it did in fact on anyone living in the country. It was an uncomfortable and insecure existence. Apart from rare official occasions there was practically no contact between western diplomats and Russians. We did not even meet them except for those delegated to have contact with us, such as the members of the protocol department of the Ministry of Foreign Affairs; or casually in shops, restaurants etc. We did have Russian language teachers and Russian servants provided by the department of the foreign ministry delegated to look after foreign diplomats, known as *Burobin* (*Buro po usluzhivaniu innostrannykh*). *Burobin* provided everything, accommodation, servants (who were more or less obligatory and were there largely to watch what their employers were doing and report back), teachers, theatre tickets, train or plane tickets, hotels, or even a whole sheep for the Argentinian Ambassador's barbecue. Very little could be done direct or without the intervention of *Burobin*.

The standard of living was very low. The country was still struggling to recover from the enormous losses of men and material caused by the war. Although strides had been made in industrial development, agricultural production did not keep pace and the food supplies were still very inadequate. There was considerable disagreement over the implementation of the agricultural policy among leading members of the Politburo. Stalin may even have been prepared to countenance this disagreement in order to prevent the leaders from combining too heavily against him.[1]

Accommodation for the average Russian was very poor. Apart from the elite members of society most lived in communal flats, where as many as forty people might share one large flat and the kitchen and bathroom facilities. Rooms which contained more than one family would be divided by partitions or hangings of some kind. There were few consumer goods to buy in the shops and what was available was in great demand. In the winter many people still wore the traditional felt boots, *valenki*, and padded quilted jackets to keep themselves warm in what seemed to be then invariably temperatures of -15° to -20° degrees centigrade.

First impressions of Moscow in the 1950s from Sally Leyland, a member of the Russian Secretariat were of a dismal drabness.

There is little colour to be seen in the streets or Metro. This impression of drabness is strengthened by the appearance of the buildings which are shabby and in need of paint and repair; entrances and stairways leading to flats are stark whatever the locality. There are no attempts to beautify private dwellings as far as one can judge from outside, but the public buildings such as the Palaces of Culture are better cared for and the *Agitpunkte*, whose doorways are framed in red bunting and illuminated like the cinemas, provide a break in the dun-coloured monotony. Drabness plays no part in the theatrical production where spectacular effects, mechanical invention, massed crowds, the continual changing of scenery are the order of the day.

Visits to the big universal stores provided surprises. I had not expected to find such a range of non-utilitarian goods available. There are coloured dresses for big and small; hats plain and hats elaborate; coats, costumes, nylon stockings; cosmetics, perfume, scented soap. All these goods are shoddy by western standards, but they were eagerly pounced on by the Soviet citizen. Stores are always overcrowded and there would appear to be a shortage of shopping space.[2]

* * *

Under the rules set out in September 1948 all foreign diplomats were required to tell the Ministry of Foreign Affairs 48 hours in advance where and when they were going outside the 50-kilometre area (later to be reduced to 40 kilometres) around Moscow. If the authorities did not wish the visit to take place for any reason, some excuse would be given, that the trains or planes were full, or there were no rooms in the hotels. This would happen even in areas officially open to travel by foreigners. About one third of the Soviet Union was declared out of bounds. This included all the coastal and frontier areas except Leningrad and Odessa, most of the non-Russian areas of the Soviet Union and most of the industrial areas – the Urals, Donbas and main Volga towns. All the Moscow oblast outside the 50-kilometre limit was out of bounds for travel by car. There was no objection to travelling by train or plane through a forbidden area provided no stop was made. In 1951 the position deteriorated and members of the Embassy, particularly the Service Attachés, failed on many occasions to obtain tickets for places officially permitted.

A despatch from the Embassy in Moscow to the Foreign Office written in January 1951 describes the sort of thing that could happen to travellers attempting to venture into 'those parts of the Soviet Union which they are not formally forbidden to go but where their presence is not desired. It is sufficient to say that they are treated there in the same way as unprivileged Soviet citizens.' They had to wait in the street for several days, unable to use the waiting room at the station, not allowed to sleep there and only allowed in one hour before the train left. During their visit to the autonomous republic of Dagestan they were not allowed to stay anywhere in Mahachkala or Derbent and spent two nights and a day walking the streets and sitting in cafés. Finally they gave in and bought a ticket back to Moscow. A letter from Sir William Strang, Permanent under Secretary at that time, said that the King had read the account with much interest.[3]

However Russia is a very big country and in spite of the restrictions there were large areas open to travellers. Travel was one of the best ways of finding out anything about the country and the people, how they were living and what they were thinking. On trains, aeroplanes and buses it was easier to talk to Russians, who knew that they would probably never see us again and therefore were less inhibited about talking to foreigners. In spite of the restrictions members of the Embassy were able to visit a wide range of places. In the two years that I was in the Soviet Union I was able to travel from the White Sea in the north to the Black Sea in the south, and as far as Kazan and Kurgan in the east and Tbilisi in the Caucasus. After Stalin's death we were allowed to travel much further and large areas in Central Asia became open to foreigners, particularly the cities of Samarkand, Bukhara and Tashkent in Uzbekistan.

The official Intourist hotels only existed in the bigger towns which were open to foreigners but we were also allowed to visit some of the smaller old, historic towns to the north of Moscow, such as Zagorsk, Kostroma, Novgorod, Pskov, Vladimir and Suzdal. Here the hotels were very primitive, often without indoor toilets and with communal washing facilities. I remember quite interesting conversations with visiting party secretaries as they shaved and I had a discreet wash.

The city of Moscow was much smaller than the modern city of today. It virtually finished at the *Sadovoe koltso* (Garden Ring). None of the large radial roads extending out into the suburbs, constructed in the time of Khrushchev and lined by the blocks of apartment buildings, existed. There was little traffic. The wide streets and squares, which could only be crossed at specific places or at the risk of being stopped and fined by the militiaman on duty, were substantially empty.

* * *

Contact with local people was not possible except on the most ephemeral basis. Otherwise any Russians known to have more than casual contact with western diplomats risked serious trouble. As a result members of foreign embassies led a very inward looking social life. For those who spoke Russian, the compensations were the theatre, and also excellent ballet and opera. There was skiing in the winter and in the summer tennis on the Embassy court, which also doubled up in winter as a skating rink. For the more adventurous there was skating along the paths of Gorky Park. If one had a job during the day and was interested in Russian literature and culture, it was an interesting if restricted and unreal life.

Iain went out to Moscow as a 3rd Secretary in September 1951, when Sir Alvary Gascoigne was Ambassador. I arrived in 1952 to be the librarian/archivist and the most junior member of the Russian Secretariat, which was concerned with the internal affairs of the Soviet Union. Also in the Secretariat when I arrived were Tom Brimelow, the head, Sally Leyland (to be replaced after a few months by Jill Sheppard) and Dick Freeborn, a Russian scholar and academic who was to become Professor of Russian Literature at London University. For some reason the Ambassador was known to refer to me absentmindedly as 'that nice Miss Church who lives at the bottom of the garden'. It was of course not my name.

The normal means of transport in those days was by sea from London (Tilbury Docks), often on the Russian boat, the *Beloostrov*. This was a week's journey through the North Sea and the Kiel Canal, with pleasant stops, if the boat was making good time, in Stockholm and Helsinki. The boat was small with not many passengers. It was not luxurious nor was the food *haute cuisine* but it was a pleasant journey in reasonable summer weather and gave one time to prepare for the changeover from western culture to the limitations of life in the Soviet Union in the early 1950s. It was also, incidentally, after the death of Stalin, an opportunity for the personable young first officer to make overtures to the young unaccompanied female passengers.

* * *

The period covered by Iain's letters was not an easy time either for the Russians or for the foreigners living in Russia. It was the height of the cold war. They were the last years of Stalin's life. The party had struggled to regain its absolute hold on the country, which had been somewhat relaxed during the time of the war. In spite of the disasters in the early part of the war, Stalin had managed to set himself up as the saviour of his country. The purges of the 1930s had ensured that most of his possible opponents had been eliminated and had made his position even stronger than before. The death of Zhdanov in 1948 followed by the execution of Voznesensky and the elimination of the 'Leningrad group' had further strengthened his position. Stalin saw Leningrad as a rival to Moscow and a danger to his power, and for this reason he got rid of party leaders and Soviet officials who were arrested and executed.[4]

This still left many leaders of the party who had been in power and working together for many years, including some who were possible successors. Several people suggest that Stalin was considering another purge before his death but that he died before he was able to carry it out. There were undoubtedly differences of opinion among the Politburo members over questions of policy, and rivalries among them for the post of Stalin's successor (the main candidates being Beria and Malenkov), rivalries that Stalin no doubt used to his own advantage. In 1949 several of Stalin's closest colleagues had been deprived of their ministries, although they were appointed or remained deputy prime ministers of the USSR and there had been no question of demotion. This included Molotov in Foreign Affairs, Bulganin in Defence and Mikoyan in the Ministry of Foreign Trade and belied a possible lack of confidence and suspicion of these close associates.[5]

The American historian, Adam Ulam, writes that 'An impenetrable mystery appears to surround the events of the last four years of Stalin's life and reign'. An ageing despot, who had always ruled by imposing fear and mystification, he now found himself isolated and alone and anxious to avoid the company of those who would see that he was becoming old and no longer constantly alert; and that he was losing his self-confidence and physical vigour.[6]

Into this atmosphere of fear and suspicion Stalin launched his treatise on linguistics, an attack on the accepted authorities on the subject, except that the major exponent of linguistic theory whom he attacked, Professor Marr, died before Stalin could do him any major harm. Stalin's main argument was that Russian should be the ultimate language for the proletariat. But it was not only in linguistics that Stalinist theory was paramount. All the arts suffered under his dictatorship. Through Zhdanov he had attacked writers, particularly those from Leningrad such as Zoshchenko and Akhmatova, and musicians such as Prokofiev and Shostakovich for failing to live up to Marxist-Leninist norms. 'Stalin's last years marked the nadir of intellectual and cultural life in the USSR. Both Marxism and Russian nationalism were raided to produce a crude, reductionist and paranoid view of the world, which was made obligatory for every artist and scholar, indeed for anyone who wished to get into print.[7]

Zhdanov was said to be an intelligent and well-read man, but was used by Stalin to carry out the policy of cultural suppression. His death, though unexpected, was not considered to be sinister, although it is said that Stalin attributed it to incompetence of the doctors attending him. Zhdanov was apparently asthmatic. His family survived unharmed after his death although his son was in fact married for a while to Stalin's daughter, Svetlana Allilluyeva, but they were divorced after a short time.

* * *

What other events stand out in this period of 'impenetrable mystery'? In domestic affairs one of the chief areas of difference of opinion was that of party policy on agriculture and the production of food, a problem that was never to be solved during the lifetime of the Soviet Union. During the early 1950s party policy was to amalgamate the collective farms into bigger units largely with the aim of providing stronger and firmer party control in each farm. This control had become lax during the war years when many peasants had hoped that the collective farms would be dissolved. However, plans for amalgamation went ahead. By 1950 the 250,000 collective farms had been reduced to 121,400 and by the end of 1952 there were only 94,800. Many peasant farmers lost their private plots and were forced to work for minimal wages on state farms. Workers on collective farms had to give so much produce to the state that they had nothing left for themselves. Grain harvests improved very slowly and by 1952 the harvest was still below 1940 levels.[8]

Steps were taken to restore the strong grip of the party on all spheres of life. Party schools were set up with training centres for party secretaries, instructors and propagandists. There was little freedom for the average Soviet citizen and practically no choice. From the earliest age children were subject to the party cell system. Each row of desks in kindergarten or primary school competed with the rest for best work and behaviour awards. From this smallest Communist cell they graduated to be members of the Pioneers, the All-Union Lenin Pioneer Organisation, the youngest Communist children's organisation, for those aged from ten to fifteen, and from there to the Komsomol (the All-Union Communist League of Youth), which could lead in later life to membership of the Communist Party itself. Without that membership it was difficult for young people to graduate and move into prestigious higher education, and finally into good jobs and membership of the party. Without membership of the party it was impossible to reach the higher echelons of one's profession or be allowed to travel abroad or enjoy any of the privileges of the elite. This was the more positive side of life. What was more unpleasant was what could happen to those who infringed the rules of the party, or even to those who failed to report infringements of others. This was still very much the period of the middle of the night knock on the door and the disappearance of anyone who did not wholly support the regime, or did not comply with communist ruling, or perhaps even who had dared to displease the leadership in some way.

To ensure that Soviet citizens could not develop any kind of friendship with westerners without being in serious trouble, western diplomats in Moscow were usually followed by members of the MGB.[9] This certainly happened if they went outside the 40-kilometre limit. Service Attachés and senior members of the Embassy were constantly followed, junior members less so.

The effects of the cold war were obvious everywhere. There was anti-western propaganda in the press and in public notices and slogans in the streets. There were constant references to the 'American–English war mongers'. The large-scale development of the armaments industry, which continued after the war and which discouraged any increase in consumer goods production, was deemed essential against any attack by the United States. Stalin feared war and did not want war and trusted that the Americans would not wish to initiate conflict with a nation by then armed with nuclear weapons. But it was necessary to take precautions. When in 1950, North Korea attacked South Korea and was supplied with arms by the Russians, Stalin had not expected that the South would be supported by American troops. The Korean war dragged on until after his death.

* * *

Iain mentions in his letters the introduction of greater restrictions on the movements of foreigners in the Soviet Union, which reduced the areas open to travel. He also talks a lot about his visits to the Bolshoi Theatre and the very high standard particularly of the ballet. Visits to the Bolshoi were also a welcome distraction, even if one did meet the same people in the intervals. They were also a relief from the drabness of Soviet life outside. They provided beauty and colour and wonderful music, a kind of fairyland compared with the streets of Moscow and there was Russian champagne and caviar to be had in the interval.

* * *

Iain's first letter to his parents in Cults, Aberdeenshire, after his arrival in Moscow for the first time in October 1951, describes his impressions of the city and the country at this time.

Moscow, Thursday October 1951

Dear M & D,

We arrived this morning. Yes, in Moscow. If I open the windows of the comfortable room where I am writing, double-paned against the cold, and look across the Embassy garden, I can see the dark square block of the Embassy building, which was once the imposing mansion of a merchant prince; and just beyond the porch and the uniformed guards at the gates, the dark slow-moving waters of the Moskva River lap against the embankment. And on the other side they wash the ramparts of the Kremlin. From the window I can see two of the great red illuminated stars which shine at night from the pinnacles of the spired towers at this side of the great fortress-town. For it is vast, an assembly of palaces and towers and domes rising above the long, red, crenellated ramparts: and one of the most beautiful sights in the world. It is quite breath-taking as one comes upon it suddenly, driving along the broad rather empty streets, with dark drab-coloured people on the pavements, and past the tall modern buildings which line the main

1. View of the Kremlin from the Embassy, 1950s.

11

thoroughfares, and which on the whole seem to be built in a rather tasteless flashy style. But I have not seen the city properly in daylight – only a rapid drive from the Leningrad Station before lunch, and another this afternoon, along Gorky Street, across the Red Square, across the river and along the bank to the Embassy. So I first saw the Kremlin across Red Square, which one knows so well from photographs. The squat square-stepped structure one had seen was there in the middle, like the entrance to some concrete dug-out built by the possessors of modern alien weapons to threaten the golden domes and the delicate oriental crenellations of the walls behind. The tomb of Lenin. And even as in the photographs the drab dark-clad people had formed into a long straggling line across the square queuing to see the dead, mummified body of their leader. I believe if I produce my little grey diplomatic card I can break that queue. For I have priority, and am one of the privileged here. Life in the Embassy is a weird contrast of privileges and restrictions, both equally fantastic. Since I landed yesterday at midday at the quay at Leningrad, I have experienced some of the privileges. I have travelled in the streamlined Intourist taxis; I lunched in the Hotel Astoria in the ambassadorial suite, where the chairs are covered in pink satin. I travelled in the rather uncomfortable but curiously ornate first class sleeping coaches of the 'Red Arrow', the Moscow train, and woke this morning to my first Russian countryside; miles and miles of open forest, irregular areas and clumps of pine and larch broken by glades and little valleys and grey green marshes. And amongst them the most beautiful birches with silver white stems you have ever dreamed of, and all now in the different golden yellow shades of autumn. And in the forest here and there, but more often in wide clearings, villages of wooden huts with log walls and carved eaves, and thatched or felt roofs, some painted blue, some yellow, mostly grey and weather beaten and picturesquely dilapidated. Yes, the whole was very picturesque, and in a remarkable unfamiliar range of oranges and blues and browns which I have seen in no other countryside. It was very beautiful under the cold light of an autumn dawn. And at the same time excessively gloomy and depressing. The poverty is very great. Or perhaps it is squalor rather than poverty. I have seen Indian villages which were certainly much poorer but seldom anything which so lacked animation. Perhaps it is the influence of the climate, and the drab shapeless clothes which everyone wears even now when it is comparatively mild. The villages on the route today reminded me somewhat of pictures of sixteenth or seventeenth century villages in the west or perhaps of a period much earlier, before the enclosures – each with its flock of geese, its lean cows, complete lack of made roads and unfenced fields. And then suddenly one would pass a power plant or a vast untidy dump of scrap iron or the large concrete silage towers of a collective farm – then again the forest and the thatched huts.

I have nowhere yet to stay here. A large party came with the Ambassador, more with us and there is very limited accommodation for diplomats. So I was to have put up in a hotel until the middle of November. But the Metropole Hotel informed the Embassy this morning that they could not put up a person like me in their limited room at the time of the Patriotic Celebration of November 7th.

So I am staying in the flat of one Robin Farqhuarson, 3rd Secretary and the Ambassador's private secretary, who lives by himself in a very comfortable kind of mews flat behind the Embassy Garden. I had an excellent supper alone, served by his maid, a Volga German from Kuibishev. He is leaving fairly soon, but it is doubtful if I should get this flat. But what does seem certain is that I shall have to share a flat and I will not be in a mess or anything equivalent. Elizabeth (Richardson, later Hammarskjöld) is sharing a flat in a fairly new block where I had lunch, with a girl in the Soviet Press Reading Section. The two second secretaries in Chancery have a kind of bungalow in the country outside Moscow and come in every day and it is possible I might get a vacant place there. Resumed Friday but with a very short time in which to write. So I must put off any description of Leningrad till next week. We had time after lunch and a drink in the lavish tasteless hotel to walk through some of the very beautiful streets and see the Neva and the Winter Palace: we even had time to see the first two acts of *Swan Lake* in the exquisite Marigny Theatre.

With love, Iain

Vakhtangova 9, Moscow, 1 November 1951

Dear M & D,

I must accustom myself to eighteenth century habits of writing – to the fact that posts do not come and go several times in the week, and that I cannot hope for answers in under a fortnight. I can of course use the post boxes at the street corners, but letters so sent must be assumed subject to Soviet scrutiny.

When I wrote I had scarcely settled down here. I write now from the drawing room of the flat which belongs to Colonel Prynne, the Military Attaché. But flat is a rather inadequate term to describe the ground floor of what must once have been the large town house of a member of the Russian nobility or some high merchant. And the

13

room is of noble proportions which hold over seventy at a cocktail party and has three full-length double width and double thickness windows. Few if any Russians live in rooms like this. For most of such old houses where they still exist are now institutions of some kind or another – children's crèches or worker's clubs. To own such a flat is of course here a mark of some wealth and privilege. For the housing shortage here is appalling by English standards. Moscow does not cover a large area on the map, less than one third, I believe of that covered by London and it is remarkable how soon one can drive out into the country. But seven million live here. I do not intend now to attempt to describe Moscow. My contacts and views so far have been almost entirely within the Embassy; my knowledge of the city and the Russians confined to a few walks round the streets and to talking to some of the servants and drivers and occasionally asking my way. It is easy to get lost not that it is a difficult city, at least in the centre, but no maps are ever posted up, nor is it possible to buy one as none are published.

I resumed this today Wednesday. I still write at Colonel Prynne's in his large and dignified drawing room. Here I am no doubt much more comfortably off though his spare room is rather large and bare, and like nearly all interiors here overheated and excessively dry. Dryness is one of the chief enemies here indoors. Woodwork and pictures crack, glasses suddenly shatter and people drink copious quantities of orangeade – usually from what I have seen, with gin as well. And when I arrived the Colonel was greatly concerned for the sounding board of his new clavichord. He is one of the twelve persons in England who play the lute, and his own treasured instrument lies in a glass case behind me beside a large collection of Elizabethan music. He constructed the lute himself. He is also an expert on hawking and a student of mathematical chess. He has a family in England and lives here alone. He has an intimate knowledge of wild flowers and their cultivation in gardens. But he is not what one might have pictured as the senior Military Attaché from Britain to the USSR.

When I leave here I may go to live at a place called Perlovka which is out in the country about 15 kilometres from the Embassy. The three bachelor members of Chancery live in this large wooden-built dacha or country villa set in an extensive garden and a copse of pine trees. The area was on a very long lease to the firm of Metro-Vickers in the early 1930s and after the Trials and the withdrawal of Vickers it was donated by them to the Embassy. So it is the only accommodation for which HMG does not pay fantastically high rents. It is a delightful rustic kind of shooting lodge with wooden walls and tiled peasant stoves and Bukhara rugs on the walls and a private skating pond outside the windows and a special member of the Ministry of the Interior's militia to patrol the gates on 24-hour watch. I had lunch there on Saturday. But it would be rather inconvenient to live there without a car. Two of the others have obtained Soviet driving permits, a difficult task which includes an explanation of the workings of the internal combustion engine in Russian.

Moscow is not an easy place to drive in. There is not a great deal of traffic in the broad streets of the centre of the city. Except for the trolley buses and a few lorries all modern Russian models are of about five different kinds; all fairly large and new looking. They must look new because old cars are not allowed on the streets, and they must be clean and tidy because you can be fined if your car is not washed and polished.

I should not jump so from subject to subject and then revert to the kind of description which I declared I should postpone. But it is easy to write intelligibly about flats and families and members of the staff, about their lunches and the lives they lead because there one can assume a measure of knowledge, one can assume that even if you do not know what kind of lunches we have, you will know that we ate with knives and forks and talked about the voyage out, and the Moscow theatres, and the trip made by Robert Longmire last week to Novgorod. You may not know that we have always had wine at our lunch parties and today Caucasian champagne. You may not know that Mrs Dobbs' little boy understands Russian better than English. But these things fill in an intelligible picture. But for Moscow outside that of the streets, the theatres, the shops and the people this is very, very difficult. I can mention unusual features which would probably astonish you in many ways. But I cannot assume that you will equate these to their background. And as so many fantastic pictures have been given of life here, you may take these peculiarities as typical whereas it is more than often the similarities between what one sees here and what one has seen every day in London and Paris and doesn't quite expect to find here, which are most surprising. If I said that the four enormous many-storied blocks of offices which they are constructing in the centre of the city have the most extraordinary castellated turrets and spires on top you would probably assume that they are strange in other respects. In fact they are otherwise rather like the central building of London University or some of New York's skyscrapers. If I say that there are no private shops in Moscow at all, even old apple-women with trays have signs on their boards saying they are section so and so of the distribution branch of the fresh food group of the Ministry of Alimentation, you may imagine that the shops are utterly different from those in Union Street which would again be untrue in most respects, or that they all resemble one another like so many Woolworths. By the way you can buy much more than the post report suggested, but most things are shoddy and everything is dear. So descriptions of Moscow must be very full in order not to be misleading to one who has not been here. And even then it must always be remembered they are descriptions by witnesses who are prevented from asking those questions and receiving the answers which are normally regarded as essential before one starts to make remarks and judgements about other people's natures.

Love, Iain

Embassy, Sofiiskaia Naberezhnaia, Moscow, USSR

Dear M,

Three letters this morning. The King's messenger was delayed in Warsaw by snow and with him your letters. So I write in much the same haste as last week from the office. This has been a week of farewells at the station, not counting the Air Commodore who died of pneumonia. Fred Warner and Philip de Zulueta left the day before yesterday, first and second secretaries who lived out at the dacha at Perlovka. Today a further party leaves to join the *Belo-Ostrov*, the bereaved Mrs Bird, wife of the Air Attaché, the energetic Miss Flynn, Sir David Kelly's secretary, and Mr and Mrs Dobbs whom I am very sorry to see go. He has been head of the Secretariat here. His replacement (Tom Brimelow) arrives tomorrow from Cuba with wife and two children. He knows Moscow and was here in the worst period of the war, in the Kuibyshev days.

Very cold now – fur hat and lined coat days with minus twenty centigrade on the thermometer at the dacha garage. Icy surfaces on the roads and little children skating on some of the main streets. The river has frozen over in front of the Embassy. The tennis court at Perlovka has been flooded and I tried out my new skates on Sunday last when we had a lunch party with ice hockey. On Wednesday I paid my first visit to the Bolshoi and there saw the State Ballet Company in what was certainly the most lavish and magnificent performance I have ever seen on any stage – in the ballet *Romeo and Juliet*. It was exceedingly moving, the chief role being taken by Moscow prima ballerina Ulanova whom many critics consider to be the greatest living dancer. The costumes and settings were beautiful, the vast stage often held well over a hundred dancers at a time and none of the supporting cast was in any way second-rate as is so often the case in London. The ballet follows Shakespeare very faithfully which is more than can be said for a play, *Mnogo shuma iz nichevo (Much Ado About Nothing)* which I saw at the Vakhtangova Theatre on Monday. This was downright bad, acting, interpretation, décor and all. But I have not yet seen the Arts Theatre or the Maly which are considered excellent. These, the Ballet, the Circus and the Puppet theatres are the highlights of Moscow entertainment. Everything else and literally so, is created as propaganda.

Love, Iain

Perlovka, Saturday evening 24 November 1951

Dear M & D,

Today is Saturday so I have not been in to Moscow. Indeed I lay late abed after a very late ride back in Tom Sewell's car last night after the 12.30 train had steamed out of the Leningradsky Voksal (station) with some departing members of the Embassy. It is a ritual that departing officials are seen off at the platform and last night's consignment were given a send off by a party of over fifty, including members of other embassies and legations. I had come from the American Embassy and arrived early, stumping up and down the platform in my flying boots with Father Brassard, the Moscow Roman Catholic Priest. The temperature was -20°C.

I write alone in the wood-lined sitting room of our dacha with only Pushkin the large yellow-eyed tabby cat to keep me company. Nikolai, the doorman and woodcutter, and Tania the cook have gone to their small wooden home at the end of the garden. Our guardian militiaman will still be outside – on the other side of the fence, stamping his feet to keep out the cold. Tom has just gone off to Moscow taking home a young Swedish girl who came out to lunch and stayed to supper, she the lively daughter of a distinguished Swedish Military Attaché here. Mark Alford, the naval lieutenant our other *dachnik* has not returned. We cleaned the layer of snow from our rink this afternoon and re-flooded it. So tomorrow we can hope for some skating, when the Talbots come to lunch. You asked for some personalities so I shall give you them. But the Talbots you know as the new Naval Attaché and his family who came out with me on the *Belo-Ostrov*. One advantage of my present position of no fixed abode is that I incur no entertainment obligations but at the same time benefit from those arranged by others – a lazy and selfish attitude. Had dinner last night at Robin Farquharson's, behind the Embassy. Lunch with

Kenneth Parsons the visa officer, who took Russian at Oxford when I was there, and his wife who also works in the Embassy in their flat at *Narodnaia*. This is another block of 'diplomatic' flats on the embankment of the Moskva river. There is another called *Sadovaia*. Both are blocks entirely occupied by members of western embassies. The Poles and the Chinese etc. are similarly contained only in different blocks. There is also a 'democratic peoples' section at *Sadovaia*. The flats are pleasant and light and recently built only they suffer from that lack of finish which one finds everywhere in constructions here. The imposing front of *Sadovaia* is entirely spoilt by the fact that the covering layer of concrete has never been applied to the béton of the balconies. Doors seldom fit and electric installations are incomplete or defective. Elizabeth shares a flat at the *Sadovaia* block.

Monday. Yes we skated yesterday as I had hoped. But the surface of our rink was uneven. We sprayed it when there were too many degrees of frost and it froze unevenly. It is strange that the temperatures which we have been having, much colder than it ever becomes in Britain, do not feel excessively so. A cold damp wind on the Mannofield Road can be more chilling and much more disagreeable. Here the air is very dry. So dry that when the rivers freeze up they steam, and enormous billowing clouds come out of the boilers of railway engines soaring up into the sky and in fact forming real cumulus masses which remain long after the train has gone. And trains here are pretty slow.

We receive a subsidised rate of 50 roubles to the pound here, whereas the official rate is 11.6 to the pound. This is to encourage us to go out and about, travel, attend theatres etc. and which makes us unusually richer than the Americans who do not receive this bonus. There is not much to buy here should I ever save any subsidised roubles after paying for living expenses. There are a few things – books, gramophone records are very cheap but of inferior quality, Bokhara carpets which are not cheap but are less expensive than in London; caviar, and perhaps linen mats and cloths and some of the strange items which find their way into 'Commission shops'. These are state-owned second-hand shops where such things as Victorian bronze figures and oil paintings, baroque candelabras and cut glass command fantastically high prices. However intrepid commission shop hunters (Lady Kelly was said to be one) have found old Tsarist jewellery, and looted Meissen china, and old masters with the marks of East German museums, sold for little or nothing. All silver is sold by weight and judging by those I have seen, oil paintings by the foot.

Last night I went to the Bolshoi Theatre to see the spectacular ballet *Bakhchiserai Fountain*. The beautiful bride is seized by the

Tartars from her palace in the Ukraine and carried off to the harem of the great Khan. Struchkova played the principal role. And nothing in any ballet can surely equal the vigour and savagery of the great Tartar dance with whips which closes the third act. This week is Uzbek Week. Moscow welcomes (and criticises) the work of the Uzbek SSR. So we have been 'covering' this from the Embassy. I went on Tuesday to a concert, dancing and choirs and the orchestra of the conservatory of Tashkent, seventy-strong, Mongolians in black ties and tailcoats playing Tchaikovsky and even Mozart on a bizarre assortment of oriental instruments. The choir was in Samarkand blue-striped pyjamas singing hymns in honour to Stalin, and the dancing troupe of very attractive Uzbek girls with long black pigtails dancing traditional intricate measures in red leather boots and silken trousers. And I visited too an exhibition of Uzbek art. *Pravda* had written lately condemning the art of this republic for addiction to idealism and bourgeois nationalism and not portraying in these paintings the great works of socialist construction. Actually a great part of the exhibition did portray these works – dam building and cotton picking and the presentation of memorials to Stalin the great teacher. There were some competent portraits of farmers and heroes of soviet labour and a few good landscapes. I was reminded of some war artist exhibitions in Britain. The crafts were very disappointing for a part of the world which once produced Bokhara carpets and Sanyassid pottery. I went to this with Mr Tom Brimelow, the new head of the Secretariat newly arrived from Cuba, who speaks excellent Russian. His last ambassador here was Sir Stafford Cripps. He has a wife and two daughters. The influx of married members of staff further complicates accommodation problems.

Hope Anne enjoyed her Boat-club Ball.

Love, Iain

Embassy, Moscow USSR, Wednesday,
concluded Friday 7 December 1951

Dear M & D,

Today is Constitution day – the day of the Stalin Constitution of 1936, and *Pravda* exhibits a half-page photograph of the leader on its front page and a full-page article on 'the most democratic constitution in the world'. I am here however in the office as I must wait until the evening before returning to Perlovka to take with me the mail which comes in this afternoon from Berlin, and also to take Cyril Ray of the *Sunday Times* who is invited to supper with us – also Mr and Mrs Brimelow the new head of the Secretariat and Elizabeth. And I am here too because last night I spent in town – until three a.m. at a party in the flat of the very pleasant Assistant Air Attaché, one Raymond Easterbrooke, and until about 10.30 chez Mrs Young, wife of the acting Air Attaché, who occasionally puts up Perlovka residents for the night. She is one of the more enterprising of the Embassy's wives who manages her two children, has learned to speak good Russian, and has travelled as widely in Russia as is possible for any of us. Easterbrooke is also one of those who see as much of and make the most of Russia as possible and is the best Russian speaker in the Embassy. He took the same course as myself some years ago and then spent six months in Paris. I have arranged to go with him to spend the Orthodox Christmas at Zagorsk, the monastery town north east of Moscow which was one of the greatest and richest foundations of the Russian Church and is still a place of pilgrimage.

Glad to hear that you are both well and hope you enjoy the Royal Scots dinner.

Love, Iain

Perlovka, Thursday evening 20 December 1951

Dear M & D,

Tomorrow's the last bag to go before Christmas. Yesterday's brought me a large tin box with a currant bun which we shall eat out here over the holiday. Perlovka is popular on holidays especially when there is skating and the self-contained flat on the ground floor where people camp out on weekends will be full for the next fortnight. Kenneth Parsons the visa officer and his wife Monica will be coming out with their ancient green car, and Elizabeth and Sally Leyland from the Secretariat, and possibly Cyril Ray from his lonely room in the Hotel Metropole. So we shall have a fairly full house for some days.

At Christmas there is a surfeit of parties and entertainments. And tomorrow morning I have to go in earlier than usual as I am going on a visit round the Kremlin. Last night was the Embassy staff Christmas dance which I had to attend. In order not to be there for the first half I arranged to go to the Bolshoi Theatre and saw for the second time Prokofiev's *Romeo and Juliet*. I went with a small party including Clara Hall, the last of the unfortunate Soviet wives to have contact with the Embassy. She now lives with her little boy at the bottom of the Embassy garden and dare not go out alone on the streets, and we had last night to take considerable precautions. You will remember the story of the wives of British subjects, mostly airmen, who were married in Russia during the war and who were never permitted to leave the country. Only a fortnight before I arrived there were two of these girls employed in the Embassy. But as you may have read in the press at the time the other left. The Soviet version which unfortunately was reproduced in most of the British press said that she left of her own accord and did not wish to return. The truth is that pressure was put on her relatives and that she was finally arrested one night by a whole troupe of militiamen. I think I have mentioned before the other virtual prisoner in the Embassy, George Bundock, the store man who has not been outside the gates for over two years. Strangely enough and typical of this country of anomalous contrasts Clara was not the only Russian at the Embassy dance, for contrary to expectations (Moscow citizens scarcely ever accept invitations) the Russian dancing teacher and light opera star turned up for this function in the hall of the Press Reading Section.

On Christmas Eve there is a carol concert with the Americans; and on Christmas day a service conducted by the Anglican bishop of Fulham who flew in today for a short visit. Moscow lies within his diocese together with Scandinavia and most of Europe as far as Switzerland. Fulham strangely does not. I was a little relieved that I was not given the job of accompanying him some time this week as interpreter on an official visit with a letter from the Archbishop of Canterbury to the Patriarch of All Russia, as my ecclesiastical vocabulary is very inadequate, and does not improve by reading the Soviet press. I did, however, pass my Russian exam and so have an extra £100 to my salary.

With best wishes for a Merry Christmas and for 1952,

Love, from Iain

Moscow, Thursday 27 December 1951

Dear M, D and Anne,

The last few days have not seen much time for writing, despite the holidays; so much time spent eating and entertaining in addition to filling in some work. We had five or six guests including the Parsons,

Elizabeth, and Cyril Ray. Christmas was complicated by the stay in Moscow of the Bishop of Fulham and a series of services and entertainments; carol singing and a party in the Ambassador's drawing room on Xmas Eve. And the party at the old British Consulate building and now the home of most of the junior female staff on Saturday lasted till five in the morning. Yesterday to the great monastery at Zagorsk, north east of Moscow (60 kilometres) with Tom Sewell in his car following the Bishop, Sir A. and Lady Gascoigne, Bob Longmire and the two poodles in the Rolls. All back to Perlovka to tea; and later minus the Ambassador's party, to skate on our pond at midnight. On Sunday a skating party with most of the members of the Dutch Embassy except the Ambassador and some Italians including the Conti di Gropello. The last is a very charming man who is not exactly a favourite of Sir A. Gascoigne as he used to organise Fascist riots and attacks on the British Consulate General in Tangier during the war when Sir A. was in charge and he was Italian consul.

Last week's visit to the Kremlin was put off at the last moment and I went this morning with Sir A. and Lady Gascoigne and the Bishop and some more. A visit of over four hours sightseeing is very tiring acting as interpreter the whole time. We were very fortunate in being the first party from the Embassy here to have seen the recently restored Uspensky Cathedral. We also saw the Blagoveshchensky Cathedral though not the Archangelsky. There are three cathedrals and five or six chapels within the Kremlin area. We saw the Great Palace and the Armoury Museum, the last contains the richest collection of silver and gold plate in the world.

But I must stop and send my love, Iain

(A letter from Iain written on black bordered paper after the death of King George VI)

Thursday 21 January 1952

Dear M & D,

This week I find myself at my desk in Chancery, partly because Elizabeth and Bob Longmire and Sally Leyland, three of the five members of the Secretariat staff made off for a three-day trip to Leningrad and left me alone in the left wing and Tom Brimelow in the library. All this must be very obscure no doubt to those who do not know the Embassy or the people in it. The Embassy was once, before the Revolution, the home of a wealthy extravagant manufacturer of bizarre tastes and was known as the 'Sugar King's Palace'. His tastes are revealed in the vast heavy brass chandeliers which hang in what is now the typistry, in the dark Gothic panelling of the hall and in the library with its balcony in the 'English' style which now houses the Secretariat. I was interested to read that M. Litvinov, recently dead, once occupied the Embassy building and lived very modestly with his wife and dogs on the second floor of the newly requisitioned mansion. It is there that Sir A. Gascoigne, his wife and dogs now live as Ambassador.

Love Iain

Sofiiskaia Naberezhnaia, Moscow, USSR, 31 January 1952

Dear D & M,

Yesterday a dinner in the evening; consultations with Monsieur Hureau, the French chef; correction of Miss Lugg's seating plan (she is Sir A.'s private personal assistant). And then attempts to entertain the wife of the Afghan Ambassador in conversation, not an easy matter as she only speaks Pushtu and German. The Ambassador is a pleasant old rogue, but she is rather unapproachable. It was he who is said to have remarked on one occasion that had he known Moscow was such a social place he would never have brought that wife with him. And we also had an emaciated French counsellor called Brionvall, an urbane character who has spent most of his career in Peking. Lit by candles on the long polished table with silver candelabras, the ornate Embassy dining room looked well and the frayed patches on the red damask on the walls were not visible.

Having sent you so scrappy a note last week I am somewhat behindhand in writing. Did I say that there have been further restrictions on the movement of members of the outcaste diplomatic community? You may have read of this in the newspapers. The noose has been tightened, symptomatic of the gradual worsening of relations. The ring round Moscow has been reduced in radius to forty from fifty kilometres. A long list of towns has been placed on the 'out of bounds' list for foreigners. Some of these, like Yakutsk, it has never been possible to visit, as there had always been found some excuse to prevent the issue of rail-tickets, or accommodation had been denied. But others like Kharkov, Omsk and Pskov, with its famous churches, have been visited several times by members of the Embassy in the last few years. Now they fall within the great area of Russia to which permits are never granted.

Another very disagreeable note from the Ministry last week ordered the withdrawal of the passport of one of the Embassy maids, that of the very able and pleasant Volga German who worked for Robin Farqhuarson in this very flat. All Soviet citizens of Moscow must possess the precious document of an internal passport; without it they can remain in none of the large towns of the Union. So Bertha had to set off for Karaganda in Siberia to join the rest of the Germans who were hunted out of their autonomous region in the Volga during the war and sent en masse to Karaganda. Against such persecutions of Soviet citizens who work for the Embassy we are quite powerless.

I hope you are both well and I wish you a happy birthday for today the 1st.

With love from Iain

Moscow, Thursday 7 February 1952

Dear M & D,

The Embassy flag at half mast today and a very busy one for the private secretary, receiving from early in the morning until late this evening the heads of nearly every mission in the capital, at least every friendly mission. The weekly mail arrived last night but work was almost impossible with the constant arrival of Ambassadors and Chargés and Ministers in large cars with the flags of France or Finland or Ethiopia or Venezuela flying at their bonnets; crowds in the Embassy hall to sign the Book of Condolences and a constant stream of visitors to the Ambassador; a large dinner party last night cancelled and mourning and black ties until further notice. All this of course has no effect on our relation to the country and the people around us. True Mr Gusev called amongst the throng this afternoon and a note came for me to translate from Mr Vishinsky (Foreign Minister), but no Poles, Czechs or Chinese. And two lines on the back page of *Pravda* announced the King's death.

Two letters came from Woodhouselee in the Queen's Messenger's load. One almost expects a messenger with that title to arrive at the gallop, and handing his reins to the doorkeeper at the Embassy steps, to come in with his leather despatch case slung over his shoulder in the uniform of a Crimean officer.

Love from Iain

ARRIVAL IN MOSCOW 1951-52

Sophiiskaia Naberezhnaia 14, Moscow,
the British Embassy, 29 February 1952

Dear M & D,

This week I have returned to the Bolshoi Theatre. On Tuesday I went to hear *Prince Igor*. On Wednesday to the ballet there, to see for the second time *Bakhchiserai Fountain*, the modern Russian ballet which opens with one of the most magnificent of all scenes in any ballet. This is the scene in the garden and on the terrace of the house of a 15th century nobleman when the betrothal celebrations of the beautiful daughter of the house are interrupted by the incursion of a band of Tatar marauders. The betrothal is marked by dances by the principal guests of exquisite mazurkas and spirited Polish steps: the raid leads to the most violent but the most remarkably controlled fight I have seen on any stage. The daughter is carried off, the nobles are slain and terrifyingly real smoke and flames consume the palace. The Bolshoi scenic artists are famous for their productions of flames and of water. It is literally quite impossible to believe that the back-curtain and the scenery has not been consumed by fire and I am told that similarly the waters in the opera of the *Bronze Horseman* which creep in over the stage and mount into mighty breaking waves beating against the plinth of the statue of Peter the Great are such that they are absolutely convincingly watery. Last night the daughter, the princess who is carried off to the harem of the Khan of Bakhchiserai, was played by the great Ulanova herself.

I am still private secretary to the Ambassador and this involves much work on bag days. It has snowed every day during the last fortnight and continues cold, very cold by British standards, fairly cold by Moscow (-12 °C). I hope to go to the Cathedral to hear the Metropolitan on Sunday, this being the first in Lent and a festival day. Tetya Polya, our cook, celebrated Shrove Tuesday by giving us a special lunch with *blini* (pancakes) fried in butter and served hot, after salted herring and smoked salmon. The pancakes are accompanied by caviar, and sour cream which is poured on top and the pancakes folded over. They should be eaten with vodka as accompaniment. I wish I could send you some. I hope that you are not too restrained by rationing.

I hope you are well, love, Iain

4 March 1952

Dear M,

Written Friday evening on a particularly busy day, after a busy week. I was away for two days in Ryazan, a provincial town about 100 km away on the banks of the Oka. It was a poor place except for its crumbling cathedral and some blocks of new flats. I could write more, of how we spent one night in an agricultural workers hostel, as they did not wish us to stay in the hotel; how we saw an old film of Tarzan in what was once the pillared ballroom of the Assembly Hall of the Nobility; how it raged a blizzard of snow most of the time we were there; how we played hide and seek with our plain clothes followers and how we came back by sleeper on Thursday morning.

This week was very full indeed, with the coming to Moscow of the members of the Moscow Economic Conference. The British Delegation is a very mixed assortment of 6 people of whom we have seen very little but hope to see more. Their leader is Lord Boyd Orr. As their status is unofficial and their presence officially disapproved of by HMG we may not see as much of them as we would like and as they are very closely shepherded by their Russian hosts it is difficult to contact them. There is the fairly well known economist Mr Maurice Dobbs, Communist Cambridge don, Miss Joan Robinson economist and a party of MPs including Sidney Silverman and Emrys Hughes. You will probably have seen reports in the press.

Love Iain

'Embassy' Moscow, 18 March 1952

Dear M & D,

Back to hasty notes. I had reckoned at least on having lunchtime today to write but was invited at the last moment to have lunch with the Ambassador and his two guests of honour, Mr and Mrs Gromyko, on the eve of their departure to London. Both, especially she, were very affable. She does not go now but stays to complete a course in librarianship at the Moscow University.

The week has been a pleasant one, starting with my weekend with Bob Longmire in Stalingrad. I flew there on Saturday morning at dawn, a $3^1/2$ hour flight across the flat steppe country of the Middle Volga. There it was warm and it has a southern gaiety about it and a semi-tropical air which contrasts with Moscow. The people seemed on the whole more prosperous, due no doubt to the almost complete lack of old people in what is virtually a new town. The Park of Culture was filled with crowds on Sunday evening, the Volga full of bathers and ferryboats. The shops were well stocked but still very crowded.

There is still much destruction. I was not so impressed with the new building as I had expected. Whole areas lie in ruins and outside the town centre families still live in holes in the ground covered with corrugated iron and others in the remaining rooms of otherwise burnt out blocks of flats. We were there under the auspices of Intourist, the Soviet organisation which shepherds foreign visitors in Russia. We were not very well treated in the hotel however, being suspect diplomats. The Volga is magnificent, about 1 mile wide with a number of low islands and a great deal of river traffic.

Love Iain

British Embassy, Moscow, 24 March 1952

Dear M & D,

Last week was very busy with the Russian note on the German Peace Treaty early in the week with the Ambassador (and me) called out at eight in the evening to see Gromyko and much ensuing translation, consultation, telegraphing and minuting; and even busier with the presentation of a note of our own later in the week on the Austrian Treaty – synchronising and comparison with the similar French and American notes. The Austrian note has not as much as been mentioned in the Russian press. The German one has held the back page of *Pravda* ever since and the headlines it has shared with the bacteria infected insects which the American butchers have, they say, dropped on the people of Korea and China.

We were busy too with these minor matters which take up as much time, somebody arrested out skiing, a British sailor tried for hooliganism in Lithuania, a cocktail party for the staff (no outsiders as we are still in mourning). The Ambassador's chauffeur was taken to hospital with his head split open by the Ambassador's footman in a quarrel over the latter's wife; a great number of people sick with the flu which comes with the first thaw and the Ambassador away by plane to France on leave.

Thank you for Wednesday's letter. No word from Anne, in fact no word since I came to Moscow.

Hope you are all well, love Iain

Moscow, c/o the Foreign Office, Downing Street,
London, SW1, April 1952

Dear M & D,

The governmental economy cuts have hit the Embassy and mean some reduction of staff. The accountant is leaving and the finances will be in the hands of that strange slow-moving but likeable character, Mr James, who is one of the permanent members of the Embassy, having lived in a small flat across the courtyard from ours for some fifteen years with one interruption only, when the Germans came to the gates of Moscow and the Embassy moved to Kuibyshev. He has grown more and more portly and more and more long winded and one wonders how it was he who went with Mr Churchill to Yalta as his personal shorthand writer and translator. His little daughter visits us each Sunday afternoon with Nicky Hall, the son of the last of the 'Soviet wives' and sometimes, but not always, Petya the suspicious eyed son of the huge Tatar doorman at the Embassy is allowed to come too.

The Ambassador missed the busiest fortnight since I came here, with the exchange of notes on the German Peace Treaty, differing drafts and late conferences with the French and the Americans. I went myself with Paul Grey, the Minister, when he received the last Soviet reply and sat through the half hour interview as Vyshinsky went through the text; this at 11 o'clock at night which is not an unusual time to be called to the Ministry here.

The Economic Conference brought 500 or so foreigners to this city which apart from the permanent diplomats had not seen such a gathering from beyond the borders for some time. The British delegation was a strange assortment of business men of different kinds, trade unionists, economists, Quakers; some came for information, some to further the World Peace Movement, some in search of markets, some for the free holiday. In the main the conference was organised for the benefit of the Chinese, who made large offers for goods which they had consistently refused to buy through Hong Kong and the traditional trade channels. It was refreshing to meet some people who were not members of the diplomatic staff. I saw most of Peter Wiles to whom George Richardson had given an introduction, a don from New College, and Emrys Hughes, the MP for South Ayrshire, a very Scottish Welshman and one who had been in Russia immediately after the revolution. He had not been regarded very favourably in later years by the Soviet authorities, as a friend of the exiled Trotsky.

Love, Iain

Sofiiskaia Naberezhnaia 14, 22 May 1952

Dear M & D,

I write on Thursday. I shall not be here in Moscow tomorrow as I hope to get tickets to go to the small town of Michurinsk by train and stay there over the weekend with one Pat Black from the Canadian Embassy. The town is the birthplace of and is dedicated to the biologist Michurin who is one of the great and honoured fathers of Soviet science. His pupil, the contemporary Professor Lysenko is a name possibly better known in the west.

I spent last Sunday at Zagorsk, a town some 40 or so miles outside Moscow, the religious centre of Russia and the headquarters of the Moscow Patriarchate. In the great Troitsa Sergei Monastery there are several old churches with blue onion domes painted with silver stars; there is also the Patriarchate Museum and one of the few religious schools in Russia. There are some fine icons in the cathedral including the Rublëv Trinity which hung for so many years over the fireplace in your room at Gray's School of Art. The town is untidy and undistinguished but the Monastery with its vast fortified red brick walls is imposing and picturesque, situated on high ground in the centre of the town with a great cobbled square in front and heavy towers with steep pitched roofs along the walls.

Love, Iain

British Embassy, Moscow, 28 May 1952

Dear M & D,

I spent the last two evenings at the Bolshoi Theatre; on Wednesday to see *The Red Poppy*, a political ballet with Lepershinskaia, one of the finest of the younger ballerinas. The ballet is about China, the oppression of the western overlords, the arrival of a Soviet ship in the Chinese port representing the revelation of a new world and a new hope for the people. Despite the propaganda there is some very fine dancing and the décor is magnificent. *Boris Godunov*, last night is probably the most lavish production on any opera stage in the world; also one of the longest.

We enjoyed the weekend in Michurinsk, some eight hours south of Moscow. We stayed in the only hotel (pre-revolutionary), furnished in the usual heavy Victorian style and with the usual very primitive

29

communal washing facilities. We were followed wherever we went and prevented from even visiting Michurin's house which is now a museum. We spent Sunday evening at a 'Bear Circus' in the local 'Park of Culture' where we heard a whole series of political songs and monologues, the finest from a striking girl from Ulan Bator directed against the Americans and bacteriological warfare. This was followed by what was very little removed from the 18th century sport of bear-baiting.

I hope you are all well, love Iain

British Embassy, Moscow, 7 July 1952

Dear M & D,

This week I was away in Kaluga, which lies south west of Moscow on the banks of the Oka. You may remember it from wartime communiqués. I intended to spend 2 or 3 days but could not obtain a room in the hotel – an inconvenience almost certainly laid on by the local militia and the MGB. So Thursday night we went in the train arriving at 6 a.m. and Friday we left at 1.30 a.m. I went with Prudie Mennell, wife of 1st Secretary Peter Mennell and niece of Lord Vansittart. Both her mother and brother are artists and have painted in Plockton.

Kaluga is a pleasant town with large numbers of parks and trees and steep ill-kept cobbled streets of wooden houses, many carved with fantastic intricacy, leading down to the river Oka. The parks contain even more than the usual number of the stock statues – Lenin with hand outstretched to the horizon, Pushkin looking pensive, the buxom Soviet sportswoman in running shorts, the solid square cut granite Stalin and girl in the gym tunic and pioneer scarf. These are found in every village and town throughout the land. The nave of the crumbling 18th century church had been turned into a cinema. But three other churches were still in use and in one we watched a baptism – not a common event in the new Russia. The screaming infant was plunged into a great brass vessel by a dignified old priest with long white hair.

It was difficult to get food, the station buffet was the only place classed as a restaurant but was far away and the day was very hot. We intended to go to the local theatre but the performance was cancelled (not I think just to annoy us) so we went down to the river and took out a rowing boat and rowed through the town and along green meadows. Unfortunately we did not notice how fast the river ran and when I turned to go back to the boathouse and our train, I rowed and rowed but the current ran almost as fast and we made about 200 yards in half an hour; the rowlock began to bend in the gunwale and the only thing to do was to abandon ship, beach it and make our way back by foot. Fifty roubles and much argument, and, I suspect a hint from one of our sleuths (who had no wish that we should miss the train) gave us back our passports left as security. One of the sleuths we had seen previously following us disconsolately along the bank, running into considerable difficulties where it was intersected by steep ravines. So we did catch our train and returned yesterday morning rather tired and sunburnt.

I am arranging to buy a car from Per Schoyen of the Norwegian Embassy in August. I shall probably be home at Christmas, mid-December to mid-January but this is not definite yet.

Last week I had the strange task of taking a marble urn containing the ashes of Mr Alfred Gibbon to a wretched flat in an outlying part of Moscow, and presenting them to his disconsolate Russian wife. Poor Gibbon died last week and I had taken his corpse from the morgue and'had travelled across Moscow with his coffin last Thursday. The Muscovites stopped and stared at us as we crossed Dzerzhinsky Square, past the Bolshoi and the Kremlin with his poor wife sitting beside me and a great Union Jack draped amongst the wreaths. One has a strange variety of duties. Tomorrow I must pay a visit to the Butyrskaia prison – the one which became well known in the days of the purge trials of the thirties – and visit a British seaman who is now doing his fifth month of imprisonment for being drunk and disorderly in a dockside restaurant.

I must now to bed, goodnight, with love from Iain

British Embassy, Moscow, 7 & 8 August 1952

Dear M & D,

I have just come by train from supper at my old home in Perlovka where James Davidson and Peter Knapton (Assistant Naval and Air Attachés) now live on one floor of the dacha. Elizabeth lives in the top flat now with her black poodle, one of Lady Gascoigne's. Taking advantage of the English bank holiday last weekend I went off for three days to the town of Vologda, some 400 kms north of Moscow with Sally Leyland and Mrs Brimelow and had much the most enjoyable excursion so far. We received no attention at all from the police or their friends. The weather was clear and sunny and Vologda proved to be the most picturesque of towns. I have no time now to describe V. and its 42 beautiful churches, all but two used as factories, military stores or derelict, its cathedral with magnificent frescoes; nor to tell you of the delightful walk we had out of the town to the ancient Prilutsky monastery.

I hope you are well, love Iain

19 August 1952

Dear M,

I have been to the ballet to see *Don Quixote* – on Sunday with Elizabeth; and on a very pleasant picnic the previous day in a birch wood with some Dutch and Americans and the new girl here, Jean [sic] Nutt. Have received my Volkswagen.

Very busy this week indeed with the Ambassador catching up on last week's papers on his return from his tour and the announcement of the 19th Session of the Communist Party, the first since 1939; the arrival of the Chinese in Moscow and the despatch of my special charge, the imprisoned seaman. He stayed with me last night and I saw him off this morning on the Helsinki plane. Robin leaves next week and I have to leave my flat, with some reluctance.

Love Iain

British Embassy, Moscow, early September 1952

Dear M & D,

Already September and I shall soon have been here a year. Robin left on Sunday morning, having stayed rather longer than the usual spell, almost 2 $^1/_2$ years. I am still in my flat in the Embassy garden, not sure where I shall stay. The new head of Chancery has arrived. Grace Kennan has left for the start of term at Harvard. I have not left Moscow this week, only going beyond the centre on Sunday last to Kuskovo, a large pleasantly situated house in a sad state of repair which was once the seat of the powerful family of the Sheremetevs. They owned, according to the records, 780,000 serfs in the 18th century. It is now a museum for Russian porcelain; picnicked in the grounds which are pleasantly wooded.

Love Iain

* * *

During Iain's first year there was continuous speculation about the state of Stalin's health and consequently great interest in any foreigner who had the privilege of seeing him. A new French Ambassador, Monsieur Louis Joxe, was appointed to Moscow in April and shortly after his arrival he was granted an audience with Stalin. Sir Alvary Gascoigne was much affronted by this but perhaps somewhat mollified by the fact that Andrei Gromyko accepted an invitation to lunch at the British Embassy before leaving to take up his post as Ambassador to London. It was many years since a Deputy Foreign Minister had come to a meal with a British Ambassador in Moscow. Reports by Louis Joxe on his interview with Stalin were that Vyshinsky, who was in attendance, was almost too frightened to speak and the interpreter scared stiff. Such was the power which Stalin exerted upon his menials.[10]

In May the new American Ambassador, George Kennan, was also received by Stalin. The Indian Ambassador had an audience with Stalin before his departure for India to take up the post of Vice President. He was not considered by diplomatic circles to be the most reliable of persons in relating what had taken place. When asked about the Generalissimo's health he remarked that he had observed nothing more than that Stalin appeared to be ageing but was not losing his grip. He moved slowly but his mind was very alert. Vyshinsky also gave a lunch for the Indian Ambassador, an honour not accorded to Sir David Kelly or the US Ambassador on departure.[11]

Rumours continued to circulate about Stalin's health and his ability to continue to hold all the reins of power. At one stage a story went about that Stalin had proposed a plan for a meeting of Heads of State of the USSR, USA, France and Great Britain but this was not confirmed and was later denied by TASS, the Soviet news agency. Ulam speaks of conflicting emotions in Stalin during his old age, on one hand a desire to give up his duties before he would be found incapable of doing them and on the other a clinging to power and a desire to prove that he was still strong and powerful.

2

STALIN'S DEATH AND AFTER, MOSCOW 1952–54

My journey to Moscow in August 1952, almost a year after Iain, was by the same sea route on the *Beloostrov*. It was pleasant and unremarkable, but exciting for me. At last I was actually to see this country whose language I had been learning and whose history, literature and culture I had been studying for several years. The ship made the scenic trip through the islands to Stockholm, where we had a few hours stop, long enough to have an excellent lunch at the Grand Hotel. At Helsinki there was no time to go ashore and we continued through into the Baltic Sea to Leningrad. After what seemed an interminable wait in the customs shed at the port we were finally taken to the Astoria Hotel to wait for the Red Arrow train to take us to Moscow in the evening.

There was an even longer delay in the hotel for lunch so that I gave up waiting for the second course and went for a walk, to visit the statue of the bronze horseman which features in the eponymous Pushkin poem. When I got back to the hotel they were still waiting for their dessert; a good introduction to the general slowness of Russian service in hotels and restaurants.

Various members of the Embassy met us at the Leningradsky station, mostly there to greet Captain Talbot, the Naval Attaché and his wife, returning from leave. Iain Sutherland was one of the greeters who afterwards told me that he thought I had very untidy luggage. This included several boxes containing the hats which I had been told would be obligatory at diplomatic functions. I was taken to a flat in the

Sadovaia Samotechnaia block, which I was to share with another girl who was working in the Joint Press Reading Service (JPRS), producing daily translations from the Russian press. This was just off the Garden Ring road, more or less the limit of the town in those days and about twenty minutes' drive from the Embassy. I lived there for the first few months until I was transferred later to the flat at the bottom of the Embassy garden, where Iain had spent the first year and which I shared with the Ambassador's new private secretary, Elizabeth Richardson. I also spent a short time out at the dacha in Perlovka which Iain describes in his letters.

Perlovka was a beautiful place in those days, a village surrounded by forests, and quite rural. It had the disadvantage of the distance from Moscow and the problem of waiting for trains at the level crossing, sometimes for nearly an hour. A sepulchral voice would emanate from the darkness to announce, *'poezd iz Moskvy'* (train from Moscow), and we would sit waiting for yet another noisy, steaming, old-fashioned train to make its way across. Now Perlovka is no longer rural but more or less part of Moscow, the level crossing is long gone, and the Embassy had to give up the dacha many years ago.

The atmosphere in the cold war years of the early 1950s was not exactly friendly. However the members of the Embassy were kind and welcoming and made it their business to see that everyone, and particularly junior members of the Embassy, were well looked after. For there was always the fear that if they were lonely and unhappy they might be vulnerable to the attentions of the Soviet intelligence organisations. The amount of social activity plus the heat of the summer weather and the very strangeness of the place took some getting used to. But I gradually became accustomed to the situation and began to find out what one could do and which things were interesting and worth doing.

One of the events which I remember most clearly in the first few weeks after my arrival was the departure of the US Ambassador on leave and his speech at the Berlin airport which resulted in his not being allowed to return. George Kennan writes in his autobiography that 'he is thunderstruck' when he is told by the American Consulate General in Geneva, 'the embassy has just received a note from the Soviet Foreign Office saying that I am declared persona non grata, which means that they will no longer recognise me as ambassador and I shall not be permitted to return to Moscow. Within six months, now, of his own death Stalin is apparently in a strange state of anxiety and suspicion; and presumably he suspects me of God knows what.'[1] In Moscow at the time there was shock and surprise but not so much that the Russians had declared Kennan persona non grata but that he had allowed himself to be so frank in public, and at such a time, about what was happening in the Soviet Union and the restrictions which were being put upon him. A letter from the Embassy to the Foreign Office on 7 October 1952 says that 'his comparison of the system prevailing in Moscow with that prevailing in Germany under Hitler was one which the Soviet Government would always consider unpardonable'.[2]

George Kennan's expulsion from the Soviet Union in his absence ended his diplomatic career.

> I live quietly through the winter at our farm in the country. The weeks go by. Finally I come to Washington to see the new Secretary of State. He receives me civilly, and casually tells me that he knows of no niche for me in the department or in the Foreign Service. I am, in other words, fired. No reason is offered. I ask him how it is proposed to announce my dismissal to the press and the public. The secretary says I should go to see his press secretary – he will work it out.
>
> I go to see the press secretary. He professes helplessness. 'Honestly, I wouldn't know what to say,' he says. 'Would you have any suggestions?' I tell him that I would like to have a few minutes to think about it. So I go to a restaurant for lunch, take out a piece of paper, and draft, so to speak, my own death warrant – the terms of my dismissal from the Foreign Service. I take it back to the press secretary, who reads it and says to me, 'Geez, Mr Ambassador, that's elegant – I couldn't have written that.'[3]

In August the arrangements for the holding of the XIXth Party Congress in October were announced. There had been a gap of 13 1/2 years since the last Congress although according to the current statutes of the All-Union Communist Party (Bolshevik) they were supposed to be convened at least once every three years. In the 28 years since Lenin's death only six congresses were held. The XVIIIth Congress was held in 1939.

There was no explanation offered for the long lapse of time between the 1952 Congress and the last one. The 1952 Congress was to approve the draft directives of the Five Year Plan for the period 1951–55 and the draft of the revised Statutes for the Communist Party of the Soviet Union. It was always Stalin, except once at the XIIIth Party Congress in 1924, who was the spokesman of the Central Committee and who gave the political report of the Central Committee. In 1952 this had been changed and the report and keynote speech was to be made by G.M. Malenkov. Research Department suggested that it was perhaps considered time 'for the Generalissimo to withdraw from the direct exercise of some of his powers and to assume a more or less honorific position'.[4] Or was it that he did not wish to appear ageing and ailing?

The party was to change its name from the All-Union Communist Party of Bolsheviks to the Communist Party of the Soviet Union (CPSU). The selection of Malenkov as the Committee's rapporteur led to considerable interest and speculation about his prominence in the party ranks. The main administrative changes were the abolition of the Politburo and the Orgburo. These were to be replaced by the Presidium and the Secretariat. Party Congresses were to be held every four not three years and the Secretariat was to take over the direction of party work and the function of selecting party officials. Research Department did not expect there to be changes in Soviet policy. They considered that the Presidium would make the workings of the central machinery of the party even more obscure and that it was too large to be constantly in plenary session.[5]

Pravda of 30 October produced the usual list (67) of slogans for the 35th Anniversary of the Revolution (there were only 60 in 1951) but there was not considered to be anything of great significance in them. A Chancery letter drew attention to No. 15, which 'hailed the foreign policy of the Soviet Union' and listed one of its aims as the development of business relations with all countries. No. 48 called for the introduction of science into agriculture, a sign of the times. Soviet agriculture was traditionally backward and forever needing improvement. Otherwise slogans urged – 'Long live peace between the peoples!' 'Down with warmongers!' 'Fraternal Greetings to all the peoples fighting against imperialist aggressors, warmongers – for peace, democracy and socialism'.[6]

At the ceremony on 6 November in the Bolshoi Theatre to celebrate the anniversary of the revolution, Stalin's attitude was one of boredom, with occasional impatient movements. He sat inconspicuously in the second row on the platform. Speeches reflected statements by Stalin and Malenkov at the recent Party Congress.[7] There was nothing new. The celebrations had been overshadowed by the Party Congress.

* * *

The Embassy, 17 October 1952

Dear M & D,

Over the last few weeks I have sent you but stray postcards, from Moscow, from Leningrad, from Tiflis and from Moscow again. Now

I am back to the Embassy routine – a busy one with the current Party Congress, a run of extra political work and a number of new arrivals and the normal series of functions and entertainments.

Tonight I write on my return from the Bolshoi Theatre where I saw one of the less interesting ballets in the repertoire – on a French revolutionary theme called, 'The Flames of Paris'. Few diplomats there and a good number of Party congressmen attending after their last session in the Kremlin two nights ago and spending a few more days in the capital before returning to their native Moldavias or Azerbaijans. Or so we thought, being given seats less favourably placed than those usually accorded to the Embassy. Also crowds of Chinese. I went with Elizabeth who now occupies my former flat in the Embassy garden block.

I am now not alone in my flat in the Sadovaia. A new young 3rd Secretary, replacing Robin, arrived on the *Belo-Ostrov* – Murray Simons – and he now lives with me. I hope we shall not have to change house again. We have a not very efficient maid and hope for some new furniture. Murray is a small, shy, dark person, but quite companionable, who has just completed much the same course as Elizabeth and I took last year, and has spent the last two months in Paris.

But the chief news of the last few weeks has been my travels. I was first in Leningrad as you know for a week, first on duty with Tom Brimelow. I stayed another two days buying books for the Embassy and was joined by Henrietta (Dutch Embassy) and the Blacks (from the Canadian). With H. I went on to the old town of Novgorod – an overnight journey, one night there and then back via Leningrad and Moscow. Weather none too good but most enjoyable. I had scarce returned to Moscow when I set out again this time for Tiflis, by air with James Davidson, the Scots Assistant Naval Attaché. Henrietta insisted on coming also, but had to leave after three days in order to return to Holland.

Tiflis itself is a town of much charm and the days were warm and sunny. We did see Gori, the birthplace of Stalin and Mtskheta, the ancient Georgian capital with its 10th century Georgian Christian cathedral. Outside the town boundary one is in the hands of Intourist entirely and any attempt we made to elude them was frustrated. However we did find much of interest in Tiflis. We saw the Georgian ballet. We ate much *shashlik*, meat on long skewers, and Georgian cheese. We bought two silver daggers from an ancient bearded silversmith whose home we visited. We went up the funicular railway to the high hill above the town where there is a magnificent view of the surrounding mountains and where a new restaurant has been built by Beria's sister, and a park with a huge statue of Stalin. We ate walnuts and peaches in the *kolkhoz* market. We found an Armenian musical instrument maker and from him James, who plays the Scottish variety, bought a set of Caucasian bagpipes. We had a set of *shashlik* sticks made at ironsmiths. We had an uncomfortable flight back in the plane – five and a half hours with lunch at Rostov on Don.

My next trip will probably be to Britain. I think of coming via Vienna.

Love Iain

A Christmas letter from Moscow...

Sadovaia Samotechnaia, Wednesday 24 December

Written on the 24th, Wednesday. Because of the holiday the bag closes today. Sometimes as last week, when I returned together with the courier, the incoming bag is diverted from its route. So it was that last Wednesday bad weather forced us northwards and we landed at Vilno in Lithuania, the first western visitors there for some years, as it lies well within the area forbidden to foreigners. There we were put up with

2. Elizabeth Richardson (later Hammarskjöld), Tetya Polya, Jeanne and Tonya in the Embassy garden, 1953.

39

our 33 bags of mail in the ancient hotel Bristol, still so called. We were entertained there very lavishly and treated more like delegates than diplomats in the SU and were quite sorry to leave next morning. Vilno must once have been one of the most attractive towns in Europe. It still has many of the old baroque churches, palaces and streets, but alas over half must have been utterly destroyed during the war and less has been reconstructed than in similarly damaged Berlin where I came from the previous day. There I had spent Tuesday shopping and passed the night in the sedate old Savoy Hotel.

I have little time to write now. In half an hour I must go to Perlovka, preparatory to going out there for the Christmas weekend. I shall think of you at Cults on Christmas day and hope you enjoy yourselves.

Love from Iain

British Embassy, Moscow 30.XII.52

Dear M & D,

I have now been back ten days. There seem to have been very few working days in that period and I really think that I might well have continued on leave till after Christmas. Thursday last till Sunday were free, except for a skeleton staff which I did not join; and over this holiday I went with nine others to my old home, the dacha at Perlovka. With several car loads of bedding and turkey and wine and skis and cake and Christmas decorations we went out on Christmas day and did not return till the night before last. Myself and Simons, James Davidson and Knapton and Dick Freeborn from the Secretariat, with Elizabeth and Jean [sic] Nutt and Jill Sheppard, the new book buyer and Russian expert, and two girls from the Australian Embassy. The party in fact contained all the unmarried diplomatic staff of the Embassy except the redoubtable Miss Conolly, a little Irishwoman and Foreign Office adviser on Soviet affairs who is out here temporarily while Tom Brimelow takes his hundred days accumulated leave; and she came on Sunday. And on the night of Boxing Day we increased the number by some twenty or thirty more for a party under the tall Christmas tree, which stood in the central hall and stretched up to the roof of the first floor. Perlovka with its wooden log walls, its ski-lodge hall, open tiled fire and wooded garden makes an excellent place for such a party in every way, were it not for the difficulties of reaching it and the long wait at the level-crossing on the way. And so I spent a very festive and enjoyable Christmas and have not had so much time to find Moscow, as most of those who return from leave find it, a little depressing when one comes for the second time, knowing its limitations and restrictions and no longer with the adventure of first discovery before one.

The Berlin mail was not our only Christmas present. On that evening we also had a note from *Burobin* (the Bureau for servicing the diplomatic corps) telling the Embassy that it will have to vacate its present premises. We have known that this is likely for some time as the island on which it stands opposite the Kremlin is due for replanning as a park. But we did not expect our notice now. In fact we cannot and will not move in the three months stipulated. But I fear the move will take up much of our and my time in the next year.

Lady Gascoigne's New Year's Eve party, to which all members of commonwealth missions were invited, was a great success, despite the efforts of the spiteful Mrs Ford, wife of the Canadian Chargé d'Affaires and sworn enemy of Lady G. Mrs F. had organised another party to coincide with that in our Embassy and had sought to outshine ours by ordering a real band. All my best wishes for 1953, with love, from Iain

Moscow, Wednesday, 21 January 1953

Dear M & D,

I set out this afternoon with the new visa officer in his car to see if we could visit a People's Court. But being the anniversary of the death of Lenin all were closed, although the day is no longer a full holiday in the Soviet Union. So we went on to look for the Dostoyevsky museum, found it in a very squalid block of flats – also closed.

The new visa officer is called Terence O'Brien-Tear. His wife comes from Stornoway and was at the University in Edinburgh, which further increases the number of Scots in the Embassy. The most patriotic of these is James Davidson who conducts the Monday evening class in Scottish dancing of about 40 strong and which even I have attended. Indeed I shall be co-host with him, Mr Tommy Banks from Edinburgh, the Military Attaché's clerk, Irene Hogg, Miss Imray from Aberdeen, Elizabeth – not very Scots although the daughter of a Presbyterian Minister and Jock Cargill, the Chief Chancery Messenger, who was actually born in Cults, at a Burns Night dance this Sunday. We are assisted by the two new Canadian girls, named Jamieson and Mackenzie, the Canadian archivist Mackinnon, and the wife of the French 1st secretary Delahaye, also from Edinburgh.

Love Iain

Sofiiskaia, Friday 23 January 1953

Dear M & D,

On Saturday I went with Irene Hogg to a dull concert of Russian songs and to a restaurant where we fell into conversation with a colonel in the air force who had actually fought in Spain in the International Brigade. This was one of the most extraordinary conversations I have had here. The officer was later warned not to converse with us further and we are afraid he was right when he said that he would probably be in serious trouble the following day. Unfortunately I cannot write all he said, before he drank a toast in farewell, kissed Irene's hand and we left the restaurant.

The story of the Jewish doctors, which has caused much speculation here, and judging from last Sunday's papers even more at home and of a very wild kind, was published the following day.

I hope you are both now well,

Love from Iain

* * *

We do not know exactly what the mysterious air force colonel said to Iain in the restaurant that night, but on 13 January TASS reported what became known as *The Doctors' Plot*, the 'unmasking' of a diversionary group of Soviet doctors who allegedly killed Zhdanov and tried to kill Marshals Vasilevsky, Govorov, Konev, General Shtemenko and Admiral Levchenko.[8] Seven out of the nine doctors accused were Jewish. They were accused of wrecking, terrorism and acting as American spies, echoing the accusations of the purges of 1936–9 and adding fuel to the suspicion that Stalin was contemplating another set of purges, to rid himself of some of the established party and government cadres which had been building up during the last 15 years, and presumably to replace them with younger and more malleable members. The changes made at the XIXth Party Congress when the ten members of the old Politburo were 'swamped by relatively younger newcomers' in the formation of the Presidium, was later interpreted by Khrushchev as introducing less experienced persons 'so that these would extol him (Stalin) in all sorts of ways. We can also assume that this was also a design for the future annihilation of the old Politburo members ...' The security services were also accused of lack of vigilance, which indicated that Beria himself might also be in danger of arrest.[9] As it happened, of course, Stalin was to die quite soon after *The Doctors' Plot*, before he had time to go any further with whatever plans he had for purges.

* * *

Sadovaia, Wednesday 4 February 1953

Dear M & D,

Wednesday evening and just returned from the weekly film show at Kropotkin house, which I do not often see. Tonight I had to go and supervise the delivery of the projector and the film was Cocteau's *Eternel Retour*. Kropotkin house is a building in the older part of Moscow, the area of the *pereulki* or narrow streets where many noble families once had their town residences. It is here that the anarchist philosopher was born and here he spent the early years described in the first chapters of his *Memoirs of a Revolutionary*. It now houses the JPRS, the Anglo American press service, and the children's centre. It was here too we held the Burns Night dance on Sunday, when the militiamen at the gate found an evening of Scottish reels a change from their usual tedious guard in the bitter cold, and we served a company of fifty with whiskey and turkey, rum punch and tinned haggis.

The Embassy is still much concerned about its forced removal. The only building offered which is remotely adaptable contains no residence for the Ambassador, no garden and is excessively gloomy, right in the centre of Moscow, in a small back street.

Love Iain

Moscow, Friday 6 February 1953

Dear D,

Two nights ago the thermometer at Perlovka read -35°C. Too cold for walking much in the street even with one's beaver collar up and the earflaps down on one's fur hat; the snow squeaks underfoot, the river is frozen solid; the Embassy is none too warm despite central heating and a log fire in Chancery. It is dangerous to walk abroad in nylon stockings, which are said to stick to the skin. It is difficult to find a taxi in the streets as I discovered after a concert on Wednesday night at the Conservatoire to which I went with Jeanne Nutt from our Russian Secretariat. This was one of the concerts organised by the Union of

Composers to play and criticise works written in 1952. The most interesting work was a cello concerto by a young Georgian named Tsintsadze played by Shafran, one of the finest cellists alive.

Some lucky members of the Embassy this week paid a visit to the State Ballet School of the Bolshoi Theatre. Unfortunately I was not among them and the party was limited in number. Colonel and Mrs Prynne, the Military Attaché and his wife, were there as their elder daughter is at the Sadlers Wells School in London. You will remember an article in the 'Listener', which Lady Kelly wrote last year on the visit when she was here.

It seems most likely that I shall leave Moscow next winter, though I might be asked to stay till the spring.

With love to all, Iain.

* * *

(Undated)

The weekend was bitterly cold. I went out yesterday afternoon to Tsaritsino for the first time this year. This is the place where there are woods and slopes and many members of the diplomatic corps go to ski over the weekends. The slopes were quite icy and rather difficult for a beginner like myself. On Saturday evening I had been to an Ostrovsky play at the 'filial' of the Arts Theatre with Jan Bosić Serbian third secretary at the Yugoslav Embassy.

There are only three, at present two, at the Yugoslav mission, and as communists but anti-Soviet, they are worse treated and more closely watched than any other members of the corps. Bosić is a pleasant and intelligent person. A Bosnian with broad Slav features and a shock of black hair.

Earlier in the same day I had been to the Tretyakov gallery to walk round the annual exhibition of the all-Union Society of Artists with a Russian and his wife whom I met last week at the opera. He had greeted me there in English and I recognised him as a man with whom I had talked last July on the train returning from Vologda. He was a translator of English books into Russian, his wife whose spoken English was excellent, was a teacher at the Institute of Foreign Languages. They were very anxious to speak with one whose native tongue was English; whether they were 'licensed to talk to foreigners' or not I cannot say.

I hope you and D and Anne are well, Love from Iain

STALIN'S DEATH AND AFTER

Sadovaia Samotechnaia Flat 35, Thursday 5.III.1953

Dear M & D,

The dramatic bulletin, which was first broadcast early yesterday morning announcing Stalin's illness, has been the principal event of the week and the chief topic of conversation and speculation in the Embassy. We kept a portable wireless set in Chancery yesterday, but nothing further till 2 a.m. today. An event of this kind emphasises the isolation of the Embassy from the population here. We cannot tell what people think. It must have been a very great shock to hear that the leader, the great father of the people whose name is on every hoarding, whose picture is in every office and public building, whose genius is praised in nearly every newspaper article printed, was stricken and with little hope for his recovery. But we only have the opinion of chauffeurs and maid to consult. Our Varya was obviously distressed. My old Aunt Polya who served Robin and me in the Embassy flat and now cooks for Elizabeth who is both a very staunch supporter of everything Soviet and very religious said to me that God has his appointed time even for the Godless. But Moscow looks very normal and feels normally cold, after last week's warm sunshine. I gather some of our correspondents, the few poor press agency correspondents who still function in Moscow, have been sending back pretty sensational stories and speculations on the barest material. Certainly nothing much appears in the Russian press. For not only are we cut off from the population, but they are as effectively cut off from the Kremlin. Apart from bulletins not a single word has been published, and the editorials, which are of course very different from those in the British papers, make no reference to the event at all. But that is what one would expect. The Ambassador was going on leave tomorrow but has postponed his departure. I intend to go up to Leningrad for three days next week – a short stay, going by air and returning by train.

With love from Iain

* * *

Life was so extraordinary and at times unreal during those last few years before Stalin died that although it is a long time ago now, it is unforgettable. And Stalin's death was even more unforgettable. Those of us who were there at that time, and who are still alive, still meet together and greet each other like members of a club.

45

If the last years of his life were surrounded in mystery, Stalin's death, it now transpires was no less of a mystery. It was not therefore surprising that little was known of the progress of his illness in the days before he died and that everyone was waiting with baited breath for an announcement. When the Ambassador visited the head of protocol department to convey his personal sympathy and hope for a speedy recovery he was given no news.

Finally, on 6 March, the Russian newspapers which it was my duty to distribute among the Embassy staff were delivered very late, which meant that something serious had happened. They were all edged in black. Stalin had died on the 5th but no announcement was made until a day later. This was entirely in keeping with the atmosphere of secrecy and lack of openness which we were used to. What followed too was not unusual – at first the lack of organisation and not knowing what was to happen and the crowds surging on to the streets; then the overwhelming security precautions and the immense presence of the militia preventing any Soviet citizen getting anywhere near the lying in state in the Hall of Columns or later the funeral. Fairly typical too was the last-minute issuing of passes and information for those diplomats who were permitted to see all these things.

Although not unexpected, Stalin's death was a great shock to the people of the country. For years they had been subjected to his strong and tyrannical control. Now they were afraid and apprehensive of what would happen next and who would be the new leader. The reaction of shock and fear was mixed with relief for some who had suffered most under his regime, bewilderment, anxiety and curiosity about who would replace him, and an overwhelming desire to see him lying in state in the Hall of Columns. Hence the pouring out of people onto the streets and the eventual crowds and stampedes which caused so many casualties.

There was individual grief, particularly among the elderly and women, like the two ladies who looked after the flat where I lived. But there was no sense of general mourning. Those diplomats who managed to get through the barriers of militia into the Hall of Columns in the first hours after his body was taken there reported tense expectancy but no real grief. The atmosphere was more that of a holiday, or even as I felt, a football match.

Despatches poured out of the Embassy in the days following Stalin's death. Sir Alvary, an ambassador very much of the old school, complained that his secretaries had been up all night before the funeral trying to get the necessary passes but felt he should excuse the protocol department for lack of preparation because of the very short time which was left between the death and the laying of his body to rest in the mausoleum with Lenin. He was also very concerned that 'the loss of Stalin as helmsman of the Soviet ship of state might well carry with it unpleasant possibilities', that the United States or any other power might take advantage of a time of uncertainty to 'abandon their containment policy in favour of more positive action'. There was of course much speculation about a successor. Was it to be Molotov or Malenkov or even a small committee of members of the Politburo?[10]

The Ambassador was the only one to attend the funeral. He wrote, 'to say that I was impressed by the funeral ceremony would be an understatement. The lying in state in the Hall of Columns, while it was a somewhat sinister and barbaric display, with no religious atmosphere about it, brought back with full force the history of Communism and of those who have invented this particularly vicious but powerful form of ideology. Stalin will, I presume, rank in history as a cruel, cold-blooded and ruthless tyrant. And yet there was no gainsaying he was a great man'.[11]

* * *

Wednesday, 11 and Friday 13 March 1953

Dear M & D,

Our news this week, as yours also, has been the death of Stalin. Ever since I came here, ever since I studied the affairs of this country, the Soviet Union, the Kremlin, the direction of affairs has been identified with Stalin. An interview with the great man has been one of the cherished goals of every diplomat in Moscow. Now they have all seen him – but laid out in State in the Marble Hall of Columns surrounded by wreaths, or again, where he lies now next door to Lenin in a perspex covered sarcophagus in the mausoleum in Red Square.

On Wednesday and Thursday last week we had waited for the bulletins, we had kept a wireless in Chancery to listen for announcements. Stalin died on Thursday night. But there was no announcement till the early hours of the following morning. I knew when I looked out from my bedroom window across the broad *Sadovaia*. Red flags edged with black were already fixed in the brackets along the walls of the new apartment block on the opposite side of the street. Varya our maid arrived late, brought the fried eggs in for breakfast but they were uneatable. When I said something to console her she burst into tears and fled from the room. The old woman, who sits at the bottom of the lift shaft and opens the doors, was sobbing into her shawl.

When we drove through the town to the Embassy a few people had begun to congregate around the Kremlin gates, but later as the morning went on, when the newspapers were published saying that the lying in state would be in the Hall of Columns, thousands of people began to converge on the centre of the city till there were vast crowds in Red Square and the roads leading off. By the time we returned for lunch the central squares had been cordoned off. Thousands of security forces and police appeared and thousands of lorries.

Moscow is constructed in a series of concentric rings, the centremost of which is the wall of the Kremlin itself. The inner rings also correspond to former defensive walls, first that of the Kitai Gorod, the mediaeval boundary, then the line of the wall which stood in the days when Napoleon invaded Russia, now marked by the 'boulevards' which circle the city. The outermost is the ring road of the broad *Sadovaia* on which I live. Soon the Kitai Gorod was cordoned off, lorries head to tail blocked all the entrances. By the afternoon this was extended to the boulevards. By Monday, the day of Stalin's funeral and on Sunday also, the whole area enclosed by the *Sadovaia* was barricaded by lines of vehicles thrown across every street and closely guarded by the military.

I went out in the evening to see the crowds and to see also if we could get to the Hall of Columns. All day and through the night parties from factories, schools, clubs and from the outlying districts marched through the streets. All were presumably bent on reaching the centre but few can have done so. We used our diplomatic cards and succeeded in reaching as far as Dzerzhinsky Square, but we could get no further. Organised parties were being allowed down Gorky Street. But here there were just close-packed throngs – few I must say showing much grief; most seemed to treat it as a kind of vast holiday; a fair number were drunk and there were a good many ambulances taking away those who were trampled on or thrown heavily from the lorries when they tried to climb over. But on the whole the troops seemed good-natured and were unarmed.

It was the next day that we all went to see Stalin. I thought at first that I was not going to be able to go, as I did not have a top hat. The Ambassador wanted everyone to be correctly dressed, but later relented. And as it turned out only the senior members of the Embassy had them and I think the doyen of the corps, the Swedish Ambassador. Most unsuitable they were too with the temperature at minus fifteen and an hour's wait on the exposed Revolution Square. Each little Embassy group took their place in the long queue. The Bulgarians and the Koreans and the Poles and their like all had enormous wreaths. So had a few of the western missions including the Swiss. There was a tremendous run on flowers in Moscow, real and artificial. The Swiss wreath suffered a minor adventure when it was stolen from the flower shop by the Albanians. The British group had no wreath but were marked out by their sober garb and the top hats.

When at last, frozen by cold, we reached the Hall, we mounted two staircases. Rows of police stood outside, and soldiers of the MVD troops stood all the way up the stairs. There were more troops at the top of the stairs – smart, picked men from the Kremlin garrison – and along the two broad corridors through which we went. Piles of wreaths lined the route. The way was lit by candelabras draped in black tulle, but as we turned into the main hall we were blinded by blue searchlights shining directly at us as the cameras took their pictures of the show. The searchlights added to the impression that it was like a fantastic film set from one of Mr de Mille's films. One could hear the music, and when one's eyes became accustomed to the glare saw that there was a symphony orchestra at one end of the hall playing soft but not very solemn music, and half-smothered in banks of bright artificial flowers. The hall was filled with people. There were numbers of senior officers. The newspapers later said that soldiers, scientists, artists, party men all took turns to stand beside the coffin. There were others seated on benches at one side who were supposed to be relatives of the deceased. But we had no time to stand and stare. The queue passed quickly and was hurried on by the officials. I peered into the lights and the flowers and looked for Stalin. And raised above more banks of flowers, not altogether easy to distinguish at first, they had set the coffin with the body. He was in his marshal's uniform with the medals on his breast, his hands folded in front and his feet towards us. The face was greyish in colour but had the familiar benign expression, the hair and moustache a darker grey. But there was not much time and we were soon in the next room. As we turned away, Mrs Talbot, the Naval Attaché's wife, who was in front of me suddenly asked 'Where's Stalin?' She had walked through without seeing him.

Some members of the Embassy went back later for a second round but I didn't. One American is said to have gone through six times. The guards showed great respect for diplomatic cards. But only a fraction of the hundreds of Russians who waited in queues all that day and the next could have seen him. One of the journalists reported that the queue on Sunday stretched over ten miles. The Military Attaché estimated that there were about 250,000 troops engaged in keeping the populace from seeing Stalin.

The funeral was fixed for Monday, but by late the previous night we had no news of the details. Only at 1.30 a.m. did I learn that the Ambassador had to be on parade next morning at 8.50 a.m. Only at 5 a.m. did I finally get the necessary tickets and passes from the Ministry of Foreign Affairs. I did not see the funeral. Only the Ambassador took part. Only the Minister and Service Attachés were in the square. Indeed it is remarkable how few Soviet citizens can have seen it; diplomats, delegates, officials and soldiers in the centre of an area barricaded off from the rest of the city – an area set within an enclave of virtually deserted streets.

I conclude on Friday – the bag is a large one – there are many official letters and despatches and not much time. There is not much news except Stalin. By Tuesday all had returned to normal. On Wednesday the Rolls drove up to the Kremlin with the Ambassador to see Molotov.

Moscow, Thursday 26 March 1953

Dear M and D,

The Embassy flag is continually at half-mast these days. It remains there this time till Monday or Tuesday whichever is the date of Queen Mary's funeral. In accordance with the usual custom we opened a book of condolences, which is placed on a special table with a desk lamp in the gloomy wood-covered entrance-hall of the Embassy. The book is the same one hastily discovered when the King died, and decorated with a new length of black ribbon. The oldest signatures of all are the most interesting in this book, as it was originally the visitor's book of the English Club in St. Petersburg. But today the members of Chancery dressed in black striped trousers led in the representatives of different countries to add their signatures to the latest list. So we ushered in the spruce young Mr Bravo, the Argentinian Ambassador, the last diplomat to see Stalin alive, the obese repulsive looking M. di Stefano, the Italian, the rubicund Mr Jelal from Baghdad, and a dozen more.

The sky is blue and clear and sunny though the temperature is still below zero. On Saturday I went out along the Kaluga road in my Volksvagen with Elizabeth and Jeanne but there is … and here my ink ran out after lunch.

Since lunchtime a few more dignitaries called to present their condolences. Most difficult of this afternoon's mourners was the

Afghan Chargé whom I presumed could speak at least some Russian when he answered me in that tongue, saying 'I do not speak English', on my greeting him in French. But ushering him into the Ambassador and following as interpreter I discovered that he could only repeat 'I do not speak Russian' when I translated the Ambassador's remarks of thanks. So in a moment of inspiration I repeated those words of thanks in Urdu, but it cannot have been very clearly, for he registered comprehension, but immediately delivered a long speech in what I presume to have been Persian, which the Ambassador, thinking he was speaking Russian, desired me to translate.

I hope you are all well, Love Iain

Sadovaia Samotechnaia, Thursday April 1953

Dear M & D,

Your news arrived on time last night and then I read of your being honoured with the John Knox Cap of Aberdeen University. No, we do not have the *Scotsman* in the Embassy. I was most pleased to hear of the LLD. One of your fellow recipients I see from the Press and Journal cutting is a former professor of Law at Oxford.

The Ambassador returned from London today, after over a week away from Moscow. I did not go to meet him at the airport, as we had some exchanges with the Ministry about Captain Holt and the internees from Korea who are due to come across Siberia this week to Moscow. Lady G. came back last week, the day Sir Alvary left for Berlin. The chief event in the Embassy during her absence was the destruction of the cats in the Embassy basement, the day before she returned. She is a great animal lover as everyone knows, the founder of the Japanese RSPCA, and has no sense of smell. The cats and kittens in the Ambassadorial kitchens and cellars below the Embassy offices multiplied and strayed all along the passageways where there are store-rooms and workshops and the place where we keep the Commissariat of food and drink. So something had to be done, as people refused to work there. Returning, Lady G. accused poor Dr Haigh of dreadful things and suspects that all the members of Chancery are implicated. The Ambassador's first words on entering the Embassy this evening were 'What is this I hear about the cats?' The story is well known to the diplomatic corps and according to one Grozny, a Russian teacher, who lunched with the Mexican Chargé, is well known also to Moscow University.

We had four nominally free days over Easter. I had planned to go away as only in that way would they have been free, but could not obtain accommodation at Murom on the Oka where I intended to go. On the Sunday, which was beautifully sunny, I went to Zagorsk, where the green roofs and the red walls were particularly beautiful. I went by train and took a picnic and Jeanne Nutt.

The fortnight has been extremely busy. Internationally there have been a few gestures by the Soviet Government of a rather more conciliatory nature, which I see the press in Britain has seized upon as indicative of a complete change of policy. There may be some changes in tactics; there have been very dramatic changes in the internal administration of which we only have echoes, but it is too early to say how they will affect general relations. The possibility of an armistice in Korea opened up by Chou En-lai's offers is the most important. If that succeeds we shall see.

With love from Iain

Moscow, Monday 20 April 1953

Dear M & D,

I write this letter earlier this week. But I shall not stay late this evening for last night I returned late and rather tired after being out with the Burmese Ambassador to a performance of *Evgenii Onegin* at the Bolshoi and to supper at the Ararat. The Burmese Ambassador, Mr Maung Ohn, is a rather an enigmatic figure, once Secretary and protégé of Aung Sang, the socialist leader, and later in the declaration of independence the first Ambassador of the Burmese Union in London. Despite all this he still looks about twenty-five, though he must certainly be older. He walks with a limp, from a wound he received when someone tried unsuccessfully to assassinate him, and he does walk too, all over Moscow, when few ambassadors move a step without their large cars with the flags flying on the mudguard, except of course our own who goes out regularly from 2.30 to 4 each day. In winter the Burmese Ambassador is a familiar figure in his huge black furry hat, his stick and his ever-benevolent smile, waiting in bus queues or in bookshops standing observing the populace. He is a Buddhist, and as he eats neither flesh nor fish and drinks no wine he has usually to be made a special omelette at Ambassadorial dinner parties. Actually Buddhists are not denied meat or wine unless they are priests, but Mr Maung Ohn likes to cultivate an air of special holiness, withdrawal and tolerance. Occasionally he entertains at the 'Ararat', Moscow's most sympathetic restaurant and most westernised, other ambassadors and sometimes just third secretaries. Last night I was there with James Garvey, an attaché at the Americans, and Ursula Dooley from the Australians to whom he has recently become engaged. After caviar, and sturgeon salad, and Armenian devilled trout and *shashlik* and Georgian wine and cherry juice and much more we all felt very full. One is of course at a conversational disadvantage as the Ambassador himself only eats potato salad, an egg and mineral water.

The bag closes as I write, Love Iain

Moscow, 23.IV.53

Dear M & D,

I had intended to go off on the weekend but we awaited the arrival of the party of civilian internees including Mr Holt from Korea. Actually they came on Monday morning, 10 days in the train from Antung via Mukden and Manchuria and the Trans-Siberian. Their arrival and departure was the chief event of the week. The Ambassador and Lady G. and most of the staff went down to the Yaroslavsky station to meet their train. I did not go, but saw much of them during their day and a half here. A special RAF aircraft was brought in to evacuate them to England. It was hoped that they might in this way reach home on Tuesday. Unfortunately the captain of the plane brought with him a packet of letters for the internees; the Soviet customs objected to this and for three hours they were all delayed there on Monday night. They proved to be a wonderful group of people; they had suffered a great deal during the first year of their imprisonment but were in fairly good health when they arrived. I took Mr Holt and Blake, the Vice Consul in Seoul round Moscow on Monday afternoon and we attracted much attention on Red Square and in the Metro as they were still dressed in the strange, ill-fitting khaki suits which they had been given in Pyongyang.

The most interesting members of the party were Philip Deane, the *Observer* correspondent (there should be something by him in next week's issue), Monsignor Quinlan of the Maynooth Irish Mission (who left for his native Ireland with the others which he was going to see for the first time since he left for China in 1932. Of his 20 years in the Far East he had spent one year a prisoner during the Chinese Civil War, some years a prisoner in the Chinese Japanese war, 4 years in Japan during the last war, and now three more interned in Korea) also the 73 year-old Bishop of Korea who was still wearing his purple chasuble in which he was captured.

I go off tonight for the weekend to Murom on the Oka.

Love Iain

* * *

The Soviet leadership moved swiftly after Stalin's death and on 7 March details were announced of the appointment of the new rulers. Although Malenkov was appointed Chairman of the Council of Ministers and Secretary of the Central Committee of the CPSU, general comments from the Foreign Office assumed government by committee. First after Malenkov came Beria as 1st Deputy Chairman of the Council of Ministers and Minister of Internal Affairs. He was followed by Molotov, also a 1st Deputy Chairman and Minister of Foreign Affairs, then Bulganin, also Minister of War, and Kaganovich. Mikoyan was appointed Minister of Internal and External Trade.

Instead of a Presidium and Buro of the Presidium there was to be one body, the Presidium of the Central Committee of the CPSU, with ten members and four candidate members. The members were Malenkov, Beria, Molotov, Voroshilov, Khrushchev, Bulganin, Kaganovich, Mikoyan, Saburov and Pervukhin, and the candidate members were Shvernik, Ponomarenko, Melnikov and Bagirov. Voroshilov was appointed official head of state, Chairman of the Presidium of the Council of Ministers, in place of Shvernik, who was relieved of this post.[12]

A despatch from Sir Alvary on 13 March analysing the changes said that the haste in announcing the changes pointed to ensuring 'uninterrupted direction of the State and Party organs' and 'the prevention of any disorder and panic'. There was no playing up of Malenkov as new chief and 'Voroshilov, the aging trusty comrade of Stalin was safely out of the way in honourable retirement as titular head of state'. Khrushchev was described as 'a somewhat enigmatic figure of obvious ability whose future should certainly be watched'. Brezhnev, who had been appointed Head of the Political Administration of the Ministry of the Navy, was seen as 'a party politico with a rather unsavoury record' who seemed to specialise in cleaning up any branch of the party apparatus, which was not functioning correctly. 'Contrary to all prognostications and forebodings there was no period of chaos doubt or hesitation following Stalin's death, due to the firmness of tone and action of his disciples.'[13] By 14 March Malenkov had asked to be relieved of his duties as Secretary of the Central Committee of the CPSU. Was this because he simply 'had too much on his plate' or was this the beginning of a move against him?[14] Leonard Schapiro writes, 'It is a matter for conjecture whether Malenkov was forced out of the Secretariat by his colleagues, or whether, faced with the choice of relinquishing one of his two offices, he chose to retain the government post in the belief that the government machine had now become the more influential.'[15]

In the following months life in Moscow became slightly easier and more relaxed. The threat of having to abandon the Embassy site on Sofiiskaia Naberezhnaia evaporated as on 4 April US and British spokesmen announced the rescinding of the Soviet order to their respective embassies in Moscow to move from their premises. On 2 April the 15 Soviet doctors arrested because of supposed conspiracy were all released. On 11 April the new US Ambassador Bohlen arrived in Moscow, after a long period during which there had been only a chargé. On 12 May Ambassador Bohlen was received by Gromyko, who had recently been appointed 1st Deputy Minister of Foreign Affairs, and been replaced as Ambassador in London by Malik. On 23 April the British Ambassador was received by Molotov. Exchanges of delegations began to take place. British and Irish delegations arrived for the May Day celebrations. Soviet miners went to Porthcawl. There were visits of women's organisations, students, writers and trade unionists.

Most memorable was the arrival in Moscow on their way home, of the internees from Korea, which Iain has mentioned in his letters. The Soviet Union had agreed to intercede with North Korea for their release. They had survived their ordeals because of their character and resilience to the terrible deprivations they had suffered. For this reason they were truly remarkable people, Mr Holt the Minister from the British mission in Seoul, Philip Deane, the *Observer* correspondent, Monsignor Quinlan and of course the former Vice Consul, Blake. It was only later that we were to learn that he had been brainwashed and changed his allegiance during his internment.

On 5 May George Bundock was allowed to leave the USSR and to go home, under the amnesty of 23 March 1953. George had been a prisoner in the Embassy for over four years after being accused of passing a sexual disease to a Russian woman and being tried and convicted in his absence. He had continued to work in the Embassy as store man and general factotum and occupied himself in his spare time by acquiring a wide collection of music, on long-playing records as they were then called, which he was always happy to share with other members of the staff.

* * *

British Embassy, Moscow, 29 April 1953

Dear M & D,

The publication of Eisenhower's speech on Saturday last means some extra work, despatches on the *Pravda* article, which replied to it. In addition there are some new appointments. The Ambassador had another interview with Molotov, and there is the usual activity before the great May Day parade.

Over the weekend, Friday night to Monday morning I went to Murom. It is about 280 kilometres away but the train travels slowly. Returning we left at 10 in the evening, travelling 'hard' and came into the Kazan station in Moscow at 9.30 a.m. Travelling 'hard' means having a bunk or sleeper of very solid wood, three tier in long open compartments. We had three at one end of the carriage and shared the corner with two of the fussiest silliest women you could find in any bourgeois society who changed the positions of their suitcases and their bedding and their clothes at least once every half hour throughout the night, and a drunken youth and his girl friend who were later turned out by the woman attendant for creating a 'scandal'. I went with Jeanne Nutt who suffered from being bitten by fleas at the Murom Hotel and Jill Sheppard who escaped.

Murom is an old town, very down at heel, on the high western bank of the Oka. The other bank is low and the land beyond was flooded for miles and miles owing to the quick melting of the snow this year, and sitting on the Murom bank above the little river harbour one could imagine that you were on the seashore. On Sunday there was a special *kolkhoz* market – the only 'free' section of the Soviet economy. But this was a special day when crowds of peasants had come in from the surrounding countryside on carts or buses or bicycles with produce to sell – butter, vegetables and poultry. There was a special area in front of the old cathedral, now a fire station, and beside the picturesque old church of the Blessed Virgin, the only one still in use, where piglets were sold in special wicker baskets. We decided in the end not to buy one, but we did purchase a basket each and some large semi glazed pots in yellow or green of the kind used by peasants for pickling cucumbers. We bought also some provisions, *tvorok* (cream cheese) and eggs and black bread and port wine in the Gastronom shop, and with them went a-picnicking to a place beyond the boundary of the town on the banks of the Oka.

The paths and the roads were exceedingly muddy but the sun shone and the wind was not too strong on the grassy slopes facing a neat little village of wooden houses with carved lintels and eaves and a greensward street between, along which the *kolkhozniks* had sunk a row of wells, each with a carved well cover. The village was, I think, part of a neighbouring state farm of some size where we saw large numbers of horses and pigs, the *kolkhoz* of the Paris Commune. The town of Murom away from the river is dismal, scattered and industrial. Most of the houses are wooden. The streets are cobbled in the centre and beyond just earth, many of them mud and water when we were there so the taxi had to make long switchback detours on the journey between the hotel and the station. The largest building is the Murom Museum where we went on Sunday when it rained – arranged chronologically from the mammoth bones dug out of the Oka mud, to a model of a power station and a little furnished room described as the house of a *peredevoi kolkhoznik* (an advanced agricultural operative). This of course had portraits of Lenin, Stalin and Pushkin in it.

And here I'm afraid I must end, Love, Iain

* * *

From this time Iain was busy with work and a good deal of travelling, sometimes with me, sometimes with other members of the Embassy. He did not have so much time for writing long letters but would frequently send postcards. It became a busy time for the Embassy staff as the cold war began to thaw, more and more visitors came to Moscow, and there was much more official contact with Russians than we had had before.

One of the first instances of this contact was at the Ball, which the Ambassador gave on 2 June on the occasion of the new Queen's coronation. It was attended by Molotov and Gromyko as well as dozens of other Soviet officials, including many military personnel and also dancers from the Bolshoi Ballet. There are photographs of a 3rd Secretary of the Australian Embassy dancing with Lepershinskaia, one of the leading ballerinas, and a story that he saw her home to find her husband waiting up for her on the balcony of her flat. All members of Russian-speaking staff were told that they must consider themselves on duty until the last Russian left the party. The military were the most difficult to entertain as they were unwilling to talk, eat or even drink.

The dancers were the most relaxed. The party went on until the early hours of the morning and as daylight dawned we, the junior members of the Embassy, had breakfast in the flat where I lived at the bottom of the garden.

On 9 June two Russian-born wives of US citizens were granted exit visas by the Soviet government. On 17 June more wives were granted visas. On 22 June a number of travel restrictions were lifted for foreign diplomats in the USSR. On 10 July Beria's dismissal from his post as Minister of Internal Affairs and trial was announced in the local press. The reasons given were that he was a traitor to his country because of his assistance to foreign imperialists, that he had attempted to override party and government decisions and to govern the country himself through his ministry, that he had tried to delay decisions relating to collective farms, that he had made attempts to undermine good relations between the various groups forming the USSR and that he had tried to restore capitalism in the Soviet Union. The government team now consisted of Malenkov, Molotov, Bulganin and Kaganovich. Moscow remained quiet and there were no signs of anything unusual. Beria was succeeded by Kruglov who was not a member of the Presidium. It was possible that Beria had been in trouble already when Stalin died but no steps were taken earlier in order to preserve the façade of unity.[16]

A despatch from Sir Alvary reports that the Soviet armed forces remained loyal in support of the Central Committee and its action in dismissing Beria,[17] and a letter from Sir Alvary to Paul Mason in the Foreign Office wonders whether this was a Malenkov/Beria struggle, with Malenkov sure that the army would get rid of the head of the secret police.[18]

'There is no doubt that the elimination of Beria put an end to the position of the security organs as a state within a state which they had acquired under Stalin'.[19] 'According to Khrushchev, he was shot on the spot, to forestall any attempt by the security police to rescue him; other sources say that he was executed in December after a secret trial.'[20]

* * *

Moscow, Thursday July 1953

Dear D,

I enclose a few photographs taken at the Moscow Embassy Coronation Ball. You will be disappointed to observe that IJMS does not appear in them. He was either at the front door or entertaining the Rumanian Ambassador to beer in the garden. We have however the Ambassador and Lady Gascoigne, the Minister and Mrs Grey and some others from the Embassy.

I hope to fly to the Northern Caucasus with Terry O'Bryan Tear and his wife Sandra, the person from Stornoway. And then go across the Ossetian Highway over the Mamison pass and through the valley of the Rion to a place called Kutaisi and thence to the coast at Poti and Sukhumi. Unfortunately Lady Gascoigne and Elizabeth and Mrs Brimelow who went a similar way last week appear from a telegram to have failed to get over the pass but we do not know why.

Moscow is losing its isolation. To lunch at the Ambassador's today we had Mr John Gordon, Editor of the *Sunday Express*, and Lord Verulam, President of Enfield Cables. We had a delegation from the National Society of Woodworkers visit the Embassy last week. We had some British oilmen and some fur buyers. At the same time most of the regular agency correspondents, kept in Moscow for years now with Russian wives who were not allowed to leave, have been enabled to go. Gone too has Bob Tucker, the editor of the Press Reading

3. The Russian ballerina, Lepershinskaia, dancing with the 3rd Secretary from the Australian Embassy, Bill Morrison, at the Coronation Ball, British Embassy, Moscow, 2 June 1953. On the left are the Ambassador, Sir Alvary Gascoigne and Lady Gascoigne.

Service and his Russian wife. Clara Hall alas has had no luck in her applications to go.

Love Iain

The next two paragraphs are from postcards from Sukhumi, in the Abkhazian Autonomous Soviet Socialist Republic, part of Georgia.

The Abkhazia Hotel, Sukhumi, 21 July 1953

Dear M & D,

I write from a 'Luxe' room on the third floor of the Hotel on this card. The balcony looks out on the Black Sea, which is blue. But the heat is such that one cannot stand there long. We flew this morning (35 minutes) from Kutaisi, having come yesterday by bus (10 hours) from Shovi in the Rion valley. We had arrived there the previous night on foot from the other side of the Mamison pass (14 hours), our luggage on horseback. Love Iain

Hotel Abkhazia, Sukhumi, ASSR, 21 July 1953

Dear Anne,

I expect you are back from Iona. I write from the shore of another sea – the room I have looks out over the Black Sea. I and the O'Bryan Tears, from the Embassy, arrived here this morning by air from Kutaisi. The previous day 10 hours in a bus from the high Caucasus down the beautiful Rion valley. The day before that with two horses and two Ossetian drivers we crossed the Mamison pass. Love Iain.

* * *

Wednesday, Sadovaia Samotechnaia 12/35, August 1953

Dear M & D and A,

The Embassy is much reduced. This week only myself and Peter Mennell in Chancery. Murray Simons, relieved of his post as Ambassador's Secretary with Sir A.'s departure, set off immediately for Tiflis. Prudie Mennell who was to have gone with him has fallen ill. The Head of Chancery, Tony Rouse, has gone on leave to England. So has Jeanne Nutt. So also Peter Knapton who flew away in the Ambassador's crowded plane. Terry O'Bryan Tear is still in

Stockholm, so I have to issue visas to Russians wishing to enter Britain or New Zealand or Libya or a lot of other strange places. And with notes on Germany and the aftermath of the Supreme Soviet meeting this last week has been busy. And of course the Ambassador has also gone. On Tuesday morning the whole staff went out to the airport at Vnukovo to see him off in the early morning. Most of the heads of other missions here were there too, and an official from the Ministry of Foreign Affairs. Lady Gascoigne was presented with a large bunch of flowers on the airport steps. The large four engined RAF plane, which had come in the previous day in a terrific thunderstorm was waiting for them, being critically inspected by a large crowd of Russians, pilots and airport staff and groups of passengers going to Riga or returning from Tashkent. It had a strange appearance as the wings and tail were painted over bright red for special identification. Inside it must have looked even stranger for it was a transport plane and was loaded to absolute capacity with all the Ambassadorial crates and only a very small space was left for Sir A. and Lady G., Peter Knapton, the chef, the butler and the five poodles. The Ambassador was not really sad to leave Moscow, though conditions here are much better and both more hopeful and more interesting than when he arrived just under two years ago.

I went to see the Indian Art Exhibition, which is at present the sensation of Moscow. Have you ever known an exhibition of pictures, and not a very good one at that, when crowds waited on the street four deep all day in a queue several hundred yards long and there were six policemen at the door? Needless to say we did not wait in the queue. A diplomatic number plate on the car and the policemen cleared the way and ushered us in. The Russians sent a show of modern Soviet painting to New Delhi last winter, many of them vast realistic canvases of happy *kolkhozniks* and factory interiors. It was pretty severely criticised by artists there but achieved considerable success with the public. This is a return visit sponsored by the Russian Ministry of Culture. Three Indian artists have come with the show and are constantly in attendance with interpreters conducting parties round the crowded rooms.

Another recent visit I made was to the new University on the Lenin Hills. This was a special parting request of Lady Gascoigne's to the Protocol Department and despite the fact that the furniture is not yet in position nor some of the floors laid we saw some of the interior of the great central block of the skyscraper. The block contains only the Geology, Geography and Physics faculties and the Scientific Library. There are also residence quarters for students and lecturers. Perched atop a hill overlooking Moscow it is 36 stories high and although in elevation it is topped by the Empire State Building it is, we were told, in cubic capacity, the largest building in the world. The view from the 17th storey was truly magnificent.

Love from Iain

The Bear Hotel, Yaroslavl, Monday 10 September 1953

Dear M,

I am waiting in a room in the Hotel *Medved'* overlooking the main square of Yaroslavl and the theatre shown in the postcard I put in the box yesterday for you. It has been raining pretty steadily since we arrived here yesterday at lunchtime. We should have left early this morning but there have been difficulties in obtaining petrol. We had hoped to visit the Ilinskaia Church, which contains some of the finest, if not the finest, frescoes in Russia. Perhaps the finest are or were in another Yaroslavl church of Iona Predtechi in Tolchkovo, which we tried to visit yesterday. Yesterday when we had walked there we found it in the centre of a large square of elegant early 19th century buildings. It has two dissimilar bell towers and five very graceful cupolas with the net-like tracery on them, which is characteristic of the Yaroslavl style. An old woman who lived in part of what must have been the crypt could not open the doors. The key, she said, was in the museum. The museum, it being Sunday, was shut. We went there this morning but no key. We were directed to the architectural department of the *oblast* (district) Committee, which occupied one range of the elegant buildings along one side of the square. It was not there. They said we should go to the town committee in a street in another part of the town. We walked there in the drizzling rain. We were directed to the office of the chief architect, and sent from there to another. He was on leave. In any case we would have to have the chief architect's permission. He was away on business, his deputy was on leave. The deputy's deputy was away at lunch but just as we were going he turned up but told us, quite politely, however, that he could not give the required permission. We would have to go to the office of the town surveyor. We knew where this was because we had already been there yesterday. But it had been Sunday and it had been closed. Perhaps today we would have more luck. The office was even very neat and clean with a library and an old distinguished looking gentleman with a beard sitting at a desk. He would have to ring up the architect's office where we had been already. He phoned but as we knew could get no decision. So we had to return to see if the petrol had arrived. And so we look like leaving Yaroslavl without seeing the interiors of any of its churches. I do not think anyone had tried to prevent us entering them but just that Yaroslavl is not organised for curious tourists.

At Rostov-Yaroslavsky the hotel is very primitive and it was there that we spent last night. 'Tsarkov's Inn' they call it in my Baedeker, 'en face du Kremlin'. And it cannot have changed much since pre-revolutionary days. The eating house was on the ground floor with crowds of workmen and schoolgirls sitting at very dirty tables, thick tobacco smoke and hoards of flies and a few individuals who had drunk too much vodka; there was a strong smell of garlic and borsch and burnt fat and old quilted jackets wet by the rain. The rooms looked out on to the square, beds clean enough but as usual much too short and very hard. We looked out from our windows and were rather puzzled. In Lady Kelly's book there was a photograph of the view from this very window. But we could not identify the view, for Lady Kelly's Kremlin was bright and shiny and well preserved. We saw a shambles of wrecked roofs and overturned domes and crosses. Only one cupola was left on the Uspensky Cathedral where there had been four. All but one had gone from the ancient bell tower. On the Church of John all had disappeared and the metal roofing had been ripped from the covered cloisters round the walls. We were most puzzled and dismayed. It looked as if a bomb had exploded in the precincts. We asked the director with the wooden leg and he told us the strange tale of a whirlwind, which had struck the little town of Rostov the previous week. Only three minutes it had lasted, and the breadth of the area affected was only about two hundred yards. But it had swept straight across the town uprooting trees, lifting the roofs off wooden houses, stripping the metal from the shops in the market and hitting the Kremlin with full force before it passed on to Lake Nero, beyond where it raised a waterspout some hundreds of feet high. Some people were killed and many injured. Nothing was mentioned in the press, but such events never are. Acts of God are not news here or perhaps they do not occur.

With love from Iain

Thursday – Sadovaia

I shall be coming back to UK in October, probably on the *Belo-Ostrov* leaving Leningrad on October 19. I shall be in London and have to join China-Korea political department on the 17 November, which means that I shall have some leave between 26 October and 17 November and shall carry some forward.

The Embassy is still in the throes of repairs and resounds to the sound of hammering in preparation for the arrival of Sir William Hayter on 3rd October. Moscow is now wet and cold, the year's tennis is over and the Bolshoi Theatre season has begun.

With love from Iain

British Embassy, Moscow, 1 October 1953

Dear D & M,

This week we have just come from welcoming in the new Ambassador at the airport. And last night I had just arrived back at 9.30 p.m. from Alma Ata. I had left at 5.30 (Moscow time) the same day and had been in the aircraft all day with stops at Karaganda, Kustanai (in Kazakhstan) and Uralsk. I have no time now to describe my travels. Did you get a card from Samarkand? We went there first, then to Tashkent (Uzbekistan), Stalinabad (Tadzhikistan), Frunze (Kirgizstan) and Alma Ata (Kazakhstan). All these places are further from Moscow than Moscow is from London. I went with Dick Freeborn and Dick Woolcote of the Australian Embassy who stayed on for a few extra days in Alma Ata.

My plans for return remain the same. Ex Leningrad on the 19th. I hope you are enjoying your holiday, Love from Iain

British Embassy, Moscow, Friday October 1953

Dear M,

Tomorrow morning, Saturday, I go with the Embassy party to the Kremlin Palace for the Presentation of the Ambassador's Credentials; morning coats, top hats, uniforms and a series of handshakes; a party for me at the Mennells the night before that; a party by the new Ambassador for the staff on Monday. There have been difficulties over sending my car and I may not take it; a great disappointment yesterday, nearly all the photographs I took on my trip with my new camera were blank. I foolishly left the exposed spools in the hotel at Alma Ata and the police must have found them and exposed the negative to the light.

Love Iain

* * *

Iain left Moscow in October 1953 soon after I returned from leave in the UK. In fact he was away on his long Central Asian trip when I came back. There were no commitments in our relationship at this stage, but there was an agreement that we would meet up again when I returned to the UK the following year. I missed him as we had got used to doing things together, whether it be going to the theatre or travelling to strange places that we had never seen before.

However there was much of interest happening in the Soviet Union at this period. The distinct thaw in relations with the west provided many more opportunities for visitors to come to Moscow. We had much more contact with Russians too and Russian speakers were in demand, either interpreting for the Minister of Foreign Trade, Mikoyan (at one such meeting we together mixed a special 'Mikoyan' cocktail) at receptions for British businessmen or looking after non-Communist student delegations visiting the USSR.[21]

The thaw had an effect not only on the diplomatic community but also on the Russians themselves. Less rigid collective leadership with Malenkov as Chairman of the Council of Ministers and Khrushchev as Secretary General of the Party – improvement in conditions in the camps after riots and disturbances took place – the break up of Beria's empire and the splitting of the security forces between Ministry of the Interior (MVD) and the KGB – produced a relatively more relaxed atmosphere in the country. Some Soviet personalities began to attend diplomatic functions. I remember having my hand shaken by Bulganin and Voroshilov as they were leaving a national day celebration at the Indonesian Embassy when they were so drunk that their eyes were not focusing. Members of the Embassy continued to travel more widely than before. It became possible, in theory, to travel by car, although little was known of the state of the roads and lodging places en route. Four of us were to find out with some discomfort when we planned a journey in mid November to the south, destination Sochi, on the Black Sea coast, supposedly the Riviera of Russia. We had visions of sun and blue sea. This was where the Soviet leaders had their summer dachas and sanatoria. Even junior party members or trade union officials might be lucky enough to enjoy a week or two's holiday here in the summer. We thought that in November there would still be time to enjoy these delights. Peter Mennell, Jim and Barbara Barker, from the Canadian Embassy and I, packed ourselves into Peter's Vauxhall, together with the driver, Volodya, and luggage and supplies for several days. Barbara recorded our journey in a letter to her parents.

November/December 1953

Dear Mum and Dad,

Our idea was to drive to Kharkov and spend the night there, the next day to Rostov and the next to Sochi. We were going to spend four days in Sochi, and then we were going to put the car and ourselves on a ship to Yalta. Peter, Jeanne and I were going to spend a couple of days in Yalta and then drive back to Moscow. We were pioneers on this trip; since the travel restrictions for diplomats in Russia have been lifted everyone has been vying with everyone else to see who could be first to visit each place. People had been to Sochi and Yalta before but no one had been by car.

We set off in the best of spirits, it was a lovely day and the sun was shining. We made very good time for the first part of the day, which was a good thing as Kharkov is 1100 kms away. About the middle of the afternoon we got to Oriel. While Volodya went to the gas station we thought we would find someplace to have a cup of tea. Never in my life have I seen such a dismal place. Deseronto looks like paradise after Oriel. Also it was cold as the dickens by this time and the sun had gone and everything looked horrid. We had lunch in the car after Oriel, quite a tricky operation that we did every day in order to keep on driving and not lose time. But if you have tried to slice bread or carve chicken or open tins in the back of an English car with three people in it... We got better at it later on in the trip but were always covered with spilled coffee and crumbs and kept losing food down around our feet and didn't have room to bend down and hunt for it. About this time we started to feel cold in the car, and for the whole of the rest of the trip we were constantly frozen. We each had a rug but it didn't seem to make any difference. Peter and the driver were all right because they had a heater but the heat didn't reach the back. They also had to keep the two front windows open so the windshield wouldn't fog up. It is my most vivid memory of the trip – I have never been so cold for so long in my life. We stopped a couple of times for bathroom privileges always out in the country. It was cold but not so bad as it might have been and infinitely better than a Russian john.

About five o'clock we got to a place called Kursk and were very cheered because it was only forty miles to Kharkov, and we thought we would be there in no time. Little did we know. It had just got dark and all of a sudden it started to snow, pretty as all get out at first, and then a wind came up, and blew harder and harder and within about half an hour it had developed into the worst blizzard I have ever seen in my life. Really and truly it was just terrifying. We were in the Ukraine at this point in the middle of a flat plain (not the steppe, that was the next day!). There wasn't a tree or a house or even a bush for miles and miles and so there was nothing to stop the wind blowing the snow across the road in white sheets. We couldn't even see the nose of the car. We kept going slower and slower until finally we were doing about 2 miles an hour. It was bitterly cold and howling so that you couldn't even talk normally. Then we discovered we were the only ones still travelling on the road. We passed, I think, 36 trucks and buses, mostly off the road on their sides or some of them had just skidded and stopped in the middle of the road and their drivers had decided just to wait for the morning. All we needed was a pack of wolves on our trail to complete the perfect picture of winter travel through Russia. And I will never forget Peter, who was marvellously calm with his nose pressed against the windshield singing abstractedly to himself and directing Volodya to the left or right. 'When the deep – *na leva* (left) – purple falls over slee – *na prava* (right) – py gardenwalls'. Then all of a sudden we saw a little white light that looked like a parking light of a truck that had parked on the road facing us. So Volodya swerved to the right to go around it and suddenly we were on our sides in the ditch. Well… We thought we were there for the night, but by some miracle a truck had gone off the road just a few feet further along the road and it was full of men who rushed over to help us out – everybody shouting directions and all of them having a wonderful time. Jeanne and I stayed in the car but Jim and Peter got out to push, Jim in a light trench coat and Peter in one of those navy duffel coats that aren't built for blizzards. After about twenty minutes of frenzied pushing and all wading in drifts up to their waists they finally got the car on the road again and we went on. Finally after driving for six hours through the blizzard, forty miles, Kharkov appeared and never have I been gladder to see any place in my life.

The hotel by Russian standards was a very nice one, an Intourist one which means that they usually have a bathroom with at least a couple of the bedrooms, and even soap and towels. It couldn't have looked lovelier to us if it had been the Waldorf Astoria. Jim and I had the biggest room, typically Soviet with a grand piano, twelve chairs, a couple of round tables with rugs over them, orange lampshades, chrome plated beds, and a bedside lamp made out of marble in the shape of an owl, with the light coming out of his eyes. We all had dinner in our room, Wiener schnitzel and lots of vodka to thaw us out.

We had planned to leave about nine that morning but Volodya had to get gas first and when he got to the place he found they wouldn't have any until eleven. So we wandered round the stores and looked at Kharkov and finally about eleven thirty got under way again. Had to fight our way through a crowd of about sixty people all milling around the car trying to see what it and we looked like. That day was the best day we had for driving. It snowed quite hard for a little while and then stopped and turned to slush. We kept driving through tiny villages with about twelve little shacks to each, quite picturesque but perfectly dreadful really, tiny little one room shacks made out of mud with thatched roofs. Once in a while they would be painted but mostly they were mud colour and sitting in absolute seas of mud. They often were double buildings, one for the cow and chickens and the other room for the family. They were the poorest most miserable looking peasants you have ever seen, old women out digging or carrying two pails of water from the community well. We kept getting bogged down in the middle of flocks of sheep wandering down the road, or a family of geese that wouldn't make up their minds where to go, or old men driving prehistoric wagons. We were driving through the black earth district of the Ukraine and it really was coal black and wonderful for growing I guess. We stopped at a gas station and Jeanne and I saw an elegant looking privy out behind which we thought we would try. It looked so nice, made of stucco with trellis all around it. But once inside it was the same old thing, two holes in the ground and the most overpowering smell, just indescribable. We looked down the holes (don't ask me why) and found it was built over a concrete pit about 12 feet deep and square. They must have been building for posterity!

We got to Rostov on Don about 10 o'clock. We weren't nearly so tired that night and thought it would be fun to have dinner in the hotel restaurant and absorb some local colour. However after we looked in the door and saw about three brawls and people being sick we decided we would forego their company and eat in our rooms again. This hotel wasn't Intourist and it wasn't nearly as good. Jim and I had a bathroom to ourselves (no soap and towels or toilet paper, bathtub stained up to the top the colour of very strong tea and when you took the plug out the water just ran on to the bathroom floor and down a hole in the middle). Volodya had all his meals with us, which was fun. In Moscow they hardly dare to smile at you because if they are seen to be getting too friendly they are told to leave, but on a trip with none of the other chauffeurs around to tell tales he could relax and he is such a nice guy. All our dinner table conversation was the most dreadful mixture of English and Russian but it never seemed to be any strain and V was pretty smart at getting what we were driving at. Jeanne's Russian is very good, Peter's appalling but very fluent and Jim's and mine practically non-existent but everyone seemed to know what everyone else was saying.

The original plan had been to drive right to Sochi that day. It was about 300 miles and we had done that many the day before from Kharkov, but everyone we talked to said that the road was really not that good and when a Russian says that you can be sure it is practically impossible. So we decided that we would just go as far as Krasnodar, which was only 100 miles away and we were sure that even if the roads were very bad we would easily make it by late afternoon. Ha, Ha! For about the first ten miles it wasn't too bad and then it started. I've never seen anything worse, mud about a foot deep and slippery and slimy. It was just like driving through a freshly ploughed field in the early spring: deep, deep ruts and mud right up to the hubcaps. It was bumpy and we kept getting stuck and could only go about ten miles an hour. It was worse than the blizzard really except that at least we could see where we were going. By this time we were really on the steppes, the Kuban steppes, absolutely flat country. You could probably see for fifty miles in all directions and not a single tree or bush or blade of grass, just miles and miles of mud. The villages we went through were even poorer than the ones the day before and the little houses were sunk nearly up to the one window in mud. It began to snow again, the kind of snow that melts as soon as it hits the ground but it was cold and wet and miserable. We kept crossing railway tracks and every time we did we would have to sit and wait until some old scrunch came out of her little shack to lift the barrier; and every time we had to stop for a railway crossing we would get stuck in the mud again and the boys would have to get out and push. And when they lifted up their feet a big lump of mud about a foot square would come up with them, and then all that came back into the car. You can just imagine what we and the rugs and the car looked like. Then we stopped to put the chains on, for mud not for snow, and V got really covered, practically lying in the mud.

Sometimes we just drove through the fields and not on the road at all because the fields were a bit harder. And then in one village something happened to one of the chains and it got wrapped around the axle and we had to stop and take the wheel off. We stopped very suddenly much to the discomfort of the NKVD (People's Commissariat for Internal Affairs) men who were following us. They stopped too close and not back a block or two the way they usually do and they had to stand around out in the cold pretending that there was something wrong with their car too. Finally Peter went up to a house to borrow some water for hand washing and the faithful watchdog rushed out and bit him on the leg. This was the last straw but we went on and on thinking that Krasnodar must be just around the corner, and then we would see a sign saying we had another hundred kilometres to go! Then all of a sudden about nine o'clock in the middle of a tiny little village V stopped the car and said he had had it. He was falling asleep at the wheel and said we would just have to spend the night in the car and go on again by daylight. Jim offered to drive instead of V but neither Peter nor V was in favour and since it was Peter's car we had to give in. It wasn't quite so bad for them because at least in the front they could stretch their legs out but we couldn't move anything except our heads.

They promptly went to sleep but the three of us thought we had to get out and stretch our legs for a few minutes. If there had been a single light on in any of the cottages we would have knocked at the door and asked if we could spend the night on their floor. However, I guess they all go to bed as soon as it is dark because every house was in pitch darkness. We wandered around and were covered in snow and soaked to the skin. So we squeezed ourselves back into the car, and tried to go to sleep and I have never known such a long night in my life. We'd all lean one way and then the other, and we were absolutely frozen and wet and couldn't get warm. We'd sleep for about five minutes and then be awake for half an hour. And for some reason the car was parked on a slant and Jeanne was on the bottom side with the full weight of Jim and me on her and her face pressed into the handle of the door. Somewhere about midnight Jeanne very firmly said, 'Jim you'll have to change to places with me', which we did without getting out of the car, how I'll never know.

It didn't get light until about seven o'clock and then we started on the same nightmare driving again. As it turned out the village where we had spent the night in the car was only twenty-five kilometres from Krasnodar but it took us from seven until noon to get there. At last we arrived in Krasnodar expecting the worst but there was a hotel and it wasn't bad at all. Jim and I had a huge suite with about twenty chairs and the beds in a curtained alcove. We didn't have bathrooms but there was a not too smelly one down the hall. We asked if we could have a bath and they said we could have a shower if we waited while they lit the fire in the wood stove, which they did in a lovely big square flat topped *pechka* like the kind you always read about the Russians sleeping on top of. The shower was in a little sort of wooden cubbyhole and you stood on a piece of slippery rubber matting under the shower, while an old scrunch stoked the fire on the other side of the wall.

The next morning Jim had to go back to Moscow. We were supposed to be in Sochi by Wednesday and this was Friday. We all kept saying 'oh never mind, pretty soon we'll be in Sochi in all that sunshine and sea bathing'. So we drove off and left Jim in front of the hotel clutching his Aeroflot ticket in one hand and 'Brush Up Your Russian' in the other. I was quite sure I would never see him again and if it hadn't meant leaving Jeanne by herself with Peter and Volodya would have been delighted to go back with him. As it turned out he got as far as Rostov that night and then the weather was too bad to go any further so they put him up at the airport guest house and he got back to Moscow on Saturday noon. Meanwhile we started off again. Everyone said the road was excellent as far as Novorossiisk, but from there to Sochi was through the mountains and if there was much snow the road would be closed. We decided that if the road was closed we would have to spend the winter in Novorossiisk. Anything would be better

4. Stuck in the snow and mud outside Rostov, on the drive to Sochi, autumn 1953. The driver, Volodya, putting on the chains watched by Peter Mennell, Jim Barker and Jeanne, from the car.

71

than going back the way we had come and we thought we would take a chance on it.

Just on the outskirts of Krasnodar we found the loveliest traffic jam. About a hundred trucks and buses were stopped on the road because it hadn't been ploughed and there were only two deep ruts in the snow and nobody could pass without getting stuck in the ditch. Jeanne and I stood it for about half an hour and then suggested to Peter that we might go back to Krasnodar, arrange to put the car on a flatcar on the train and go by train to Sochi. So with a great deal of difficulty and much help from Russian bystanders we turned the car round. They practically lifted it up and turned it round. It was just lovely because our followers were stuck about forty cars back along the road and couldn't see what we were doing, and if you could have seen the surprised look on their faces when they saw us passing them going in the opposite direction.

We went back to Krasnodar and to the station where Jeanne and Peter and V all went in to negotiate with the stationmaster. Jeanne said he was most cooperative and in about ten minutes she had us all arranged to ride in the car on the flatcar on the train. Then Volodya got talking to some of the people who were sitting around listening to all this and they told him the road was just fine once you got past the traffic jam outside the town, and V got the bit in his teeth and before Jeanne knew where she was at he had talked Peter into trying it again. So much against Jeanne's and my better judgement we set out again. Needless to say the road was lousy. We never did get past the traffic jam; it was continuous nearly all the way. About two feet of snow had fallen so there were two deep ruts, which were too high for our car and scraped the bottom, so we had to drive on a slant most of the way, again about ten miles an hour.

We were out of the steppes by this time and into the foothills of the Caucasus, pretty rolling country and the villages we went through were much prettier, still mud houses but painted now, pinks and blues and greens with fancy carving around the doors and windows, and shutters to match. We saw an awful lot of oil derricks and figured this must be a much more profitable part of the country. Our followers had by this time changed out of their Pobeda into a jeep, which we thought was very smart of them. It was bad driving but not as bad as the day before and much as we missed Jim Jeanne and I did have room to move in the back seat! We finally arrived at the hotel in Novorossiisk. This was the only one we hadn't wired ahead to and when we first went in they said they couldn't give us any rooms. After a lot of negotiating the militia must have told them to give us their best rooms or else, and we were given two, one for Jeanne and I and one for Peter and Volodya. It was just a tiny hotel, mostly truck drivers, and the rooms were rather like monks' cells but not too bad. The john itself was unspeakable but the washing facilities were interesting. There was a big old bath tub full of cold water and a rusty gallon pail which you dipped full of water and poured it into a little container, which had holes in it and the water sprinkled out of it and fell into another rusty pail underneath. We got kind of hysterical trying to wash there; also there was an inch of water all over the bathroom floor.

The manageress was suddenly conscience stricken at having foreigners in her hotel and came in and began mopping up the water on the floor. She went into a long tale about how during the war Novorossiisk had been very badly bombed by the Germans and how there had been hundreds of fires, and that was why things weren't quite as nice as they might have been and why there was water all over the floor.

The next morning we started out, this time really on the last lap of our journey to Sochi. We couldn't believe it. The mountain road was open we found out and there was practically no snow in Novorossiisk so we thought the sunny south was practically in sight. It was 175 miles to Sochi, all through the mountains and we were looking forward to it. We had an old Baedeker with us, which said that 'the drive is interesting and very picturesque but rather tiring for ladies'. Jeanne and I pooh-poohed this and said that Baedeker's ladies lived a long time ago and weren't nearly as tough as we were. Well... It was all up and down mountains, and all hairpin bends. We counted them and there were eight to a kilometre, about three thousand that day, not just curves but real hairpins bending right back on themselves. Jeanne and I were desperately seasick all day long – couldn't even speak we felt so awful. It would have been lovely if we hadn't felt so terrible, all along beside the sea and the mountains with snow on the tops.

For the first hour or so we drove through the most terrific storm, wind howling and the waves lashing against the rocks, and rain and then sleet and hail and a sort of eerie yellow light. And on the lonely mountain road it looked just like a setting for a murder story. I don't think we passed another thing on the road all day long and the men following had a miserable time trying to hide from us on the mountain road. It took us forever to get to Sochi because we could never get up any speed. It did finally end about eleven o'clock at night. We found the hotel, a very elegant one, quite big and right on the sea. The outside was very impressive and the inside too by Soviet standards, but by ours pretty terrible with the same dreadful furniture and lamps and the same Russian smell and the same sloppiness.

We found out that night that the ship which we were supposed to take to Yalta the next day and which we had nearly killed ourselves racing to Sochi to catch, was not going to come in at all because of storms on the sea, and there wouldn't be another one until the next Friday. So we either had to drive back the way we had come or stay in Sochi for a week. Nobody could bear the thought of going over any of those roads again, but we didn't relish the idea of staying on either and Jeanne had to get back to Moscow for work. So we decided that Jeanne and I would fly back home on Wednesday and Peter and Volodya would take the next ship to Yalta and drive home from there.

The next day we woke up to the most dreadful storm raging, a terrific gale blowing in from the sea and rain, sleet and hail all alternating at half hour intervals. This was our wonderful Sochi that we had nearly bust ourselves to get to for the sunshine. And it was bitterly cold, just as bad inside the hotel as outside. They had no heat on in the hotel because they said this was most unusual and they never had weather like this until February. We couldn't go out so we spent our time wrapped in blankets playing canasta in Russian, which Jeanne taught Volodya and I still don't know how she managed. We went to a very old movie, 'The Three Musketeers', in English with Russian subtitles, tried to go to a concert but the weather was so bad the artists never arrived. When the rain stopped we went for a walk along the promenade by the sea. Sochi looks a bit like Torquay. It is all palm trees, beautifully laid out gardens and paths and lovely wide streets with beds of flowers running down each side. It must be perfectly lovely, in the summer. Enormous waves were breaking against the sea wall with the spray flying up about forty feet into the air. Peter and I were not looking closely enough and suddenly a tremendous wave sneaked up on us, crashed up right over the wall and rolled in about twenty feet inshore. And there we were with the water swirling around our hips and bits of seaweed streaming past us and Jeanne and Volodya laughing so hard they nearly fell in too!

The next day it was snowing and even colder. We went to the Aeroflot office to get our tickets for Moscow. This took a long time because they had to get permission for us to fly back when we were meant to drive. Also we had to send about six telegrams to Moscow, telling them when we would be back and asking for more gas tickets for Peter as he had run out by this time. This had to be done in Russian so Jeanne wrote them out roughly and we each copied them on to the forms. Finally we spent hours in the market arranging to have boxes of tangerines shipped back to Moscow (the ones on the trees were covered in snow by this time!). By this time we were frozen and had to return to the hotel to recover and play more canasta. Fortunately the food was good. It was the only place in the Soviet Union where you found yourself really looking forward to eating. We went to another movie, this time a Russian anti-American one called 'Mountain Outpost', quite good too and you couldn't help cheering for the Russians because all their soldiers were nice clean cut, clean living, shiny faced boys, while the Americans were ugly, drunken and always pushing young ladies off mountains and beating their dogs and horses!

We thought we should see a sanatorium so we asked to visit one. It really was very impressive. Every trades union, district and organisation maintains its own sanatorium, some are medical and some are just rest homes for holidays. The one we saw was for coal miners and was medical. There was a swimming pool and an underground funicular down the side of the mountain to the sea shore where there was a bathing beach and a solarium, a tennis and a squash court, a gymnasium and an outdoor summer theatre and an indoor summer theatre. There wasn't a single thing you could find fault with. And it is almost free, i.e. paid for by the unions. I forgot to tell you that the Sochi hotel had bedbugs. We all got bitten and couldn't believe it because it was supposed to be such a high class one and we hadn't found any bedbugs in any of the other perfectly dreadful places where we stayed.

The next morning we got up early and Peter and Volodya drove us to the airport. Jeanne and I each took two seasick pills because we had heard that the road to the airport was a continuation of the hairpin drive, which it was. So by the time we got to the airport we were both so sleepy we couldn't even talk, and Peter and Volodya helped us staggering across the field to the plane. We felt rather mean leaving them to brave the drive home by themselves but not mean enough to change our minds. We couldn't wait to get back to Moscow. And in about six hours we were there. It seemed incredible when it had taken us six ghastly days to get down there. We weren't even conscious on the flight back – slept all the way thanks to the pills. And there was Jim's cheery face waiting to meet us at the airport and I have never been so glad to see any person or any place before. The trip was certainly interesting but far more fun to think back on than it was while we were doing it.

Love, Barbara

* * *

I made other trips between November 1953 and when I left in August 1954 but nothing quite so adventurous and difficult. I went to Georgia with Patrick Regan, who took Peter Mennell's place in Chancery, where we saw Stalin's birthplace at Gori, Mtskheta, the ancient Georgian capital and centre of Georgian culture and religion with its magnificent 15th century cathedral. And we enjoyed the good Georgian food and wine. The Caucasus was the Mediterranean of the Soviet Union. Georgians believed in enjoying life and behaved more like Italians than Russians. They would even stop to stare as you passed, look you up and down and make remarks about you. I went to Central Asia with Murray Simons, when Bukhara was still a primitive town surrounded by medieval walls and Tashkent had an old Uzbek market area with houses made of mud and ladies wearing veils of straw. On the way back we called at Alma Ata and then Kurgan and Kazan in Tatarstan. I think it was in Kazan that I saw women fighting and actually pulling out each other's hair and men so drunk in the one and only restaurant that they collapsed on the floor pulling the tablecloth and four plates of bright red borsch with them.

The most important internal event at the end of 1953 was the report of the trial of Beria and his associates, which according to the Soviet press took place between 18 and 23 December. It confirmed that sentence of death by shooting had been carried out.[22]

In November the Lenin-Stalin mausoleum was opened, and a decree was passed rescinding the prohibition of marriages between Soviet citizens and foreigners. On 28 November the Ambassador was received by Malenkov and on 21 December the Soviet government accepted President Eisenhower's invitation to participate in confidential or diplomatic talks on the control of nuclear energy. A few days later a Soviet proposal was made, that states participating in an agreement to control atomic energy should assume the obligation never to use weapons of mass destruction. However, in contrast to the attempts in recent months to try to improve relations with foreigners, a renewed campaign for greater vigilance was reported.[23]

This was a time when much greater emphasis was being put for the first time on the production of consumer goods and the increase in capital investment in this field.[24] In March there were reports of Khrushchev's virgin land campaign and the expansion of 13 million hectares in 1954–55 assimilating great areas of virgin and idle land.[25] The elections held in March for the Supreme Soviet were of little interest. There was only one candidate for each place and it served as little more than an opportunity for the usual propaganda for government policy.[26] April saw the results in Moscow of the 'Petrov' affair. As a result of the defection of a member of the Soviet Embassy in Canberra and the accusation by the Soviets of the abduction of Mrs Petrova, all

Soviet/Australian diplomatic relations were broken and the Australian Embassy staff left Moscow on 29 April.[27]

The first quarter of 1954 therefore seemed to be a series of ups and downs, steps forward in relations with the Soviets and steps backward. The Soviet government's agreement to the setting up of the Berlin Conference on 25 January became the main feature of Soviet foreign policy. Visitors continued to come; Sir John Hunt in June and in August a Labour Party delegation arrived in Moscow led by Atlee and including Bevan, Summerskill and Morgan Phillips. Malenkov gave a reception for them at his dacha, attended by the Ambassador, and a reception was given at the Embassy attended by Malenkov, Molotov, Khrushchev, Mikoyan, Shvernik and Vyshinsky.[28]

I left Moscow in August 1954 when my two-year assignment came to an end. I was ready for a change from the strange atmosphere in which we lived and a return to the more normal world, but I knew that there were many things I would miss. And I was leaving at a time when things were changing rapidly in the Soviet Union and becoming more interesting than they had been for many years. I left by air to fly to Vienna and after a night there to continue by train to Venice where I was to meet Iain.

5. The wedding of Jeanne and Iain at the Crown Court Church, 15 October 1955, with left George Richardson, best man, and Susan Evans (later Harley) and Anne Sutherland, bridesmaids.

3

BLOODSHED AT BLED,
YUGOSLAVIA 1956–59

I ain and I were married in October 1955 in London and our first
posting, to Belgrade, came only five months later. We had expected
to stay considerably longer in London. Iain was to be 2nd Secretary
in the Economic Section of the Embassy, his first (and in fact only)
non-political posting. It was my first posting as a non-working member
of the Embassy (Foreign Office wives were not allowed to work in
postings abroad in those days) and I should probably have felt this
change more acutely if I had not discovered soon after my arrival that
I was expecting our first child; but it took some time to get used to not
having an occupation during the day and thus being a target for wives'
coffee parties and even, as I discovered after one embarrassment when
unknowingly I took Iain with me, wives' lunches.

As we were told that we had to arrive at the end of March, just before
Easter weekend, we set off on the Orient Express, the normal means
of transport at that time. Neither of us had ever been to Yugoslavia or
knew very much about the country. We did not speak the language and
had no instruction in it before we left. However, as we spoke Russian we
thought we would manage to make ourselves understood, and as it
was a communist country we would be prepared for the sort of life we
would have to lead. This turned out to be only half true. The language
spoken in Belgrade, known as Serbo-Croat in those days, although a
Slav language with the same Cyrillic script and many similarities with
Russian, is not at all the same and it soon became apparent that
we would have to learn it as a new language. As far as communism

was concerned, compared with the USSR the Yugoslav variety was completely different.

Tito had been expelled from the Cominform, the organisation which coordinated the policies of the ruling European Communist Parties – and those of France and Italy, in 1948 because he resisted Stalin's and the Soviet Union's interference in the Yugoslav economy and pursued an independent foreign policy especially in the Balkans. 'Tito and his colleagues were, moreover, shocked and repelled by the duplicity and the arrogant power politics which they felt characterised the Soviet Union's attitude towards its allies and fraternal Communist parties.' This expulsion from the Communist club forced Tito to find his own methods of economic planning and to take Yugoslavia's 'own road to socialism'. Popularly elected People's Councils controlled most local functions, including economic enterprises, investment and production; enterprises were run by Workers' Councils elected by the workers by secret ballot; agriculture became mostly private or cooperative.[1] In the years following the expulsion from the Cominform Tito showed considerable courage and skill in pursuing an independent path, resisting the Soviet threats and threatening force himself if necessary. Later there was some reconciliation between Tito and Khrushchev; but never becoming too close.

The Yugoslav government and party moved away from the Soviet pattern and developed economic ties with non-communist countries, which led to a much less rigid form of communism and much freer social intercourse with foreigners from the west. As western diplomats we were able to make friendships with Yugoslavs from all sides of the political spectrum, from members of the party and government to members of the *ancien regime* and opponents of the present leadership. We were able to travel freely without restrictions throughout the country and to make our own arrangements for transport, hotel accommodation and hiring servants. To Iain and me, used as we were to the Soviet variety, this did not seem like communism.

The six republics which made up Yugoslavia in the 1950s, Serbia, Montenegro, Croatia, Slovenia, Bosnia-Herzegovina and Macedonia, had considerable autonomy in such areas as economics, education, culture and social welfare, but were held together firmly in matters political and military by Tito and the central government. Any attempt to stray away from the party line was severely stamped on. While I lived there I always felt that the ethnic differences between the various nationalities were not a problem and that they all intermarried and lived side by side in considerable harmony. I was therefore the more shocked when the wars between the various nationalities began in the early 1990s. Perhaps as suggested by Dushko Doder in his book, *The Yugoslavs*, the nationalistic struggles were not easily apparent to a western diplomat living in Belgrade and consorting mostly with bureaucrats and officials. His book was written in the 1970s and he certainly thought that the differences were there then. In such a mixture of ethnic peoples as the Orthodox Serbs, the Catholic Croats, the Muslim Bosnians, as well as Macedonia with its separate Church, and Slovenia 'who lived under the domination of Germanic people for more than a thousand years and is clearly European', Doder believed that the chances of Yugoslav unity were slight. He writes,

> After a relatively short time (living in Yugoslavia) I discovered that not only do the Yugoslavs have a hazy notion of their common purpose, but that there is in fact no such thing as a Yugoslav. There are Serbs, Croats, Slovenes, Macedonians and others, who in some respects seem as unlike each other as people from different countries. Although of a common South (or Yugo) Slav origin, they speak different languages, use different scripts, and had never lived within a common state prior to the creation of Yugoslavia in 1918. Their history has been one of suffering and humiliation. For centuries the northwestern half of Yugoslavia had been under the domination of Austria-Hungary, while the southeastern half was ruled by Turkey. Imperial wars, invasions and colonial rule have left a landscape of Gothic spires, Islamic mosques and Byzantine domes stained with blood.[2]

To me, as I said, this did not seem so apparent; and more than 1.1 million people identified themselves as 'Yugoslavs' in the 1981 census (out of 2.2 million population). But no doubt in the 1950s the rule of the Communist Party and Tito's hold on the country, plus fear of the USSR, was strong enough to keep these differences and problems submerged beneath a seeming unity. At that time Tito was still relatively young and vigorous and the speculation as to what would happen after his death had not seriously begun. The country was poor and struggling after the effects of the war, there was much less private enterprise, private building and movement of labour between Yugoslavia and its western neighbours than in the 1970s. There were enormous differences in wealth between different parts of the country. Slovenia was far and away the most prosperous and the areas of southern Serbia and Bosnia, and of course Macedonia, were some of the poorest that we visited.

Someone has said that Yugoslavia was a country with two alphabets, three religions, four languages, six nations, six republics and seven neighbours. There was certainly diversity and considerable national feeling and competitiveness among the various ethnic groups. At times these feelings became more violent and aggressive. They existed under the surface but while Tito was president there was unity and these feelings were kept in check because of his strong grip on the country and its police state, and partly because he was respected and admired, even loved by much of the population. Tito himself was half Croat, half Slovenian, but not identified with one nationality.

As he grew older and finally died in 1980 this restraining power was lost; there was no obvious successor and the system of the yearly rotating presidency was not a success; Serbian nationalism became more pronounced; some of the enmity between Serbs and Croats which existed during the partisan struggles of the Second World War, when the Fascist Utashi regime in Croatia massacred nearly half a million Serbs, began to re-emerge. The breaking up of the federation in the 1990s was aggravated by the Croats' declaration of independence, which was hastily recognised by the Germans, and stoked the fears of Serbs living in Croatia. Bosnian Serbs were more aggressive than Serbian Serbs; added to this there was probable terrorist infiltration of the Bosnian Muslims and you have a picture of potential conflagration. With a mixture of peoples of volatile and emotional nature and a powerful Serbian army you have the unfortunate and terrible situation that ensued. Old friends and neighbours wanted to kill each other and they did.

When we arrived in Yugoslavia at the beginning of 1956 relations with the western powers were good, if 'somewhat clouded by the revival of the Djilas affair in December 1954'. Relations with the Soviet Union were 'on the mend', and were better than with the satellite countries. Attempts to bring Yugoslavia back into the Cominform had failed and in the economic field the Yugoslav aim was to move westwards. The Yugoslav ideal was that of good and peaceful relations with all countries. The return of friendly Yugoslav–American relations was confirmed by Mr Dulles' visit to Tito at Brioni in October 1955. There was a relaxation in Yugoslav–German relations. The Yugoslavs had also made friends among the so-called non-aligned nations such as India, Burma, Egypt and some of the Arab countries.

The Djilas case had been handled carefully. Milovan Djilas and Vladimir Dedijer, partisan leaders who, especially Djilas, had been close to Tito, were convicted in 1955 of spreading hostile propaganda abroad with the object of damaging the federal interests of the state. Djilas was given a suspended sentence of 18 months with three years' probation and Dedijer was given a suspended sentence of six months with three months' probation. The way the case was handled showed a 'general tendency of further humanisation and liberalisation of the Yugoslav police state. Law abiding citizens now feel relatively free of arbitrary arrest and there is an increasing freedom of discussion in public as well as private.'[3] Djilas, however, had argued that the party was the chief obstacle to the development of democracy and its power should be reduced. His trial and conviction put a sharp brake on liberalisation.

The economic situation was not as successful as the political, although it should have been a time of economic achievement, with new freedom, western support and growing tourist trade. The Yugoslav government had put the major reform of the economic system at the top of the list for 1956, the plan being to cut down on heavy industry and increase the production of consumer goods with an improved supply of tractors, machinery and fertilisers, slaughter houses and refrigeration plants.[4] Iain was to become much involved in these plans in his work with the British lend-lease programmes. This was the atmosphere, which we were to find when we arrived in Belgrade in spring 1956. At this time Iain was writing regularly to his parents and had not yet handed over to me the task of family correspondent.

* * *

British Embassy, 42 Prvog Maja, Belgrade, Friday 30/III/56

Dear M & D,

We arrived here yesterday morning. The train was late but it was still early morning when the Orient Express drew into the rather dilapidated main station of Belgrade – in general appearance not unlike what we might find in a Russian provincial town. There is much here to remind one of Moscow besides the Cyrillic alphabet and the deceptive similarity of the language; the large number of military uniforms almost indistinguishable from the Soviet patterns; the drab new cement houses, the poorly dressed peasants and the piles of dirty snow still lying in the streets. However the west is also here mixed up with the Soviet reminders – American cars, and people comparatively well dressed, some advertisements for foreign goods and a few new buildings in architectural journal styles. The people as a whole are much less drab and more attractive than the great Russians. But most of the Embassy people are agreed that Belgrade is rather dull. It is the rest of the country, which makes it worthwhile. We have met most of the members of the Embassy, introduced to them very quickly in a confusion of names at a cocktail party held for Sir David Kelly who is now here on a visit. Accommodation is their chief complaint. We are regarded as lucky in having at least the prospect of obtaining a house and by Belgrade standards I am told quite an attractive one. But we shall have some weeks in the hotel Excelsior. This is clean, expensive and largely occupied by foreigners – some there permanently. At first we were due to go to a very second rate hotel near the station, all the others being reputedly full up. But after bribing the manager we easily found a room at the better hotel. HMG is precluded from offering these traditional Balkan bribes and so the Administration Section of the Embassy is not very successful at arranging accommodation. There are all the bureaucratic complications of a communist state here, but peculation (rather than influence as in Russia) and bribery get things done. We are told that we may get the house by the end of April.

Love from Iain

Belgrade, 7/IV/56

Dear M & D,

We are still in the Excelsior Hotel, but may move into our house next week. It is an extraordinary house, built by a wealthy eccentric in the 1930s and since then it has gradually been allowed to fall into disrepair. It is quite large, but the person for whom it was built was single and this was a town villa intended for occasional visits (probably for a mistress). It has one vast bedroom on the second floor. One of the rooms is in local 'folklore' style, rather dark, rather like the public lounge in an inn. The bathroom is magnificently appointed and has indeed got a bath of black marble into which you descend by three steps. And finally there is the Turkish room, which is dark and rather musty. This dwelling will need some repairs but will be better than the hotel and might be made quite comfortable.

Meanwhile we have explored the town (architecturally drab and uninteresting) been to the ballet (mediocre) visited other members of the Embassy (very kind and helpful), been out picnicking to the east of Belgrade along the Danube (pleasant country); been to see Meštrović's huge granite memorial (very fine) on the hill of Avala above Belgrade.

With love from us both, Iain

Belgrade (written in the Embassy), 5/V/56

Dear M & D,

Jeanne wrote last week to tell you our principal news. It does not really become news until the end of the year, but naturally affects us before then too. Jeanne was a little sick last week, but this week is much better. It was I think the visit to Sarajevo which made us much more cheerful, for we were both heartily sick of the room in the Excelsior Hotel, and Jeanne of the very heavy Balkan meals there.

We leave the hotel this week; not to the house with the Bosnian carvings which I described before but for a flat in the centre of town. We were given the choice. The house had more character and a garden. But the roof leaked, the kitchen was very, very dark and dirty, and (most importantly) we discovered that the heating system was very inefficient and very wasteful of fuel. The bill would have eaten up a very high proportion of my total foreign allowance. So we took the flat of Mr Watkins, the consul, who has been posted and whose successor has not arrived.

Did you get a card from Sarajevo? We went there for the 1st May holiday and stayed with Bob and Claire Pease. He was in Moscow and is now consul there, the sole foreign representative. Nobody knows quite why we continue to keep a consul there; they were very lonely over the winter and for the first year had terrible difficulties furnishing and heating the consulate building. But in spring at last it is a most attractive town, beautifully situated and preserving more of the east than most towns in the Soviet Union with histories more truly oriental. It has a very fine great mosque and most picturesque markets; and delightful old Turkish houses rising steeply from the river. The countryside round about is most beautiful and reminded me of the Pyrenees. I could write much more about Sarajevo, but time is short. There is not so much to write about Belgrade because truly it is rather dull architecturally and the immediate surroundings rather dull too. However it impresses beyond about 10 miles so we look forward to having the car.

Jeanne sends her love and I mine, from Iain

34 Prvog Maja, Belgrade, Sunday (undated)

Dear M & D,

Two evenings ago I went to see the Moscow Arts Theatre which is paying a visit to Belgrade. The previous evening we both heard something very different – Mr Dizzie Gillespie, the inventor of 'bepop' and his jazz band playing in the hall of the Guards Regiments at Topčider Park. Belgrade provides an extraordinary juxtaposition of east and west in every sphere. The Yugoslavs take what they can get from either side of the iron curtain, whether it be orchestras or economic aid. Mr Gillespie's band played on a stage flanked by two vast busts of Marx on one side and Lenin on the other.

Love from us both, Iain

Belgrade, 23/VI/56

Dear M & D,

Spent most of last week looking after a General Sir John Hutton, head of the British Productivity Institute and former commander of the royal artillery. His wife, a most voluble person, once a Miss Emslie from Edinburgh, was once upon a time in charge of the hospital at Niš during the First World War. Anne might know her, (Lady Hutton), as she is a consultant to the Sick Children's Hospital in Edinburgh.[5] Since coming here I have encountered not a few people who had links with Edinburgh at that time, and others who came to Scotland during the First World War. Most extraordinarily I discovered only last week that the Embassy messenger, Mr Milevoijević, was once at the Aberdeen Grammar School. Like not a few of the Embassy local staff, doormen, chauffeurs etc he held a rather better position before the war, but is not exactly persona grata with the present regime. He told me that the happiest days of his life were those he had spent living in the family of Professor Soper, the then professor of Humanity at Old Aberdeen. The Embassy engineer, who came here the other day to inspect our plumbing, has a degree in Civil Engineering from Edinburgh. For whom did you design the Celtic gravestone, which is in the Belgrade Cemetery?

Last weekend we went to Kosmai, a hill to the south about 50 miles away where there are fine woods and a hotel and the most magnificent wild flowers I have ever seen. This part of the world is particularly renowned for the variety and luxuriance of its flowers. The conditions are so good that in the Voivodina (the area between here and the Hungarian border) many flowers are grown for seed, and the rivers Danube and Sava form the dividing lines between different types of flora. Serbia is also noted for its birdsong and the wooded suburbs of Košutnyak, where some members of the diplomatic corps live, are full of nightingales in the evening.

I hope you are all well, Jeanne sends her love – from Iain

Belgrade, Saturday 21/7/56

Dear Dorothy and DM,

Your holiday sounds delightful. I'm glad you had good weather in the second week and we look forward to seeing the sketches in the future.

Here life has not changed much. Many people have gone away for their holidays to the Dalmatian coast and to the islands. We have started our official entertaining with one or two dinner parties for those who remain.

The Ambassador and many other Heads of Mission have gone to Bled, in Slovenia. They spend some 6–8 weeks there in the summer as part of an old tradition when the government of the country went there. Now it is only the diplomats. They stay in hotels and villas and cause a good deal of trouble, as all their work has to be sent up to them.

Iain has been almost invisible this week again, working from early morning until late at night. We are planning a quiet day tomorrow. Last Sunday we started by exploring the banks of the Danube at Novi Sad, about 80 kms away. There is a beach and not bad swimming though it was very crowded so after bathing and picnicking we went back to the small town of Karlovtsy, full of remnants of the Austro-Hungarian Empire – old houses and palaces now turned into barracks and museums.

Love to you both, Jeanne

Belgrade, Saturday 15/9/56

Dear Dorothy,

We had an interesting trip to Zagreb last week, to the opening of the International Industrial Fair. We had little time to see the town, which is completely central European in style and not the least Balkan. We thought it far more interesting than Belgrade and look forward sometime to exploring further the old town with its narrow streets and little squares.

The Fair was rather hot and full of dull machinery but Tito came to the opening and visited every pavilion afterwards. The British pavilion was a dreadful mess with nothing in it and nothing ready for the opening. Other countries relied on an official or purely prestige exhibition.

We were all set to go off on holiday next Wednesday, having waited for this and that, when yesterday we received a sad blow. The

Ambassador wants Iain to be in Belgrade for the Consular Conference, which takes place the week after next.

Our love to you both, Jeanne

Belgrade, Saturday 5 October 1956

Dear M & D,

It is two weeks since I last wrote anything to Woodhouselee. Since then the weather has turned very much colder, the Ambassador has left for leave in England, the Marshal has gone and returned from the Crimea; the kitten has grown larger and so has Jeanne. We await mid-November and intend to go up to Vienna about the 10th. As we have not had any leave I can stay rather longer there.

It is Saturday afternoon. Jeanne has gone out to tea with the wife of the Secretary at the Israeli Legation. Last night we had a small supper party for Mr Djagar who used to be in the Yugoslav Embassy in Moscow and now works in Mr Kardelj's (the Prime Minister's) Office. But not a very eventful week. Belgrade has a visitor in Dr Thomas Balogh who used to be my economics tutor at Balliol, lecturing to the Yugoslav equivalent of Chatham House. On Tuesday I went with Bill Laver to hear the Russian violinist Oistrakh.

It is really only from Zemun that Belgrade looks at all attractive, as from there one looks across the confluence of the Danube and Sava to the walls of the Kalemegdan, the ancient Turkish fortress. Zemun is mostly industrial, but the older parts are very different in character from Belgrade for before 1918 it was in Austro-Hungary. It is, so far as it is anything now, Catholic, whereas Belgrade's churches are mainly Serbian Orthodox. The Danube is more sheltered there and it has a large fishing colony.

Jeanne also sends her love, Iain

* * *

The rule for expectant mothers at the Embassy in Belgrade, laid down by the Foreign Office medical advisers, was that their babies should either be born in England or in a designated private clinic in Vienna. The hospitals in Belgrade were not recommended for confinements or serious medical conditions and there was no Embassy doctor in Belgrade, as there was in Moscow. I had opted for the Vienna alternative, thinking that I would not thus have to be away from Iain and Belgrade for so long. But no one warned me that 10 days was nowhere near a long enough period between leaving Belgrade to travel by train to Vienna and the supposed date of the birth of the baby. As James decided to come early it was obviously not. He was born on the day when we should have been travelling and had it been a day later he might have been born in some wayside station in Serbia. Fortunately this did not happen and he was born normally in the hospital where one area was set aside for foreigners. The nurses were mostly nuns and were very kind and helpful. The doctors, as Iain has described in his letters, were perfectly adequate but general conditions were not up to western standards, particularly the plumbing. (These are rather reminiscent of the poor third world type conditions prevailing at my local hospital in north London in 2004!) In Belgrade I learned early not to visit the lavatories in the night as the cockroaches chose that time to be particularly rampant among the rubbish piled up there.

* * *

British Embassy, Belgrade, Saturday 10 November 1956

Dear M & D,

This is rather a busy day and I have not time for the long letter I am due, nor can I call on Jeanne to be my correspondent. You will have had our telegram. All was packed last night ready for the train for Vienna. Hotels were booked there, and arrangements made at the Rudolfinerhaus hospital. Then last night Jeanne had indications that our baby could not wait. We arranged a bed in the Polyclinic just opposite the Embassy where most members of the diplomatic staff go, and this morning she was delivered of a boy, 3 kilograms and in good health. She was tired but well when I saw her last before lunch. I go again in a short time.

Hope you are well, love Iain

British Embassy, Belgrade, 12/XI/56

Dear Anne,

We did not get to Vienna after all. On Friday night we were packed and ready to go when the baby gave signs that it could not wait. I called the gynaecologist. He obtained a bed in the Traumatološka Bolnica just opposite the Embassy in Ulica Prvog Maja and in the same street as our flat. He could not come himself but got hold of a woman doctor, one of his colleagues. By the morning things had really started to happen. At 11.30 the baby was born attended by no less than three gynaecologists. The Yugoslav Government has been very angry about Suez. They were going to have demonstrations in front of the Embassy last week but they were called off. Hungary is much closer to them and much more nearly concerns them, but the Russians have been given a relatively mild press. Vienna would have been very full of refugees. It would have been interesting to be there, but accommodation might well have been difficult. What does Liverpool say about Suez? We have not heard news of Susan since just before the landings and the breaking off of diplomatic relations when she was still in Cairo. She may have left via Libya.

Jeanne sends her love, I hope you are well, Love Iain

Belgrade, Friday 16 November 1956

Dear Dorothy and DM,

Thank you both for your letters and kind wishes. We are both very thrilled with the baby, although it was a bit of a shock when he arrived so soon and so suddenly. I was very unhappy at missing my Viennese 'holiday' at first but then of course later there was no time to think of that and now he fully makes up for my earlier disappointment.

I expect Iain has told you he weighed about $6^1/2$ lbs, not a very big baby. He has blue eyes at the moment and very little hair. He looks quite nice and was never red and wrinkled. We must take a photograph very soon so that you can see what your first grandchild looks like.

The news from Hungary continues to be very distressing. It would not have affected our plans for Vienna, however. The train does not pass through Hungary of course and although Vienna is nearer the border than Belgrade, it's also much nearer the west.

Love from us all, Jeanne

Belgrade, 24/XI/56

Dear M & D,

Jeanne and James are well. They came back from the hospital on Saturday. He now sleeps in our spare bedroom, which is converted into a nursery. We have a new boiler and for the first time for some months have had hot water on tap – very necessary now that the first snow has come.

As I write I hear the BBC news of the report of the expulsion of British subjects from Egypt. So far as we know Susan is still there and will be one of those who will have to leave.

The Ambassador and Lady Roberts came back to Belgrade at the beginning of the week, she very concerned about friends and relations in Cairo. She is Lebanese, but was brought up in Cairo. They will be leaving us at the end of February for Paris and they will be much missed. He is an exacting person to work for, but most lively and competent. Sir J. Nicholls, his successor, was Minister in Moscow in Sir David Kelly's day, but before I went there.

I hope that you are both well, with love from both of us, Iain

Belgrade, Sunday 16 December 1956

Dear M & D,

With Christmas comes a series of parties and invitations and we have a stack of 'request the pleasure' cards on the desk. Jeanne is now able to come out, though prefers not to stay for the kind of party, which goes on till 3 a.m. The baby's evening feed can be administered by Katica. Apart from parties, this has been a particularly busy week with Mr Kardelj making speeches and Mr Djilas sentenced to 3 years' imprisonment, and the Social Plan for 1957 announced, and a number of visitors, including Miss Jennie Lee.

Jeanne is writing separately. We both send love and best wishes for Christmas, Iain

* * *

The major event of 1956 was for us of course the birth of our son James on November 10. Had we made it to Vienna we might have been more caught up in the events happening at that time in Hungary. Many people thought in fact that we did not go to Vienna precisely because of the Hungarian crisis, but this was not of course so. As Iain mentions in his letters the Yugoslavs were much more outspoken about the events in Suez than in Hungary. They felt that Egypt had every right to nationalise the canal and run it herself.

* * *

During 1956 among official papers there are reports of problems between the various nationalities in the country. A report from the Consul in Zagreb says that 'In this comparatively wealthy part of Yugoslavia the regime has gained a good deal of grudging respect for its foreign policy, but in internal affairs the Croats and Slovenes remain profoundly suspicious and will continue to do so until the Yugoslav government comes within a reasonable distance of solving her internal problems.'[6]

In August 1956 the British Consulate in Skopje was closed and Frank Roberts in his report speaks of Macedonia as the most backward of all the republics, receiving substantial funds from the federal government for industrial and economic development, and being still a potential powder keg, although content at that moment to improve the economy and make a contribution to the development of Yugoslavia as a whole.[7] Our friend, Bob Pease, Consul in Sarajevo, just before the closing of that Consulate in autumn 1956, describes Bosnia, after Macedonia and Montenegro, as the most backward of the Yugoslav republics. When he arrived the 'plans for turning the republic from a backward area, into the most heavily industrialised one in Yugoslavia had reached a stage when construction of the principal objects was almost complete and production about to begin'. But he writes of a downward trend in membership of the Communist Party, indifference to communist ideas, poor standard of living, problems between Serbs and Croats and subdued ill will between Muslims and Christians, the Muslims looking to Nasser as the leader of Islam and supporting him over Suez. 'Both Croats and Serbs believe that it will be a long time indeed before this problem disappears, and they say that the inter-racial bloodshed of the last war would be repeated.'[8] Perhaps I was naïve and uninformed in my assessment of the country's peacefulness and unity, sitting in Belgrade in ignorance of problems further afield.

There are also reports from Albanian émigré groups in Paris to the Secretary of State in London, of Yugoslav atrocities in Kossovo.[9] These are followed by rebuttal from the Yugoslav authorities and complaints of arms being sent to the Albanian minority in Kossovo from Albania.[10] Kossovo was already making its reputation as a probable trouble spot in the Balkans. John Julius Norwich, then 2nd Secretary in the Embassy, after his visit to Priština in the 'Autonomous Region of the Kosmet' and talks with the Vice President of the Regional Executive Council, Ali Sukri, reports Mr Sukri's intention to work for the provision of Albanian language schools for the *Shiptar* minority. Such Albanian language schools did not exist before the war in Yugoslavia. They existed later on in the 1970s and 1980s when the Albanians were effectively in charge of the province before Milošević cracked down in 1989–90. Norwich's impression at the time was that 'the autonomy of the Kosmet existed more on paper than in practice'.[11]

The name *Shiptar* is of course not now used. It was officially banned by Tito in the 1970s. He also got rid of the name Kossovo-Metojia and Kossovo was given enhanced rights, not republican status though virtually the same rights as a republic. The Serbs were annoyed by this and saw themselves as losers in the 1974 constitution. Tito, as already mentioned, was part Croat and part Slovene, Ivanka was Serb from Bosnia.

Throughout the year there was continued speculation about the attitudes of Yugoslav leadership to the west and their relationship with the USSR. This was reflected particularly in exhaustive correspondence concerning Tito's critical remarks about the Baghdad Pact during his visit to Egypt.

The intention of the Yugoslav leadership during 1956 had been to deal mostly with internal problems, the improvement of living conditions, and the consolidation of the system of Communes. But external affairs dominated the scene, particularly the events in Poland and Hungary. Tito managed to keep some kind of balance between his relations with the west, the Soviet bloc and the non-aligned nations but there was deterioration in relations with the UK over the Suez and Cyprus crises. His attitude to the Soviet Union was influenced by the favourable economic agreements and loans given by them, by the unmasking of Stalin by Khrushchev, the dissolution of the Cominform and Tito's visit to Russia in June. But later events in Hungary and Poland reduced the favourable effect of the former and the year ended in difficult relations with the Soviet Union and Eastern Europe.

On the home front there were general complaints about the lack of party activity and support among the people. Development of the communal system of local government in the regions and the workers' councils within the factories had made little ideological or political progress. Tito and his followers were felt to be distant from the people, the peasants lived their own lives outside communist society and the town workers were discontented. Djilas took up these points in his articles during the year as well as that of the cult of personality and bureaucracy. In November Djilas was arrested and given three years' hard labour. His articles on the Hungarian crisis had been too outspoken.[12]

In spite of the problems Tito was still very popular, although perhaps not his followers. There was some discontent and criticism among Croats and Slovenes but no effective opposition. There was said to be a 'Zagreb' group of sympathisers with Djilas. But there was no movement comparable to Hungary's. There was a tightening of security in the country but this did not involve any restrictions on travel or contacts for foreign diplomats and there was certainly no fear as in the USSR of the 'knock on the door at midnight'. There was a widespread celebration of the Orthodox Christmas, following the New Year.[13]

* * *

c/o The Foreign Office, SW1 (Belgrade), 5 January 1957

Dear M & D,

There was an excess of parties, mostly large 'family' parties at which we played games, during Christmas week. The most enjoyable was that at the Lamberts, as it was the least crowded. John I knew slightly in London; Jennie is the daughter of Sir J. Urqhuart, who made his name as HM's very outspoken Consul General in Shanghai just after the war.

James is increasing in size and awareness. We had an enormous collection of Christmas cards, enlarged by messages on James' birth and by many New Year (and some Christmas cards) from Yugoslavs. Here the orthodox Christmas does not fall until later, but many of the older generation of Serbs celebrate the day of St. Nicholas, on December 18, with receptions called *Slavas*, in fact a pre-Christmas winter festival.

We may go away for a few weeks in February, but not inside Yugoslavia, to Austria if we have enough money. The Norwich's nanny has promised to look after James. They have a little girl of about two, called Artemis.

We will soon be saying goodbye to the Roberts. He leaves in February for Paris to be UK Representative to NATO. His successor, Sir John Nicholls from Tel Aviv will not be coming until March or later.

With love from us all, Iain

Belgrade, Saturday 26/I/57

Dear M & D,

Thank you for your cuttings on the Yugoslav Exhibition in Edinburgh. Ambassador Vevoda who opened it is at the moment back in Belgrade and had lunch in the Embassy the other day. I believe the Yugoslavs want to have a return exhibition here. Despite the lack of appropriate galleries Belgrade has a surprising number of foreign exhibitions. At the moment there is a large show of modern Italian Art.

The Ambassador leaves for Paris and NATO on the 4th. As yet it is not known when his successor Sir John Nicholls will arrive.

With love and best wishes from Iain, Jeanne and James

(British Consulate, Sarajevo) Belgrade, 18/III/57

Dear M & D,

The Consulate at Sarajevo is closed, so we have fallen heir to its old notepaper. I was very busy last week with the Annual Trade Talks, and arrangements for Saturday with the sudden death of Moša Pijade just on his return from London. Today is the funeral, so all shops and most offices closed, except for ours, and the centre of the town impassable because of the crowds. Peter Hayman has gone in the Rolls, but not all the staff. Pijade was President of the Assembly, No 3 in the government and chief party theoretician. He was also quite well known as a painter. I met him at the Embassy party three weeks ago to celebrate the delegation's departure for London – a little wizened, white-haired man of Spanish–Jewish origins.

Here it is suddenly spring. Almost summer with temperatures in the 80s this morning. Yesterday we went for our first Sunday picnic of this year to the hills called Fruška Gora, north of the Sava and south of the town of Novi Sad (Neustadt if your map is pre-1918). The woods were full of snowdrops. We took James in a basket at the back of the car. It was his first picnic ever.

Later this week we have Mr Barritt the Labour Attaché from Vienna on one of his periodic visits and again I am doing a tour with him. This time we go south and west, to Sarajevo first, then to Mostar in Hercegovina and thence on to Split on the Dalmatian coast. This will be my first sight of the Adriatic from the Yugoslav side. Unfortunately Jeanne cannot come with us, for this should be a most interesting tour. We have plans to go later to the coast on holiday in May with James.

Hope you are all well, with love from Iain, Jeanne and James

BLOODSHED AT BLED

Beograd, Saturday 27 April 1957

Dear M & D,

We were away last weekend; left James with the Urquarts and went off in the car to South Serbia. It is a whole day's drive from Belgrade to Sopoćani, our destination, and the roads for the most part are poor. We stopped at Kraguevac and Kraljevo on the way and in each place bought 3 local pots. That part of Serbia is well-known for its earthenware, although less and less of the traditional types are now being made. Sopoćani is famous for its monastery, and the monastery is famous for the magnificent series of 13th century frescoes which are the best-known examples of early Serbian art and some consider to be the finest existing examples of Byzantine painting. There is a very fine and quite well preserved Pieta of which you may have seen some reproductions. An exhibition of copies of these and other Serbian and Macedonian frescoes was held in the Tate Gallery some years ago.

The monastery at Sopoćani lay roofless for many years and only recently has anything been done in the way of preservation. The restoration has been pretty ruthless. Everything inside the church except the tomb of King Uroš has been cleared away and the exterior is spoilt by a new metal roof. It is no longer in the care of the Church so all the peasants from the surrounding area who had gathered in the monastery precincts on Easter Sunday according to their ancient customs were forbidden to enter it. They held their service in a miserable little chapel outside the walls. We spent two nights at the well-appointed little tourist hotel, which has been built nearby. On the Monday we went westwards into very wild country over very mountainous twisting roads. On the way we visited another monastery at Mileševo, which is still in use as a church. There are frescoes here also, rather earlier than those at Sopoćani and in a poor state of preservation. The monastery is in a most delightful situation set among some precipitous hills. Behind perched on a sheer pinnacle there are the ruins of an ancient fortress and below this a 16th century mosque, also still in use. In this area the majority of people were and still are to some extent Moslems. Near Sopoćani the town of Novi Pazar is almost entirely Turkish in character and much less modernised than Sarajevo. The night of Monday we spent at Titovo Užice, a partisan centre during the war and for a period the only town held by them. The hotel Zlatibor was not very good and had fleas; back on Tuesday by Veljevo to Belgrade and to James.

I enclose a photograph of the old Turkish Bridge in Mostar in Hercegovina, photographed during my trip last month with the Labour Attaché. It has a family resemblance to Balgownie.[14]

Jeanne and James send love, from Iain

British Embassy, Belgrade, 25 May 1957

Dear M & D,

This week and next are full of engagements and parties, for various members of the Embassy who are leaving soon, including the Norwiches who are bound for Beirut. At the end of next week we have hosts of visitors from Britain, including the Oliviers in *Titus Andronicus* with a 60 strong cast, about 100 British delegates to the World Power Conference, which opens on June 4, some Australian officials to look after Hungarian refugees, and a large party due on June 2 with the inaugural flight of BEA to Belgrade. This includes Lord and Lady Attlee and Air Chief Marshal Sir William Elliott, now the Head of Chatham House. I shall be going with these last to Dubrovnik for two days.

We have some leave at the beginning of July and plan to go to the coast, probably to the island of Korčula.

With love from Iain, Jeanne and James

6. May Day 1957 in Belgrade.

British Embassy, Belgrade, 21 June 1957

Dear M & D,

This has been a quiet week, after a full fortnight. We have seen off the British delegation to the Power Conference, the BEA party and the Oliviers. We have finished with the annual garden party for the Queen's Birthday on the 13th. We have celebrated my birthday. Next week I have a Congress of Workers Councils, a special congress to discuss and criticise the system of industrial management, which is peculiar to Yugoslavia. The TUC delegate is the Mr Carron of the AEU, whose name was on everyone's lips at the time of the strike earlier in the year.

At the end of the week we shall set off on holiday. We shall drive down to Dubrovnik, staying a night in Sarajevo. From D. we shall take the boat trip to our island of Korčula and stay there for three weeks, probably taking a day or so away in the middle to visit the Dubrovnik Festival. We take Katica and James in the car with us and leave the car in Dubrovnik.

James and Jeanne join in sending love. Yes, why don't you come out to Yugoslavia in the spring? I expect we shall be here at least until next June.

Love Iain

Korčula, 2 July 1957

Dear M & D,

Our holiday on the coast is nearly over. We had intended to return on Monday morning to reach Belgrade on Tuesday, but we find that the car battery is flat and the only place where it can be charged on the island is the shipyard and that is closed for two days. For this weekend all Korčula is on holiday. The civil authorities celebrate the 27th July, the day of the uprising against the Germans and the Italians during the war, or so it is described in the posters. It is also in fact a religious holiday and there is still a procession of the town's three religious orders through the streets on the 29th. That of course is not advertised. On Sunday, in the evening the traditional *Moreshka* is danced on a flat space to the south of the town. This is a dance which has been held here in Korčula for the last 300 years in which the performers dress up in Moorish costume and brandish short swords. No one is sure of its origins but it dates from the days when K was part of the Venetian Republic. There is much evidence of the Venetian influence in the architecture of the old town. The altarpiece is by Tintoretto. But the available space within the old fortifications was so small that, as in Dubrovnik, the streets are very narrow and most buildings of four stories or more. There are some fine old palaces with little courtyards, but most are in the last stages of decay and ruin. One of these is the house of Dr Arneri, a lawyer and pre-war mayor, who has, on two evenings shown us round the town and whose family is one of the oldest on Korčula. One half of the family palace is open to the sky with fig trees growing through the windows. I think M once read Rebecca West's *Grey Lamb-Black Falcon*. Dr Arneri and his wife figure in the chapter on Korčula. He is there described as 'the cardinal'. Like Kapellina's (not Katelina as we originally thought) the family name has an Italian sound to it. Just before the war the Italian government tried to prove that many of the island families were in fact Italians and that their sympathies lay on the other side of the Adriatic. But for many generations they have spoken Croat, and in most cases both here and in Dubrovnik, the Slavonic form of their names is older than the Italian.

The Kapellinas are much with us here. She is the daughter of one of the two old ladies in whose house we are staying. He has a small motor boat. We went yesterday in their boat across the strait to Orebić on the Pelešac peninsula. This is the long neck of land which runs parallel to Korčula. Pelešac is for the most part barren mountainous limestone (even more barren than Korčula and Hvar where the hills are covered with the low evergreen scrub or maquis common to so many Mediterranean islands). But wherever there is a little earth or wherever the stony hillsides can be terraced there are vines. The finest Dingač, the best known of Yugoslav red wines, very strong and heavy, comes from this area. However the attractive well built stone houses with their neat clean interiors and little flower gardens (unlike the usual Yugoslav untidiness and squalor) which one finds along the edge of the sea at Orebić and the other coastal villages owe their existence to the sea. They are the houses built by the mariners of the Association of the Captains of Sabioncello (which is Italian for Pelešac) who in the days of sail commanded a large proportion of the vessels under the Austro-Hungarian merchant fleet. Many others served under the Russian and United States Flags. We visited one of these houses on Orebić and were shown around its 20–30 rooms by a little man who is a friend of the Kapellinas, the son of one of these captains. The house was crammed with an extraordinary collection of bric-a-brac gathered from every part of the world, and the walls covered with paintings and murals by the old captain, who was also an amateur artist. The son is also curator of a local maritime museum full of old sailing prints and figureheads and mariners' certificates. But many of the old houses are not kept up in this style today. The retired captains have lost their savings and no longer come from California or New Zealand, although not a few have relatives abroad who send remittances. But this last is true not only of Orebić but of the whole Dalmatian coast and particularly so of the islands. Great numbers of people have emigrated. In the centre of Korčula there is a town called Blato which once had 15,000 inhabitants and now has about 2000 or less. Today few can obtain visas, but some leave illegally. However there are few families without relatives abroad, mostly in America and Australia.

Belgrade 3 August (cont)

I did not finish this letter in Korčula. We are now back in Belgrade. We left on Tuesday, rather late in the day as the car battery was flat. We then had difficulty in getting a boat to take us back over the water to Orebić. It was 3 before we set out in the hope of making Sarajevo by late evening. After 40 kms the exhaust pipe fell off and had to be tied on by wire. By 6 p.m. the battery again ran down so we changed plan and made for Split along the easier coast road. We got there after midnight to find no rooms in any hotel in the town. We went on, making for a hotel at Castel Stari some kilometres to the north. Half-way, about 2.30 a.m., near where the once great Roman town of Salonae stood, we stalled. Nothing would make the engine start. Finally we succeeded after an hour's wait with the help of a tow rope and some drunken sailors in a jeep. Next day we went to the Consul for money and help and wandered round Diocletian's Palace (i.e. the centre of Split) while the car was being repaired. We made good time on the return trip on Thursday via Jajce and Banja Luka. Belgrade is sombre and murky after the sea and the coastal towns. Today, Saturday, it is raining.

Love from Iain, Jeanne and James

* * *

Korčula was a very beautiful, unspoilt place in 1957, with donkeys in the street, no cars and no tourists. We stayed in rooms belonging to relatives of friends in Belgrade who took us out fishing or to visit other islands nearby. Someone persuaded us to take our car across to the island on planks on a fishing boat. Besides the perilous crossing that was very foolish as there were only 25 kilometres of road and it was very difficult to recharge our flat battery when we wanted to leave. That, plus the fact that we had hit a stone on the notoriously bad Orebić peninsula road on the way down meant that we had a nightmare drive through the night with no lights and no way of starting the engine if we stopped.

* * *

Belgrade, September 1957

Dear M & D,

We were very busy last week with the visit of the Secretary of State, Selwyn Lloyd. I went with the visiting party to a farm on Saturday. It was to a co-operative in the village of Stara Pazova, north of Belgrade in the Vojvodina, the most fertile part of the country and a village with a majority of inhabitants of Slovak origin. It ended up with much drinking of plum brandy in the village club and songs by both parties. Sir William Hayter, now Deputy Undersecretary, who was Ambassador in Moscow, was of the party. We have had two series of farewells for the very popular naval attaché, Captain Ferguson and his wife and daughters who left by train the night before last to the strains of bagpipes on the platform. John Graham who has taken the place of John Julius Norwich is a keen and adept player. Next week we have less welcome visitors who cause even more work than the Secretary of State – the Foreign Office and Treasury inspectors.

Jeanne and James look forward to seeing you and we all send our love, Iain

* * *

Belgrade, Saturday 27 October 1957

Dear M and D,

I have not written a proper letter to Woodhouselee for a long time. I have been away and Jeanne and James have seen you. Jeanne has a letter to put in this envelope. James sends his love and a wet kiss. The journey which John and Jenny Lambert and I took in the south ended up with our being summoned back to the coast to Risan on the Boca di Cotarro where Lord Aberdare was killed. We were in Sarajevo when we were told and had to cut short our visits there. This was a sad business as his widow, Grizelda Harvey of the films and radio and his wife for only a few weeks, was in a very shocked state, although not injured beyond bruised. The car, a new Bentley, went over the edge of a bridge into a small stream which is normally dry but which the recent rains had filled. We spent two nights in the hotel at Kotor and travelled many times backward and forward along the coast road to Risan during our stay. There was the hospital where they were taken after the crash, a brand new well furnished place for which all the equipment had been donated by a local emigrant who had made good in the United States. But it had few doctors and fewer nurses. Fortunately the cook spoke English and so could interpret for Lady Aberdare during the 24 hours before we arrived. The coast there is beautiful and most romantic but terribly depopulated. The town of Perast, half way between Kotor and Risan once boasted one of the largest fleets in the Mediterranean and even beyond, but its trade and ships were ruined by the British blockade during the Napoleonic wars. Its great renaissance palaces stand empty and roofless. But we had no time to see the monuments. The body was flown back from Titograd and I had a rather hair raising journey in a 1927 vintage taxi up the road from Kotor into Montenegro proper which has 17 consecutive hairpin bends as it rises up from the Bay. We had the coffin roped to the roof. John Lambert and I returned to Belgrade by car. Jenny and the widow returned by plane.

Since then we have had the Embassy inspectors from London and the Embassy Play. Marshal Zhukov has been and gone, to return to Moscow no longer Minister of Defence.

With love from Iain, Jeanne and James

Belgrade, Saturday 10 November 1957

Dear Anne,

James and Jeanne are both well and settled back in Prvog Maja. He has a pair of tartan trousers from Woodhouselee in which he can now stand up and walk some paces. We took him out this afternoon in the pale but still pleasant November sun along the road that runs coastward from Belgrade down the Danube. Winter has been slow this year. The maize is harvested and vines. But the fields are still green and all the leaves have not fallen.

Since Jeanne came back much time has been spent and many hard words spoken about a play, written by Lady Nicholls, the Ambassadress, which is to be put on before Christmas. Rehearsals are serious. Jeanne is the wife of the Etruscan Ambassador in this diplomatic melodrama.

Belgrade, Thursday 29 November 1957

Dear Dorothy,

A great part of my time now is taken up rehearsing for this play. It's becoming rather too serious for me now that we have found a theatre, the Belgrade Children's Theatre which holds 300 and scenery is being made and posters sent round. There was a competition for the programme cover which Iain won. I will send you a copy when they are printed. The play, *Bloodshed at Bled* is a skit on the diplomatic corps during their summer session at Bled.

Much love to you both, Jeanne

7. The coffin of Lord Aberdare being taken to Belgrade on top of an ancient Yugoslav taxi, after the accident when he drove into a mountain stream and was drowned in his overturned car, while on his honeymoon with the actress Grizelda Harvey, Autumn 1957.

BLOODSHED AT BLED

Belgrade, 4 January 1958, Saturday afternoon

Dear M & D,

There have been many entertainments and functions these past weeks. It is pleasant to have a quiet Saturday evening with nothing to do, the first for sometime. We had the Play, Christmas, New Year; we had a series of parties to say goodbye to Peter and Rosemary Hayman, the counsellor who left last night by train. Today we had only a funeral,

8. Cover for the programme for *Bloodshed at Bled*, designed by Iain, December 1957.

9. Carnival masked ball given by the Urius, Counsellor at the Japanese Embassy, February 1958. From left to right, Iain, Jeanne, Chibi Stewart, Jenny Lambert, and in front, John Lambert.

the funeral of the brother of the *Times* correspondent here. We did not know him well, but knew Desa and her husband, Eric Bourne, who is the correspondent of the *Daily Express*. She is Yugoslav. It was a long orthodox funeral with seven bearded priests and a vast carved baroque motor hearse.

On Christmas day we had a party mostly for the Embassy, including the Ambassador and Lady Nicholls and most of the guests stayed until about 3 a.m. and played charades. And then we had another large party at which we were again joint hosts, this time for the Haymans. Our flat was the venue as we have most room and it lent itself best to the parody of Lady Nicholls' play, which was presented to the company. She did not take it amiss.

With love from Iain, Jeanne and James

* * *

There are several references to the Play, *Bloodshed at Bled*, the take-off of diplomatic life, written by Lady Nicholls to be performed by members of the Embassy. It caused much distress among Embassy families as usually one member of a couple was commandeered to take part and there were endless long rehearsals for these amateur actors. Emotions ran high and there were not a few hysterical outbursts. I managed to get away with a not too demanding role, having avoided being cast in a romantic role with my least favourite member of the Embassy. Iain spent long evening hours in some office painting a backcloth. It was eventually performed for three nights in a small theatre, one night to an invited Yugoslav audience, including rather embarrassingly the Foreign Minister, Mr Popović.

Throughout 1957 there were the usual ups and downs in Yugoslav relations with the Soviet Union and the west. The Ambassador's remarks in his annual report, to the effect that there had been a restoration of friendly relations with the UK were not accepted by the Foreign Office who retorted that 'the Yugoslavs are continuing to oppose our policies and criticise us at the United Nations and in the press, notably on the Cyprus issue'. It seems illogical to expect complete support from the Yugoslavs, after all a communist country, of all western policies. There was no doubt of course considerable irritation when the Yugoslavs were prepared to take financial aid from both sides as it suited them. 'In the 10 years between 1949–59 Yugoslavia received $2.4 thousand million in aid from the west – it took the forms of loans, of credit for buying heavy machinery for industry, of fertilisers, seed and stock for farmers, of American surplus wheat and flour for bread, medical supplies, military equipment, service aircraft, naval and merchant ships and many other vital needs for a modern state. A novel feature was the offer for Yugoslav specialists to be trained in the United States, Great Britain and other western countries.'[15]

There was great joy in Belgrade when Malenkov, Molotov, Kaganovich and Shepilov were expelled from the Soviet Central Committee, but the removal of Marshal Zhukov, following a visit to Yugoslavia, was considered to be an insult and Tito claimed illness as an excuse not to attend the 40th Anniversary of the Revolution.

The Yugoslavs had to deal with some 20,000 Hungarian refugees after the Austro-Hungarian border was closed but most were dispersed eventually among western countries including Canada and Australia. The long overdue Congress of the Union of Communists of Yugoslavia was postponed from November to April 1958, possibly because they were dealing at that time with another Djilas crisis. In October he was tried again, after his book, *The New Class*, had been smuggled out of Yugoslavia and published in the US, and this time sentenced to seven years' imprisonment. The severity of the sentence succeeded in alienating western socialists. His fellow Montenegrin, Dedijer, refused a passport to take up a lectureship at Manchester University.

* * *

Belgrade, 22 February 1958

Dear M & D,

Last night the Urius, the Japanese Counsellor and his wife, who are very westernised, gave the most lavish party Belgrade has seen for many years – a masked ball to celebrate Carnival or Fasching. There was a magnificent array of costumes, many in the national dress of various parts of Yugoslavia. Jeanne had a dress from the Baranja, that part of Croatia near the Hungarian border. It came from a friend of the cook.

Jeanne has told you that we have a plan to drive to Istanbul at Easter with the Lamberts. We would go by car staying one night at Sofia on the journey. She has also said that we might come home on leave in May or June. As yet I do not know when we shall leave Belgrade permanently. I should prefer on the whole, to go this year.

With love from Jeanne and James, Iain

Belgrade, 15 March 1958

Dear M & D,

Thank you for your last two letters. We have had a visit from the C in C of the Mediterranean Fleet. We have speeches and preparations for the elections two weeks hence. We have a delegation of directors from Massey Ferguson, including the Mr Charles Calder of Kirkwall who entertained me at Coventry before I came out here. One of the others, a Canadian called Mackay, comes from Caithness, from where they are putting up the reactor. We had them all to supper on Thursday. We may be going to Skopje for a few days from the 26th when the Labour Attaché comes down for one of his periodic visits from Vienna. Our plans are now firm for the visit to Istanbul at Easter.

Love from James who has just had his bath and is going to bed. Love from Iain and Jeanne

* * *

Like so many places in the 1950s Istanbul was a fascinating city with no tourists and we had a delightful week visiting mosques and museums and the colourful open-air fish market along the river. We took a boat to the Principe Islands, where we had exotic Turkish food in a quiet restaurant where no one spoke English and we spoke no Turkish and we had to guess what to choose from the menu.

We spent the night on the way back in Sofia, which seemed very grim and Soviet with militia at every street corner. It was the time of Orthodox Easter and we were amazed by the large crowds assembled in the streets at the time of the midnight mass. We stayed in the one hotel available for foreigners where we picnicked in our rooms on tinned sardines brought with us from Belgrade, as there was nothing to eat in the hotel restaurant. Soon after our return, in May, we left by car to drive across Europe for our annual leave. We took our excellent Yugoslav maid with us, who by this time had become James' nanny and looked after him full time. Katica, who had hardly been outside her village before coming to work for us in Belgrade, was fascinated and particularly impressed by the rows of identical houses as we drove through the suburbs of south London on our arrival.

While we were visiting Turkey and preparing for our journey to England the 7th Party Congress, postponed from the previous November, was taking place in Ljubljana. There emerged only minor changes in party policy, a slight liberalisation for the ordinary party member, less jargon, a less aggressive view of the progress of socialism; they advocated 'the use of persuasion as the essential method of work'. Disciplinary measures were eased, membership was not excluded by the employment of labour in businesses or by religious attendance and the congress was to be held every five years. However strong remarks were made by Tito and other leaders concerning the continuance of the Yugoslav independent way, which antagonised the Russians and they refused to attend the Congress, except as observers.[16]

* * *

Belgrade, 20 July 1958

Dear M & D,

Bill Laver left the day after we returned so I have been very busy in the Embassy. The Ambassador is in Bled. There is much concern over the situation in the Middle East. And the heat is such that it is not very pleasant to work. Belgrade is a little dead – so many have gone on holiday; as many at the coast; the theatres are closed. Many of the Ambassadors have departed for Bled. The journalists have been in the north seeking news from Brioni of Nasser's movements.

We returned to Belgrade to find James and Katica had had a good flight and were well. Ivka the cook had filled the flat with flowers. Mitz the cat came back the following day but has since spent most of the time hiding from James and the heat.

Our journey back was pleasant but as we had to make Belgrade by the Thursday, we had to go fast. On Tuesday we saw a little of Munich and did some shopping and then over the mountain roads by Salzburg on a glorious day to spend the night at Graz. From there but a short run on Wednesday to the Yugoslav frontier, through Slovenia, looking very pretty, and the dull straight road from Zagreb to Belgrade.

Brussels was most enjoyable. We had a full day and a half there. In some ways I enjoyed the town more than the Exhibition. It is a distinguished city. The old central square with the town hall and the 17th century Guild Houses is magnificent and for the Fair it has been regilt and painted and hung with traditional heraldic flags and at night lit by concealed lighting. And the main thoroughfares have all been decorated, not haphazardly, but with mile long garlands of coloured lights.

Jeanne, James and Katica all join in sending their love – from Iain

Belgrade, 9 August 1958

Dear M & D,

We returned from the north on Monday in the evening. We had driven to Bled where the Ambassador is ensconced in a villa. They had a party on the Friday night to which came all the other Ambassadors who conduct their affairs from Slovenia away from Belgrade's heat. We took back the diplomatic bag on Saturday, but only as far as Zagreb. Monday, being bank holiday we spent two nights at a place called Plitvice some 3 hours' drive from Zagreb where there is an extraordinary formation of lakes and waters set in hilly wooded country. It is limestone karst rock and the rivers run part underground and burst out of the earth in the most unexpected places. Below the new hotel where we stayed there is one large lake and above it no less than sixteen others, each tumbling into the next in a series of very spectacular waterfalls. And the lakes are of the most bright blue colour even on a dull day and strangely not all of the same blue, but some bright turquoise and others dark blue green.

Love from Iain, Jeanne and James

Belgrade, Saturday, 18 October 1958

Dear M & D,

I write by the light of a candle as most of the electricity in our block of flats has fused. This happens not infrequently at some times of the year, but this is the first time for some months. It must be the result of the sudden cold weather and extra demands on power. It was still clear and sunny this afternoon and we went with James and Katica down by the Sava in the grounds of the Belgrade Fair. But it has turned cold.

We had a farewell party here for Bill Laver last Saturday with the Ambassador and Lady Nicholls and a three-instrument band. (The lights have come on again) Bill goes to Oslo at the beginning of December. The new Economic Counsellor, Mr Rogers, comes from Madrid, but is known personally to no one here. He does not arrive until just before Christmas. The Nicholls have concocted another play for this year but Jeanne is spared acting in it because of baby No 2 and I am spared another 30-foot backcloth because there are no outdoor scenes or balconies, and James is excused because he cannot speak very well.

Love from us all, Iain

Belgrade, Saturday 20 December 1958

Dear M and D,

Jeanne promised to send you the programme cover for this year's play. I send it as a not very appropriate Christmas card which may not reach you before the 25th. The plate was a little fudged so the final version came out grey instead of black and white. The plot of the play concerned four counsellors who tried to prevent the Celtic (British) Ambassador putting on another play. The story was rather esoteric and not readily intelligible to the Yugoslavs who were encouraged to buy tickets. Not very many did and the second two nights had rather thin audiences despite some packing with complimentary tickets and parties of cooks, maids and their relatives.

Jeanne went to Trieste on Thursday as soon as the play was over and returned on Sunday with Christmas tree lights, bananas and shrimps. I could not go being very busy in the Embassy and awaiting the arrival of the Rogers, who take Bill Laver's place. He arrived just as we announced that £3 million was to be given, or rather lent, to the Yugoslavs, rather less than they had asked and hoped for.

James joins Jeanne and me and Katica in sending you both love and best wishes for a happy Christmas and New Year, Iain.

Belgrade, 3 January 1959, Saturday afternoon

Dear M & D,

This is James' New Year Card to you, which he made himself with green crayon dipped in ink. I think they are Japanese crayfish or perhaps nothing so definite. We have some Christmas cards from Yugoslavs, or rather greetings cards, for they do not usually mention Christmas, which are much less naturalistic. There are also very dull ones with nothing on them but *Yugoprodukt* or the Secretary of the Central Committee of Yugoslav Trade Unions or perhaps a visiting card with p.f.n.a. discreetly pencilled in the corner.

Jeanne and James are out to tea with the Browns who arrived just before Christmas to replace the Starks. The Rogers (new Economic Counsellor) came a few days later. They have not yet found a flat so are living in the hotel where we stayed for our first six weeks. They have no children. They come from Madrid. She is younger and paints. We spent New Year's Eve at home with a supper of hare shot by Mrs Garvey's 14-year-old son now home from school. He was there with Terence and Rosemary Garvey (the son is an O'Neill for she was married to Con O'Neill, until recently the Chargé d'Affaires in Peking) and the Stewarts. We saw the New Year in with a bottle of champagne, the cork from which we shot out into Ulica Maršala Tito below us. There were not many people about then, but later the streets were thronged with revellers and there were still some stragglers when I walked to the Embassy at 10 the next morning.

With love from Iain.

Much love to you both, Jeanne

British Embassy, Belgrade, 31 January 1959

Dear Anne,

You have a niece, born January 29 at 7 a.m. 3 kilos, 300 grammes at the Traumatološka Bolnica, Belgrade. No name yet. Alexandra, Alison, even Anne have been favoured. It is a healthy, soft, greedy little baby and is said to have pretty ears. It is rather nice. James calls it his baby and wants to pull its nose and hair. Jeanne is quite well and sends her love to you. I write in my office, which is not 50 yards from the hospital on the other side of Prvog Maja and I am now going to see Jeanne.

Love from all four of us, Iain.

Belgrade, 21 February 1959

Dear M & D,

Thank you for your letter of Thursday. Jeanne has written separately. She has told you the news of our staying on. The Stewarts are also staying until later in the autumn. We are disappointed. We had thought that by April or May we should be pleased to go; the baby would be able to travel but not to crawl away. We should have been home in the early summer. I do not know if the decision is immutable. It may be connected with the delay in setting up the mission in Cairo, which has kept a number of people waiting about for many months in London. I had made some soundings about Tom Sewell's job in Madrid. Our new Counsellor came from there and Peter Mennell is Head of Chancery.

Sandra (as James calls his sister) is well and growing bigger. He seems to like his sister and even the cat, who was very jealous of James, is reconciled to the second one. We have not been out much, but have had a spate of visitors anxious to get a share of the loan granted to Yugoslavia at the beginning of the year. We do go out for the first time since Alexandra, as an exception, to a 50th birthday celebration for Eric Bourne, the *Daily Express* and *Christian Science Monitor* correspondent whose wife, Desa, writes for the *Times*.

With love from Iain, Jeanne, James and Sandra

Belgrade, 1 April 1959

Dear M & D,

Last week was Easter. We did not go away, not being able to leave Alexandra, and Tom Rogers took his car and his wife to Dubrovnik via Sarajevo, so I had to be at the Embassy. However, next week on the tenth we plan to make a trip to Macedonia. More than once before I had hoped to be able to go to this, the most southerly of the Republics and the only one which I have not visited, but have each time been thwarted. We shall spend a few days in Skopje, the capital, I making some official visits and calls and then go by Veles and Prilep to Lake Ohrid. It should be a good time of year with the spring flowers out and as yet not too much dust on the roads. James, Alexandra and Katica will go to stay with the Garveys. The Garveys went to Skopje for Easter.

We did go off for a picnic on Easter Monday. The plum and almond blossom was out in the country and the fields were gay and colourful. We went south to places called Lazarevac and Arandjelovac in the rolling agricultural country south of Belgrade and had our lunch on the top of a hill. The peasants were out ploughing in preparation for the maize crop sowing, with horses or oxen, for there is little or no mechanisation in this area.

This has been an agricultural week. The Ambassador has been away for three days visiting farms. We have had some meat men with plans to buy your roast from Yugoslavia instead of the Argentine, accompanied by an expert from Smithfield and a cattle breeding expert. Other visitors to Belgrade this week included Mr Louis Armstrong and his band who had a rousing near-hysterical ovation in the hall of the Trade Unions – but we could not get tickets for the performance. Also Professor A.J. Ayer with whom we had lunch yesterday at the Garveys. He is the first western philosopher to lecture here since the war. I had heard him as a visiting professor at Oxford. He is now at University College London but is due to take the chair of Logic at Oxford this autumn.

Jeanne, James and Alexandra join in sending love, Iain

Belgrade, 21 April 1959

Dear Dorothy,

Macedonia is quite fascinating and I was so glad I had been able to go and grateful to the kind Garveys for making it possible. I expect Iain will write you a letter about our travels when he has got straightened out. We were very busy, getting up at 6 and going to bed at 1 a.m, seeing farms and factories, monasteries and churches and climbing the hills in motor cars and on foot, with our Yugoslav friends.

We spent four days in Skopje and Iain did some good work, as a representative of the economic section of the Embassy, which had sent no one to Macedonia for some years. We also visited three or four monasteries in the surrounding country and explored the old Turkish town and the gipsy quarter of Skopje, both very busy and colourful.

James and Alexandra are very flourishing. James has much more colour and seems to have had a wonderful time digging in the garden all day and being taken to see his other friends who live near the Garveys. He was not missing us. Alexandra is much fatter and quite adorable.

Ohrid was a beautiful place and we very much enjoyed our two days there. We visited the trout hatchery and the wood carving atelier, as well as the three old churches in the old Turkish town and one closer to the Albanian frontier, about 20 miles away. Altogether we saw a fine selection of the frescoes in Macedonia, from 11th and 12th centuries up to the 16th and 17th. And we met a very varied selection of interesting people, from the head of the National Bank to the French consul in Skopje, directors of Macedonian factories, farm cooperatives and strange American tourists in the provincial towns. We spoke a lot of Serbian and spent more time with Yugoslavs than we usually do in a month in Belgrade. And we both enjoyed ourselves enormously.

We have still no news of our move and have no idea where and when.

Much love from us all, Jeanne

Belgrade, Thursday 25 June 1959

Dear Dorothy,

In spite of our exciting news this week I don't think Iain has written to you. He has had the Trade Delegation here all this week. Every day they have meetings and usually there have been lunches and dinners as well. I haven't seen him much lately.

The news is our posting to Havana, which we heard about by telegram last Saturday. We are both delighted, more than anything by the prospect of such a complete change from anything we have experienced and from Eastern Europe. One cannot help thinking of blue sea and skies, sunshine, sugar and cigars! As well of course there is bound to be great heat, much corruption and an occasional revolution. But we persist in thinking ourselves very lucky and most people we talk to seem to agree.

Much love to you both from us all, Jeanne

Belgrade, Ulica Suboborska 27, Senjak, Sunday 12th July 1959

Dear M & D,

I write from the Graham's house, to which we moved last week and in which we are to spend our last month in Belgrade. John Graham and his family have gone on leave, and it is a great advantage to be able to live here while the packers are in our flat, and avoid having to go to a hotel. Suboborska 27 has a garden, which is excellent for James and Sandra in this hot weather.

We have both been excessively busy for the last ten days. I had much to do following the trade negotiations. Many visitors come at this time of year. There is a great deal to do packing up after 3 years. However the main packing – all the boxes for Cuba have been finished yesterday. Today we took the day off, it being Sunday, and went for a picnic to one of our favourite places, the ruined monastery of Hopovo on the way to Novi Sad, at the foot of the Fruška Gora hills. There was a large party, the Browns from our Embassy, the Thabaults from the French and John Thibault from the Canadian.

I send this airmail. Looking forward to seeing you soon. Love from Iain, James, and Sandra.

The Ambassador's Villa, Bled, Wednesday 22 July 1959

Dear Dorothy,

We are staying two nights in Bled in the villa, which the Nicholls have taken for one month. We came up yesterday by car as courier and we return tomorrow. We are also making our official farewell.

We are still making, unmaking and changing our leave plans. We have left the children in Katica's care at the house, with many friends keeping a friendly eye. James was very angry when he saw us going off with a picnic basket. It's his favourite form of entertainment at the moment.

The Ambassador is about to close the bag, Iain is writing 'official' letters. But he sends his love, as we all do – to you both. Jeanne

* * *

We were happy to leave Belgrade but we had much enjoyed our three years in Yugoslavia, particularly the country outside Belgrade and the mountains and the sea. We were leaving at a time when the country seemed to be on the upgrade. There were reasonable relations all round, with the Soviet Union, the west and the unaligned nations. Agriculture was improving due to the new methods and machinery and the standard of living was continuing to improve. The then Minister at the Embassy, Terence Garvey, sums up the situation in his report written at the beginning of 1960. 'Yugoslavia is not yet a free society nor is it clear that it will ever become such. But communism in Yugoslav hands has become something less dangerous and more humane than the classical communist state.'[17]

4

CUBA YES, YANKEE NO! REVOLUTION AND COMMUNISM – CUBAN STYLE 1959–62

'I don't understand why it should have been the Cubans. They are so individualistic and they had the highest standard of living in Latin America'[1]

We were never quite sure why we were sent to Cuba. Perhaps it was because I had persuaded Iain to put Mexico at the very end of his post preference form, a list of choices, which each member of the Foreign Office was asked to give when reaching the end of a posting, not that they were necessarily taken into consideration. We had asked to have a change, a break from communist countries, where we had previously served almost exclusively. Before leaving Belgrade we had discussed taking our excellent Yugoslav nanny with us but thought that she would be lonely in Cuba. Little did we know that less than a year after we arrived the Yugoslav Embassy residence would be situated in the street next to us. The posting turned out not to be such a change, politically. It was communism, Cuban style.

We arrived in Havana in autumn 1959. Castro had come down from the Sierra Maestra in January 1959 and entered Havana in triumph. After years of fighting between the Cuban army and the Castro-led rebels, the former President of Cuba and dictator, Fulgencio Batista was gone and Castro was in power. 'While the bells tolled in Havana, the bearer of the future was preparing to' begin a triumphal six hundred mile march to the capital. Fidel Castro, a legend at thirty-one, had made his way into those mountains three years before with only twelve men. Now an almost unanimous Cuban public hailed him as something close to a Messiah, or at least an apostle of a new order of justice.'[2]

The transfer of power had been remarkably peaceful and the US government recognised the Provisional Government as early as 7 January. 'Positive signs emerged with the announcement of the Provisional Government's first cabinet on 19 January. No overtures were made to the USSR and though legalised, there was undisguised contempt among Castro's 26th July Movement for the communist P.S.P.' (the *Partido Socialista Popular*).[3]

Castro was ruling with the help of many liberal-minded Cubans who were hoping for a democratic government after the years of dictatorship. By the time we arrived in September 1959 he had certainly not set up a communist state in Cuba. The revolution had been successful, most of the government consisted of young people who shared Castro's political views but the only major reform, which had been carried out so far, was the agrarian reform, the giving of land to landless peasants. However, despite the outward signs of friendly relations between the US and Cuba during the first half of 1959, the agrarian reform itself (many of the large landowners in Cuba were North American) and later the intervention in US-owned businesses led to deterioration in relations. In April 1959, when Castro visited Washington at the invitation of the American Society of Newspaper Editors, President Eisenhower refused to see him and Castro was received by Vice President Nixon.

The situation was of course to deteriorate much further as time passed, as further reforms were introduced and as Castro began to move closer towards the Cuban Communist Party, the PSP.

Herbert Matthews, the *New York Times* correspondent and editor, and friend of Fidel Castro, questions whether the Cuban Revolution was a communist revolution and emerges with the answer that it was not. 'The problem that future historians will have to face lies in the fact that the Castro regime was not communistic in its early stages but gradually moved deeper and deeper into the communist camp.' In 1959 Cubans put a special stamp on their letters to the US with the following words in English, 'Our Revolution is NOT COMMUNIST, our Revolution is HUMANIST.' During 1959 and 1960 Castro probably did not want to get involved with communists but was trapped by his revolutionary aims and the attitude of the US and the American peoples. He either had to go with the US or accept help from the Soviet Union.

A State Department White Paper on Cuba in April 1961 stated that, 'the character of the Batista regime in Cuba made a violent popular reaction almost inevitable. The rapacity of the leadership, the corruption of the Government, the brutality of the police, the regime's indifference to the needs of the people for education, medical care, housing, for social justice and economic opportunity – all these, in Cuba as elsewhere, constituted an open invitation to revolution.' Matthews says that what they were seeing was a revolt against a small, corrupt, wealthy ruling class whom the US had put in power and helped to keep in power. Even in 1958 the US still controlled 35% to 40% of the sugar production through sugar import quotas. 'In 1958 US interests controlled 80% of Cuban utilities, 90% of the mines, 90% of the cattle ranches, all of the oil refining and distribution (with the Royal Dutch Shell) and 40% of the sugar industry.'[4] An American friend once told me that an afternoon's entertainment for one of her wealthy Cuban woman friends might be to go to one of the casinos with $500 to gamble. It is not surprising that the Cuban people, who lived on very little, were ready to rise up against this small but very wealthy minority. It was interesting that it should have happened in Cuba as it had a higher standard of living than most other countries in Latin America.

* * *

When we arrived American influence was still very visible. The cars in the streets were American, products in the shops were imported from the US, the plumbing and electrical equipment were all American, and in fact the effects of the long years of American economic influence were paramount.

After the sea crossing from Liverpool on the SS *Parthia*, which was the normal route across the Atlantic for Foreign Service staff at this time, we were intended to arrive by car from New York, driving down through Florida and the keys to Havana. This journey never materialised as the strike of New York dockers, which had started during our sea journey was not solved before we had to leave. We waited some time in New York to see whether we would be able to get our car off the ship but we were finally obliged to repack our cabin luggage, which we had carefully arranged so as to be stowed in the boot of the car, and travel to Havana by air. By this time James was three and Alexandra (known at that time as Sandra, which was James' name for her, but to be known later as Alex) was nine months old.

My letter to my mother-in-law describes our arrival.

CUBA YES, YANKEE NO!

Havana, 15 October 1959

Dear Dorothy

I'm glad you got our letters from the boat. You haven't had many since from us and we haven't even the excuse of the long journey because we came here from New York in six hours – by air. The longshoremen's strike prevented us getting the car off the boat and we finally had to take an air passage. I was really quite relieved as the close contact with the family on the boat and then for four days in a New York hotel had been quite enough and I was hoping the strike would last long enough so that we would not have to drive.

New York is as expected big and noisy but much shabbier than we expected somehow, apart from 5th Avenue and around that area. We went *en famille* to see the view from the Empire State Building, but after that decided sightseeing was too exhausting without a car. We've had a terrific welcome in Havana in spite of arriving 5 days early and we've been out almost every evening since we arrived. Everyone is very friendly, almost overwhelmingly so. The Ambassador and Mrs Fordham have already invited us three times.

Love from us all, Jeanne

Havana, Friday 23 October 1959

Dear Dorothy,

Amazing that we have been here over two weeks. Now we are official as the Olivers left last week. We had a busy time until then as we became involved in all their farewell parties. Since we moved into their house last Tuesday we have been house hunting. We are looking in the suburb of Miramar which is half the distance away and has many nice houses. We are considering one at the moment and waiting to see if anything else turns up.

Thursday. This letter has been interrupted by a series of unfortunate occurrences which upset what we thought was going to be a few quiet days. The car broke down, then the bathroom door stuck and could not be opened, and finally the cook fell and damaged her leg. I had to go with her to the hospital (a nightmare journey following the Cuban ambulance through the narrow streets of old Havana and not knowing where I was).

Iain is still very busy – gone are my illusions of this as a 'holiday' post. Castro has been making speeches. I watched one on television

119

on Monday. It is certainly an extraordinary performance. He speaks for some 3–4 hours with no pause and no notes. There was a gathering of about a million people outside the palace on the last occasion.

* * *

Our car has arrived from New York by sea now and we hope to have it out of the customs any day. The past few days have been rather confused because of our own incidents and the national ones which have been very depressing, but more so for the Americans than us. I have not been to see houses this week. Yesterday James and I went to the big Biltmore Club which is near here and spent the morning on the beach. This was the really good side of life in Havana. Hot sun, blue sky and clear blue sea on a gradually sloping beach. The water feels just cool enough to be refreshing and make the sun bearable on one's back. James had a rubber ring and thoroughly enjoyed himself, swimming around. He is completely unafraid.

We took two visitors from the Board of Trade to dinner in one of the many Spanish restaurants in Havana; there is wonderful shellfish. We have tried one Cuban speciality several times – black bean soup, very thick, with white rice and raw onion. It's known as *Cristianos y Moros* (Christians and Moors).

Love from us all, Jeanne

10. Crowd scene in the Plaza de la Revolución, during one of Fidel Castro's speeches.

CUBA YES, YANKEE NO!

Havana, Sunday 27 December 1959

Dear Dorothy,

I was tempted to write May or June because that is how it feels here. Our first tropical Christmas seemed very odd but the day turned out to be wet and dull which helped in the end to give the right impression and to eat the traditional turkey and Christmas pudding. But the days before and today are delightful – sunny and not unbearably hot and the evenings are just cool enough to wear a wrap.

Sorry to send belated birthday wishes – much love from us all, Jeanne.

In his letter to my sister-in-law, Anne, my father-in-law, David Sutherland, describes the house from photographs sent to him.

(Undated)

An important event this week was a letter from Jeanne enclosing half a dozen snaps of interest – 2 of them shows more clearly than in any previous photos the kind of house they live in – Calle 36, Miramar, Havana. It is a palatial looking house in the Spanish style, the walls plain white; on one wall a typical Spanish religious symbol, the Madonna and Child in relief, with a broad black frame, the whole protected from rain and weather by projecting V shaped roofing. The garden, or court has extensive cement floorboard – large squares like a draughtboard. Numerous white painted metal tables and chairs with wrought iron decorative spirals like grapes; Sandra holding a flower looked a small figure standing in this setting; Jeanne, James and Sandra and Stritzi, the small terrier dog – a very good one.

Havana, Wednesday 17 February 1960

Dear Dorothy,

The weeks fly past and it is a pity you are not able to see the children changing. James is at this moment calling out of the window to the ice cream vendor, trying to persuade him to deliver some ice cream; all in his newly acquired Spanish, which is quite good now. He spends most of the day in Spanish and only speaks English when I am at home.

We have had a dinner for 17 and a cocktail party for 60 this week. The dinner was a sort of return of hospitality to the

121

various ambassadors who had entertained us, Dutch, Canadian, our own and some more people to mould it together. We had the head of Shell, Maurice Baird Smith, and one man from Esso and his wife who was very kind to me when we arrived, and the new Yugoslav couple.

The cocktail party was rather a tricky mixture, consisting of the four Cuban journalists who are going on a visit to England, arranged by the Central Office of Information, their wives, some of their friends and some more newspapermen plus some of the prominent British businessmen here and some of our Embassy.

This weekend we are planning a rest. We hope to leave Havana on Saturday morning for the nearest and most famous Cuban resort, Varadero, which is said to be extremely beautiful and have sand like sugar.

Much love to you both from us all, Jeanne

11. 'Cocktail Party', given by the Sutherlands for Cuban journalists going on a visit to the UK, February 1960. From the left Iain, Jeanne; centre José Aníbal Maestri (dean of the National College of Journalists), Isabel Fordham, Asunción Cordero de Maestri; right, Enrique Labrador Ruiz and Ambassador Stanley Fordham.

CUBA YES, YANKEE NO!

Havana, Monday 22 February 1960

Dear Dorothy,

We had a pleasant weekend at Varadero. It's a small town of no great distinction on a promontory with sea all round and miles and miles of sandy beaches. There all the wealthy Cubans built houses with the front on the beach and the back to the canal where they kept their yachts. The houses and the yachts varied in size and magnificence according to whether the owner was a millionaire, billionaire or whatever. In between there are some large and splendid hotels. There are very few yachts now.

Love from us all, Jeanne

Havana, Tuesday 8 March 1960

Dear Dorothy and DM,

I write to you both as official correspondent. No we did not yet receive the photograph taken at Catterline, but things arrive here very slowly by sea mail. Some things destined for the Embassy were blown up in the docks on Friday. The explosion was a terrible disaster. However one's first rush of sympathy was somewhat dampened by the local reactions, at first gruelling and repetitive commentaries delivered with horrible relish, followed by the political twist which was developed on Saturday and continued until it came to a climax with Castro's tirade at the cemetery gates. The Cuban-American situation seems very bad at the moment.[5]

Much love from us all, Jeanne

Havana, 5 April 1960

Dear Dorothy,

Iain is still very busy though not quite as harassed as before. The Clarks have now settled into their house just two blocks away from us and besides being delighted to have them as neighbours it is considerably easier to have two cars. Iain and Alan Clark drive in to the office in one and we keep one around here for errands.

The International Festival of Ballet continued here last week with the American Ballet and we managed to go on Thursday evening. It

123

was a good programme but even so not good enough to prevent me dropping off a bit in the last part. It is billed to start at 9.30 but never starts before 9.45 or 10.00 and finished after midnight. The American Ambassador gave an enormous party in his magnificent residence for the Ballet Company on Wednesday. We were to go on the Saturday night to a midnight party given for them by the head of Shell. However the party was changed to Friday night and I funked it, as we did not get home until 11.15 that night from a reception given by the Brazilian Ambassador for the Cuban President on the occasion of the visit to Cuba of one of the Brazilian Presidential candidates. This was a most extraordinary mixture of people, including the most reactionary and the most left wing sections of Cuban society. Castro had indicated that he was coming but although the party was from 7.30 to 9.30 he arrived a little before 11 o'clock and left, we are told, after 1 a.m. There was some trouble letting Castro and his friends in to the reception until they had removed their guns.

We all send our love to you both, Jeanne

Havana, Wednesday 29 June 1960

Dear Dorothy,

It has been a very busy week with parties to say goodbye to the Fordhams every night and our own at the end. We had sixty people, all sitting down to a meal in the garden. The four-piece Cuban orchestra turned out to be excellent and the party seemed to be a success as it did not end until 2 a.m.

On Sunday we had to attend a special meeting of the West Indian Cultural Association in honour of the Fordhams and at which Isabel was presented with their Distinguished Service Order for the work she has done for the West Indian community in Havana, and particularly for setting up their Old People's Home. It was rather like an English village gathering with recitations and singing and speeches, except that all the participants were black and the speeches were full of colour and excitement and some of the songs sounded almost like calypsos.

Much has been happening here in the last few weeks, some published and some not yet. All the members of the government have been making speeches and we have been translating them.[6] Iain has been sending telegrams and generally being very caught up in it all.

On Sunday evening about 7 o'clock there was the most terrible bang followed by smoke billowing up into the sky. The explosion shook the house and knocked plaster down from the roof, although it was miles from here. An ammunition dump on the other side of the harbour blew up. It was a much larger explosion than the one on board the *Coubre* (the French ship) but fortunately in an isolated place so that there were not many casualties. But windows were blown out of shops miles away.

Love from us all, Jeanne

There follows a rare letter from Iain to his parents:

Havana, 5 July 1960

Dear M & D,

I imagine that even the *Press and Journal* has had a word about Cuba this week on its front page. Usually of interest to the British Press for only a few sensational articles under the over-used headline 'Our Man in Havana', the wires have been buzzing this week. We have correspondents from most of the British papers – Holden from the *Times*, Cunahan of the BBC and one Sherman of the *Observer* are expected for supper. It's difficult to see them during office hours.

Our own telegraph traffic has gone up also and there has been much overtime in the cipher room. The Ambassador presented our Note on the 'intervention' of the Shell refinery to the Cuban Foreign Minister at 10.30 p.m. last night. The previous afternoon Jeanne and I had taken the head of Shell here, Maurice Baird Smith and his assistant Lloyd-Hirst to the airport to see them off, and as a precaution. We knew them both well. Maurice B.S. was a bachelor who lived in a splendid house in the Country Club area of Havana (only it is no longer called 'Country Club' which is too American, but 'Cubanacan' which is Siboney, the language of the original natives of Cuba who were all killed off by the Spaniards). Lloyd-Hirst was from the Argentine, from the large English colony there, but his wife came from Stornoway and could be persuaded to sing Gaelic songs at functions like St Andrew's night. The leader of the Scots community, or at least the host on that occasion was however the Canadian Ambassador, Alan Anderson, who was born in Aberdeen and went to the Grammar School, then to Canada in his youth and was in Cuba many years ago as a clerk in the Royal Bank of Canada.

(The letter ends here)

* * *

Relations between the Cubans and the Americans deteriorated rapidly during 1960, as Castro carried out his plans for nationalisation of the large foreign companies, most of them North American. The expropriation of land had started in 1959 with the agrarian reform, according to a law under which there were to be no private estates of more than 1000 acres. The reform was organised by the INRA, the Agrarian Reform Institute, headed by Castro himself but directed by Nuñez Jimenez. Castro had promised that the land would be given to those who cultivated it and there was no mention of cooperatives or state farms. In fact large quantities of the big estates were made into agricultural cooperatives. The US government, while admitting that the Cuban government had the right to expropriate foreign land, protested strongly that this could not be done without adequate compensation. Castro had rejected the American note demanding prompt compensation and offered only $4^1/2$ per cent bonds, with no fixed period for payment.[7] Cuban ministers who opposed the agrarian reform were dismissed. Philip Bonsal, the American ambassador, who delivered the American note was a moderate and continued to believe that he could negotiate with Cuba; but in temperament he was the complete opposite of Castro and the two were never able to get on.[8]

In July 1959 a surprising event had occurred. Castro had resigned from his position as Prime Minister and called for the resignation also of the then President, Urrutía. For a period Cuba remained without either Prime Minister or President. Castro remained in charge of the army and the INRA. Finally Osvaldo Dorticós became President. 'He was to prove invaluable as a nominal leader of the Cuban revolutionary regime. He was the only member of the cabinet to keep office hours and the only one indeed who was used to regular work.'[9] At the big 26 July meeting when Castro spoke for four hours, Dorticós announced that Castro would resume the post of Prime Minister. Castro had said that it was a decision for the people to make.[10] Dorticós (who was 47) and the Foreign Minister, Roa (53) were older than all the other members of the government who were mostly in their early thirties. There was never any consideration of elections. When asked about this on his visit to America, Castro had said 'they would follow when the agrarian reform was complete, when all could read and write, when all children went to school and all had free access to medicine and doctors'.[11]

At this time there was still constant speculation as to whether Castro was communist. But by the middle of 1959 he had stopped making anti-communist comments, which had previously cropped up in his speeches;[12] but in July 1959 Stanley Fordham was saying, 'The only ones that can with some confidence be called crypto-communist are Raul Castro, Che Guevara, Nuñez Jiménez, and possibly David Salvador. I still doubt that anything closely resembling a truly communist state will evolve under Castro's leadership.'[13]

At first in 1959 the country was being led by a mixture of rebel leaders, liberals and some communists. Not surprisingly they did not always see eye to eye. There were arguments between Castro and the communists and between Castro and the trade union leaders. Liberal leaders who had supported Castro at the beginning began to turn against him, particularly as he moved closer to the Communist Party. They were gradually dismissed from their posts. Very soon the exodus began, first with the *batistianistas* (followers of Batista), then 'the frightened rich', such as the owners of the house we rented and many others, who mistakenly thought that by letting their houses to foreign diplomats (and receiving incidentally a rent in dollars) they would be saving them from the takeovers. The main exodus 'started in the spring, speeded up in the summer and took on the proportion of mass flight by the end of 1960'. Following the earliest refugees, and after the large scale appropriations in summer, the business community began to leave, also teachers; after the takeover of the trade unions there were also former pro-*fidelistas* and finally members of the 26th July Movement and sympathisers. By 1961 there were over 100,000 political émigrés in the US and these were only a fraction of those who had tried to get out. If all could have gone there would have been 250,000, out of a population of 7 million.[14]

As relations with the Americans deteriorated over the expropriation of land and businesses, and the liberal supporters of his regime resigned or were removed, Castro moved gradually closer to the communist groups in the country and to the communist bloc abroad. In January 1960 Mikoyan visited Cuba and an economic agreement was signed. Russia was to buy sugar and also lend £100 million to Cuba for 12 years. They were also to supply Cuba with crude and refined petrol and other commodities and to provide technical aid. Cuba was to export fruit juices, fibre and hides. The agreement was vague and Hugh Thomas does not think that the Russians at this stage were eager to have a communist Cuba.[15] Soon after this the US made offers of military assistance to stop exile aircraft coming from Florida but Castro rejected this offer because he did not trust the US. He had asked Russia for arms which they had (perhaps reluctantly) agreed. At the same time

Eisenhower had agreed to accept the CIA's recommendation to begin to arm and train Cuban exiles.

By now there were very few opposition voices left in the country. Most of the television stations and newspapers had been taken over by the government. Only the Church remained in open opposition. A labour law had been passed requiring the registration of all employers, employees and self-employed in order to regulate labour in the country. In May Cuba resumed diplomatic relations with the Soviet Union.

The final crunch came when Castro asked the foreign oil companies to process Russian oil. After some consideration they refused and as the Esso and Shell refineries were taken over by Castro, the US decided to cut the sugar quota and suspended the 700,000 tons remaining of Cuba's 1960 quota.

> Having decided to escape from the sugar quota Cuba's problem was to derive the maximum benefit from US abrogation of it. It was therefore desirable that the abrogation should have been unilateral and like an act of aggression. For years afterwards ill-informed, if well-intentioned Liberals justified Castro's communisation of Cuba as a response to Eisenhower's sugar policy. But that policy enabled Castro to respond with a series of counter-measures which might not then have occurred (or just possibly might never have occurred) and would have been more difficult to justify, even to Cubans.[16]

By September 1960 Castro had expropriated all enterprises and properties owned by US companies and individuals. The Cuban Council of Ministers passed a decree in July granting the President and Prime Minister powers to expropriate all property of US firms and nationals in Cuba, when deemed to be necessary in the national interest. Compensation was to be made in the form of bonds with interest of not less than 2%, the money to come from 25% of the exchange received by Cuba from sale of sugar to the US. If the money was not available from this fund for payment of interest in any one year the interest for that year was to lapse.[17] But it was not just a case of expropriation of American-owned companies. In October Law 890 nationalised 376 all-Cuban enterprises, 18 distilleries, 5 breweries, 4 paint factories, 61 textile factories, 16 rice mills, 11 movie theatres and 13 department stores.[18] In October Castro nationalised another 116 US enterprises and Ambassador Bonsal left Cuba never to return. In January 1961 the Americans broke off diplomatic relations.

CUBA YES, YANKEE NO!

*** *** ***

Havana, Tuesday 19 July 1960

Dear Parents All!

Last week you got nothing more than a mere bulletin on the state of affairs. The reason was an unexpected cocktail party for 50 people, which we ended up giving last Tuesday for all the visiting British, Australian, Indian and other journalists who have been waiting for something to happen and to whom Iain has no time to talk during the day.

There was finally very little time for Iain to be Chargé. He complains that he was not able to write even one despatch under his own name. Stanley Fordham left on Friday last week and the new Ambassador, Bill Marchant, arrived yesterday evening. We had a little supper party for him, which was completely disrupted by Fidel who decided to get up from his sick bed and speak from 8.30 until midnight. The Ambassador was fascinated of course so no one spoke the whole evening and my carefully planned dinner was eaten in snatches round the television.

Love to you both, Jeanne

Havana, Monday 29 August 1960

Dear Dorothy,

Yesterday we went out for the day with James. We went to *Pinar del Rio*, which is the westernmost province of the island and has mountains and pine woods as its name suggests. We went as far as Artimisa and Candalería where we turned off just at the foot of the mountains at a place called Soroa. Here is what they call a 'Tourist Centre'. There is a restaurant and a place where you can picnic by a waterfall and some walks up the hills and a private garden with what is supposed to be the largest collection of orchids in the world. Near this they are building a place for 'popular tourism', that is somewhere where ordinary Cubans can go (before there were only places for wealthy American tourists).

I continue to act as interpreter to Mrs Marchant on her calls on Ambassadresses. Last week we did the Czech, Yugoslav, Costa Rican, Panamanian, Japanese and Peruvian. One of the chief topics of conversation with the Latin American ladies is the number of

129

uninvited guests they have, i.e. asilees, Cubans who have decided that they are no longer safe outside. Thank goodness we are not involved in this strange reciprocal arrangement, to which the South Americans subscribe, whereby they take in each other's nationals at times of revolution. It must be a terrible strain. Once the Peruvian lady had eleven at the same time. [Later, other embassies such as the Brazilian had embarrassingly large numbers.]

Time is up and I must go into town before the banks shut. I hope your holiday ended well and you managed to do a fair amount of sketching.

Love from us all, Jeanne

Havana, Monday 5 September 1960

Dear Dorothy,

This morning I was busy finishing a translation of the 'Declaration of Havana', which is part of Fidel Castro's reply to the Costa Rica Agreement and he really let himself go. He seems to be back to health again and he spoke the usual $3^1/2$ hours.

As you will know he broke off relations with Chang Kai Chek and agreed to set up diplomatic relations with the Chinese communist government. Everyone now wonders what will happen to the many thousand Chinese in Cuba, most of whom were not communists. More and more people are leaving as the American firms are taken over and it looks as though we shall soon be just the diplomatic corps left.

It is a dreadful grey day with the rain pouring down – the effect of the cyclone, which is moving around the Atlantic. This morning they seemed to think that Cuba might be affected but no bulletins have been issued so far. I think a hurricane now on top of everything would be too much.

Very much love to you both from us all, Jeanne

Havana, 17 September 1960

Dear M & D,

Sunday evening – this morning Fidel Castro went off to New York: I went for a brief visit to the Embassy. Yesterday and the preceding days more of the American colony left – including some we know quite well – following the expropriation of the American banks. The two

Canadian banks remain. The only other foreign bank, the bank of China remains, but has changed Chinas. Some of our British friends have gone too – the people in Shell of course and those in American firms – but most of the British colony remain. One couple who did leave last week and whom we entertained to dinner on Tuesday were the Rabbi Solomon and his wife, British by nationalisation, German Jewish by birth. Besides being a Rabbi, he is also a painter of some merit who exhibits under the name of Solomonski.

I am sorry that the weather for your holiday was not as good as it might have been. Here people do not talk about the weather except to complain of the heat. But I omit another important exception – except when there is a hurricane in the offing. Two weeks ago when 'Donna' was sweeping across the Caribbean, we had warnings that it was making straight for Havana along the north coast. We papered all the windows and put up boards and laid in hurricane lamps (yes, that is why they are called h. lamps) and bought some extra tinned food (not so much available now that imports from the US are restricted) and anchored the lamps on the balcony with guy ropes and waited. And 'Donna' then veered away and went up the coast of Florida instead.

Love from Iain

Havana, Monday 19 September 1960

Dear Dorothy,

We waited all day Thursday and Friday for the hurricane but nothing happened here; it went instead to the States where it did a lot of damage. Here they say that Fidel sent it to America. On Saturday they confiscated all the American banks in Cuba. Out of 5000 Americans who used to live here I think there are now about 2000. Many of the wives of the American Embassy have left too, especially the ones with children of school age. They seem to be afraid that their children will have to learn Cuban history or be indoctrinated.

The great excitement now will be the United Nations meeting with all the leaders from the Eastern countries. I would like to see it. The Americans have restricted the Russian and Cuban delegation to Manhattan Island for security reasons ostensibly. So the Cubans yesterday, for no reason except reciprocity, confined the American Ambassador to Vedado, the part of Havana in which his Embassy is situated. But they have to let him go home so he is allowed to drive by an approved route to the Country Club district where he lives.

Cuban cocktail parties are getting all the time more like Europe. On Friday night at the Mexican National Day there were the recently arrived Russians (the Ambassador, Kudriavtsev, is the man who was 1st Secretary in Ottawa when the Canadians threw out all the Russians after the spy trial there); the Czechs and the Yugoslavs formed their own little circle with the Arab Ambassador and the Cuban foreign minister. The English are so far still speaking to everyone, so we can have quite an amusing time, moving from side to side.

Love from us all, Jeanne

Havana, 26 September 1960

Dear M & D,

As promised I enclose some photos from the last set to be developed. I wasted much of this afternoon watching Fidel Castro deliver his 4$^{1}/_{2}$-hour speech to the UN. It was relayed on Cuban television. He did not put on one of his best performances in that more formal atmosphere. His violent oratory is better suited for the crowds of several hundred and thousands, which he assembles in the main square of Havana. It is not known if Mr Khrushchev will come here but I think not. Nasser probably. Tito not so likely.

Love Iain and Jeanne

Havana, Monday 20 February 1961

Dear Anne,

Life here is very busy and usually interesting, sometimes exciting. Recently we have had a series of quite interesting visitors, O'Donovan of the *Observer*, Monsieur Aron of *Le Figaro*, an eminent French journalist and professor, and Miss Evelyn Irons of the *Sunday Times*, and for dinner with us yesterday the recently arrived Kingsley Martin of the *New Statesman*. Iain is by now the expert on Cuba in the Embassy so we spend most of our time discussing politics. In fact one hardly ever discusses anything else.

In the last months I have seen more of the country than in all the first year, having been to the extreme eastern province, Oriente, to Santiago de Cuba and last weekend to the west and Viñales, a charming valley among the hills. The weekend was cool and we enjoyed an active weekend walking, exploring the hills and riding.

Do write soon and tell us all your news, much love from us all, Jeanne

Gradually times became more difficult in Cuba, for the Cubans and for the foreigners living there. Food became scarce and it was a constant search to find enough for a balanced diet for the family, let alone food for diplomatic entertainment. Cubans of all kinds continued to leave. There were tragic scenes at the airport as families tried to pass their most treasured possessions to their friends or relatives seeing them off. They were not allowed to leave with anything more than their clothes and a wedding ring. Besides those who left openly there were many others who left secretly because they were known to be in opposition to the government and for whom it was not safe to stay. These included ex-members of Castro's army or administration who could not countenance the increased ties with the communist bloc. Many of these were recruited by the counter-revolutionary movement, which was growing among the exiles in Florida.

The constant threat of invasion caused tension among both the Cubans and the foreigners. And the incidents of sabotage and small-scale rebellion inside the country caused anger and hatred among Castro and his followers. But of course life went on. It was a beautiful country with a warm and pleasant climate except for the hottest months of the summer. Even then the sea and swimming pools were never far away. And even though Castro made four-hour violent anti-western, particularly anti-American speeches, there was never any feeling of personal hostility; we never felt threatened physically. The Minister of Justice lived in the house next to us in Miramar, with armed guards outside day and night. Our children played with the Minister's children who were often looked after by the guards. The children would climb all over them and I would pray that the catches on their rifles were firmly closed. The city was full of guns. They were piled up near the cash desks of the supermarkets, available to be picked up by their owners who would be going on militia duty after their work shift.

In the US there was considerable disagreement about what to do about Castro and Cuba. Some were against an embargo of goods as they thought it would drive Cuba further into the Soviet bloc. By November 1960 probably half the Cuban professional population had left. During the Eisenhower administration a serious exile force was being built up outside Cuba, which was supported by the CIA with arms and money. By the end of 1960 the US was on the verge of a presidential election and towards the end of his presidency it is said that Eisenhower was not always kept informed of the plans for the building up of an invasion force.

Kennedy inherited this difficult position, at first coming out strongly against Castro. As President elect he was told about the invasion plan in

November 1960. The plan at that time was to establish a bridgehead and then to destroy the air force. It was believed that the country would rise up against Castro and welcome the invasion force. There was much discussion about whether the invasion should go ahead. It was finally agreed that the Cubans should go ahead with the least risk to the US and that no US military would participate. Kennedy was told that they were just helping the exiles and it was not a US operation, which was not quite the truth. Meanwhile, in Guatemala where the invasion force was being prepared, there was confidence and optimism. A remote suggestion for the renewing of relations with Cuba in January 1961 came to nothing.[19]

In March 1961 the Cuban Revolutionary Council was set up under Dr José Miró Cardena, which included exiles of a wide selection of political beliefs, from *batistianistas* to ex-*fidelistas*, but all united against the 'betrayal of the Cuban revolution'. There was much confusion in reconciling the various anti-Castro elements outside Cuba. There was a sense of haste and urgency that something should be done before the large-scale increase of Soviet bloc arms in Cuba, and this did not leave enough time to reconcile the different sides. 'The invasion force was given such priority that anti-Castro forces inside Cuba were virtually ignored.' Poor intelligence about the state of popular rebellion meant that the invasion came as a surprise and discouraged anti-Castro forces from doing anything until they knew what was happening. By then it was too late.[20]

Back home in Cuba a parade in Havana in January featured Russian tanks and other weapons. Ambassadors had arrived from China and from all other communist countries. In July Cuba and China signed a commercial treaty and in September entered into diplomatic relations.

Some land had been given to the peasants but the majority had been organised into cooperatives, which the farmers did not like although they were generally better off than they had been before. There were attempts being made to diversify agriculture and to introduce crops other than sugar. By spring 1961 over one third of farmland in Cuba was probably run by the state. However inexperience and lack of organisation led to poor results from the cooperative movement, and lack of trained managers and accountants, who had fled to the States, made things more difficult. From November 1960 food became short and from spring 1961 very short.[21]

* * *

Everyone had underestimated the difficulties Cuba would have in running the country itself after years of US economic control. They not only had to run existing industries but also plan for self-sufficiency and expansion and they had to find new sources for the essentials and luxuries which had previously been imported from the US.

However rural unemployment had almost ended. New hospitals, schools and houses had been built and INRA had also built shops, clinics, clubs and libraries. Nearly all country dwellers and most Cuban town dwellers thought that they were better off than in the past. Clubs, hotels and beaches were open to the public. A hotel in Varadero cost $15 instead of $50 a night and the Havana Biltmore Yacht Club 50 cents for the day.

There was great unhappiness and despair among the middle class but the worst aspect of all was the imprisonment of opponents of the system. By 1961 there were possibly 10,000 political prisoners in Cuba and conditions were seriously bad and overcrowded. The administration of justice was a problem as many of the judges were anti-Castro and had gone into exile. All through the winter of 1960–61 there were attacks by CIA and exiles, rumoured invasions and violence. Many Cubans were said to have been shot by the government by October 1960. Deserters were imprisoned or executed. Castro was, as always, 'audacious and on the move, verbose, egotistic, careless of human life and above all charismatic, dazzling simple and sophisticated people alike, and always an amazing orator'.[22] His speeches were long and repetitive. They were wonderful lessons in Spanish because he repeated everything several times in a slightly different way and his style was slow, deliberate and emphatic. His style is unforgettable, 'cado niño, cado Indio, cado negro, cado mujer...'[23] as he would list the social minorities and the underprivileged in his usually rather gruff and hoarse voice.

* * *

Letter to my father-in-law from:

Foreign Office, 8 Carlton House Terrace, London, SW1

Dear Mr Sutherland,

You will be pleased to hear that we had a phone call this morning from Mrs Sutherland, the wife of the Head of Chancery, to say that all members of the staff and their families are safe and well.

Yours sincerely,

(A.F. Maddocks)

Havana, Thursday 27 April 1961

Dear Dorothy,

At last we have a courier leaving Cuba, and it happens strangely to be Iain, who is going to New York and possibly to Washington for four days. He is to take the mail and to tell them all the things, which no one has had time to write about during the last few weeks.

This week has not been as long as the last thank goodness, but we are left with the reaction and almost anti-climax. Everything appears to have returned to normal, even more so than before, as now there are hardly any bombs at night or shooting to be heard in Havana. On the other hand hardly anyone thinks this is the end and so there is still a good deal of tension and apprehension. 'Will the Americans do anything or not?' is what most people think and some more thoughtful ones add 'And what would happen if they did, would it mean a general conflagration?'

There are several unpleasant aftermaths of the invasion, the worst being the nightly interrogations of the prisoners taken in the battle areas. These appear on radio and television and you may watch these poor, tired men trying to argue against a panel of communist theoreticians who twist their questions so as to make the prisoner answer the way they want; brainwashing in public. However last night Castro at least said that he was only going to shoot one or two. This seems to be in response to the pleas from the other Latin American countries.

The arrests, which were the most terrible part of last week, have abated. Some say 50,000 have been arrested. The prisons are bursting and the conditions are appalling. Iain comes home at all hours and tells me fantastic stories of the people he manages to see and find and even get released if he is lucky. Nine or ten British subjects have been held during the last two weeks. I can't remember how many are left in now, not many. A lot of time last week was spent comforting, protecting or just cheering British subjects.

Personally we are all very well here. The children were too young to be frightened by the noises we had a week last Saturday and the odd bursts later in the week. It was all quite a long way away, the Saturday bombing, but it woke us up with a start and we rather stupidly and unnecessarily woke the children. But they liked it and jumped up and down saying, 'bang, bang'. For several nights James went to bed with his toy pistol under his pillow. He was prepared to shoot anything, which came along. However it is very quiet now, perhaps rather ominously quiet?

We have had no formal entertainment since the 'invasion' but endless consultations over coffee, tea or drinks. At night we did not go out much unless it was urgent. The first week everyone got very little sleep because of all the phone calls in the middle of the night, (the press does not mind about the time difference) or looking for lost people, or bangs in the night. So we are a little tired. It will do Iain good to get away if they don't work him too hard.

We have the West Indian couple, the Barnetts, staying for ten days, as it is rather unpleasant for them in a hotel. They are looking for a house but I think they will have to return to a hotel as no one has time here at the moment to find houses.

* * *

Herbert Matthews wrote, 'The ill fated invasion of Cuba last April was one of the rare politico-military events – a perfect failure'; and he adds, 'It was an appalling example of intelligence agents making their "information" conform to the plan they were determined to work out.'[24] It was all based on the premise that the country would rise up against Castro as soon as the invasion started and that there would be little need for fighting. The Cuban exiles mostly believed this, and many also believed that the Americans would at least give them support. The Americans were ambivalent about the whole exercise and there was a distinct lack of communication between the CIA and the government. The enterprise was put in jeopardy by the air attacks on Havana, San Antonio de los Baños and Santiago de Cuba, which took place on the Saturday, 40 hours before the invasion was due to start on the Monday. This gave time for Castro to prepare his forces, raise the army and the militia and arrest anyone who had anything to do with opposition to his government plus many who did not. And Castro certainly used this time to get rid of anyone whom he thought might possibly support the invasion.

Between the air raid of 15 April and 17th 100,000 people were arrested. Many British citizens were caught up in this widespread sweep up of anyone who was remotely suspect, even though they were completely innocent, and released soon afterwards. People were held in crowded prisons, theatres and cinemas. Iain, in his letter to Robin Edmonds of American Department, FO, tells how when searching for detained British subjects at the Cuban Army Investigation Department he came across Peron's ex-Minister of the Interior, Señor Borlenghi, produced by a semi-literate guard who did not know the difference between *Gran Bretaña* and the Argentine. Iain informed the Argentine Ambassador who said that there was nothing he could do for him except to offer him an alternative prison in Buenos Aires.[25]

Hugh Thomas describes the ill-fated enterprise. The invading brigade consisted of about 1200 men, all aged around thirty, mostly middle and upper class, although there were about 200 working-class Cubans. Political allegiance varied from extreme right to centre, a cross-section of those opposed to Castro. Some had no training at all, some a few weeks. The landing at Cochino Bay was mismanaged and the surrounding area consisted of swampy ground occupied by armed charcoal burners. At dawn there was a Cuban air attack on the landing craft and ships in the Bay, some ammunition and supply ships were hit and some withdrew. The brigade was deserted by the supply ships, which had removed themselves and mostly refused to return. By the night of 17–18 April, instead of the planned consolidation of the attack that had been planned, there was fierce fighting between the attackers and the Cuban government forces. The invaders believed that US support would arrive but it never came. The CIA cancelled the instructions for the supply ships to return without consulting Washington. The US refused any air support except of the most inadequate kind and the situation became too bad even for evacuation. By mid afternoon on 18th Kennedy allowed the US navy to try to evacuate survivors but it was too late. 'The US government had shown itself divided, ill informed and careless of detail.'

Castro's forces captured the surviving invaders and took 1180 prisoners (1297 landed). Eighty men were lost in the fighting and 30–40 in the disembarkation. Castro said that they lost 87 men. The invaders said this figure was much higher. The prisoners were not shot, except for a few *batistianistas*, and after interrogation on television, they were imprisoned in poor conditions and finally released a year and a half later, in exchange for medical supplies. 'For Castro the defeat of the invasion was a triumph. After the defeat came the celebrations, the parading of prisoners on television, the jubilant announcement on 1 May that Cuba was a socialist state and there would be no more elections. The revolution, he explained, was the direct expression of the will of the people; there was not an election every four years in Cuba but an election every day.'[26]

Havana, 30 May 1961

Dear Dorothy,

I went into town to have lunch with Iain at the American Club. It still exists although there are only about three Americans each day and it is largely supported by the small British and Canadian colony who were previously allowed in on sufferance.

The school is now entirely for foreign children. All the Cuban schools closed on 28 April and are not likely to open until January 1962, as all the teachers and the older children have been sent to the villages and the mountains to teach the illiterate members of the population, who are to learn to read and write this year, *El Año de la Educacion* (The Year of Education). With the help of the diplomatic corps and the head of James' school, the energetic old French lady, we finally managed to get an 'International Diplomatic School' going with

12. Jeanne, James and Sandra in the garden, Cuba, 1961.

about 20 pupils. We have now formally notified the Ministry of Foreign Affairs in the hope that they will give it their blessing and allow it to continue until the end of the term and start again next year if enough children are all here. The Russians have their own school and in the 'year of education' it seems a pity that our children should be without for nine months.

Encouraged by the partial success with the school I am now trying to persuade the Board of the Anglo-American Hospital to try to do a deal with the Cubans rather than just close down at the end of the month. The idea would be to offer the hospital to some Institute of Medicine on the condition that so many beds were put at the disposal of the foreign community or those foreigners who wished to use it.

With a school, a hospital and a beach life might be possible. The beach we nearly lost last week when the Militia arrived to take it over, like nearly all the private clubs. Then five days later we heard that the intervention had been suspended and the Club was to return to the members. We suspect the intervention of many diplomatic members. Among these diplomats the United Arab Republic is heavily represented and they may have had some influence.

We send much love to you all, Jeanne

* * *

The prisons were full. All private schools were to be nationalised. Cuba now moved closer to full membership of the communist alliance and 'old' Cuban communist leaders came to the fore. At the 26 July 1961 meeting the unity of all parties was proclaimed in *El Partido Unico de la Revolución Socialista* (The One Party of Socialist Revolution). Blas Roca, the Organisation Secretary of the Cuban Communist Party published a book, *Los Fundamentos del Socialismo en Cuba* (*Fundamentals of Socialism in Cuba*) with a prologue by him in which he refers to the unification of all revolutionary forces and their setting out on the road to communism. Roca was to be seen on the left hand of Castro at the May Day celebrations when the revolutionary leaders paraded the streets.[27]

In December Fidel proclaimed for the first time his belief in Marxist-Leninism. This is an excellent example of his rhetoric and his repetitive style.

> Do I believe in Marxism? I believe absolutely in Marxism! Did I believe in it on 1 January? I believed on the 1 January. Did I believe it on 26

July? I believed in it on the 26 July. Did I understand it as I understand it today, after almost 10 years of struggle? No, I did not understand it as I understand it today. Compared with the way I understood it then and the way I understand it now there is a great difference. Did I have prejudices? Yes I had prejudices! On 26 July? Yes. Could I call myself a mature revolutionary on 26 July? No, I couldn't call myself a mature revolutionary. I could call myself almost a mature revolutionary. Can I call myself a mature revolutionary today? This would mean that I felt satisfied with what I am and I am not satisfied of course.[28]

* * *

The economic situation worsened and the shortages of food, household goods and even houses became more acute. Public transport was very poor. There were poor harvests and the state farms did not work. Soviet aid in 1961–62 reached $570 million. The shortages finally resulted in food rationing, which, as can be seen from the letters, was not very successful. There was discontent with the Russian advisers and technicians and Castro played Russia and China off against each other. But he needed Russia for economic help.

It was a difficult situation for everyone, Cubans and foreigners alike. The foreigners had access to outside supplies but they had to bear all the inconveniences of the situation usually without the Cubans' belief in the revolution and Castro. Every day life was difficult as the shortage of food, and later medical supplies, worsened. It was much helped by the use of the Embassy house at Jibacoa (which had been donated for the use of the Embassy by an exiled Cuban before leaving); by the availability of the former *Miramar* beach club and the odd weekend away at places such as Varadero and Tarara.

* * *

Havana, 7 July 1961

Dear Dorothy,

Marie Boissevain, the wife of the Dutch Ambassador, has invited us to spend the weekend in Varadero with them. We shall leave some time tomorrow, if all goes well, and arrive back on Monday morning. We are invited to stay in the Dupont house. This is an enormous modern castle built by the multi-millionaire, Mr Dupont, of nylon stockings I think. He made a fortune and built this fantastic house at the furthest point of the beach in Varadero, standing in its own vast park and with its own golf course. He hasn't been for nearly ten years they say, but he keeps on all the servants and pays them regularly. Presumably because he still brings in so many dollars the Cubans have not so far touched the house. It is supposed to be quite extraordinary, inside and out, has the most wonderful selection of tropical plants of all kinds and, something not so common here, families of iguanas living in the grounds who used to be very tame when the family lived there. It should be an amusing weekend. I am told that the same cocktail is served at lunch and another at dinner, as Mr Dupont had when he visited.

Fidel made a speech about shortages this week, explaining how it would not hurt the Cubans to eat less fat and that they could do to lose weight, and being particularly cross about the Americans whose fault it is that they are short of food, especially cross as the Americans refused to allow several million tons of lard to leave the States for Cuba this week.

Love from us all, Jeanne

Havana, Thursday 20 July 1961

Dear Dorothy and David,

On Tuesday evening we had a supper for the Granada Television team, who are here for a month and are making four twenty minute programmes starting on September 28th. They all seem very won over by revolutionary Cuba and we spent a lot of time reminding them that this was a system which allowed of no opposition, no choice but to join in, support the government, leave or go to prison.

The country is going through a very difficult period. As Iain put it, they are nearer than they have ever been to an economic crisis. We now have serious shortages of meat, fish, bacon, eggs, butter, cheese, oil and fats and even scarcity of oranges and grapefruit. They have made an attempt to start rationing fats and we have all filled in our forms but so far nothing has been distributed. We are living on our small reserves imported recently from the States, but it is obvious that this time it is not going to be a question of weeks, but months, and everyone is thinking that something will have to be done to ensure that supplies are available for the Embassy staff.

Much love from us all, Jeanne

CUBA YES, YANKEE NO!

Havana, 2 August 1961

Dear Dorothy,

We had some news about us in this week's bag – at long last. After the initial shock, and with some reservations, because I had hoped to come back to Europe and because I am not quite sure about living in the States, I think it is about the best thing that could have happened to us. We are to go to Washington and Iain is to be the Latin American specialist First Secretary in the Embassy in Washington. I really only wanted to go to Spain and that was pretty impossible.

The job seems to attract him and it has certain advantages. It is a reasonably normal country where you can buy things when you want them. We don't have to learn a new language; except for the children who will have to learn to speak English, but they would have to do that some time anyway. I am not sure about living in the States for a long period. They have rather peculiar politics and diplomacy, but I am sure we shall make some good friends and find people with the same tastes as ours.

So far the news of our transfer has not been made public and we are not telling anyone here until the dates are more settled and much nearer the time for us to leave. Also it is still possible for things to change.

Much love from us all, Jeanne

Havana, Sunday 3 September

Dear Dorothy,

There is to be a great gathering of *alfabetizadores* soon to prove there will not be one illiterate Cuban left by the end of the year. The sad thing is that they only learn to read selections of Fidel's speeches and anti-American slogans. In fact most of their textbooks are full of indoctrination and translations from the Russian.

These are the things we spend our time talking about and sometimes arguing about. Visitors come out from England and tend to see only the campaigns to end illiteracy and to build the peasants houses, teach them to cook and sew and sing and play the guitar. They do not hear about the means used to achieve this end nor the fact that there is no possible way to disagree with the government except from Miami or prison; and that there is no opposition and not one single opposition newspaper left; and to resign from one's job in protest means that one will either starve or be arrested. We have two staunch members of the Liberal party here at the moment, Sir Andrew Murray, an ex-Lord Provost of Edinburgh and Miss Sykes, an unsuccessful Liberal candidate for Ipswich. We had some difficulty in explaining that there was not much liberalism here.

Iain invited Sir Andrew to meet some Havana Scots on Tuesday evening at 7.30. They were still all there four hours later, having spent the time arguing at the tops of their voices and occasionally shouting at each other and hurling insults across the room. It was a very hot night. But they all said they hadn't had such a good time for ages nor enjoyed themselves so much for a long time, and they went off arranging to meet for lunch the next day. So in a strange way it must have been a success.

Last Sunday 12 members of the Embassy hired a boat and went off fishing, in the direction of Cabañas where there is a beach. The boat and the fishing were very successful. Everybody went home with something to help out the week's rations and it was beautiful sailing along on the blue sea in the bright morning sunshine. But at Cabañas we were not so successful. We were told that there were sharks round the quiet beach where we decided to swim and at the same time the Militia swooped down on us and the clouds opened and poured with rain as we were about to put our feet in the water.

We were shot at, at one stage, from the shore, presumably mistaken for would be escaping Cubans, but we were fortunately out of range; all this in spite of our being on an excursion officially organised by the *Instituto Nacional de la Industria Turistica* (the National Institute of the Tourist Industry).

Love from us all, Jeanne and Iain

Havana, Wednesday 22 November 1961

Dear Dorothy,

We have been going along fairly quietly but pretty busy. A lot of the time is taken up with finding supplies. The Chinese, however, do not seem to have a problem and at their national day party the tables were absolutely groaning with food of all kinds, a rather poignant contrast with life outside.

Now that we have little more than two months left here we really feel that we are near to leaving. We shall need a base this time as no one can have us for three months and we cannot afford to live in a hotel. The idea is to find a house in the country not too far from London and from which we can visit or have people visit us. There is a slight complication, however, as it seems highly likely that the Sutherland family is to be increased by a fifth member at the end of May or beginning of June – this I may add not according to plan!

Hope you are all well, much love from all of us, Jeanne

Havana, 28 December 1961

Dear M & D and Anne,

We all hope you had a merry Christmas and M. a happy birthday. Here we spent Christmas Eve at the Embassy residence where the Marchants gave a party for the staff and the much-dwindled British colony. Turkey and mince pies at tables round the extraordinary indoor swimming pool which is part of the building.

We had Christmas with James and Sandra and 4 grass widowers including Robin Byatt who has come to take Alan Clark's place and whose wife arrives tomorrow, and some of the British businessmen left in Cuba. On Boxing Day we entertained some Cuban friends, mostly of the *ancien regime*, and not those celebrating their first 'socialist Christmas' with trees adorned with hammers and sickles.

We have still not fixed a house for leave. Nor have we been able to make final arrangements for travelling the Atlantic. The plan to go via the southern Caribbean calling at Caracas and the Port of Spain would take too long and be too expensive. I have therefore booked the family on the SS *Camito* (Elder Fyffes) from Kingston on February 1. This booking still stands but in the meantime the FO have suggested that I go officially on my way home to Caracas, Santo Domingo and possibly some other places. I shall have to do this alone, but I am waiting to see if we cannot all arrange to cross together on a boat from Panama.

With love and best wishes to you all and greetings for 1962.

* * *

The last year in Cuba had been a difficult one; obtaining food and medicines, and even the services of a doctor caused problems with young children. The closing of the schools, the growing communist ideology, the problems of the hundreds of asilees, and the guns everywhere made life very difficult but the beauty of the island, the cheerfulness and friendliness of the people always made it a pleasant place to be: The British Ambassador's summary for 1961 reads, 'Officially designated the Year of Education, 1961 was in fact the year of widespread indoctrination'. He in fact gives few marks to Castro for positive achievements and concludes, 'the story of Cuba in 1961 marks the establishment of a form of Communism in the New World that must, I believe, affect the course of history in the whole of Latin America, whatever may be the fate of the present regime in Cuba'. He also reminded us that during the year Costa Rica, Venezuela, Columbia and Panama broke off diplomatic relations with Cuba and that on 22 September the British businessman, Mr R. Geddes, was tried and sentenced to 30 years' imprisonment on charges of working as a US intelligence agent.[29]

* * *

The Sutherland family finally left Cuba in February 1962, by air to Jamaica and then by sea in a Fyffes' banana boat, that is the $2^1/2$ children and I; by this time I was five months pregnant. Iain went by air from Jamaica to visit some of his new parish in Latin America, and arrived home after us. The sea voyage was pleasant and remarkably smooth for that time of year. The 100 passengers were better looked after than by Cunard on the *Parthia*. There was one unusual event when the ship's engines broke down and we drifted for some 24 hours. This was not unpleasant as the passengers spent the time sitting out on deck and the crew went fishing and caught a shark. Aircraft from the American base at Guantanamo Bay, which was by this time not far away, flew over the vessel, curious to see what we were doing.

5

THE MISSILE CRISIS AND
THE CRIME OF THE CENTURY,
WASHINGTON 1962–65

Our move from Cuba to Washington took over five months as we had much accumulated leave and we were awaiting the birth of our third child. Most of this time was spent in Hill House, in Eversley, Hampshire. Iain came back to England some time after me, following his familiarisation tour of the Latin American countries with which he was to be concerned in the Embassy in Washington. He also left before me. We spent a very happy leave, punctuated by visits from members of the family and friends instead of the constant moving and staying with relatives which had characterised our last few leaves.

Elizabeth Anne was born in Wokingham hospital on 29 May. Iain had to leave 12 days later. When she was about four weeks old, I packed up and followed with the three children and the nanny, Ann Trease. In those days to get to Washington by air from London involved flying to Baltimore and travelling by road from there. Dulles International Airport was not opened until 1963.

I had little time to prepare myself for life in the United States. At least, I felt, we would be able to speak the language and understand what was going on, even if I was not too well informed on the aims of the Kennedy Administration and the 'new frontier'. James, who was on his fourth country, (Yugoslavia, Cuba, England and now the US), did for a while think it was a new language he had to learn and copied all the most extreme forms of American construction he heard. But he sorted himself out eventually and he and Sandra survived with a mild American accent.

* * *

The letters start with one from Iain who is preparing to receive the family in Washington.

Washington, 17 June 1962 – Sunday

Dear M & D,

Lois Clark was at Baltimore airport to meet me on Monday evening when I arrived by BOAC jet. I was plunged straight into the work of the Chancery, depleted by several people being absent on leave. I also set out straight away to look for houses so that I might know as soon as possible whether Jeanne and the family could come out on the 26th. On Friday I decided that we should take the house which belongs to a member of the US Embassy in London. It is most attractive in a convenient and excellent residential area. North West Washington is much the most attractive suburban city I have seen with many parks and trees and an unexpectedly high standard of architectural distinction. The house has a weatherboard frontage with green shutters and fine old poplars in the (not very large) garden. In the meantime I have been staying with the Clarks (who were in Cuba)

13. Elizabeth Anne, newly born, with grandparents Dorothy and Tom Nutt, in the garden of Hill House, just before departure to Washington, June 1962.

who have been very kind. I shall probably impose upon them until Jeanne arrives.

I hope that you are both well.

With love from Iain

2831 44th Street, Washington DC, Monday 30 July 1962

Dear Dorothy,

I have just sent off Sandra and the baby for a walk with Ann. James refuses to go as he is playing with the boy next door. There is very little time with all the children around and I have not managed to do much since I arrived. How do people manage with five or six?

Iain has a large group of countries in his remit at the moment as so many people are away. Eastern Europe would really be Tom Brimelow's responsibility. The Barnetts, the Jamaicans who stayed with us in Havana, have arrived in Washington. Jamaica is just setting up an Embassy and we are invited to the Independence celebrations next Monday. Jamaica will then be one of Iain's countries (he also does the Caribbean) instead of the Colonial Attaché's.

Yesterday we made a short expedition with James and Sandra to Mount Vernon, the home of George Washington, but unfortunately it poured with rain as we arrived and there was a half hour's wait to go round the house. We walked round the grounds and saw the gardens, stables, tomb, etc. in a truly English downpour, afterwards cheering ourselves up with ice cream at the cafeteria. Next time we must choose a sunny day and go by boat down the Potomac River. The house has a lovely situation overlooking the river.

Love from us all and a crooked smile from E. Anne, Jeanne

2831 44th Street, NW Washington 7 DC
(Undated probably August)

Dear Dorothy,

We gave our first cocktail party on Tuesday. It went quite well except that we had too much food and fewer guests than we had anticipated. We also did our first exploring outside Washington last Sunday. We drove east towards the sea, to the Chesapeake Bay, but there are very few beaches along both sides of the bay. We went across the seven-mile Bay Bridge, which is extremely impressive (you really have the strange impression of being suspended over the sea), and on to a small town called Oxford. It was attractive and picturesque, a town of small boat owners and fishermen. The little harbour's sail boats made a pretty picture but it was a very hot day and there was nowhere really to swim. Even James the intrepid found the water too dirty. There were few tourists, but also not many places to get anything to eat or drink on a Sunday. Obviously a delightful place to spend the weekend with friends who have a summer house and a boat to take you sailing. Now I understand why the Americans do not regard the Bay as seaside.

Much love from us all, Jeanne

Washington, Monday 1 October 1962

Dear Dorothy,

So sorry to have been so long writing. I need about twice as long each day to fit everything in. I believe, however, Iain has sent a few postcards reporting briefly on our doings. These have not been very extensive or ranged very far yet. The one trip to Chesapeake Bay on a hot summer's day was interesting but not equal to the Caribbean for beautiful beaches. The other was a weekend in the Shenandoah National Park, with its trimmed edges and beautifully cambered roads and really attractive mountain scenery and woods.

I have managed to visit the Phillips Art Gallery which consists almost entirely of nineteenth century French art, laid out in a private house where you can sit in an armchair, and even smoke, while looking at the Renoir, Monet, Manet, and Pisarro etc. There were one or two Graham Sutherlands and a few modern German and American, some completely incomprehensible. I also made a brief visit to the National Gallery of Art with an American friend where we saw an exhibition of American lithographs and etchings and a few rooms of the English and French permanent exhibition.

Lots of love from us all, Jeanne

* * *

The first few months in Washington were understandably very much taken up with the domestic side of life, settling in with three small children in a new house and a new environment. The British Embassy was very big. Instead of being number two in seniority, head of the political section and Consul General, as in Havana, Iain became about number 22. We did not see all the other members of the Embassy as we had in Cuba, in a family kind of situation. We saw the ones with whom Iain worked and whom we already knew from other posts. We could make friends as we wished and with people we met from many walks of life.

Iain was the 1st Secretary in Chancery responsible for reporting on affairs in Latin America and the Caribbean and we arrived in Washington at a time when Cuba, about which he obviously knew more than others in the Embassy, was still of great importance to the US government. John F. Kennedy had become president just before the ill-fated Bay of Pigs invasion of Cuba by anti-Castro rebels trained in Guatemala and supported by the CIA and the Pentagon. One of the first decisions he had to make was to allow this invasion to go ahead, badly planned and inadequately resourced as it was. The repercussions in international politics and imminent dangers of third world war were to follow soon after we arrived and became Kennedy's second most difficult decision.

Decisions over the fate of Cuba and its ties with the Soviet Union were not the President's only worries by mid 1962. He had come to power on the famous slogan, *The New Frontier*, a successor to the New Deal and Fair Deal. 'The New Frontier,' he said 'sums up not what I intend to offer the American people but what I intend to ask of them. It appeals to their pride, not to their pocketbook; it holds out the promise of more sacrifice instead of more security. But I tell you the New Frontier is here whether we seek it or not... uncharted areas of science and peace, unsolved problems of peace and war, unconquered pockets of ignorance and prejudice, unanswered questions of poverty and surplus...'[1]

The sense of excitement and expectation among the President's supporters was still very strong in Washington society when we arrived in July 1962, in spite of a year with many setbacks for the President, particularly in his inability to get bills passed through Congress, one of the main difficulties of his presidency. An Art Buchwald column in September 1962 made fun of the President's inability to get his laws passed, saying that he could probably not even pass a law to prevent people walking on the White House lawn. 'The President is the supreme centre of power in the tradition of strong presidents like the Roosevelts,' writes Sir David Ormsby Gore, the British Ambassador, and again, 'The burden of the President from this arrangement is immense. So far excessive delays in taking decisions has not resulted. But it remains the most obvious danger.'[2]

The 'missile crisis' was brewing by the time we arrived in Washington. Throughout 1962 relations between Cuba and the US had been worsening. In January the President announced an almost complete embargo on US trade with Cuba; and later in the same month the Organisation of American States (OAS) Council had formally excluded Cuba from OAS affairs.

On 29 August a U-2 plane discovered evidence of SAM (Surface to Air Missiles) in Cuba, assumed to be there for the protection of offensive missiles. By September the President had issued a warning against the placing of offensive weapons in Cuba and that the US would have to act if offensive ground-to-ground missiles were introduced. On 8 and 15 September two Russian ships arrived in Havana with lorries on the top deck and a number of medium range ballistic missiles beneath. They were unloaded at night. On 13 September Kennedy warned that if Cuba was to gather an 'offensive military capacity from the Soviet Union, the United States would do what had to be done'. By 18–21 September secret reports began to arrive of mysterious activities in the San Cristobal area and on 14 October photographs showed that sites for ballistic missiles were being prepared at San Cristobal and sites for IRBMs of 2000 miles radius were also being prepared. U-2 flights confirmed that there were three IRBM fixed sites and six mobile MRBM sites, guarded by Russians not Cubans, altogether 30–55 missiles.[3]

During those weeks after the first sighting of missiles in Cuba there was tremendous tension in Washington. The atmosphere became very oppressive, particularly as something very serious was obviously happening but nobody knew precisely what. At evening functions wives appeared but practically no husbands came, or at least not until very late in the evening. And no reason was ever given for lateness or for where they had been. By 17 October Kennedy and the government had still not decided whether to attack the Cuban missile sites by air or to blockade Cuba. The British Ambassador, Sir David Ormsby Gore was told about the crisis on 21 October before any other allies. The US Congress was not told until 4 p.m. on October 22. Finally the choice was made for a blockade, on the basis that this choice, while preventing further missiles arriving, would give time for alternative solutions. In Kennedy's speech on 22 October he said that a 'quarantine would be imposed to prevent further weapons being shipped and Khrushchev was to be asked to remove the bombers and missiles and to abandon the sites'. A large naval deployment was set up from Florida to beyond

Puerto Rico, which could stop and disable Russian vessels and the quarantine came into force on 24 October. The world then waited for the Russian reaction. By October 23 two medium range missiles were ready in Cuba and 20,000 Russian troops. The first Russian response, which was the same as the Cubans', was to say that all the weapons in Cuba were defensive. However, 25 Russian cargo ships were moving towards Havana. The suspense grew as we watched the television screens showing the Russian vessels making towards Havana harbour. When they halted or altered course the relief was palpable. The days and weeks of the crisis had been a time of immense stress and anxiety.

On 27 October a U-2 plane was brought down by a SAM missile in Cuba. Kennedy took no immediate action but a huge invasion force was made ready in Florida. 'Our little group seated round the cabinet table in continuous session that Saturday (27th) felt nuclear war to be closer on that day than at any time in the nuclear age'. During the night of 27–28 October Khrushchev confirmed his first proposal and ordered the dismantling of the missiles. And so the crisis ended. Castro felt completely betrayed. The US never gave a promise not to invade and Kennedy seemed to have won a victory. But Khrushchev was not humiliated and Castro was not overthrown.[4]

***

A letter to my mother-in-law describes the anxiety and fear which we all felt during the Cuban missile crisis.

Washington, Monday 29 October 1962

Dear Dorothy,

It is amazing how one gets used to crises. The first few days last week I found it impossible to concentrate on any plans for the future, even as near as a few days away, and I lost several pounds in weight. It was very unpleasant here. I wonder what it was like in England. Things relaxed a little with the fairly calm letter from Khrushchev to Russell; and then went up and down for the rest of the week. It was a busy time for the whole Embassy and for Iain particularly of course. I saw him only in the evening at functions, when he managed to get to them. Extraordinary how he manages to attract work. And

I thought Washington would be a reasonably calm assignment. It certainly isn't at the moment, but, as I say, one seems to get used to it and I can think about the future again now. Although it's early days to consider the whole affair settled.

How unpleasant it must have been for all our poor friends in Havana. I am glad I wasn't there. One of the things that used to console me about Havana was the thought that in case of world war we were further than most from nuclear warfare. One of the unpleasant things here was the excitement with which all the news reporters told of the troop movements in Florida etc. One misses the unemotional BBC reporting. Not the only thing to criticise here of course. (Letter ends here)

2831 44th Street, Washington N.W., 13 November 1962

Dear M & D

The Embassy building here is a large modern block finished just over a year ago, not a very distinguished addition to the buildings of a town with great architectural distinction. It is rather like a large secondary school with the addition of a strange circular structure like a gasometer, the Rotunda, where meetings and receptions are held. The Ambassador's residence and the old Chancery next door are overshadowed. They were built by Lutyens in more expansive days with steep gables and tall (largely false) chimneys and carved lions.

The Chancery is on floor 3 of the new office block and in the days of the Cuban crisis that is where I have spent a great deal of time even on weekends and evenings, when not driving down to the State Department in town or across the river to the Pentagon. All these journeys point to the need for a second car and we have ordered a Ford Falcon station wagon.

The week before the Cuba crisis we had as visitors Paul Scott and his wife who caught the last plane out to Havana before the commercial air services were withdrawn. He is my successor's successor there as Keith Oakshott who took my place fell ill. The Scotts had a somewhat abrupt introduction to Castro's (or Khrushchev's) Cuba.

We had our first snow last week and it has turned colder. But this is the best season in Washington, when all the trees are the most brilliant deep autumn colours I have seen anywhere.

Love from Iain, Jeanne, James, Sandra and Elizabeth Anne

THE MISSILE CRISIS AND THE CRIME OF THE CENTURY

Washington, Saturday 22 December, 1962

Dear Dorothy,

We have invited some friends to Christmas lunch, Vanessa and Hugh Thomas. Hugh is the author of *The Spanish Civil War* and is currently writing a book about Cuba, where we met him; and another couple from the Embassy, the Brigstockes. He is Shipping Attaché. They have four children, ranging from 8 to 1 year. The wife, Heather, is an old friend of Susan Evans.

It snowed all day yesterday and part of the night so we may have a white Christmas. It's very pretty but it makes everything twice as difficult as Washington traffic gets into a terrible mess as soon as it begins to snow.

One week later.

I'm sorry this was never posted – we ran out of stamps and never got around to buying more during the week. It is now too late to wish you a Happy Christmas and Many Happy Returns of your birthday. We can wish you a Happy New Year and maybe even a chance of seeing you.

I think Christmas was enjoyed by all except perhaps me. (I didn't have time to consciously enjoy it.) But it seemed happy and pleasant. The children had wonderful presents, James was thrilled with his Sutherland tie and has worn it to a tea party and today to the White House to see the Christmas tree – a party organised for diplomats' children. Must stop as I have to change to go to a cocktail party and dinner.

Love to you both from us all, Jeanne

* * *

I struggled somewhat during the first weeks and months in Washington. Looking after a household and three young children at the same time as being expected to provide and attend official entertainment for Iain's contacts was quite demanding. I did not have the domestic support I had become used to in Yugoslavia and Cuba.

On a higher scale President Kennedy was struggling too during 1962. He had his problems with Congress, economic problems after the Black Monday on the stock exchange in spring, he had lost his battle for medical and hospital care legislation and his Tax Revision bill was emasculated; this without mentioning his problems with foreign affairs.[5]

An extract from the annual review despatch from the Ambassador, Sir David Ormsby Gore to Lord Home sums up the presidential year.

The year 1962 has been fully satisfying neither to the Kennedy administration nor to the US people as a whole. The year started with the President firmly in the saddle with widespread popular support and assisted by a team of undoubted competence. The apprenticeship was over; the economic soothsayers confirmed the omens were good, surely the persistent problems of domestic and foreign affairs would yield before this determined and gifted administration? In the event it was 12 months of considerable frustration and disappointment, and by the year end most of the spectres that haunt the average American had still to be banished. But this is not to imply that the year was without special significance. The steady recovery of the stock market after its steep decline in May, the sharpest since the war; the passage of the Trade Expansion Bill with partisan support, and the Cuban success, were major developments which will have a lasting influence on the Administration's thought and policies.[6]

Another area of great importance in the 1960s was the civil rights issue and the desegregation of education. In November the black student, James Meredith was enrolled in the University of Mississippi, 'a bastion of extreme white racism'. Desegregation had increased and many changes were being made without violence. The rights of the freedom fighters were being protected and more action taken against discrimination in employment. Most blacks were avoiding violence but their slogan had become 'freedom now'; and there still remained the contentious questions of private discrimination and the ghettoes in the cities. The Administration was considering further legislation against housing discrimination but little had been done yet to solve the basic problems. When Meredith arrived at Mississippi demonstrations broke out. Two people were killed and several were wounded.[7]

* * *

2831 44th Street, Washington D.C., 4 February 1963

Dear M & D,

Last weekend we were all in bed with varying degrees of flu and different temperatures. We rose on the Monday to welcome Bill, now Sir Bill Marchant and his wife on a visit from Havana, to give them a party that evening. This was rather too much for Jeanne and she went back to bed and to lose her voice until yesterday. All this has been set off by the bitterly cold weather which returned to Washington the previous week. But judging from your letters and the British press you have not had it any better. The *Times* for 1 February describes January as the worst month for low temperatures and dullness since 1814.

The Marchants came up to Washington for a five day visit and stayed at the residence, although they saw little of the Ambassador, and go back to Cuba via Mexico City after a few days holiday there. They came out on one of the aircraft chartered by Mr Donovan and his mission which ransomed the Bay of Pigs prisoners with medical supplies and baby foods. Cuba, they say, is now a rather grimmer place than it was when we left almost exactly a year ago.

The previous weekend, as Jeanne has reported, we motored north just into New England, to a small town called Wilton in Connecticut, to attend the wedding of Miss Onora O'Neill whom you will remember having met at Hill House. She married an American economist and philosophy lecturer whom she had known in Oxford and her mother, Rosemary Garvey, whom you also met on the same occasion, came all the way from Peking to attend. Terence Garvey is currently chargé d'affaires in Peking. We stayed two nights in Connecticut, one in an old English type inn in a most English part of the States and the second with the journalist friends at whose house the wedding took place. Rosemary came back along the turnpikes with us to spend a day in Washington.

We all send love and best wishes from Iain, Jeanne, James, Sandra and Elizabeth Anne

Washington D.C., Tuesday 12 February 1963

Dear Dorothy,

After three attacks of flu I finally went to the doctor who told me I was recovering from viral pneumonia so no wonder I felt odd. Unfortunately this has not been the end of our chapter of illness. We have James in hospital with nephritis since last Friday. He had barely recovered from his long drawn out flu before he became ill again. He has really been quite sick but is responding to treatment, looks much better and is a bit happier about hospital. If you have time I'm sure he would love to have a PC from you at the Children's Hospital.

With love from us all, Jeanne

2831 44th Street N.W., Washington D.C., 3 March 1963

Dear Dorothy,

We have not done much of interest lately. We have seen *Billy Budd*, the Melville story made into a movie and we visited a semi-night club show called the *Shadows* where we heard an amazing African singer called Miriam Makeba singing African and American folk songs of a very strange and spectacular nature. We had met her before at a Ghana Embassy party and she was such a quiet shy little person. Then on the stage these amazing sounds come forth.

My mother and father are very excited about their forthcoming trip. They are to arrive by the Queen Elizabeth and return by BOAC about a month later. We are hoping to get away with them for a week or so while they are here, possibly taking the children and ourselves to the beach in South Carolina.

Love from us all, Jeanne

2831 44th Street N.W., 6 March 1963

Dear M & D,

James was delighted with his illustrated letter with vignettes of painting at Woodhouselee. It is now difficult to contain him in his bedroom where he is surrounded by jig-saw puzzles and Lego, two goldfish and two terrapins and much cut paper.

Yes, I have been much concerned with such things as the protests over raids in the Bahamas mentioned in your letter; and the previous week much taken with some not very successful negotiations with the Americans for some naval facilities in the same islands, which were attended by two of the local members of the Legislative Council, two of the Bay Street boys of Nassau who control the economy, make their money out of prohibition and boast descent from pirates. I hope to go away myself for a week or 10 days at the end of the month, but further east to attend the annual meeting of the Heads of Mission in Central America. The conference takes place from April 2 in San Salvador. I plan to spend a day in New Orleans on the way and a day or two in Guatemala City on the way back.

Love from Iain and Jeanne

Washington, Sunday 8 July 1963

Dear M & D,

Your last letter announced that you had decided to stay on with Anne to celebrate the 4th July, your wedding anniversary. I send belated congratulations. I regret that I spent most of the 4th, here a general holiday, working in the Embassy. But in the evening James and I set out to sit with many others on the steps below the Lincoln Memorial to watch the traditional rockets and fireworks which are set off on the green spaces between the White House and the monolith of the Washington Memorial. The pillared Lincoln Monument with its huge illuminated seated marble figure is a good vantage point, as the coloured lights and the rockets are reflected in the artificial lake which stretches between there and the monument to Washington. Two days earlier, on Tuesday, we bade goodbye to Tom and Dorothy Nutt who flew back to London by BOAC.

I think they enjoyed their stay here and also their long bus trip into Canada. Last weekend we took them off on a long car run to the Shenandoah valley and spent Saturday night in a State Park across the West Virginia frontier, in wild wooded country which we had not previously visited – reminiscent of central Europe. It is in fact an area of German and Swiss settlement. On the way we called at a log house or cabin (about $2^1/2$ hours out of Washington not far from Winchester, but amongst the first range of hills) which we have been offered at a very modest rent for the last two weeks of July and the first of August. The owner, James Reston, is one of the editors of the *New York Times* and he has gone to spend his holidays at Rogart in Sutherland. He comes originally from Scotland and is generally known as Scottie Reston.

Also on Tuesday last the Brimelows left us. He has been appointed Minister in Moscow.

With love from Iain, Jeanne, James, Sandra and Elizabeth

The Mill House (by Fiery Run), Hume,
Fauquier County, Virginia, 21 July 1963

Dear M & D,

I write from James Reston's cabin in the foothills of the Blue Mountains. It was described as a cabin but in truth it is a sizeable house constructed of old wooden beams on the foundations of what must once have been a farm or mill house. We drove out on Friday night, Jeanne with the children and Ann in the afternoon in the white car, I later in the blue. It is about 2 hours drive out of Washington but very far from any main road and set deep in rich rolling pastoral country. The hills rise to 2–3000 feet not far away. There are fine pastures on the lower slopes and in the valleys where there are herds of Herefords and Aberdeen Angus. In the flatter country to the north-east there are some well known stud farms and the area of the hunt patronised by the Kennedy family. Our house has a large paddock with trees and a white fence and wooded slopes beyond which flows the Fiery Run (in this part of Virginia this is what you call a stream or burn, cf. Bull Run of Civil War fame, which one crosses on the way from Washington). This was the region of some of the fiercest battles fought between North and South exactly a hundred years ago. Jeanne and the children will probably stay until 5th August. Ann Trease is to return to England at the end of the month. I shall come out at the weekends whenever I can.

With love from us all, Iain

14. Jousting in Virginia, US, near the cabin of Scottie Reston, July 1963.

THE MISSILE CRISIS AND THE CRIME OF THE CENTURY

Washington, 24 August 1963

Dear M & D,

Last Saturday we set out again with James and Sandra to revisit our retreat at Hume. On this occasion it was only for the day. Our object was to watch the annual tournament attended by most of the local horse owners and farmers who compete in the ancient sport of tilting at the ring. The competitors are mounted and, bearing lances, they gallop down a meadow and attempt to spear small rings suspended from gallows like structures set in the field. James saw again his friends at the farm where he had riding lessons. It was very warm and the ground was even more parched than when we had left the week before. After the tournament there was a grand barbecue in the grounds of the local school. We returned back to 44th Street late with James and Sandra very tired.

This is a place of many visitors. I have the new British Ambassador to Peru to look after next week, and two weeks hence the successor to Bill Marchant in Havana. Today we had Martin Buxton who was in Far Eastern Dept with me in London and who is attending a conference on China. John Lambert, who was in Belgrade, came out for talks on disarmament.

Love from us all, Iain

* * *

The summer was a pleasant relief from all our illnesses. I much enjoyed my parents' visit, the first time any member of the family had managed to come and see us during one of our postings abroad. Their plan to travel one way by sea and return by air was an excellent one. I was able to go and meet them in New York although I did not arrive in time to greet them in the docks, due to the fact that I left in a great hurry without my wallet. I did not realise this until I reached the Baltimore tunnel and started looking for money to pay the charge. I had just enough to get me through the tunnel but not enough to pay the obligatory tolls on the highways and buy the petrol to get me to New York. In America this was a big problem because all the banks are very local and it was impossible to cash a cheque on a Washington bank once outside the town. I knew if I went back I would never get to New York that day so I struggled on and finally after many stops and entreaties at motels and banks along the way managed, tearfully by then, to persuade a fatherly looking bank teller in Havre le Grace to let me have some money.

The rest of their stay was not so stressful and we had a very good holiday at Pauley's Island in South Carolina, at that time an unspoilt small fishing town, now I understand a flourishing tourist resort. We rented a house, we went fishing, sometimes for crabs with a piece of string on a stick, and at other times deep sea fishing and we enjoyed the delicious sea food in the local restaurants.

* * *

Washington D.C., Friday 11 October

Dear Dorothy,

Here we are all well and full of vitamin pills. Sandra likes her new Episcopal School where they swear allegiance to the American flag every day, not so usual in private schools here. We have had our Jamaican maid, Carmen, for two months. She is kind and willing but

15. British Ambassador, Sir David Ormsby Gore, signing documents with American officials, 11 October 1963, with Iain in background.

alas does not have much control over the children. I still long for the magic formula to take over the household.

The season has started again and we are out 3 or 4 nights a week. Iain is going to be away in November at a conference in Sao Paolo. It would be lovely to go but impossible at the moment both domestically and financially. I am consoling myself with a cookery course run by the Adult Education Department of the YWCA, called *Cooking for Entertaining*.

Latin America as usual figures very largely in the news here. The latest hurricane has wreaked havoc in Haiti and Cuba. It has been an interesting time in the States too, the year of the negro [sic] revolution. Everyone is very conscious of the situation and even the children now ask questions and offer comments on racial questions.

James was very thrilled with his letter and will I hope write back soon. We are going tomorrow to Gettysburg, home of the important Civil War battle, about 50 miles away, with an American family with three children.

Much love from us all, Jeanne

* * *

Much was going on in the US during this period. On the home front the 'negro' revolution continued. The President was determined that his civil rights policy would prevail and that desegregation in all forms and in all places would come about. 'He was revered in many Negro homes and reviled in many white Southern homes as the first President, in the words of Richard Rovere, "with the conviction that no form of segregation or discrimination is morally defensible or socially tolerable".'[8] Under his jurisdiction more black members of the population were appointed to top Federal jobs than at any other time in history. A single President's Committee on Equal Employment Opportunity was set up. In June 1963 two black students were enrolled in the University of Alabama without incident but with a high degree of preparedness. The summer culminated in the march to Washington. This turned out to be a peaceful assembly on the Washington Monument grounds on August 28 when 230,000 people, the biggest public demonstration ever held in the capital, sang, chanted and listened for hours to their leaders and Martin Luther King made his famous 'I have a dream' speech.[9]

But desegregation was only one of the administration's problems. As Kennedy said, at the height of his civil rights campaign, 'many leaders did not understand that he had to work simultaneously on his tax bill, on the Test Ban Treaty, on the threat of a railroad strike and on Vietnam'.[10] And that did not include relations with Latin American countries, negotiations with the European countries, France, Germany and Great Britain over nuclear deterrents and NATO, and of course the ever present Cold War. How large should the US strategic nuclear force be? Could the Soviet Union be trusted not to continue nuclear weapon testing? Foreign affairs took up vast quantities of time and were said to be of greater interest to the President than domestic ones.

* * *

Washington, Sunday 27 October 1963

Dear M & D,

Later this afternoon I take the plane from Washington airport for New York and by 8.30 tomorrow morning I shall be in Rio de Janeiro, Brazil. I go on the same day to Sao Paulo and shall be there for about 3 weeks attending the Annual Conference of the Inter-American Economic and Social Council, on the small British observer delegation. I shall probably not stay there all the time, but return to Rio for a few days from the 6th or 7th, returning to Sao Paulo for the week November 11–16th. I shall visit Brasilia, the new capital, for the day, Caracas for two days and get back to Washington on the 20th or 21st.

This has been a long hot autumn and now around our house all the gardens are carpeted in brown, yellow and red leaves. We had a visit a short time ago from the Byatts who stayed with us on their way home from Havana. They go back now to England and to Hill House at Eversley.

Monday. Iain had to leave before finishing his letter to you. He must be in Sao Paulo by now and getting ready for the opening of his conference on Tuesday. He was very thrilled to be going to Brazil and it is a little sad to be left behind. James is trying to be the man of the family (when he remembers) and we have a cosy half hour together after the other children are in bed. He started art classes at the Corcoran Art Gallery. The teacher said he was very creative and she was pleased to have him in her class.

Much love from us all, Jeanne

Washington, Thursday 28 November 1963

Dear M & D,

I arrived back in this country at Idlewild airport, New York, by American jet on the afternoon of last Friday having left La Guiara airport, Caracas, early the same morning. At Idlewild, waiting for the plane for Washington I went to the book stall and there I heard over the salesgirl's transistor radio that President Kennedy had been shot in Dallas. Later the same evening I was met by Jeanne, James and Sandra at Washington airport, having been away for almost four weeks in Brazil and Venezuela. Since then Washington and the Embassy have been preoccupied with the assassination, the funeral and the delegations which came here to pay homage and respect to Mr Kennedy. Being duty officer I spent much time on Sunday night at the State Department trying to collect tickets and places and find out what arrangements were being made for the British party which included Prince Philip, the Homes and Mr Wilson. And on Monday early I had to go round delivering messages and tickets to Mr Wilson and others. The long funeral ceremonies were all shown on television (for once free of commercials) and I did not myself join the throng on the route. It has been a great shock to everyone, not least Sir David Ormsby Gore, the Ambassador, who has long been a close personal friend of the Kennedy family. The Princes, Kings, Prime Ministers and others have now mostly departed. President Johnson has said that he will try to carry through the policies of his predecessor, but everyone will continue for long to feel the loss.

My conference in Brazil was most interesting, but went on rather too long. I glimpsed the extraordinary new capital Brasilia only on my return flight, which took me for a few hours also to Trinidad on my way to Caracas. In Caracas I stayed with Robin Edmonds whom I had known in the FO in London.

With love from Iain and Jeanne and kisses from James, Sandra and Elizabeth

* * *

The death of President Kennedy shocked the world. It seemed that only the Chinese were unmoved and produced a cartoon in the *Worker's Daily* saying 'Kennedy bites the dust'.[11] A British newspaper is quoted as saying, 'It is incomprehensible that people like Stalin die in their beds

165

whereas people like Abraham Lincoln and Kennedy meet death with violence'.[12] Iain's description of trying to collect tickets and arrange places at the funeral for distinguished visitors is somewhat reminiscent of Stalin's funeral in 1953; but with many differences.

As I waited at the airport for Iain to arrive back from Brazil the television sets played and replayed the scenes which had taken place that afternoon in the streets of Dallas. In fact we never had such brilliant television in America as during the days following the assassination on 22 November, 1963. Not only were there no commercials, but it was all live, which was rare on American television. Not only of course did we see the assassination and all that happened afterwards in Dallas but we also saw the return of the President's body to Washington and the swearing in of President Johnson aboard the presidential plane. The new President declared 'I will do my best. That is all I can do. I ask for your help and for God's.' The most extraordinary thing was seeing the shooting of the President's assassin, Lee Harvey Oswald by the former gangster from Chicago, Jack Ruby, on Sunday 24th.

Oswald had a life history of being unwanted. His father died before he was born and his mother felt her children to be a burden. He had attended seven schools and often played truant. At 16 he declared himself to be a Marxist and at 17 he joined the Marine Corps and learned Russian and how to shoot. When he tried to defect to the Soviet Union he was only allowed to stay on sufferance. He finally returned to the US with his Russian wife, Marina, and child. He later made attempts to return to the SU and also to go to Cuba but was again rejected, and so returned to Dallas where he got a job at the book depository.

Much has been written about the death of Kennedy and there have been many conspiracy theories, none of which has ever been proved. Ruby asserted that his action in killing Oswald was entirely his own initiative but many believed that it was part of a plot, or it was meant to silence Oswald. A Commission, set up by President Johnson to investigate the possibility of a conspiracy, carried out 20,000 interviews and took 10 months. Forty years later no one has come up with any other sustainable theory.

Sorensen, who was a great admirer of Kennedy, sums up his presidency. 'He left the nation a whole new set of basic premises – on freedom now instead of someday for the American Negro – on "dampening down" instead of winning the cold war – on the unthinkability instead of the inevitability of nuclear war – on cutting taxes in times of deficit – on battling poverty in time of prosperity –

on trade, transportation and a host of other subjects. For the most part, on November 22 these problems had not been solved and these projects had not been completed.'[13] Sorensen does not mention some of the less fortunate aspects of Kennedy's career such as his handling of the Bay of Pigs invasion or his legacy for America of the Vietnam problem. Nor does he mention the mafia-like way in which the Kennedy family secured the nomination of JFK for president and his election; nor the darker sides of his character, the womanising and the wheeling and dealing. These matters were kept from the public during his presidency but have come to light during the years since; particularly his connections with the mafia. A book recently published about Frank Sinatra reveals his connections with Kennedy and 'his role in connecting him with organised crime – a link that may have led to the President's death'.[14]

Sir David Ormsby Gore, British Ambassador and friend, but perhaps a little less biased than Sorensen, writes in his review of 1963, 'The story of 1963, as of the rest of his Administration, was much the story of President Kennedy himself'.[15]

* * *

Washington, 29 December 1963

Dear M & D,

This being after Christmas I took out my skates, unusual since Yugoslavia and went with Jeanne and the children to the frozen Chesapeake Canal which runs for miles alongside the Potomac River from Georgetown in Washington to Great Falls. Today the canal was solidly frozen and the river was also iced up. Had we wished we could have skated for miles, but there were few people. The crowds go to the reflecting pool in front of the Lincoln Memorial in the centre of the city. Having spent a family Christmas we yesterday asked a crowd of friends and their children to punch and cold turkey at mid-day.

The week before Christmas was almost entirely occupied (so far as I was concerned) with a series of long discussions at the State Department between delegations representing the British and Guatemalan governments. They did not achieve much. At the end of the discussions diplomatic relations between the two countries remained severed, all over the question of the status of British Honduras.

With love from us all and best wishes for the New Year, Iain

Sunday, 2 February 1964

Dear M & D,

Sunday evening with a log fire in the sitting room. Sandra and Elizabeth and even James now asleep. Not so cold with all the snow gone from Washington and a clear sunny sky today. We went in the afternoon on a short run south in the car along the Potomac shore to Fort Washington – a vast brick structure by the edge of the river, built against the British in 1814 and added to during the Civil War. A favourite place in the summer but not many people there today.

Sandra celebrated her birthday on the 29th with a party of friends from the Embassy and from her school. I had unfortunately to go to a special meeting of the Pan American Union so could not participate. I also have had a series of visitors from various Embassies in Latin America. The week after next there will be even more to do in the Embassy with the almost simultaneous arrival in Washington of the Prime Minister, Mr Butler, Mr Wilson and the Beatles.

With love from Iain

***

R.M.S. Queen Elizabeth, Sunday 7 June 1964

Dear M & D,

On board the Queen Elizabeth four days out of New York; tomorrow at 10 a.m. we reach Cherbourg, and in the late evening, Southampton. Too late to disembark the same night, we take the boat train to Waterloo the following morning and expect to be in Richmond by lunchtime.

The last week had been much occupied with packing. The new house is very close to Washington Cathedral, one of the biggest Anglican cathedrals in the world, commenced before the 1st World War and still not complete. The style is entirely traditional. The central bell tower with its English bells and a carillon (which may be just a little too loud for comfort on a Sunday evening from the Sutherlands' address in Lowell Street) was finished last year. Like the house on 44th street it is a 'frame' dwelling of wood in the New England style – not so picturesque as its predecessor – but rather larger and with an enclosed garden. The owners are going to Bombay. The Embassy has taken it on for us for two years but it is possible that we shall not remain so long.

The crossing has been very smooth and I have heard of no passengers who have failed to turn up for the gargantuan meals. James has made friends with another James whose father is an artist in an advertising agency in New York. Sandra has made friends with the waiter at our table who comes from Lancashire and Elizabeth has tried to make friends with everyone awake or asleep in the deck chairs along the starboard side.

We look forward to seeing you soon; with love from us all, Iain

* * *

The leave in England worked well in spite of our not this time having a base. The Hutchinsons' Richmond house was big and comfortable. Later we managed to fit into my parents' house at Weymouth where they had settled after my father retired, and where he kept the *Orion*, his converted life boat, in the harbour. My father took us out for day trips. Iain and I even had a week on our own visiting the Loire valley, leaving the children with Lillian and my parents.

The whole holiday was made easy and relaxed with the help of our American au pair, Lillian, who was very good with the children, thoroughly enjoyed her visit to Britain, and got on very well with all the grandparents. We returned to Washington in autumn 1964, a year since Johnson had taken over the presidency. He was the fourth vice-president to be elected president because of an assassination of a predecessor. His was a very different background from Kennedy's, born as he was in central Texas, where 'he felt the pinch of rural poverty as he grew up, working his way through Southwest Texas State Teachers' College; there he learned compassion for the poverty of others, teaching poor students of Mexican descent'.

'From 1953 he served in the House of Representatives and later entered the Senate, becoming the youngest minority leader in history. And the following year, when the Democrats won control, he became majority leader.'[16] He pledged to continue the aims of President Kennedy after his death but was not content simply to continue what Kennedy had begun. He had his own vision of America's future, contained in his concept of the Great Society, a war on poverty and American racism. As part of this campaign he set up educational programmes for the black population, in one of which Lillian, our au pair used to take part in downtown Washington, sometimes taking Elizabeth with her to the nursery section for two-year-olds.

The introduction to the Foreign Office files on the Johnson years refers to them as 'one of the most fruitful periods of legislation in American history, with 226 of his 252 requests successfully passed by Congress. He came to office determined to address the pressing domestic problems of poverty and race relations. But whatever his radical intentions to remodel American society, he will always be remembered as the President who committed American combat troops to the war in Vietnam.'[17] In November 1964 Johnson was re-elected with the biggest majority ever, which encouraged him to continue his domestic reform programme and to succeed in passing a mass of welfare legislation – in medical care for the aged, education, housing and urban development, conservation and immigration.

In March Jack Ruby was convicted of the murder of Lee Harvey Oswald and sentenced to death. In September Martin Luther King won the Nobel Peace prize. Cuba continued to be isolated by America and the countries of the Organisation of American States (OAS). In fact in February US military aid to France, Yugoslavia and Britain was stopped because of their continuing aid to Cuba. US navy planes continued to bomb Vietnam.[18]

**

3508 Lowell St. N.W. Washington D.C., Saturday 17 October 1964

Dear Dorothy,

It is just about lunch time on Saturday – a very wet and windy one which has brought down a great many leaves all around us. Fortunately there are not so many in our present garden to be picked up, nor is the area so large. I am confined to the house with my first laryngitis of the season, sucking throat tablets and taking antibiotics in order that it should go no further. It must not as we have arranged to give our first cocktail party of the season on Tuesday – in honour of Mr and Mrs Stewart, our new Minister and his wife. They arrived a week or so ago. She was a member of the F.O. in her own right, a contemporary of Iain, I imagine, and her husband is older. Thursday was indeed a day of excitement, what with Mr Jenkin's arrest, Khrushchev's 'resignation' and the election results. (Mr Jenkins was an aide of President Johnson's and was arrested for 'immoral conduct.')

I think it was time we had a change of government in England but it remains to be seen how Mr Wilson shapes up as Prime Minister and what he can do with such a small majority.

I hope to go to Mexico with Iain in November, now that we have Lillian living in the house. We shall try to visit somewhere on the way.

Love from us all, Jeanne

3508 Lowell St. N.W. Washington D.C., 13 December 1964

Dear M & D,

Since I returned from Mexico I have been exceedingly busy with visitors. I was not personally much involved with Messrs Wilson, Gordon Walker and Healey at the beginning of the week, but had briefs to prepare and meetings to attend. Immediately after my return I had Jack Rennie who travelled back from Mexico via Washington. He was Economic Minister when we arrived and is now the Under-Secretary in the FO concerned with the western hemisphere.

At the Conference we had over thirty Ambassadors, Governors and High Commissioners and visitors seated at the long table in the Embassy beneath a copy of Orpen's portrait of Lord Cowdray. The Embassy was formerly Cowdray's house – before the expropriation of the oil companies. The participants came from all the countries round the Caribbean including the colonial territories. There was not a lot of free time from meetings and the various social functions which accompanied the conference, but on the Sunday after our arrival Jeanne and I did attend the Plaza de Toros – the largest bullring in the world. Earlier the same day we had climbed up to the Castle of Chapultepec, once an Aztec fortress, but totally rebuilt in the 19th century by the ill-fated Emperor Maximilian. In the great park which surrounds the castle there are the famous waterworks with a huge mosaic by Diego de Rivera partly submerged; also a new vast gallery of modern art completed this year. The chief new attraction of Mexico City is however the Museum of Archaeology and Anthropology which was opened only a few weeks before our arrival and which is still not complete. It was described in the *Times* as the finest museum in the world and 100 years in advance of anything in Britain.

Jeanne and all the family join in sending love and best wishes for Christmas.

Love from Iain

Washington, Monday 28 December 1964

Dear Dorothy,

Christmas is over thank goodness. I always breathe a sigh of relief and this year there seemed to be so little time to organise everything after we got back from Mexico. Yesterday was a pleasant relaxed day when there was no one to entertain, no presents to be wrapped and not even any food to be cooked. We took James and Sandra to a very soothing film all about living under the sea and taking wonderful photographs of life below by some French men who lived for a month 35 feet down. It was so gentle and soothing that I must admit I fell asleep twice!

We had an amazing Christmas weather-wise, in the 70s during Christmas Eve and Christmas Day. We were glad we had not given the children skis for Christmas. Tomorrow there is a party at the White House for diplomatic children, organised by the Hospitality and Information Service when the children are taken to see the Christmas decorations and given drinks and buns afterwards. The Johnsons are not in residence I believe. On Saturday we take the children to see the Nutcracker ballet.

Love from us all, Jeanne

British Embassy, Washington, 28 February 1965

Dear M & D,

The principal news this week is a letter from the Foreign Office received in the Embassy on Friday stating that I should expect to leave Washington, probably in the second week of September, to return to the Office in London to take up a post as assistant head of a department as yet unspecified. We are very pleased at this news. Much as we have enjoyed Washington it is a good thing to return home.

If the weather continues fine we think next weekend to drive down to the North Carolina coast to the area of Roanoke Island where Sir Walter Raleigh established the first English colony near Cape Hatteras. If and when Anne comes out in May we might spend part of the time in New England. In the meantime next week will be busy with a visit from Adam Watson, the present Ambassador in Havana; another from Denis Greenhill who was Minister here until last year and is now Assistant Under-Secretary in London. On the 13th we say goodbye to Lord Harlech, the Ambassador who has been here throughout our stay in Washington, and before the end of the month will welcome Sir Patrick Dean as his successor. He was formerly British Representative at the United Nations in New York.

Love from us all, Iain

* * *

Johnson's State of the Union message in January 1965 was mostly dedicated to domestic affairs, but he also reaffirmed his commitment to Vietnam, his support for the reunification of Germany and the increased commitment to the Alliance for Progress. The aims of the *Great Society*, keeping the economy growing and improving the quality of life were still of the greatest importance.[19] The valedictory despatch of the British Ambassador, written in March 1965, claimed that the Kennedy era had brought about a change in the attitude of the world towards the United States and that the accomplishments of the time were outstanding. Of the present he thought that the chances of success for the *Great Society* were good. Race relations were the biggest domestic problem and there was no sign of a solution. President Johnson was not at home in foreign affairs but we should not expect isolationism.[20]

Lord Harlech's replacement as Ambassador, Sir Patrick Dean, in his annual summary, called 1965 a year of domestic prosperity with legislature passed on education, health and public welfare, which brought about improvements in social conditions, especially for the blacks, and guaranteed them their right to vote. It was marred by the escalation of the war in Vietnam; by May of 1965 there were 42,000 American troops involved in the conflict. Race riots continued in some areas, including in Los Angeles in August, and there were demonstrations against the war in Vietnam across the country. These particularly involved the black population, who made up a large section of the American troops, but also included liberals, intellectuals and civil rights leaders. The unpopularity of the war and the increase in intervention by the US affected the President's popularity and reduced public support for him.

There were also some worries about the health of the President following his heart attack.[21] These were of course unwarranted and he served as President until March 1968, when he decided not to seek his party's nomination and retired from political life to live on his ranch near Johnson City, Texas, to 'work for peace' and to write his version of his presidential years, *The Vantage Point*.

* * *

508 Lowell St. N.W. Washington D.C., Sunday 4 April 1965

Dear Dorothy,

I have not been a good correspondent lately. With the teaching and everything else there is not much time for letter writing. It is pleasant to be out of the house and a job is more stimulating than constant childcare and endless housework. But teaching 1st grade is not what I would choose to do permanently.

We have some rather disturbing news this week. Life had seemed to be fairly well organised when we were to go on leave in September. James was to go straight to school, I was going to put Sandra and possibly Elizabeth temporarily in too and set about house hunting. Now we have heard that Iain is wanted to start work in August – as Assistant Head of Northern Department – and if he is to get this job he must leave much earlier.

Today was fine and we went with the children and Molly, their teacher, and her spaniel to an old ruined fort overlooking the river whence the Americans turned their guns on the English in the War of Independence.

Love from us all, Jeanne

Postcard from Iain, 12 June, Washington

Dear D & M,

We left Wellfleet, Cape Cod, on Wednesday morning for Boston where we spent a night with the Consul General in Old Chestnut Street. We left Anne next day in New York and slept ourselves in a motel half way on the turnpike to Washington, arriving here yesterday in time to attend the annual Garden Party on the occasion of the Queen's Birthday. By the time you get this you should have had a telegram saying that we have decided with some reluctance that it would be best to go from our boat on 9 July to spend a week at Bodrhyddan with Anne.

Love Iain

* * *

After a pleasant holiday at Cape Cod with Anne, where we ate fresh lobster, dug clams out of the sand at low tide to make clam chowder, we returned to Washington for our departure via New York, Toronto and Montreal, sailing down the St Lawrence River on our way home to Liverpool.

As in the case of most of our postings we were sorry to leave Washington and yet ready to move on, this time for a period in London, the first time for nine years. When we left there were two of us and when we returned we were five, plus at least five times as much luggage; and with no home to go to. My long-suffering girl friend, Elaine, allowed us to stay in her mansion flat in Swiss Cottage for three months, while we house hunted and finally found, bought and moved into the house in Highgate where I am still living.

6

AFTER SUKARNO AND
KONFRONTASI, INDONESIA 1967–69

T he posting to Indonesia came too soon after our return from Washington to be really welcome. It was less than two years since we had bought and moved into the house in North London and it was the first time I really resented being asked to move. But as usual in the Foreign Service, a move meant promotion and to refuse risked losing that. Iain was to be promoted to the rank of Counsellor and number two in the Embassy. I was not happy, however, about uprooting the whole family, leaving the house in the hands of some unknown tenants and going off into the blue.

We planned to travel by sea which would have taken some weeks and given us some sort of holiday, but the Arab–Israeli War (The Six-Day War) erupted in June 1967 and the Suez Canal was closed. Without the canal the sea journey was going to take over five weeks via the Cape on a small cargo boat and the office would not agree to such a long voyage. We eventually compromised by travelling by air and breaking the journey in Athens for five days and in Singapore for about a week.

***

Indonesia is the largest and most populous country in Southeast Asia, made up of thousands of islands extending along the equator between the Pacific and the Indian Oceans. The five largest islands in the archipelago, Sumatra, Java, Sulawesi, Kalimantan (two thirds of Borneo) and Irian Jaya (the western half of New Guinea), make up 90% of the land. Large sections of the country are mountainous, covered with rainforest or mangrove swamps and there are over 300 volcanoes, many active. Two thirds of the over 200,000,000 population live in the lowland areas of Java and Madura. Being on the Equator most of the country is hot all year round, with little variation of temperature. The average temperature for Djakarta, at approximately sea level, is 79° F and the hottest recorded temperature 96°, but it often feels much hotter because of the humidity. The average temperature in Bandung, which is 2200 ft above sea level, is 72° F.

The climate is tropical monsoon and agriculture makes up the largest sector of the economy. Indonesia is among the world's top producers of rice, palm oil, tea, coffee, rubber and tobacco. It is the world's leading exporter of natural gas, and a major exporter of tin. Indonesia remains, however, a relatively poor country. Ethnic tensions and civil unrest are hindering economic development.[1]

There are very great differences in the density of the population, 'which is closely related to the fertility of the soil. Only western Sumatra, the Lesser Sunda Islands, and especially Java, have soils which can support large numbers. Some of these areas have densities as high as 3000 to 4000 to the square mile; Java has over 1200. But Borneo (Kalimantan), for example, the world's largest island after Greenland, has less than 50 people per square mile. So also with the smaller islands; some are virtually uninhabited, others, such as Bali, are intensively cultivated'.[2]

Travelling anywhere on the island of Java one was always aware of the density of the population. There were people everywhere. If you went on a mountain walk you would meet itinerant sellers of *sate*, if you stopped in a car on the side of the road you were always immediately surrounded by groups of people, standing and watching. Whereas in Sumatra for instance you could travel for miles without seeing anyone, or indeed seeing anything except forest or jungle.

* * *

The earliest people of the Indonesian islands lived in small communities, employed in rice growing or fishing. Later there developed a series of kingdoms which are mentioned in the Hindu epic the *Ramayana*. The earliest outside influences seem to have come from India and with them the Hindu religion. Later trade was carried on with China and with it came Buddhism. Hinduism/Buddhism was introduced into Java and

Sumatra in the 8th and 9th centuries. The great Monument of Borobodur in central Java was built at this time, and later Prambanan. In the early 15th century Islam spread along the northern coast of Sumatra and the north coast of Java. The Indonesians, who always seemed to manage to take what they wanted from the latest religion and keep what they wanted of the former, 'accepted Islam without abandoning their previous Hindu-Buddhist practices'.[3] Bali alone remained Hindu-Buddhist.

The next adventurers to reach the archipelago were the Portuguese, followed by the Spaniards. Then came the English, but more importantly the Dutch. The United East India Company was formed in 1602 which gradually took over more and more of the territory of the East Indies. Between 1650 and 1680 all the Indonesian states of importance came under the power of the Company. From 1705 until 1941 the Dutch controlled events in Indonesia. The political centre was Batavia, founded by the first Governor General of the Company. Atjeh, in northern Sumatra, remained independent until the beginning of the 20th century and there were constant crises and conflicts between local rulers and the Dutch. But by 1755 most of Java's three and a half million were governed by Batavia. Batavia was renamed Djakarta in 1944 when Indonesia became independent. Souvenirs of Dutch rule remain in many of the buildings and in the canals which cross Djakarta. (In our day they were used for everything, from sewers to places for people to wash and clean their teeth. The town still did not have a sewage system although the pipes for it, supplied by the French, were lying in the streets, mostly used by the inhabitants as water resistant accommodation and largely better than cardboard boxes.)

Under the Dutch the production of crops of all kinds increased but without the country's becoming much richer or the standard of living improving greatly. They continued their policy of annexing the other islands of the archipelago and by 1910 all came under Dutch rule. In spite of further production booms the peasant economy failed to improve and the lack of education, little industrialisation and the very large increases in population among the peasantry prevented an improvement in their living standards. From time to time there were outbreaks of hostilities against the occupying forces but these were suppressed. During the early 20th century nationalist movements emerged and political parties were set up, such as the *Sarekat Islam* (The Muslim Society), the National Indies Party and the Indies Social Democratic Association. Leftist elements from these parties joined with others to form the PKI (the Communist Party of Indonesia). In 1927 members of the 'study club' in Bandung formed the Indonesian National Party with Sukarno as chairman. He was arrested with other leaders in 1929 and served two years. He was again arrested in 1933 and exiled for more than eight years.

Independence came to Indonesia only after the war and after the Japanese occupation. It was encouraged by the Japanese who had put the Europeans into concentration camps and released Sukarno. As they gradually lost the war the Japanese allowed the Indonesians greater power and promised them independence. After the dropping of the bomb on Hiroshima in 1944 the Japanese Supreme Commander in Southeast Asia authorised the handover of power to the Indonesians. On 17 August Sukarno and Hatta declared Indonesia independent.

That was only the beginning. There followed years of conflict and argument even after the Dutch had agreed to Indonesian independence. Apart from Dutch intransigence, there was opposition from non-Javanese members of the country, particularly Atjeh which has always been, and still is, fiercely independent. The task of combining the conglomeration of multi-cultural, multi-religious peoples, who for years had not been given the task of ruling themselves, was enormous. They had never had a unified system of education, they had largely been the workers and producers for a foreign European occupier who administered their country and took the profits of their labour. They were divided in all ways. They had only been united by 'common colonial experience' as President Sukarno called it.[4]

By 1960 Sukarno was in complete control of the country and was supported by the Soviet bloc nations. Sukarno was an undoubtedly charismatic character, emotional and with wild and extravagant tastes in everything.

> He dismantled parliamentary democracy and destroyed free enterprise. His personal and political excesses, as epitomised eventually by his infamous cabinet of 100 corrupt and cynical ministers induced a continuous state of national crisis. Sukarno narrowly escaped recurrent attempts at assassination. Regional insurrections broke out in Sumatra and Sulawesi. Inflation escalated the cost-of-living index from 100 in 1958 to 18,000 in 1965 and on up wildly to 600,000 in 1967. In 1963, Sukarno all but broke with the U.S. After having exacted U.S. $1,000,000,000 in Soviet armaments and other items, he next affronted Moscow. On 20 January 1965, Indonesia formally withdrew from the United Nations because the latter supported Malaysia, which Sukarno had vowed to crush as an imperialist plot of encirclement.[5]

The struggle between Malaysia and Indonesia over the island of Borneo which lasted from 1962 to 1966 was known as *Konfrontasi*. It involved the plan to combine the two British colonies on the island with Malaya to form Malaysia, a move strongly resisted by Indonesia, but eventually to be accepted by them if the UN referendum produced a majority vote in favour. However Malaya jumped the gun and announced that the federation would be created before the referendum vote was announced. This caused a strong Indonesian reaction. Rioters burnt the British Embassy, sacked the Singapore Embassy in Djakarta and conflict broke out between Indonesian and Commonwealth troops in Malaysia. In September 1965 a coup initiated by Sukarno-led communist factions 'caused six top army generals to be kidnapped, tortured, mutilated and murdered. General, Suharto, the commander of the Djakarta garrison, swiftly reversed the coup. There ensued a contest for power between Suharto and Sukarno while some 300,000 or more Communists and alleged Communists were being slaughtered.'[6] In March 1966 Suharto took over from Sukarno and the war with Malaysia gradually ceased. In May 1966 a peace treaty was signed.

* * *

It was at the tail end of all this that we arrived in Indonesia. Most Embassy families had been evacuated from Djakarta during the troubles and we were among the first to return. Most of the accommodation was in very poor condition as is apparent in the first letter home. In our house the walls were filthy, the furniture was decrepit and the cushions on the terrace seats were full of holes.

After the fall of Sukarno and the coup the Indonesians had broken with the eastern bloc countries and had not yet managed to get financial help from the west. The parlous state of the electricity supply in our street was only to improve substantially nearly a year after we came, after the arrival of the World Bank office lower down the road. Then the supply was considerably upgraded and the continual cuts stopped. Without electricity we had not only no air conditioning but no fans and no water, and many mornings I had to take water from the small garden pond in order to wash and then to drive to the electricity substation to ask them to reconnect us.

c/o DSAO, King Charles Street, London, SW1,
Friday 27 October 1967

My Dear Mother and Father,

We were due to move to our house on Sunday but when we went round to see it the condition was so bad that Commander Merrin, the Naval Attaché, in whose house we were staying, who went with us, declared it uninhabitable. So we all went back again. This produced on Monday morning an army of painters and scrubbers, electricians and plumbers, and we finally moved in on Wednesday. The water and electricity failed for 2 hours but we now have water most of the day and electricity 2 out of 3 nights.

We have 5 servants – a cook, house maid/nanny, houseboy, washer woman and gardener. They work all day and every day (not very hard or very fast) and cost about £20 a month altogether.

Djakarta is not a very attractive town although it has more large buildings and wide streets than I imagined. Sukarno built some extravagant monuments and a dual carriage way through the main part of the town, but on either side life is very primitive. We live in the residential suburb of Kebayaron where there are a lot of pleasant houses. Ours is quite attractive, now that it is cleaner, and is built round a garden including a terrace, shrubs and grass and the swimming pool.

On Saturday we were taken to the mountains. There the villages are gay with stalls of fruit on all sides and as you climb the air gets deliciously cool and you can swim in a freezing cold pool. At the top of the pass we had lunch and looked down on pine trees, roses and many European flowers and the hill slopes are covered with tea plantations.

We all send our love, Jeanne

* * *

Djakarta, 28 October 1967, Saturday

Dear M & D,

This week we are still in some disorder as we have just moved into the house my predecessor occupied. As Jeanne has written it was not really fit to move into when we arrived. He was a bachelor and there are only 3 bedrooms. We are looking for something larger but larger houses are very hard to find and very expensive. So we shall make ourselves as comfortable as we can until our heavy luggage arrives. This may not be until Christmas as it is still held up by the strike at Liverpool docks. And in any case the house is by no means small and in a tropical, Californian sort of way is quite attractive.

We were very well looked after in Singapore during our five day visit, in the Goodwood Hotel. We were welcomed by a friend, Reg Hibbert and his wife. He once worked in Northern Department and was in Ulan Bator. The small Foreign Office advisory group there is engulfed by the vast military establishment and the offices are in the Far East Headquarters in Phoenix Park.

Love, Iain

Djakarta, Saturday 4 November 1967

Dear M & D,

We have now been here over two weeks. I cannot say that we have truly settled in yet. Our house remains very bare and must remain so until our heavy luggage eventually arrives. Servants come and go; we gesticulate and smile and hope that we are understood with our few words of Indonesian when we talk to them and to others who do not know English. I cannot say that I am yet master of the very complicated political situation with its bewildering multiplicity of factions and parties, usually referred to by strings of initials.

Our new Cortina station wagon is on the road and plies back and forth along the crowded four mile road between the Embassy in town and the suburb of Kebayaron. We have met a good number of our colleagues in the diplomatic corps – en masse at several national day functions and more intimately at various dinner parties. With the Ambassador I have called on others such as the Ministers of Finance and Power, both army generals. Elizabeth and Sandra have started at the so-called international school, also in Kebayaron, and set off in our new car each morning with the chauffeur at 7.30 with their thermoses of drinking water.

November sees the beginning of the monsoon season and today we had our first tropical downpour. The brown grass, the red croton bushes and the large mango tree look fresher. The streets, up till now dry, hot and dusty, were partly flooded when we all drove into town on a shopping expedition this afternoon and returned with, among other things, a bamboo model of a three-master ship and a painting from Bali (£4), to bring some colour to our marble floored sitting room with its sparse Ministry of Works furniture.

Despite the rains it is still very hot. We could do with some of your snow. We are much dependent on the two air conditioners in the bedrooms which serve the double purpose of keeping one cool and discouraging the mosquitoes. Unfortunately the electricity supply is not always to be depended on and the large generator is still out of action for want of parts.

Djakarta has a considerable number of passing visitors who take up much of the time of the not too numerous Embassy staff. There is a constant stream of business men attracted by the more stable political situation and hopes of contracts despite the parlous economic state of the country; others come to investigate or negotiate the terms on which they may return to take back estates and businesses sequestered during confrontation. We even have had several official visitors from London since we arrived. This weekend we have US Vice President Humphrey.

Love from us all, Iain

c/o DSAO, King Charles Street, London, SW1,
Thursday 16 November 1967

Dear Dorothy,

Most of this week has been taken up with the bazaar. This was an international effort by all the embassies to raise money for the local cancer fund and the children's playing fields. There is certainly plenty of poverty to be helped but one is never quite sure where the money raised will get to and even if past the organisers' pockets.

The economy here is based on the price of rice which has just gone up from 27 to 37 rupiahs a kilo in 2 weeks. The servants', and everyone's wages are based on rice, which is the staple food, and it is really complicated keeping track of what they are to be paid. You feed them, clothe them, look after them when they are sick and pay them practically nothing.

It has just started to rain – and it is torrential. Some evenings are quite pleasantly cool now and it seems that the months of December and January are going to be the most pleasant. We are trying to fix the swimming pool but it needs painting and some form of filtering to make the water safe. Meanwhile I am always being dragged off to the Embassy pool. Our greatest excitement this week was that we got hot water; still no sign of our luggage; so annoying to sit here helpless. The house has charm and will have great possibilities when we have our possessions. It is U-shaped and built round the garden which is still fuller of workmen than tropical plants but we hope to rectify that.

We all send our love, Jeanne

Djakarta, Thursday 7 December 1967

Dear Dorothy,

We are still working on our house, we and our servants and workmen. We have to have a major overhaul of the electrical system. There is a possibility that someone has stolen part of our electricity supply. Here, apparently they steal anything, from silver and ornaments to the electric water pump.

The Indonesians we meet officially are friendly and quite informal from the Foreign Minister down; they are mostly government officials or journalists and all seem quite happy to come to our houses. A surprising number of women hold responsible posts in government and journalism.

There is not a great deal to do in Djakarta apart from official entertainment. There are few cinemas and the films are not good. Some English films are sent out and shown privately. There are few restaurants except for the Hotel Indonesia which has three very expensive ones and a coffee shop. Some of the restaurants in China Town are supposed to be good but we have not discovered them yet. Last Saturday we went to the *Wayang Orang* show. These are long complicated plays taken from the Hindu mythology of the *Ramayana* and the *Mahabharata*. They are usually performed by puppets but this was with actors. It's very long and slow, like a mixture of Indian dancing and Chinese opera and with a little English pantomime thrown in! Some is rather boring when you don't understand the language but some of the dancing and fights are very good. The Hindu religion is not practised in Java any more but these stories from Hindu mythology are still performed frequently.

The centre of the modern town consists of the Hotel Indonesia and the Press Club opposite, built around a large roundabout, with the German Embassy on one side and the new British one (under construction) on another. The Japanese and Australian embassies are just a little further down the road from the hotel and beyond them another square with a curious monument supposed to be topped by solid gold, and so on past the museum till you get to the station, the business and banking area and finally the port where the canal/town sewer runs into the sea. Sadly it is not possible to swim in the sea in

Djakarta. There is a splendid, colourful but stinking fish market and a sad, dirty aquarium.

In another part of the town are art shops and the one big store, *Sarinah*, where you can buy most things from east or west, at a price. Then there are markets, some open and some under cover. South from the Hotel Indonesia runs the big dual carriageway leading to Kebayaron and a little further on, just before it ends there is an enormous stadium built by the Russians for the Asiatic Games, and a flyover with the road leading southeast to the hills and Bogor and Bandung.

In the downtown business area there are some pleasant houses built in old Dutch style and some newer ones on the road called Imam Bondjol where there are many embassy residences, including ours. Scattered around in the residence garden are the temporary quarters of the Embassy offices.

Love from us all, Jeanne

Djakarta, Friday 22 December 1967

Dear Dorothy,

James arrived safely on Sunday after a long, tiring journey. The plane left late and was further delayed in Bombay and Madras, where it failed to gain height and had to land again; just as well we knew nothing of all this. James said they played hide and seek at the Madras airfield while waiting for the new aeroplane.

We have been experimenting with 'Christmas in Indonesia' and finally bought new decorations for the Indonesian Christmas tree as our own are not here. Yesterday I experimented with the kerosene stove. It went out 4 times while the Christmas cake was cooking.

Love from us all, Jeanne

Djakarta, 29 December 1967

Dear Dorothy,

Christmas is over once again. Amazingly we managed to eat roast turkey, stuffing and bread sauce in the middle of the day with no air conditioning. Then we slept it off and went to the zoo, a rather sad place but very dispersed on the outskirts of the town. There are many indigenous animals – black Javan bears which walk upright and an orang-utan which smokes; and pythons rather gruesomely being fed live chickens.

On Wednesday which was also a holiday 38 of us hired a boat (Russian built for Sukarno) and sailed to one of the nearest islands and had a most successful day swimming in the surf, collecting shells, picnicking and getting sunburnt. The island, uninhabited except for guards, was a paradise for shell hunters and had the most wonderful collection of pieces of coral. Great fun was had jumping the waves as it is shallow and without the dangerous undertow of Pelabuhan Ratu on the south coast.

Love from us all, Jeanne

* * *

No doubt one of the most striking features of Indonesian life was the poverty. It was said that some Europeans could not bear to see it and had to leave. There were always beggars in the streets, sometimes with the most horrific apparent disabilities, although in some cases these may have been contrived to get more generous donations. The standard of living was extremely low and millions lived below subsistence level. In Djakarta many lived in the open along the banks of the city's canals, or in cardboard boxes, under bridges or slept at night in their *betjahs* (bicycle rickshaws) which they rode and worked during the day. Those who were lucky enough to have jobs, even the poorly paid jobs working for foreigners (and the only justification for paying so little was that more could be employed) lived mostly on rice and vegetables with the odd piece of fish. It was true of course that when provided with *bulgur* wheat or potatoes by foreign aid most Indonesians rejected it. If you did not have rice you did not have a proper meal.

The reasons for the poverty are various. The majority of Indonesians had never benefited from modern methods of agriculture, industrialisation or general education. Under independence and Sukarno little was done to improve the situation. He borrowed large sums of money which he proceeded to squander on grandiose plans. Meanwhile the population, particularly of Java, increased by something like 600,000 a year and the already restricted stretches of fertile land became more and more overpopulated. Polomka, the Australian scientist and journalist writes of central Java in 1971,

> The residue of support Sukarno retained among its people was a major
> cause of Suharto's cautious and somewhat inconclusive handling of his

predecessor's overthrow, and the inroads the Communist Party (PKI) and the Nationalist Party (PNI) made among the region's civilian and military administrative apparatus still seriously handicap central government control. Moreover, the legacy of hate and fear arising from the post-*coup* killings, the general apathy and suspicion found among the people towards central authority, the increasing military presence, and the religious and political turmoil caused by the change in government, have all helped complicate the general situation. But the heart of the problem lies in the poverty and backwardness of the province's grossly excessive and potentially politically explosive population.[7]

The situation inherited by Suharto was not easy. Horace Phillips, the British Ambassador, writes in his summary of 1967, 'All the events of the year have shown how unrealistic it would have been to suppose that his (Sukarno's) removal from power would automatically solve the wider problems of Indonesia. His ruinous legacy to the country, stored up over a decade and more of self-seeking cannot be replaced in a year of well-ordered progress and prosperity.' Suharto was helped by much foreign credit; the Soviet Union agreed to reschedule debts, Japan and western creditors (including the United Kingdom) provided aid of $200 million and agreed to consider more. Inflation was reduced from 600% in 1966 to 100% in 1967. But improvements in the national economy did not reach the man in the street and by the end of the year a critical shortage of rice was causing steep rises in price. There was public dissatisfaction with the corruption and incompetence of the bureaucracy. Many of his generals took the opportunity to make money and Suharto had done little about this. The government was mostly made up of military, the ministries were largely in charge of generals, and there was no move to a changeover of rule by politicians; no elections were in sight and they were unlikely to take place in 1968.

The Ambassador summarises the situation in the last paragraph, 'Given the main problems – corruption and maladministration, the recent set-back to the economy, the frustration and discontent of the politicians – the régime faces a crucial year. But it has always been clear that it would take long to rebuild the political and economic ruins left by Sukarno. Indonesia can never be expected to rise to great heights, but I believe it has the resilience and resources to prevent it from plummeting to irredeemable depths.'[8]

* * *

Djakarta, Monday 29 January 1968

Dear M & D,

As you may have heard on the radio, here in Djakarta we have had demonstrations by students against the rising cost of rice which have caused the government some anxiety. The demonstrations were quite orderly, but there were attacks in the Chinese quarter against the shops of some merchants. The news agencies gave a somewhat exaggerated account and today all is calm. This week's Embassy news is the unexpected appointment of the Ambassador, Mr Phillips, to take charge of the mission in Jeddah. He served there before, knows Persian and Arabic and, as it will be a key post in these days of withdrawal from the Gulf and Aden, it is regarded in London as an especially difficult assignment. His successor here is not known.

With love and best wishes to you both from Iain, Jeanne, Alexandra and Elizabeth

Djakarta, Friday 9 February 1968

Dear M & D,

We go tomorrow to the Puntjak, to the second Embassy bungalow, over the pass of the same name below the volcano of Gurung Gede on the road down to the fertile plain where the city of Bandung is situated. It is a 3 hour drive through the town of Bogor with its once world-famous and still fine botanical gardens and where the deposed but still nominal president Sukarno lives under surveillance in the early 19th century Governor's Palace.

We have more ambitious plans for the week after next, when, the political situation permitting, I plan to drive down the island to Jogjakarta, and then to Surabaya. I hope Jeanne can come with me; we shall need to find someone to keep an eye on the children. Jogjakarta is the ancient Javanese capital; nearby too is the great ruined Hindu temple of Borobodur. In Surabaya there is a one man British Consulate where we will stay with Mr Docherty. But more distant travels which I had planned for March will have to be cancelled on account of the departure of Horace Phillips in mid-March. Only one, long, but brief journey seems possible until the as yet un-named successor arrives – that is a flight in a RAF plane via

Darwin in Australia to the island of Ambon in the Moluccas. There, on April 2, a new war memorial and cemetery is to be opened to various troops, mostly Australian.

We are having an additional electricity supply put in and we hope that, as a result, our lights will not fuse so often. We have also planted some more flowers in the garden, but most flowers last for only a day or two, except orchids and ours have not flowered at all.

The street sellers with their wares balanced on a bamboo pole across their shoulders are a feature of life in Djakarta and its suburbs. Each type of peddler has a different pitch of bell or a hollow wooden stick with a distinctive sound. There are shoemakers and carpenters and tinsmiths, men who sell food cooked on portable stoves and sellers of brushes and goldfish and antiques. The vendors of antiques, who were much patronised by my predecessor, are constant callers at the weekends. I have bought one blue and white, reported, Ming bowl and an old jar from Borneo.

Love from Iain, Jeanne and Alexandra and Elizabeth

* * *

The journey to Surabaya and Jogjakarta was the first of Iain's (and my) journeys outside the Djakarta area, not counting the weekends in the mountains. Iain was keen to see the rest of the country and for others in the Embassy to travel too. There is a report by the 3rd Secretary, Ian Morgan, which contains a fascinating description of visits by him to Kalimantan and Sulawesi. He tells of the extreme primitiveness of the people, contrasting with the possibility of prosperity; he is stunned by the corruption of local officials; the story, as in many of these distant places, is of decay, decrepitude, corruption and incompetence. In his covering letter Iain recommends a wider programme of touring in 1968 and at the end says, 'It is impossible to get this far-flung country in true perspective from Djakarta alone. Indonesia, outside the capital, is also generally more attractive. I hope therefore that we can report more tours in 1968.'[9] As so often happened, it became more difficult for Iain to get away as work built up and he was twice in charge of the Embassy in the Ambassador's absence. But we did manage to go to Bali twice, to Surabaya, Jogjakarta and Sumatra, including the northern province of Atjeh.

In Horace Phillips' valedictory report to Secretary of State, George Brown, he writes,

189

The priorities of the Service require me to return now to the familiar deserts of Arabia after a brief 20 months in tropical surroundings as unlike them as it is possible to imagine. Islam binds Arabia and Indonesia but the grass roots of the indigenous mysticism and animism of Java still grow strongly through the thin soil of Islam. To penetrate the enigma of Indonesia the western observer must not only understand something of the philosophy of Islam, but also have some knowledge of Javanese attitudes and behaviour.

The acting president rejects any form of personality cult, does not come over as a charismatic leader, and pursues his quiet, modest way. How is he to change the whole system of poverty and despair of all except the privileged few and turn around the years of maladministration and corruption into a country of prosperity and sufficiency for all?[10]

Horace has little hope that it will happen even though things may improve little by little.

c/o D.S.A.O., King Charles St. London, SW1, 2 March 1968

Dear Dorothy,

We came back to Djakarta on Wednesday morning after a quite comfortable journey on the new sleeper train with East German air conditioning. We enjoyed our trip very much. The first night in Tjeribon proved to be extremely comfortable in the newly decorated house of the British American Tobacco Company. The next morning we paid a surprise call on the Ratu and Radja of Tjeribon in their *Kraton* (palace) which is indeed a relic of the past. They live in extreme poverty but were very courteous and charming.

In Jogjakarta we stayed in the comfortable new hotel, the Ambarrukmo, complete with air conditioning and swimming pool. We visited several of the Hindu temples in the area. Borobodur is the biggest and it is said that if you put all the engravings of the Hindu mythology together they would reach for three miles. I personally liked the smaller complex better, Prambanan, where the temples to the Hindu gods are more spread out with green grass in between, and the engravings are better and easier to follow. We also visited the Jogja Sultan's palace, a much richer and more elegant building, and various other places in the town. One of the most interesting was the Batik Institute where they teach the old art of batik making. This was fascinating and we spent much time looking at the various designs and colours.

Love from us all, Jeanne

Koala Motor Hotel, Daly Street, Darwin, Australia, 1 April 1968

Dear M & D,

My first night in Australia – I arrived here this afternoon in an RAF aircraft with the Dutch and Canadian counsellors from Djakarta and a heterogeneous group of senior officers from Singapore and an Indonesian Admiral. Refuelled in Bali. Flew over the islands of the Timor Sea and was then taken on a conducted tour of this expanding frontier town. Followed by other aircraft with padres and pipers and pressmen and Australian members of parliament, we set off again at 5 a.m. tomorrow for the island of Ambon in the Moluccas there to be present at the dedication of the Commonwealth War Cemetery. I was sorry to be so short a time in the historic island of Ambon, once the centre of the Portuguese empire, scene of the massacre of the merchants of the Dutch East India Company, island of cloves and once of birds of paradise; scene of revolt in 1950 when most of the Christian Protestant pro-Dutch inhabitants refused to accept independence with Indonesia, island of the finest sea shells in the East Indies.

I say goodnight from Darwin, love from Iain

c/o D.S.A.O. etc. 18 April 1968

Dear Dorothy,

You may have seen the announcement of the appointment of Mr Henry Hainworth as our new Ambassador, although he is not expected here until the end of June. So it looks as though we shall be seeing the Embassy through the Queen's Birthday and the move into the new building. Iain spends all day in the office and we are out or entertaining guests ourselves almost every night. I have various women's functions to attend, some charity affairs and now all the children are at home. It doesn't leave many spare hours. The other members of the Embassy have been very helpful.

Did you see the news about poor Horace Phillips being turned down as Ambassador to Jeddah after all the fuss in the newspapers?

Time to stop; love from us all, Jeanne

c/o D.S.A.O. etc. May 1968

Dear Dorothy,

The bag is closing in half an hour although only Friday noon because the Embassy is being packed up to move this weekend to the new building, or rather the building which was destroyed in the riots of 1963 and has just been restored. A bit tatty was our verdict last night when we went to have drinks with the Ministry of Works representative. It's a pity they didn't destroy it completely so that we could have started again. However, it will be heaven compared with the boxes in the garden where they work at the moment. Iain is having a small opening ceremony the week after next. He decided that it would be inappropriate to give it greater publicity.

Next Thursday we celebrate the Queen's official birthday with 600–700 guests in the garden. I only hope it does not rain. The rainy season has gone on much longer than usual this year. Yesterday we celebrated our Elizabeth's birthday with 15 children, swimming, tea and a film show.

Love from us all, Jeanne

16. Duke of Edinburgh, the Sultan of Jogjakarta, Jeanne and Iain, during the Duke's visit to Bali in May 1968.

* * *

The Embassy had been burnt during *Konfrontasi*, and reputedly the then Ambassador, Andrew Gilchrist, marched up and down outside playing the bagpipes as it burnt. Iain did not think the suggestion that the bagpipes should be played again during the opening was conducive to the new spirit of rapprochement between Indonesia and the UK. So he decided on a small opening ceremony with a few people, including the Foreign Minister Malik. Anyway not all the furniture had arrived yet and the refurbishing was far from completed.

In May, during Iain's period as Head of Mission, one of our tasks was to greet the Duke of Edinburgh who spent a day on the island of Bali. We flew down with the Australian Chargé d'Affaires and his wife. The Duke was breaking his journey on the way to a Commonwealth

17. Reopening of the British Embassy, Djakarta, May 1968.

Study Conference in Canberra, flying his own small plane. Iain writes in his postcard to his parents, on 10 May 1968,

'Jeanne and I came here on Monday and spent all day with the Duke and his party exploring Bali and seeing dances in the evening. The people here are all Hindu and the beautiful island is full of temples and carvings and one luxury hotel. The Emperor of Ethiopia arrives today and we go back to Djakarta tomorrow.' The Duke appeared to much enjoy his stay except when pursued by journalists trying to take a picture of him next to a Balinese girl in national costume (i.e. naked to the waist). Iain and Michael managed to arrange a deal with them that if he would give a short press conference they would then leave him alone. After that things were better and we were able to visit a private house to watch Balinese dancers and had a midnight swim in the hotel pool without interruption, the Duke diving in and out among us in a very relaxed way.

* * *

c/o D.S.A.O. etc. mid June, 1968

Dear Dorothy, David and Anne,

The Queen's Birthday Party went off very well so every one said. Iain struggled hard to get everything done as he wanted but eventually there were floodlights in the trees, chairs and tables in the garden and then down came the rain in torrents and flooded everything. And this is supposed to be the dry season. The splendid band provided by the Australian regiment in Malaya had to be moved inside and there was one moment when the house looked as though it might burst but we survived and some people left, the rain stopped and a few adventurous people went outside and all was well. I still feel a little stunned. Yesterday was spent tidying up and giving away most of the 50 odd bouquets of flowers we received, to the English Church, the Embassy ladies, to the hospital and so on.

Just before the party began we heard the news of Robert Kennedy's death. I was very shocked and felt desperately sorry for the family with the 10 and a bit children and Jackie Kennedy whose children seem to use him as a father.

Love from us all, Jeanne

Monday 25 September 1968

Dear M & D,

Thank you for your letter received today with news of your visit to Edinburgh and the Festival Exhibitions. I fly to Singapore on Wednesday morning and take the BOAC flight to London on Thursday night. Jeanne has hired a car and will be at the airport.

Yes you are right about Horace Phillips whom the Saudi Arabians would not accept because of his Glasgow Jewish connections. He has been appointed Ambassador in Tanzania.

Love from Iain

c/o D.S.A.O. etc. Sunday 22 December 1968

Dear M & D,

Here we all are again back in Djakarta after our leave. We reached here on Saturday last in the afternoon after a hurried lunch on board the plane from Singapore. The Thai hostesses are hard put to it to serve the 3–4 courses given to the 1st class passengers – the caviar, the fish in aspic and the mixed fruits – as they speed across the Java Sea on the short flight from Singapore. James, very particular and selective in his food, prefers tourist class menus.

Friday had been spent shopping – a new tropical suit from Mr Salim; a turkey from Malay cold storage; a book on gardening in S.E. Asia from the better bookshop. Djakarta has not changed much in our absence. But we did remark that it looked much tidied up since we first drove through the city a year ago. The present energetic mayor has done much to have potholes filled in and trees and shrubs planted along the principal highways. The house at Aditiawarman was full of bunches of orchids to welcome our return and garden had been kept very well in our absence. But still no hot water and our cook had been dismissed under circumstances which we still cannot quite understand.

The Muslim holiday of Idul Fitr, or Lebaran falls just before Christmas this year. So this week the evenings have resounded to firecrackers. As I have just come from leave it is the turn of others to go to the hills over the Christmas holiday. So we remain in town. This evening we all went to a carol service in the old English Church, founded in the days of Sir Thomas Raffles. The present building dates from the 1840s. We rise early tomorrow, Monday, to go with the Ambassador and Mrs Hainworth to pay our respects to President Suharto on the occasion of the Lebaran holiday – this year a simple call at his private house.

This will I fear arrive too late to wish you a happy Christmas and to M many happy returns but we all wish you the best for 1969.

Love from etc.

> *c/o The DSAO, King Charles Street, London,*
> *SW1, Thursday 9 January 1969*

Dear Dorothy,

Yesterday we had 25 children from 6 to12 to a film show. The terrace looked wonderful afterwards with a sea of spilled coke in which popcorn floated like snow flakes. Talking of snow we thought of you digging yourselves out as we splashed in and out of the swimming pool at Samudra Beach at the weekend, and had occasional sorties into the warm but dangerous Indian Ocean.

There have been lots of young people this holiday and many parties. Most of them go back to their boarding schools this weekend. James seems to have made quite a hit with the girls and especially with the 11 year-old daughter of the actress Eva Bartok.

We all send our love, Jeanne

* * *

Our arrival in Indonesia the second year was much easier than the first. We knew more or less what to expect. I had learned some Indonesian and could communicate at least with the staff in the house and people in shops. The house had improved a great deal.

Life was not much easier for the Indonesian population where there was still great poverty. The stability which the military government was struggling to achieve was not free of crises and upsets. The influence of the military continued strong in the country under Suharto. Some sections of the population were not content and students who at first supported Suharto were becoming more rebellious and outspoken about the corruption and nepotism of the army.

A group of prominent businessmen met in Djakarta in 1968 to 'appraise the new face of the Indonesian nation as an investment project'.

The report which they drew up was presented to President Suharto. 'They were generally optimistic that there should be reasonable tranquillity.'[11] Since March 1966 much had been done to improve political relations with the west, by clamping down on the Communist Party and relations with Peking, and making peace with Malaysia. Indonesia had shown its desire to rejoin the UN and had been wooing the west for desperately needed financial aid. It had gained considerable help from western countries, not only in renegotiating old debts, but also acquiring new aid from the US and Japan and other members of the IGGI (Inter-Governmental Group on Indonesia). But in many ways things were not much better than under Sukarno, particularly in the urban areas where some of his wilder schemes had benefited the working population, as had the state subsidies on public utilities such as petrol and kerosene.

Planned rises in production were slow to happen and the rising population did not help. Increasing corruption, now also said to be due to foreign investment, was another problem, all this leading to public demonstrations in 1970.

One of the starkest stories of the post coup period was the ill treatment and in some cases large-scale killing of former communists. The actual figures are not known but numbers vary from the official figure of 78,000 to as much as one million. The killings were partly as a reaction to the very large numbers of communists in the party under Sukarno (many of them activists who became political prisoners and were, if not killed, held without trial and brutally treated for many years); partly as a result of the clashes between the Chinese guerrillas (already mentioned as being involved in the crush Malaysia campaign) and the Indonesian army; and in some cases because of clashes between the communists and the Muslim population, particularly in Atjeh.

In March 1969 President Suharto issued his second warning in just over a week that the Indonesian Communist Party was still a danger to the nation. At this time there were reports of a massacre of former communists in the Purwodadi area, east of Samarang. These came from a Dutch correspondent, Henk Kolb, claiming that mass graves were found and the population were made to assist. Another report said that 3500 alleged supporters of the PKI were executed in two months, that Suharto did not have sufficient control to stop these excesses. Foreign Minister, Malik maintained that reprisals had stopped and that 'rehabilitation and social adaptation of prisoners' had begun.[12]

Suharto's 'Address of State' on the occasion of the 24th Anniversary of Independence of Indonesia contained no renewed calls for vigilance against the PKI, but neither did it announce an amnesty for political prisoners. Two thousand five hundred detainees were to be transferred to the island of Buru in the Moluccas 'to be assisted to make a new life for themselves'. On the subject of West Irian, the people's choice was absolute and the region would have the status of an autonomous region as was the case with other regions. West Irian would continue to be an integral part of the Republic.[13]

Many Muslims had hoped for an Islamic state after the coup. In the 1960s about 90% of Indonesians were Muslim, 6–7% Christian and 3% Buddhist. There were serious clashes between Muslims and non-Muslims in Indonesia, particularly in Atjeh where Christian churches were attacked and Islamic fanaticism dominated.[14]

One major improvement to life in Djakarta was the work of the Governor of Djakarta, Ali Sadikin, who was improving the roads, tidying up the town and painting the buildings, finding money from lotteries and casinos.

* * *

c/o DSAO, etc. 23 January 1969

Dear Dorothy,

We leave this afternoon for Medan, Sumatra and places north. We are hoping to get up to Atjeh, the northern part of Sumatra, a province which for a long time held out against unity with the rest of the country and which is still very resentful of the lack of attention which it gets from the central government.

The girls are fairly settled at school and we try to keep up our extra programme of studies. Sandra now stays until 2.30 and the school has added to the curriculum French, and a delightful new American girl who teaches music and singing. She is partly English educated and lives in the Subud. We were at the Subud for dinner a few weeks ago. It is a centre of spiritual meditation, international and inter-denominational. There are people from all nationalities and religions who are engaged in finding themselves and peace. Their leader is an Indonesian, known as Pak Subud, and he and a few others are capable of transmitting this peace and knowledge. Quite a few are residents but a hundred came recently on a chartered flight from England and this was the occasion of our invitation.

Lots of love from us all, Jeanne

The Governor's Guest House, Banda Atjeh,
Monday 27 January 1969

Dear M & D,

This is written on the *pendopo*, the vast front porch of the State Guest House of the governor of Atjeh in northern Sumatra. The house, which has the date 1888, was once the residence of the Dutch governors. It must have been built soon after the Dutch established themselves in this part of Sumatra, for in the early 80s they were still fighting the last of a series of costly colonial wars against the Sultans of this fiercely Moslem province. Nor has Atjeh seen much peace since, as there were insurrections in the early part of this century; during the war it was never wholly conquered by the Japanese; for a brief period after the Japanese left it again became independent, and in 1953 there was a major rebellion against the government of President Sukarno.

We flew to Medan on Thursday and on to Banda Atjeh on Sunday in a rather bumpy flight of *Garuda* airways. In Medan we stayed with the British Consul, and shall return to his house on Wednesday. Not many visitors come to this part of Indonesia. I do not think anyone from the Embassy has been here since confrontation. So we have been received royally and, the local hotel being very primitive, put up in this spacious residence with its high ceilings, its hard beds enclosed like cages behind mosquito wire, and its huge pillared hall where I now write, painted green and chrome yellow like a British Railways' waiting room of the Victorian era. This morning I called on the Governor and the Commander in Chief. Tomorrow we go to the local university. Despite its troubled history and its isolation, Atjeh is fairly prosperous. There are rice fields in the plains and coconut palms everywhere. Like the rest of Sumatra it is much less overcrowded than Java; in the southern part of the province there is oil. This afternoon we drove to the west coast where the Indian Ocean rolls over beautiful deserted sandy beaches and steep wooded hills come down to the shore.

In Medan I also called on the Governor (of the province of North Sumatra) and on military commanders; but on Saturday we were able to make an overnight trip to another very beautiful but more frequented area – to the shores of Lake Toba in central Sumatra where there is a hotel by the edge of the water. It is quite cool there. The surrounding hills are covered with pine forests and the scenery reminiscent of the highlands of Scotland. But in fact Lake Toba is the crater of a huge volcano now extinct and there is an island in the middle called Samosir as large as Aberdeenshire. We crossed over to it in a boat and saw some of the villages there peopled by the Bataks who like the Atchinese here, are notoriously rebellious, but while in Atjeh they are Moslems, the Bataks are militant Christians. On the road to Toba one passes many plantations of rubber and palm oil, some of which have been handed back to their foreign owners by the government of General Suharto. One of these is the British firm, Harrisons and Crossfield, whose plantations we shall be visiting on Friday.

The rain has stopped and I must go inside and have my mandi, a tank or bath lined with tiles in which water is stored. The Governor of Atjeh's mandi is as large as a horse trough. Then we shall sit in state for another meal of highly spiced food and go out later to take coffee with the local army commander, a descendant of the Sultans who was once Indonesian Military Attaché in Washington and knows all there is to be known about what is here euphemistically described as 'unofficial trade' across the Malacca strait and is usually called smuggling. If you look up Banda Atjeh on an old map it will be called Kutaraja.

With love from both Iain and Jeanne

c/o FCO etc. Friday 7 March 1969

Dear Dorothy and DM,

Very few letters from you in the last few weeks. Perhaps it is the dreadful English weather. I hope it has improved now. The newspapers are less concerned with the weather this week than with President Nixon's visit and the 'Soames' affair.[15]

This week we have met the Director of the Hong Kong and Shanghai bank, said goodbye to the representative of CIBA and the Swedish Ambassador, met the new Canadian Ambassadress, had drinks with the teaching expert from the British Council, given an Embassy Wives coffee party and attended a reception to celebrate the Circumcision of the son of a Princess of the house of Solo. Her brother is the present Sultan of Solo, a town in Central Java. The reception was held in a local cinema hall but although it has air conditioning it was not turned on and it was terribly hot. The young man who is about twelve years old was present as the actual operation had been done some time previously. Masses of people there, all the aristocracy of Central Java I was told, a gamelan orchestra and Javanese dancing. In between I have attended a three hour meeting of the

School Board of Administrators of which I am the secretary and have given the first English lesson at the university for the classes which the British Embassy wives have agreed to take for 12 weeks.

c/o FCO (Djakarta) etc. Sunday 23 March 1969

Dear Dorothy and David,

It seems to have been a long week. Even with Iain away in Singapore on the courier run I was still busy. I went on a visit to the house of an Indo/Greek family who have a large collection of paintings, nearly all Indonesian. One of the most famous (here) is Affandi who paints vast and very strong oil colours which you need to see 30 feet away at least and don't fit into many houses. He uses what one of my friends calls the worm-cast technique! They are certainly interesting and some I like. Another is Suparto who paints very pale, white or almost white pictures, usually of bodies, either human or animals. One young painter called Sudosono whom I was invited to visit, lives way off the main road in a *kampong* or village. You have to walk through a maze of crowded little houses made of plaited bamboo until you find his home. One is struck by the teeming life that goes on behind every street in Djakarta.

Iain brought back lots of cheese, apples and salami from Singapore and our new cook (now a good one) made us wonderful cheese omelette for supper, followed by salad, Brie and apples.

Love from us all, Jeanne

c/o FCO etc. 1 April 1969

Dear Dorothy,

We had a nice cool weekend over the Easter holiday, driving round the mountains near Bandung. We spent one night at a bungalow near the big French built dam at Djatiluhur.

We drove to Lembang, north of Bandung and near the volcano Tangkubanprau. Here we stayed two nights in an old rather tumbledown Dutch hotel. The girls much enjoyed going down into the bubbling sulphurous volcano, right into the crater. It has not erupted for some time.

We had a visit from a young couple on their way to Surabaya where he is to be American Consul. His wife is the English girl who was Information Officer in the Embassy in Saigon and who was trapped under a bed for a week during the Tet campaign. You may remember the story.

James seems to be having a happy time travelling around. He is now with my parents for the last 10 days of the holiday. Most of the teachers are reasonably pleased with his work this term.

Must go to bed now, love to you all, Jeanne

c/o The FCO etc. 15 May 1969

Dear Dorothy,

We are in the midst of a Parliamentary Visit, something which, I believe, usually disrupts embassies. Iain attended the dinner in their honour at the Parliament building last night, followed by a performance of Indonesian dancing which went on very late. Today they have all been whisked away to Bali, Jogjakarta and Bandung and will get back to Djakarta on Monday. There is Mr Cronin, son (we think) of the *Hatter's Castle* Cronin, Mr Dalyell, Member for West Lothian, and Mr Leo Abse of the Bills on Divorce and Homosexuality and brother of the poet – the Labour members. The Conservatives are Mr Montgomery, one other and Lord Ferrers, an agricultural peer. Lord Ferrers lost his laundry in the Hotel Indonesia but it was easily found as he was the only person in the hotel with starched collars.

Love from us all, Jeanne

Djakarta, 15 May 1969

Dear M & D,

Jeanne has written separately. She has not however mentioned one item of news – better not say anything until we are sure, she says – but I think that, with due reservations, emphasising that it is for the moment neither public nor certain, I should mention that we may be leaving Djakarta rather earlier than we expected.

I have heard that I may be returning to take up a job in London about the middle of October. Do **not** tell anyone except Anne. I expect to hear definitely within the next few days and have made contingency plans to serve notice at the beginning of June on our tenants at Cholmeley Park if the posting is confirmed.

As Jeanne has written I have been more than usually busy this week with a six man parliamentary delegation. Have you met Mr

Tam Dalyell who I see from *Who's Who* is a member of the Edinburgh Arts Club? I have not had much time for private conversation with them between their arrival late on Sunday and their departure on tour early this morning. Yesterday was taken up with a series of calls, some of which I attended, including one at the Presidential Palace on General Suharto. A dinner was given in the gaunt outer halls of the vast, unfinished building which ex-President Sukarno started, to house the peoples' delegates during the many years that he never held elections. There has only been one general election in Indonesian history. Most of the present members are nominated in accordance with various complicated procedures which ensure that the government can never be defeated.

Love from Iain

Djakarta, Tuesday 10 June 1969

Dear M & D,

I am sorry to hear of all your troubles reported in the letters received in yesterday's bag. I am sorry that we are not nearer but my appointment in London is now confirmed. I am due to start work in October. The job, which is one of some importance but for which I would not have thought of selecting myself, is to be Head of South East Asia Department, responsible that is for relations with India, Pakistan, Ceylon, Afghanistan etc. Soviet and Chinese affairs are of central importance in the external relations of these countries, but I cannot claim any recent first hand experience of the area. I had asked to return to London after Djakarta and had hoped to become head of a Political Department. I had expected that we should not leave here until early next year. I shall try to get away from Indonesia as soon as possible, but it is unlikely that I can do so until early September.

Love from us all, Iain

c/o FCO etc. 1 July 1969

Dear Dorothy,

We have seen off the Ambassador and Mrs Hainworth to Bali. This evening we are to attend a reception for Mrs Indira Ghandi, the Indian Prime Minister.

We have been doing PNEU exams all this week. Now our year's programme is finished and I hope not to have to do it again. It has been quite stimulating and at least you know what your children are learning. But it's very exhausting here with all the other duties. We had to do the work in the afternoon, after their morning school and lunch and a short rest and before their other afternoon activities and my evening programme.

Yesterday we attended the opening of a new Australian milk factory by the President. They are to make sweetened condensed milk from reconstituted milk powder and later pasteurised, long life milk, but not in our time I'm afraid. In the evening we attended Mass at the Catholic Cathedral, a reception given by the Papal Nuncio, followed by a reception given by the Russian Ambassador to say goodbye to himself.

Tomorrow we have a visit from Mr David Aiers, Head of the South West Pacific Department, which deals with Indonesia, Malaysia and Singapore, and a near neighbour of Iain's new South Asia department. Iain and he are going off in the Air Attaché's aeroplane on Sunday for him to see something of the rest of the country. We are planning a trip to Jogjakarta, Surabaya, Bali and back to Djakarta by road at the end of July with the children. But Mr Nixon has now decided to make a call in Djakarta on his way to the Pacific splashdown. So we may have to rearrange it all and to go ahead with Iain joining us in Jogjakarta for the Ramayana performance.

Love from us all, Jeanne

c/o FCO (Djakarta) etc. 15 July 1969

Dear Dorothy,

I rushed off early this morning to the old Djakarta Museum which is way downtown in the old Chinese quarter of the city. Only five members of the very select *Cultural Group*, whose members come exclusively from the NATO country embassies, and for which I am supposed to be the treasurer, turned up. Maybe the others realised that it was going to be very, very hot. The museum contains much old Dutch-style Indonesian furniture and interesting prints of old Djakarta. It is on the big square which used to be the centre of the city and if you half close your eyes you can just imagine Djakarta as it was when it was one of the finest capitals in South East Asia, before it became overrun with people and all the lovely gardens were built over and the fine old houses torn down. There are some old Dutch style buildings left and some fine Chinese ones too but it is all crowded up with little *kampong* houses. Perhaps in another ten or twenty years, if the present Governor, Ali Sadikhin, keeps going, it will be a fine city again.

It would be interesting to come back in 10–15 years time but at the moment we are thinking more of our departure. I have begun the difficult task of deciding what is to be kept and what to be thrown away, what to be sent in the heavy luggage and what is needed in the air freight. It seems incredible that we are to leave in 7 weeks time and we are hoping to go away on the last trip to Bali and East Java, staying at Jogjakarta on the way to see the Ramayana ballet in the full moon at one of the Hindu temples.

Poor James, whose student ticket does not allow him to stopover, will have to go directly back to London and spend some time with my parents. The rest of us are planning to make short stops on the way back at Bangkok, Kathmandu and New Delhi. Then I and the girls go home and Iain follows a week later via Bombay, Colombo and Rawalpindi, all these being his 'new territories' in the office.

Love from us all, Jeanne

18. Opening of the international airport in Bali, August 1969.

c/o FCO etc. 29 August 1969

Dear Dorothy,

I'm sorry there has been no time to write for so long. Our trip to East Java and Bali was a very busy one and we never seemed to have time even for postcards. In Bali we saw many temples luxuriantly decorated for their festivals, with Balinese dancers and processions of girls carrying fruit and flowers on their heads as offerings to the gods. We also saw local dancing in a village with the *barong* and other mythical creatures in the processions, dancers going into a trance and stabbing themselves with the *kris*, the local sword.

We came back again to a busy office, a heavy social programme and a large reception which we gave to say goodbye to ourselves. It has been very complicated sorting our various routes home.

We now have the packers and the house is in turmoil. But we are making a last minute visit to the Thousand Islands tomorrow with an Indonesian friend in her boat. They are supposed to be very beautiful and we have never been. They are mostly uninhabited and we sleep on the beach under the coconut trees (actually not quite under because it's too dangerous!).

The bag is closing and I must stop. Love from us all, Jeanne

19. Iain and James with curious Indonesians in Java.

* * *

The visit to one of the Thousand Islands is a good note on which to end. The island, with its bright blue water and golden sands, lagoons and coconut trees, epitomised the most beautiful side of life in Indonesia. One could forget the dust, the heat and the humidity, the poverty and the teeming millions of people. Both sides of life made up the fascinating experience which two years in the country had provided. I was quite sorry to leave; I had grown fond of the country, the people and their colourful culture. But it was time to move on once more and we needed to be at home to sort out the future education of our three children. We were indeed to have the longest period of home posting so far in our Foreign Office career, nearly four years in London.

We left behind an Indonesia in a much better state than on our arrival. The country was to continue to grow economically in the following years. The buildings of the British Embassy and the Hotel Indonesia, important landmarks in the centre of the town in our day, have long been eclipsed by bigger and better ones. The town has spread out far beyond what we knew on the road to Kebayaron. Small *kampong* huts no longer surround the Hotel Indonesia.

We left behind not only economic problems but also political ones of great significance and problem areas which were to be fought over for many years; notably the struggles for independence in the Portuguese colony of East Timor and the Northern Sumatran province of Atjeh.

As I began to write about our time in Indonesia the world was absorbed by the tragedy of the Tsunami-hit areas of Atjeh, in 2004, and the problems of administering aid to a divided people. After 30 years of struggle there was news of an agreement signed between the rebel leaders and the government. This surely must have helped in the restoration of the stricken area.

East Timor, the former Portuguese colony, was annexed by the Indonesians when the Portuguese withdrew in 1975. After 25 years of struggle for independence and the death of more than 200,000 Timorese, in 1999, a UN referendum on East Timorese independence was held in which the inhabitants voted unanimously for independence. A UN peacekeeping force was set up to control the animosity and aggression which continued between the Timorese and the Indonesians. On 20 May 2005, six years after independence from Indonesia was granted, the last peacekeepers were to leave East Timor.

7

ACADEME AND WATERGATE, HARVARD 1973–74

arvard was Iain's sabbatical, a break which he very much deserved after his four years as head of an extremely busy political department in the Foreign Office. South Asia Department (SAD) dealt with the affairs of India, Pakistan, Sri Lanka, Afghanistan and Bangladesh (after the partition of Pakistan in 1972). He was in charge during the many conflicts between India and Pakistan in the early 1970s and the eventual break up of Pakistan. Several times the emergency section was located in SAD after the 1971 India-Pakistan war had caused members of the department to spend evening after evening, and sometimes nights, in the office in order to cope with the volume of telegrams and paper involved. This did not prevent Iain having to get up hastily at three in the morning to meet Sheik Mujibur Rahman when he was freed by the Pakistanis in late 1971 and arrived unannounced in London from east Pakistan to become the first leader of Bangladesh.

Members of the Foreign Service at Iain's stage of seniority were offered a sabbatical at a variety of universities in the UK and abroad. Harvard was one of the best. It meant being appointed a fellow of the Center for International Affairs (known as the CFIA to distinguish it carefully from the CIA) at Harvard University. Duties were not arduous, the sabbatical being intended as a period for reading and reflection. It meant giving an occasional seminar, attending the seminars given by colleagues at the Centre, both local and foreign (there were usually about a dozen foreign fellows at the CFIA at one time, usually from the

Foreign Service of the country concerned or senior foreign correspondents or academics) and writing a paper on some relevant subject at the end of the year.

Iain was free (and I also) to audit classes being held in the university. Iain audited courses on politics and philosophy and also one on Russian literature. I also attended the Russian literature course plus a Russian language course and one on Latin American literature. The course was given by the senior professor of Latin American literature at Harvard, a fascinating and, dare I say, quixotic character who had been a left-wing journalist in Argentina and once spent most of his lecture explaining the problems of levitation.

Iain left in August of 1973 on the *France* by sea in order to take up his place at the CFIA at the beginning of term. I stayed behind to see the three children into their various boarding schools. The youngest, Liz, was starting prep school in Dorset for the first time and was strangely less worried by the prospect than the others had been.

It was an interesting and stimulating year. We had few of the diplomatic and social obligations normally attached to a foreign posting and were free to spend our time more or less as we wished.

For the first time, sadly, we had to leave all three children at boarding school in England. I missed them very much but they were able to come out for the Christmas and Easter vacations. After a few weeks I found myself very busy with the courses in which I had enrolled, especially the second year Russian language course which was known as a 'mind blower' by some of the students, all much younger than I, and which I found much more difficult than I expected after a twenty-year gap since leaving Moscow. Lectures often started at 9 a.m. in the morning and I would leave Iain still in bed while I rushed for the bus into the university, clutching my homework from the day before.

We rented a small house opposite Freshwater Pond on Huron Avenue, on the outskirts of Harvard, a short bus ride from the university and big enough to hold us and the three children during vacations. Boston, a big city centre, with its wider and more varied activities and all its cultural and shopping facilities, was easily accessible either by car or by the local subway. Iain had to return to England before I left as sadly his father died suddenly at the beginning of September and we finally left together for America.

* * *

The year in Harvard was to be remembered politically for the oil crisis, following the Yom Kippur War; the ongoing negotiations on nuclear disarmament and especially for the Watergate scandal terminating in Nixon's near impeachment for his role in the affair and finally his resignation in August 1974, the first ever by an American President.

Nixon became President in 1968, defeating Hubert Humphrey and finally winning a presidential race after being defeated by Kennedy in 1960. After his inauguration he announced the Nixon doctrine of reducing US military forces abroad. He gradually withdrew ground troops from Vietnam reducing the US forces from 550,000 to 24,000 in order to make peace. 'The New China Policy and the change in US military strategy made possible peace with Hanoi. On 27 January 1973, in Paris, Nixon's Secretary of State, William Rogers, and Le Duc Tho of North Vietnam signed "An Agreement on Ending the War and Restoring Peace in Vietnam".'[1] About 2 million American servicemen fought in Vietnam or operated offshore. The war lasted from 1954 when the first Americans began to serve there until the last 50 were evacuated in 1975. Nixon's achievements were the reverse of Johnson's, whose domestic policy was spoiled by foreign relations and the Vietnam War; Nixon's foreign policy and successes in China were spoiled by domestic problems – namely Watergate.[2]

Nixon's greatest achievement, in foreign policy, was probably 'the reopening of direct communication with the People's Republic of China after a 21-year estrangement. In February 1972 he paid a state visit to China. This rapprochement in East Asia gave Nixon a stronger position during his visit to Moscow in May, the first by a US President. At its conclusion the United States and the Soviet Union announced a major advance in nuclear arms limitation as well as a bilateral trade accord and plans for joint scientific and space ventures.'[3]

* * *

The Yom Kippur War started on October 6 1973, a few weeks after we arrived in Harvard. It began with a surprise attack on Israel by Egypt and Syria, aided by other Arab nations, anxious to regain some of the territory lost in the Six Day War of 1967. The story at that time was that the Arab countries had chosen the Day of Atonement (Yom Kippur) to launch the attack because they thought that Israel would be the least prepared on that day.[4] At first the Arab forces made significant advances into the Sinai and Golan Heights but the Israelis counter attacked and pushed them back. Eventually on October 24 a cease fire was organised by the United Nations, after Henry Kissinger had spent much time in 'shuttle' diplomacy acting as a peace broker between Egypt and Israel. There were many repercussions. Israeli morale was boosted by their successes, aided by the Americans. Egypt was pushed towards a more diplomatic approach to the situation and finally to the Camp David talks. The actions of the PLO became more violent.

As a result of the Yom Kippur War the OPEC countries raised the price of oil to $11.65 a barrel, a price which may not seem much to us today but which was an enormous increase on the pre-war price, a factor which contributed to inflationary recession and other economic problems for the Americans. It produced oil and petrol shortages in the many areas dependent on Middle East oil. Closures of petrol pumps and queues are referred to in the letters. This all exacerbated Nixon's existing difficulties over the exposure of the Watergate affair and his increasing unpopularity with the press. Watergate had in fact made it very difficult for him to conduct any business, let alone the crisis of the Yom Kippur War.

* * *

Nixon's second term as President – he was re-elected in 1972 by one of the largest landslide victories in American presidential history – was dominated by the Watergate scandal. The name *Watergate* comes from the hotel of that name where the notorious break-in into the Democratic Party's National Committee offices on 17 June 1972 took place, and has of course given the 'gate' suffix to any public or political scandal since then. The affair was made public by the two reporters, Bernstein and Woodward, from the *Washington Post* and the informant known only as *Deep Throat* until June 2005 when the 90-year-old Mark Felt, a former deputy director of the FBI, decided to divulge his identity. The investigations, denials and eventual admissions and resignations continued for the next two years and included resignations of several of the President's closest aides, including two former cabinet officers. 'Just as it began to appear, through lack of hard evidence, that Nixon might be able to survive Watergate, a White House official sensationally disclosed that all conversations between Nixon and his aides had been tape-recorded by the President.' After a long legal battle in which Nixon claimed executive privilege, he was ordered to turn over the White House tapes. 'Woods (Nixon's personal secretary) was given the job of transcribing the tapes relating to Watergate, along with the famous expletives which sounded more like conversations between mafia hoods than the top members of the US executive.' Woods was also accused of causing the famous gap in the tapes containing the first evidence of Nixon's knowledge of the Watergate scandal and cover-up.[5]

The country was in the middle of the scandals and intrigues of the Watergate affair when we arrived in Harvard. They were constant items on radio and TV news and were discussed interminably by our American and other friends both at the CFIA and elsewhere. Would Nixon have to give up the tapes revealing his knowledge of the break-in? Would he be impeached? Would he resign? How many more senior officials would resign? As the scandals were still unfolding during our time in Harvard it seems that we know more about the complete story now than we did then.

* * *

Holiday Inn, Cambridge Mass. 02138, 26 August 1973

Dear M & D & Anne,

This will, I hope, reach Plockton in time to greet you on arrival. As you see from this garish notepaper, on my third day in Cambridge I am still in a hotel and have not moved into the house looked out for us by Miss Cox, the Secretary of the International Center. Miss Sally Cox is incidentally the daughter of Professor Archibald Cox, the special investigator appointed for the Watergate affair, whose name is now known to all America.

I have introduced myself at the Center and I have explored Cambridge. Most people are away on vacation and the majority of the other foreign fellows at the Center have not yet arrived. Next weekend, if the question of the house is settled I shall go out of town to explore into New England, but inland and not towards Cape Cod and Wellfleet. On Wednesday I shall go into Boston and visit that 18th century house on Beacon Hill which Anne will remember is the residence of the British Consul.

Between the *France* and Cambridge I spent one night in New York. I lunched with Michael Weir who is still Head of Chancery at the British Mission. Alison, his wife, has not joined him and they are now acknowledged to be separated. I also saw the Marchants who were in Cuba. He attends a special annual commission of the UN and is off on a lecture tour to California.

Love from Iain

Harvard University Center for International Affairs,
Wednesday 5 September 1973

Dear M & D & Anne,

I moved into the house at Huron Avenue on the hottest day of the year. So here I am. It is a New England frame house about 2 miles from the centre of Cambridge with a small and at present very overgrown garden, three bedrooms upstairs and a strange large subterraneous room in the basement where the owner projected films and where James may sleep when he comes out, if I can contrive sufficient ventilation.

I have bought a second hand Falcon car which should be insured and delivered tomorrow. I have engaged a student to do some painting on Mr Conant, the house owner's, behalf. I have made the journey several times on foot to the 'Star' supermarket to buy provisions and stock up with cool drinks against the heat. On Sunday I went into the country to the large rambling house of Mr Charles Jackson, the father-in-law of our tenant at Cholmeley Park. He is a well-known Boston lawyer. His daughter, who left for Highgate with her two children the same day, intends to write a paper on British gynaecological customs (from the sociological angle). Her husband, Mr Reeve Parker, our tenant will spend his sabbatical on Wordsworth's poems.

With much love from Iain

The letters continue after the death of Iain's father, David, addressed only to his mother, now living alone in a big house just outside Aberdeen.

540 Huron Avenue, Cambridge, Mass.02138,
10 October 1973

Dear Dorothy,

Here we are pretty well installed and most things unpacked and all set to go. In fact I have been doing my Russian homework for tomorrow's lesson at 9 a.m. Not only are there lessons at 9 every morning but three mornings a week there are conversation classes at 8 a.m. as well.

Monday was a public holiday so we drove through some beautiful wooded country about 20 miles NW of Cambridge to look at the small town of Concord where the first shots of the American Revolution were fired in 1775. Iain is busy getting himself involved in a variety of lectures but he doesn't have to deliver any himself just yet.

213

It's really bedtime as I have to be up so early. I do hope you are not too cold and lonely. We think about you and hope you are all right.

Meanwhile lots of love, Jeanne

540 Huron Avenue, Cambridge, Mass.02138,
Sunday 14 October 1973

Dear M,

Jeanne and I were very glad to have your letter of 10 October – delivered to Huron Avenue just before we set out yesterday morning to explore the north shore – the coast beyond Boston, towards Cape Ann. We drove to Gloucester, a historic but now rather desolate seaport town and on to the more picturesque community of Rockport, in part reminiscent of Cornwall and well known as an artists' colony but now taken over by tourism and the homes of the well-to-do retired. The brilliant reds and yellows of the New England fall were still evident. The weather continues clear and sunny but turning colder at night.

We have had a busy week catching up on lost time. I have to prepare speaking notes for a series of seminars. We attended an inaugural dinner at Kirkland House which I have joined. The Center had an evening session with T.N. Kaul, the Indian Ambassador from Washington. We had letters from Alexandra and Elizabeth who went out last weekend with grandpa and granny Nutt.

Look after yourself and remember to get enough to eat. We hope to have news again soon. With much love from Iain and Jeanne.

540 Huron Avenue, Monday 22 October 1973

Dear M,

Today, Veteran's Day, is a holiday. No seminars or classes. A beautiful brisk, clear, sunny day with the brilliant autumn colours of the New England oaks and maples. We did not, however, go far as we had driven some ninety miles or so on Saturday to Amherst in western Massachusetts and on Thursday and Friday this week we go to Philadelphia. Today therefore is devoted to homework and reading.

The trip to Amherst was at the invitation of a Professor Vali of the University of Massachusetts who is writing a book about the Indian Ocean and whom I had entertained to lunch in London in May. He is Hungarian, a refugee of 1958. He and his wife, who is a potter, gave us lunch and showed us the vast campus of the State University, considerably larger than Harvard. The coming visit to Philadelphia is to attend a conference at the University of Pennsylvania to which I was invited, also as the result of contacts in London.

No news this week from James. Elizabeth writes very cheerfully from Knighton House. Everyone here talks of the latest Watergate developments. There are interminable debates on the political and legal aspects on our old (black and white) television set. The theme has overshadowed even the news from the Middle East. (I think I told you that Sally Cox, the secretary of our Center is a daughter of the dismissed chief prosecutor).[6] In general the television is of much lower standard than in Britain and, all but one channel, dominated by advertisements.

We have guests tomorrow to meet a friend, John Wright, of the Ministry of Oversees Development, who is visiting Cambridge. No room for large cocktail parties at Huron Avenue (nor the duty free drink or the dollars) but our dining room seats 10 and informal entertainment is not too difficult. We had the Palmers (friends from Belgrade days) and their daughter to supper on Thursday.

We hope that you are looking after yourself and keeping well and look forward to your news.

With love from Iain

* * *

A day after this letter was written Nixon finally agreed to release the tapes of conversations with his aides. A letter from Lord Cromer, British Ambassador, says that it was 'almost impossible to exaggerate the vilification to which Mr Nixon has been exposed'.[7]

540 Huron Avenue etc. Wednesday 7 November 1973

Dear Dorothy,

We had a splendid day on Saturday visiting the Jacksons, parents of the tenant in Cholmeley Park. They have a lovely house with a view over the Charles River near the town of Dover. The house is on the edge of the woods and we walked there before lunch. Mrs Jackson phoned last night to offer me her ticket for the Boston symphony matinee concert tomorrow afternoon, so I shall take myself off in state to hear Tchaikovsky's 6th Symphony.

I have made several visits to Boston now, by car and by underground and begin to know my way around. The underground is quicker and there is no parking problem. These New England towns are much more difficult to navigate than the ones with the grid system where the streets run at right angles, like New York and Philadelphia. However the countryside is very beautiful and the little towns are very cute. It's a bit surprising to find Worcester, Gloucester, Leominster all mixed up with Weymouth, Dorchester and Dover and even something like Atholl from the north, or Uxbridge.

The week after next is Thanksgiving and there are four days holiday so we are hoping to go on a visit to Washington and New York.

I'm glad you are managing moderately well on your own. Lots of love, Jeanne

Washington DC, 22 November 1973 Thursday

Dear M,

This is Thanksgiving, the day when the Pilgrim Fathers had their first holiday in Plymouth, Massachusetts. It is a holiday throughout the United States and everyone eats turkey and pumpkin pie. We may have this for lunch, but we are not now in Massachusetts, but in Washington, having flown up from Boston yesterday. We stay with John and Meg Graham whom we first knew in Yugoslavia and who have been here for the past year, he as Head of Chancery at the Embassy. We went with them last night to see a play in one of the three halls of the vast new Kennedy Memorial Center for the performing arts by the edge of the Potomac. It is next door to the now famous hotel and block of flats known as Watergate. The area was waste land and park when we were here ten years ago at the time of the assassination. We return via New York on Saturday, spending two nights en route at Michael Weir's.

The children come out from London on 15th December. Elizabeth, who is our most regular correspondent, seems to have settled down quite well at Knighton House.

Jeanne joins in sending love, hope you are well, Love Iain

Sunday 9 December 1973, 540 Huron Avenue

My dear M,

Today being Jeanne's birthday we have been out to dinner at a restaurant in Cambridge called the 'Legal Fish Market'. I do not know why it is so called or whether there is an illegal counterpart. Excellent oysters and fish but plastic plates, cutlery and glasses which are just swept off the table into mobile plastic refuse bags when one has eaten one's fill.

President Nixon has enjoined the populace to turn down their thermostats to 65° and drive at no more than 50 miles per hour; the price of heating oil has risen. But there is little or no visible change in the masses of cars which crowd the roads and petrol (unlike most other items) is still considerably cheaper than in Britain. We look forward to greeting the children at Boston airport next Sunday and wonder how they will fit into Huron Avenue.

Jeanne is still busy with her Russian and I with collecting material and notes. There is also, in addition to the regular courses which I follow, a succession of seminars at the International Center. We have, too, more of a social life than I had anticipated. To dinner near Lexington with my French colleague; a lunch which I gave for Miss Nancy Balfour from the *Economist*; a farewell party for my Malaysian colleague who is here for four months only and a visit to the Naval War College at Newport, Rhode Island.

Jeanne joins in sending her love, Iain

540 Huron Avenue, New Year's Eve 1973

Dear M

We had a family Christmas and on Boxing Day invited some of our fellow Fellows with children for drinks, together with some other people we have met here. Tonight, New Year's Eve, we all go to Concord, to the house of Captain Colvin, the US Naval Fellow, who has six children ranging from 9 to 19. Here there is no petrol on Sundays and some queues but no dire consequences from the fuel shortage yet. On Friday we were able to drive to Ipswich, north of Boston, where we ate fried clams in the car by the reed-beds. James did not come as he has found a part time job helping to re-arrange exhibits in the Harvard Natural History Museum.

With love from Iain, Jeanne, Alexandra and Elizabeth

540 Huron Avenue, Cambridge, Mass, 6 January 1974

Dear M,

The snow has at last come to lie but not very deeply. And although we have frost, the ponds are not bearing and we had to go today to skate on the Harvard University rink. The children go back next Monday, 14th. If there is more snow we may go for three days before they leave to the skiing resort of Woodstock in the hills of Vermont where the Jacksons (parents of our tenants in Highgate, with the large house in Dover) have a cabin.

Did you look in the newspaper on the 2nd where in the New Year's Honours list you would see 'I.J.M. Sutherland, lately Counsellor, Foreign and Commonwealth Office', under the Commanders of St. Michael and St. George?

Hope you are well, with love from us all, Iain

CFIA, 6 Divinity Avenue, Cambridge, Mass,
Saturday 2 February 1974

Dear M,

The snow is back, deep powdery snow falling all day and, although we have cleared a way, I am not sure that we can get the car out.

The month of January has disappeared very quickly. After our splendid four days at the Jacksons' schoolhouse amongst the snows of Vermont just before the children left for London, I went off to New

20. Skiing at Woodstock, Vermont with American friend, Mollie Jackson, January 1974.

York on the CFIA Foreign Fellows' annual visit to the United Nations. Fifteen of us chartered a bus for a crowded two day visit. We saw the Secretary General and a good number of senior officials at the UN Secretariat, and also one of the three speakers at the Tuesday afternoon session at the Council on Foreign Relations.

Last week we had a visitor in Robin Edmonds who conducted a seminar on Wednesday at the Center. His visit coincided with one by Lord (Solly) Zuckerman, an old friend of Robin's, who also gave a seminar at the Center. We entertained them at Huron Avenue with other members of the Harvard Faculty. The Center has also had a large group of visitors from Moscow for annual discussions on disarmament. Another much discussed subject was the progress of the disarmament talks taking place at this time, including SALT (the Strategic Arms Limitation Talks) 1 and SALT 2. Charming words such as *overkill* and MAD were bandied about.

New England is worse hit by the fuel crisis than elsewhere in the US and long queues for 'gas' at the pumps develop on Friday afternoons and Saturday mornings. So far we have had no trouble with heating oil for the old fashioned steam central heating system at Huron Avenue but the price has gone up. New England is more dependent than any other part of the US on imported oil.

Love from Jeanne and Iain

540 Huron Avenue, Cambridge Mass.02138,
Sunday 17 February 1974

Post card from Iain

Dear M,

This is the courtyard of Boston's most extraordinary museum which curiously we had not visited until this afternoon. It is the house, in the form of an Italian palace, built by the eccentric and rich Mrs Gardener at the beginning of this century where, with some advice from John Sargent and latterly Bernard Berenson, she amassed a collection of renaissance furniture and gothic carvings and classical sculpture and paintings by Botticelli, Rembrandt and Manet and many more, all, by her command, left as they were when she lived there. And she left funds for free concerts to be given in the Venetian room every Sunday and for the courtyard to be provided in perpetuity with potted plants in bloom. This is her winter display of azaleas and jasmine and orchids which was there today. There is a glass roof. Outside there is slushy snow in the Boston streets.

Love Iain

CFIA, Thursday 28 February 1974

Dear M,

Election Day. One of the local radio stations has been persuaded by the Consulate General in Boston (encouraged by me) to transmit the BBC overseas coverage of the results as they come in and we have one or two of the local British coming in this evening to listen, including Nancy Balfour, former American editor of the *Economist*, who is my opposite number as this year's British Fellow at the Institute of Politics.

Thank you for your last letter written from Edinburgh. I shall write a longer reply soon. But there is room to tell you now that the Foreign Office in London has now confirmed that my next posting will be as Minister at the Embassy in Moscow. There could still be a change of plan, but the present intention is that we would return home at the end of June and go out to Moscow in mid-September. The appointment is not confidential; but don't mention it to all and sundry. It would be a pity if for instance anything was published in the press.

Love Iain

540 Huron Avenue etc. Tuesday 2 April 1974

Dear Dorothy,

I have not written many letters since the children arrived. We have been entertaining Iain's American Navy colleague and family and the Russian émigré family. James has got back into his niche in the Zoology Department. On Monday he went by bus to the Marine Biology Centre at Woods Hole on the Cape.

Iain is trying to write his paper which is not easy with so many people around. Glad you managed finally to get all your pictures sorted out and hope you had a good time in Edinburgh.

Lots of love from us all, Jeanne

* * *

Iain's next letter is concerned with details and discussions about pictures for his father's memorial exhibition which was being organised by the Art College in Aberdeen in October. The final letter from Harvard is to Anne.

* * *

CFIA etc. Saturday 20 April 1974

My Dear sister,

Thank you for your Easter card and greetings. Belated wishes for your birthday. The children's Easter holiday has passed very quickly and they return on Monday 22nd. Jeanne has decided to take a 21 day excursion ticket and return with them.

What are your plans for the summer? We shall probably stay in London during July but might look for a house in Scotland in August. I am due to leave for my new post in mid September. We already have a psephologist professor from MIT as a prospective tenant for Cholmeley Park.

We go out this evening to eat at a restaurant called Grindel's Den. Although the weather has been fine, as both Jeanne and I have had lectures and James lectures plus his job at the Zoology Museum, we have not been exploring again since the day at Wellfleet. Tomorrow to pack and on Monday, as Jeanne and the children leave for London, I leave with my fellow Fellows on the annual CFIA visit for 8 days to Washington – five days seeing congressmen and US officials (including Dr Kissinger) and three staying with Johnny Graham of the Embassy.

Love from us all, Iain

* * *

The weeks after my return from England were taken up by helping Iain to finish the paper he was preparing for the CFIA which he never developed into a longer thesis as was intended. The final two weeks of our stay in the US were spent on what turned out to be a galloping 7–8000 mile tour of the country, from east coast to west and back again together with Iain's French colleague at the Center, his wife and daughter in their six-year-old Ranch Wagon. It was an attempt to see some of the rest of the country which none of us had visited before and which we thought we might never have time to see again. It was a fascinating tour and with five drivers we were able to travel long distances every day.

As Iain and I were going to Washington first we cheated a little, flew to Salt Lake City and joined the others there. We drove past the lake and went on to spend the night at Provo. There followed several days driving through Bryce Canyon State Park, to Marble Canyon and finally the Grand Canyon, on through Arizona and to our destination, San Francisco. We drove through Los Angeles but did not stop, although I insisted that we drove the length of Sunset Boulevard and as far as Beverly Hills. We spent one night within the sound of the sea in the Surf Apartments in Carpinteria and another at Monterey; from there along the Californian coast to San Francisco.

We had two days in San Francisco which was more generous than in many places where we spent only half days or a few hours when we would have liked to spend a week. Through the Redwood Forest, where we slept one night in a cabin on the edge of the wood, took us on to Portland Oregon, and here we stayed in luxury in the house of the President of the Portland State University, Gregory Wolfe and his wife Mary Ann, old friends of Washington days. Into Idaho en route for

21. Jeanne in Glacier National Park during the journey across the US, summer 1974.

Coeur d'Alene proved disappointing so we moved on for the night to Lake Pend Oreille, stopped briefly at the Moyie River Canyon to photograph the falls and continued to the Glacier National Park with its nature walks of pines, white cottonwood, poplar, hemlock cedar, birch, and some bears.

We passed through cliffs of snow as we climbed into Logan's Pass and then past the still green waters of St Mary Lake, and into the Blackfeet Indian Reservation; on then into Montana prairie lands, hundreds of miles of flat or rolling country divided into strip farming. As the sun set into brilliant red we continued through lush prairie to Glasgow and finally Wolf Point, famous for its stampede, where we spent the night. The prairie continued until well after Williston and into North Dakota, where the country became more intensively farmed; into Minnesota and even more *soigné* homesteads, more familiar scenery, normal horizons and no more of the 'big sky' of Montana. After Duluth, Minnesota's iron ore and grain port on Lake Superior, we crossed into Wisconsin and the countryside became even more familiar with high banks and hedgerows, alternating with forests and lakes. At the Michigan border we stopped to see the end of a horse show, with big fine horses and riders. After sleeping in the town of Newberry we drove to Sault Sainte Marie on the Canadian border, crossed into Canada and drove through Ontario and the next day to Ottawa. We drove out of Ottawa via the Ogdensburg Bridge over the St Lawrence River and back into the US, to a tidy and well-kept countryside. Our last stop was in Vermont at *The Haven* in the town of Fairhaven, where we had two charming rooms in the house of an elderly couple, with breakfast of home-made bread, eggs and bacon and strawberry jam with fruit picked the day before. And so we went back to Boston and home to England.

There can be few routes more calculated to provide such a contrast of climate and scenery, all in one country, or such a feeling of immensity. States such as California and Montana were especially attractive, and also Oregon, but each one had its own interest. And it gave us a glimpse of that vast area of America known vaguely as the midwest.

8

SANDWICHES FOR THE CHARGÉ, MOSCOW AGAIN 1974–76

So we went back to Moscow, after 20 years. In some ways it was very different and in some not much changed. Physically the city had grown enormously and extended a long way outside the *Sadovoe Koltso* (Garden Ring) with the thousands of new dwellings built in the 1960s to house the former occupants of the communal flats who had often lived a whole family to each room. The centre of town was much the same but in some areas large main roads had replaced the former tangle of small streets, and the area where we lived, in Ulitsa Vakhtangova, was a good example. Prospekt Kalinina, the wide carriageway, had been driven through the Arbat area of Moscow and the enormous Arbat Square had been created. But the area around the Kremlin, Red Square, along the Manezh and as far as the Bolshoi and the Petrovsky Boulevard was in the 1970s still very familiar ground.

Areas of great concrete blocks had been built on the outskirts of the town to provide families with the privacy of their own, if small, flats. They were ugly and in most cases badly and quickly constructed and soon began to deteriorate. They made the Stalinist buildings which we had disliked in the 1950s seem almost desirable by contrast. These new *microraiony* were so much alike that there were probably fictional stories about people going home drunk and waking up in the morning in the wrong flat.

Politically the situation was certainly more relaxed than in the 1950s and the Stalinist years. Life was still not easy and western diplomats were much restricted in their movements. We still depended on the UPDK

224

(the Diplomatic Corps Service Bureau), the successor to *Burobin*, for all arrangements for travel and visits to theatres or other institutions. I was allowed, largely due to the influence of the then head of the English Department, the colourful and powerful personality, Professor Olga Sergeevna Akhmanova, to help with lectures at the Philological Faculty of the Moscow State University. Because of this I was able to make restricted friendships and to see at least something of normal Soviet life. I used to visit the homes of some of the teachers, but not those who were members of the Communist Party. I could only see them at the university or on official occasions. This changed of course after the fall of the Soviet Union when I was able to stay in Moscow with Russian friends and they were able to come and visit me.

Olga Sergeevna, a senior member of the Communist Party herself, in the 1970s seemed to be able to make her own rules. She ruled her teachers with a rod of iron. Many of them feared her but relied on her for their position in the department. They had to teach the impeccable English that she had been taught by her governess in her childhood, although most of them had never been in an English speaking country. They, and I, all had to teach according to her text book, *The English We Speak*. They were allowed a certain freedom of association with me, and some other wives, for the sake of their English.

Family life for Russians was not easy but better than it had been. The horrors of the collectivisation of agriculture, the purges of the 1930s and the hardships of the war years, had faded somewhat. By the 1970s if you did not stick your neck out politically you were probably left in peace, as opposed to the Stalin era when you were likely to be arrested for merely failing to report someone else's omissions. By the 1970s the Soviet Union had been through two cultural thaws, in the 1950s after Stalin's death and again in the 1960s.

In spite of the easing of tension with the US and the introduction of the policy of *détente*, emphasis was very much on the defence and aerospace industries and very little money was put into other sectors of the economy. Consumer goods were still in short supply; few people had private cars; clothes were still dull and unimaginative except for the privileged few who had access to foreign supplies; good food was difficult to obtain; there were still very few restaurants; foreigners (as well as the privileged Russians) had access to the special shops where you could buy the best available Russian goods as well as imported goods.

Shopping without these privileges was a hit and miss affair; scarce and desirable goods, such as fresh fruit and vegetables, particularly during the winter, would suddenly appear for sale and long queues would form instantly. People would join them on the off-chance of getting something often without even knowing what was for sale, and they would buy up large quantities, usually more than they needed, so that supplies would not last for long. Women carried around the *avoska*, an on the-off-chance string bag, in case they happened upon an interesting queue. Shopping in Russian shops still involved queuing for everything three times, once to choose it, then to pay and finally to collect the goods. But in Soviet shops there was not much choice of things to buy.

Brezhnev was not a charismatic leader. 'Admirers and detractors alike have found less to say about Brezhnev the leader than about the era over which he presided. His rule by the lights of the Soviet past was oddly impersonal.'[1] He had come up through the ranks of the Communist Party to become Khrushchev's assistant as 2nd Secretary of the CPSU and his heir apparent. After helping to get rid of Khrushchev in 1964 he became 1st Secretary of the CPSU and then General Secretary, but he shared the leadership for some years with Kosygin, who was Chairman of the Council of Ministers (PM), and Podgorny who was Chairman of the Presidium (Head of State). This was the situation while we were in Moscow and from very much the side lines Kosygin always seemed to be the most human. He was in fact the only one I met in the 1970s and Brezhnev I saw only a few days before he died in 1982. Of his 18 years in power the last nine he spent with serious health problems.

Most commentators divide the Brezhnev era into two parts, the period before his first stroke in 1972, when he became ill, and afterwards. He had a second stroke in 1974 after which his health deteriorated seriously. Before 1972 was the 'good' time and after 1972 things became much worse. It was not an exciting period in Soviet history. It was Gorbachev who called the Brezhnev era 'an era of stagnation' and said that Brezhnev followed 'in essence a fierce neo-Stalinist line'. Others said 'Brezhnev preserved the USSR in aspic for a couple of decades' and 'Brezhnev's rule was a one party dictatorship with no concern for human rights and brutal treatment of dissidents'. It included the Soviet invasions of Czechoslovakia and Afghanistan and a time when East European countries continued to be denied their freedom.[2] It was a period of holding on to, or consolidation of, domination of the communist bloc; maintaining parity with the US in the nuclear arms struggle, (which the SU had roughly achieved by 1969); dealing with a considerable amount of dissent, either by allowing a certain percentage of dissidents to emigrate or silencing them in some way; for example some thousands of Jews were allowed to leave the country for the US or Israel, but Sakharov was eventually exiled to Gorky, Solzhenytsin deported to Germany. There were also the notorious psychiatric hospitals where dissidents were kept out of the way. Many writers, artists, musicians, educationalists and others who were producing work bordering on unacceptable at this time had to keep it 'in the bottom drawer' until better and freer times emerged, or else publish in the west. Some like Shostakovich led precarious lives often on the edge of state displeasure but just managing to get away with music which was not outwardly or obviously controversial.

Terence Garvey was the Ambassador. He and his wife, Rosemary, were good friends of ours from our time in Belgrade and later years when we were all in London. Terence wrote a book about his time in the Soviet Union in the 1970s, perhaps a sort of post-valedictory despatch called *The Bones of Contention*. He writes, 'The Soviet Union has a good and sufficient reason for wanting relaxation of tension with the west. In a nuclear world she can no longer afford to regard war with imperialism as inevitable. The Russians want the advantages of relaxation, but resist changing their ways to obtain them. So the path towards *détente* is strewn with "bones of contention", the arms race and the denial of human rights.'[3] *Détente* and relaxation of tension with the west did not mean that the situation was necessarily easier for the Soviet people, or that they should give up the struggle to establish communism in other countries. Witness the invasion of Czechoslovakia and the Soviet interference in many of the third world countries in Africa, the Middle East and Latin America.

The question of arms control was an extremely important issue during the Brezhnev era. The main aim of Soviet foreign policy was to avoid any direct confrontation with the US. This involved a major build up of military resources as well as negotiating arms control agreement, all part of the system of nuclear deterrence. Without trying to go into complicated details of superpower nuclear armament, in 1972 the ABM treaty on the limitation of anti-ballistic missiles was signed, and at the same time SALT I, the limitation of strategic arms treaty. SALT II was signed later in Vienna in 1979. However (sadly) 'détente and arms control produced "mutually assured destruction" (MAD) and nuclear deterrence rather than arms control, mutual build up and "over kill" rather than disarmament'.[4] MAD and 'over kill' were words which were bandied about during our stay in Harvard and which still described the situation while we were in Moscow, though strangely as I went about my life, teaching at the university, trying to get my Russian to the standard of the Foreign Office intermediate exam, and all the other occupations, I did not seem so aware of the threats of nuclear war; in fact less so than in Washington during the missile crisis.

On a more peaceful note the Helsinki Summit Conference on Security and Cooperation in Europe (CSCE) took place in August 1975 but the enterprise did not last and the follow-up conference in Belgrade in 1977 ended in deadlock. The next CSCE summit ratified the end of the cold war in 1990. Trade agreements were also signed between the SU and the US but never took off as hoped, and they did not succeed in improving the Soviet standard of living. *Détente* in Russia was gradually abandoned; even MAD was rejected and a more warlike strategy adopted after 1975 (leading up to the invasion of Afghanistan in 1979, with all its attendant troubles). Although the Soviet Union seemingly wanted to keep it they were never prepared to change their behaviour in line with the spirit of *détente*, and the United States was blamed for its military-industrial build up. Both sides possessed large enough quantities of 'weapons of mass destruction' for considerable 'over kill'.

Besides his concerns with nuclear build-up Brezhnev had to deal with increasing discontent at home. Conditions in the country had not improved sufficiently since the end of the war to fulfil the expectations of the population, who were becoming aware of the superior situation in the west and even in the East European countries where many people were now able to travel. This plus the many restrictions and lack of intellectual freedom which came about after Brezhnev's tightening up on Khrushchev's cultural and intellectual 'thaw' brought about the increasing amount of dissidence, more writers and artists who refused to adhere to the principles of 'socialist realism' and eventually to the *samizdat* form of distribution of forbidden literature. The British Embassy's policy was for its officials not to have contact with dissidents, unlike the Americans who were much more in touch with them. From my viewpoint it seemed that we went around rather ignoring the phenomenon.

* * *

Iain was Minister, that is number two in the Embassy, or Deputy Chief of Mission. He was again to be Chargé d'Affaires on several occasions and sandwiches were regularly taken in for his lunch by the driver, Anatoly.

There are some letters from Iain to his mother, a lot of them concerned with the memorial exhibition of his father's work which was being held in Aberdeen and Edinburgh. He did not have a lot of time for writing and I again became the family correspondent, writing to my own parents, Iain's mother and sister and the children.

Ulitsa Vakhtangova 9, Moskva, Saturday 21 September 1974

Dear M,

I missed the first bag from Moscow. This will be taken by someone from a British delegation which has been attending a conference of the Great Britain/USSR Association in Armenia. The Garveys gave a large party for them last night. Fitzroy Maclean will probably be my courier to London. Another member of the delegation (which has been discussing the oddly assorted topics of European security and environmental pollution) was Professor Wynne Edwards of Aberdeen, whom I found a most gracious and interesting person.

I have been staying at the residence with the Garveys for the first four days since I arrived on Tuesday. I move to our flat at Ulitsa Vakhtangova today. Luggage from Boston has arrived but not the crate from London. Jeanne comes out on 1 October.

With much love Iain

c/o FCO, King Charles Street, London SWIA 2AA
Wednesday October 9 1974

Dear Dorothy,

This morning I was unpacking air freight luggage, having my Russian lesson and preparing for our first diplomatic entertainment at home, to receive members of a lively miners' delegation and their Russian counterparts.

We are gradually settling down in the flat which is very pleasant (the only big disadvantage being that the bathroom is such a long way from the 2 main bedrooms). We are in a quiet street with a small garden, the envy of most other members of the Embassy. The old house is peeling on the outside and shakes every time the metro goes by but it will I'm sure last our time.

Since my arrival we have been to a modern Russian play on Saturday with the Garveys and also with them to a dacha in the birch woods outside town, to meet the Head of the English Faculty at the University, where I am to help with conversational English. We have a very nice cook, Valya, and maid, Tonya, whom I remember from 20 years ago. Tonya remembers Miss Nutt and

Miss Richardson when she worked for Lady Gascoigne. So we are among friends.

I still feel very much a 'new girl'. Things have changed enormously since 20 years ago. One can only recognise the centre of the town and odd corners which have remained the same.

Love from us both, Jeanne

Moscow, 15 October 1974

Dear M,

I am so glad that the opening of the exhibition was a success and the pictures looked well in the larger room. I look forward to seeing the catalogue.

We have been exceedingly busy; too many official lunches and functions; many visitors, some interesting, some less so; to meet a group of British historians last night and their Russian hosts. Jeanne has started teaching classes at the University – in the vast complex of buildings on the Lenin Hills just built on the edge of Moscow when we were here last, but now engulfed in the new suburbs of many-storied buildings. This evening she has gone to Leningrad for two days with a Mrs Guinness, a guest of the Garveys. I saw her off on the Red Arrow train an hour ago. The Garveys have gone off until the end of the week on an official expedition to Kazakhstan.

Love Iain

c/o The FCO etc. Friday 1/11/74

Dear Dorothy,

This afternoon our London luggage is to be delivered so we expect to have a busy weekend hanging pictures.

On Wednesday we gave a buffet supper for 35, including about 8 Russians, three with wives. This was to introduce the four visiting negotiators discussing sites for a new Embassy and also here for reciprocal discussions about the Russian Embassy in London. On Tuesday the Russians invited them and us to the opera and we saw the very grand performance of Mussorgsky's *Boris Godunov* at the Bolshoi. The theatre had not changed much in 20 years, still as splendid in its red and gold, though without the caviar and champagne in the interval. These are now luxuries here too, alas.

I am involved two mornings a week at the University; Monday afternoon I have Russian and plenty of homework at the weekend. I do the shopping once or twice a week at the special supermarket for foreigners. We also have the Embassy Commissariat which imports English and other goodies and sells duty-free drink and cigarettes. In fact we live a very comfortable life once one knows where to go for everything.

How to get there is another problem because of the extraordinary traffic regulations involving practically no left turns in main streets and with zealous militiamen in boxes waiting to stop you if you contravene the regulations. I am learning slowly. We have Anatoly, our driver, during the week and daytime. Weekends and evenings (except for large official parties) we drive the Rover ourselves very cautiously.

Love, Jeanne

Moscow, Saturday 9 November 1974

Dear M,

Our first day of snow, not heavy, but sufficient to lie on the grass of the Vakhtangova garden and to make our flat lighter than usual when we woke this morning. There is a high block of flats across the narrow street and high trees in our garden so it tends to be dark, particularly in our large hall, which is lit by daylight only through the kitchen. Before the house was divided it must have been open to the impressive stairway.

Thursday and Friday were holidays. Thursday, the 7th, the 57th Anniversary of the 'October' Revolution with the annual military parade in Red Square. I stood on the diplomatic stands in the rain by Lenin's tomb. The leadership were in their black coats and broad brimmed hats in line on top of the tomb, the recently repaired and painted red walls of the Kremlin behind. Formations of troops and tanks and huge missiles in the parade. Customarily this is followed by phalanxes of civilians with floats and banners bearing slogans and everybody had been lined up ready since early morning. But Mr Brezhnev decided, apparently on the spur of the moment, that it was too wet and, indicating to the slightly bewildered groups of Soviet notables below that the usual popular demonstrations were cancelled, and that he was off for a glass of vodka, came down from the tomb and we all dispersed early. To dinner at the residence, having great difficulty in finding a route for the car as many of the central streets were closed for the holiday. A very damp fireworks display this November 7.

Jeanne has gone off this afternoon with Rosemary Garvey to visit some shops and to assist the head of the English Department (where they both teach part-time) who is writing a dictionary.

Send love from Iain, and Jeanne, who has returned with Rosemary

c/o FCO etc. 28 November 1974

Dear Dorothy,

I am waiting for Iain to come back to collect me for the Yugoslav National Day celebration. He is taking in another party on the way which I have opted out of. It was an invitation from the Russians to a drink with the 150 members of the British Chamber of Commerce who are visiting Moscow this week. Last week our visitors were from archaeology and science, this week business. We have also had Mr and Mrs Campbell Anderson from the Confederation of British Industry in Moscow. This morning I went with her to visit a Russian school specialising in English. When they asked her which Russian authors she had read she said Solzhenitsyn, which didn't go down very well!

No word from James since he was in the san. Liz has taken her Common Entrance for Sherborne and Alex English and Maths 'O' levels.

Love from Jeanne

24 Vakhtangova, Moscow, 5 December 1974

My Dear M,

What is our news? We have had two economists staying at Vakhtangova for four nights – here for an international meeting; lunch on Wednesday for them and their Russian hosts. I have spent much of the week visiting various Soviet institutes; dinner on Thursday with the French Minister, tomorrow at the New Zealand Ambassador's. I have still not had time to go exploring outside Moscow. News of the children – Elizabeth writes that she has passed her Common Entrance exam and she is therefore accepted by Sherborne to start in Thurston House in January. E is a king in her school Christmas play; Alexandra in the school sanatorium with a cold where she had to take her 'O' level maths exam. James, in a rarer letter, says he is going to see a Professor of Archaeology at Cambridge about the Archaeology/ Anthropology degree. He comes out on 16th, the girls on 17th.

Love from Iain and Jeanne

c/o FCO etc. New Year's Eve 1974

My Dear Dorothy,

I have been a bad correspondent lately; no nice notes for Christmas Day/your birthday from me. We did however think of you a lot. Iain was in a sorry state all over Christmas with an inflamed tooth and abscess until I sent him to the doctor for some antibiotics and put him firmly to bed for 12 hours.

We gave a 9–13 year-old Christmas party on the Monday, had 5 English students and others for Christmas dinner and 40 to cold buffet on Boxing Day. In between we have made attempts at sightseeing, skiing and skating. But we have had horrid thaws and mud. I remember Moscow in the winter as crisp and bright.

We are seeing in the new year at the Garveys with Onora, Rosemary's daughter, who is here with the children from New York. The idea is to go to Red Square at midnight where the Russians congregate as we do in Trafalgar Square.

Love to you and Anne and a very happy New Year, Jeanne

c/o FCO etc. Friday 17 January 1975

Dear Dorothy,

It was a sad wrench to see the children go back. I was really dreading the goodbyes at the airport but as it happened there were many families seeing off their children so we kept each other cheerful. It was also good that Alex and Liz went together this time. I am hoping to hear from them in the bag today. I miss them all very much.

But we have an overfull programme of lunches, dinners etc. to prepare for and visits – Sir Norman Reid from the Tate at the weekend and next week; two medical visitors have just gone back (one occupied James' bed as he left!). All this is working up to a climax of the Prime Minister, Mr Wilson's visit next month.

Today Iain is entertaining the British Press in Moscow to lunch and I am escaping to a quiet lunch with Rosemary Garvey. The Moscow winter continues a pale imitation of 20 years ago. It keeps thawing, freezing and snowing in cycles unheard of at this time of year in the 1950s.

I have got a little Russian Fiat, Zhiguli it is called, to be independent, and am hoping it will be ready at lunch time today.

Lots of love, Jeanne

c/o The FCO etc. 7 February 1975

Dear Dorothy,

Iain is working madly now for the PM's visit. It's very interesting but I sometimes wonder if it is worth working like that. I am trying to work at Russian to take the next FO Intermediate exam in three weeks. (I don't get any money even if I pass.) I am interrupted continuously to organise a meal for 12, 18 or 30 or drinks for something else or rush out to dinners or lunches and such things as editing the 'Guide to Newcomers' or sitting on various sub-committees of the School Board.

We enjoyed the visit of Sir Norman Reid from the Tate and his two friends. It was an occasion to meet various very interesting Russians.

Love from us all, Jeanne

Moscow, 25 February 1975

Dear M,

It is eight days since the Prime Minister's visit, but the Embassy is still recovering from the invasion, and adjusting to the new phase in Anglo-Soviet relations.

We not only had Mr Wilson, but Mr Callaghan (Foreign Secretary) too, and Mrs W. and Mrs C. and almost forty more not counting the RAF Comet crew. We had the Secretary to the Cabinet, and the PM's doctor, and press officers and various private secretaries including Robert Armstrong, who has been in the same job since I went to Delhi with Mr Heath in 1970; from the Foreign Office, Sir John Killick, the former Ambassador, and amongst those you know, Michael Weir to advise on the Middle East and John Thomson who negotiated a separate declaration on the non-proliferation of nuclear weapons. John and Julian Bullard, the Head of the East European and Soviet Department in the Office stayed with us at Vakhtangova. The PM and Mr C. had villas on the Lenin Hills, state guest houses which are used whenever visiting Prime Ministers and Heads of State come to Moscow, as they do with some frequency. And since the visit, *Pravda* and *Izvestiya* and the local TV have been full of all the documents and protocols and joint statements signed during the visit; and the Embassy has been trying to analyse all this and see where it leaves us. The visit was given much greater significance and much greater publicity as the result of the reappearance of Mr Brezhnev after almost two months away from the public eye while people speculated about his health and his standing in the Politburo. The talks were held in the Great Halls of the Kremlin. The official lunch on the Friday, the day after the party's arrival, was held in the so-called Palace of Facets. The return lunch on Monday last was at the British Embassy, which has not held so many senior Russians since the advent of Soviet power.

Love from Iain

* * *

Terence writes in his book that Wilson in February 1975 managed to insert a phrase in the Anglo-Soviet statement of principle which read, 'peaceful co-existence which means fruitful and mutually beneficial cooperation of states with different social systems, on the basis of full equality and respect'.[5] But soon everything reverted to normal.

22. Lunch given by Brezhnev for Prime Minister Wilson in the Palace of Facets, Kremlin, February 1975. Brezhnev is speaking, Wilson next to him and Iain next to Wilson; opposite Brezhnev is the Ambassador, Terence Garvey.

FROM MOSCOW TO CUBA AND BEYOND

* * *

Moscow, Tuesday 8 April 1975

Dear M,

Your letter of the 28th arrived on Friday. We and the girls waited with bags packed in the car until the mail was opened, before setting out for a weekend at the diplomatic dachas at Zavidovo. This is a kind of motel cum fishing lodge for foreigners some 80 miles north of Moscow where the Volga is dammed to form a large reservoir. You can stay either in one of the cottages (dachas) or in the lodge itself. In the winter there are skiing and skating on the river, snowmobiles in the woods and a sauna in the evenings.

We, Jeanne and I, have just returned from a vast Iraqi national day party at the Arbat restaurant, round the corner from Vakhtangova. There is much advantage in living in the centre of Moscow. But now the snows have gone we must try to do something with the garden which we share with the Military Attaché downstairs.

Love Iain

c/o FCO etc. 27 May 1975

Dear Dorothy and Anne,

I write quickly during a lull in activities. Yesterday we saw off Mr Peter Shore and his party. Today we have no one to stay or for meals. Yesterday we were giving lunch to Sir Nicholas Pevsner, Professor of History of Art in London, but there was a big storm and his plane never got here in time. So we ate the lunch without him.

We got your PC last week saying you were leaving for Wales on the 10th and that you had sold your *Fruit on a Red Tray*. Our news is that James continues staying with my friends the Dibbs and is reported to be working hard. His exams are scattered throughout June. Alex's exams start on the 2nd. Liz is going to Gazeley for half-term to stay with my mother and father.

We are expecting more visitors tomorrow – this time from Covent Garden to consult on ballet exchanges. Next week the writer, Mr Geoffrey Moorhouse, will be our house guest. I have today managed to read some of his book about crossing the Sahara on a camel, *The Fearful Void*. Dr (Mrs) Shore is involved in administration of the health service in UK. I went with her to discuss the Russian health service at the Institute of Social Hygiene and Public Health. Then she went with others to see homes for the blind and the disabled.

The University term has ended and with it my English classes. So far we have been so busy I haven't noticed. Now time to stop –

Love to you both, Jeanne

c/o The FCO etc. 1 June 1975

Dear Dorothy,

Thank you for your letter. James seems to have settled down to work in London and we are hoping for the best. Of course I worry a lot about them all – James with his problems and Alex struggling with 'O' Levels; less about Liz, but I miss her cheerfulness. I may come back for the 28th when Alex finishes her exams and has a free weekend and when my friend who is looking after James will be away for a week. I have to take over the house anyway on July 11 and the girls break up on 12th.

c/o The FCO etc. 18 June 1975

Dear Anne and Dorothy,

I read about your 10 day heat wave but gather it is over now. Here it is very hot again but at least for official functions we ride around in the Rolls with flag flying and air conditioning blowing. For the Garveys went on leave on Monday and Iain is Chargé d'affaires.

I am going back at the beginning of July, too late for Alex's post exam outing but, I hope, in time for James' and to take over the house. I have been trying to arrange our holiday plans but it is hopeless when we are all so scattered and will have to wait until I come back. Iain is due to arrive 8–10 August. Perhaps September would be good for Scotland?

Lots of love to you both, Jeanne

* * *

There followed two–three months leave in England and Scotland, partly in our house in Highgate and partly moving around visiting members of the family. It was not a very peaceful leave. At one stage it seemed as though the Soviet authorities would not renew Iain's visa, for no reason, other than as part of the visa games which occurred on and off between them and us during this time. One side expelled someone and the other would take revenge. As it happened we went back without any problem but it caused much anxiety during our leave, as did the problems of finding James, now nearly 19, a new place to continue his studies. He eventually went to the Central London Polytechnic to do a degree in Biology and three years later came out with a 2A and a place to do a master's degree in Marine Biology at Southampton University.

* * *

Tuesday 14 October 1975

My dear M,

Many thanks for your letter. Jeanne arrived back on 3rd, having been down to Sherborne over the weekend to see Liz. She resumes her part-time classes at the University tomorrow after a wives' coffee party at the Embassy.

By mid week we had our first flurries of snow. But on Sunday we went to walk in woods near the Moskva River where Professor Olga Sergeevna Akhmanova, Head of the English Department, has a small wooden dacha in part of a traditional Russian peasant house. There are also dachas occupied by senior members of the Soviet government and party, but they are hidden away in the woods and surrounded by high fences.

We have a group of visitors attending a conference on Art and Industry to drinks this evening – Sir Paul Reilly, Head of the Design Centre, Sir Mischa Black and others – and then dinner with the Garveys and the Chinese Ambassador. Lots of visitors from Britain; a delegation of businessmen from the north east of England; Sir Fitzroy Maclean again. A man organising a Tolstoy exhibition. Next week the London Philharmonic Orchestra. The Garveys plan to go off on a trip to Central Asia, their last journey in the Soviet Union before they leave in early December.

Oh dear…I did not finish this last night and can now only add love from Iain as the bag closes.

c/o the FCO etc. 5 November 1975

Dear Dorothy,

So far a rather topsy-turvy week. We were expecting a visit from the new Permanent Under Secretary (replacing Tom Brimelow who is retiring) but he didn't arrive. He was held up in Teheran. So all the lunches, dinners and other functions arranged for him took place without him and we took 7 members of the Embassy to the ballet last night to see *Swan Lake* and gave them supper afterwards.

Most of today I have spent trying to arrange a trip to Odessa and the Crimea for Iain and me. I have to make all the arrangements or we would not get away. In the meantime I was given a very hard toffee by Rosemary Garvey and managed to break the middle tooth of my bridge. Very depressing. I've been to the Russian dentist who says she will make me a plastic tooth as a stop gap (literally).

All this week we have had an unexpected layer of snow. The streets were blocked with traffic as the authorities were not ready with grit and snow ploughs. So everyone slithered to a stop.

James is planning to come out on 19 December, possibly bringing a school friend with him.

Love from us both, Jeanne

23. Professor Olga Sergeevna Akhmanova, Head of the English Department at the Moscow State University, at her dacha at Ekaterinovka.

FROM MOSCOW TO CUBA AND BEYOND

c/o The FCO etc. 15 November 1975

Dear Dorothy,

I arrived back on the train this morning from Voronezh, a town in
the RSFSR about 600–700 kilometres south-east of Moscow. It is not
a very exciting place, a very Russian town where no tourists go but
with a university established in the 19th century where there are at
present 20 English students and many others from countries all over
the world who go there to learn Russian. We spent Thursday night
and Friday there and left on the night train yesterday. The Ambassador
is leaving for London today and will take this letter.

We had a very interesting week's trip. We flew to Odessa, a busy
sea port on the north shores of the Black Sea, and famous for such
things as the long wide stone steps going down to the sea from the
promenade, known formerly as the 'Richelieu' steps and now as the
Potemkin steps (where the mutineers from the battleship Potemkin
were mowed down by the Tsarist troops at the beginning of this
century). At the top is a statue of Richelieu, a former governor of the
town. We made courtesy calls on the Diplomatic Representative and
the Mayor. Odessa is twinned with Liverpool and we discussed the
future programme of exchanges between them. We also went to the
very splendid opera house built in the 19th century and saw a
Ukrainian comic opera. We didn't understand a word as it was sung
and spoken in Ukrainian. We stayed in the Hotel London, now the
Odessa Hotel, in an enormous room overlooking the sea with beds
in a curtained alcove and a red flag flying from our balcony which
had not been taken down since the November parade.

We couldn't go on to Simferopol in the Crimea by train as it
goes through territory forbidden to foreigners and we couldn't take
the steamer because it stops at Sebastopol which is also forbidden, so
we had to fly in one of the little local planes of Aeroflot. We arrived
in Simferopol at lunch time on Tuesday and drove the 80–90
kilometres to Yalta, the well-known Crimean resort. It is very
beautiful, with mountains going down to the sea. The whole
countryside is heavily wooded and the town nestles between parks
and gardens which varied in colour from the bright green of
cypresses and pines to the golden autumn colours of the poplars
and other deciduous trees. Yalta has been a resort since the Tsarist
times but more recently it has become the place where Soviet
citizens from the colder northern parts of the country are able to
go and spend their holidays. So the old palaces have been turned

into museums and new holiday homes have been built up the hillside and the great *sanatoria* (as they are called) for the coal miners' union rise from among the trees, together with many others. But the general atmosphere was very pleasant and old worldly and reminiscent of the stories of Chekhov, who lived there for sometime to cure his tuberculosis, and wrote many stories about the Crimea.

We also visited the town of Simferopol and were entertained by the Mayor and several of the town council members and taken to see a factory where they made leather goods. They were all very friendly and kind and gave us lots of presents, including a bouquet of 32 carnations which I have carefully carried back to Moscow as they are like gold here, literally worth a rouble each. In Yalta we went to see the Livada palace where the Yalta Conference was held in 1945, with Churchill, Roosevelt and Stalin. And so on by air to Voronezh where we spent most of our time with the British students, visiting the University where they live and study.

Love from us both, Jeanne

27 November 1975, Moscow

Dear M,

This post card shows the hotel in which we stayed for two nights in Yalta, during the Crimean part of our visit to the south earlier this month. But the sky was not so blue and a high wind blew in across the Black Sea, whipping up considerable waves along the Yalta promenade. We saw the former Czar's palace at Livadia and the curious early 19th century palace of the Vorontsovs at Alupka built by an English architect in the style of an English castle. With a day of appointments in Simferopol we had not much time for sight seeing.

This week snow has come to Moscow, the first heavy fall this winter. The Garveys leave on the 6th December and this means a heavy round of farewell calls and functions. We shall be very sorry to see them go. On the 8th we have Sir Norman and Lady Reid (from the Tate) to stay for some nights at the time of the opening of the Turner Exhibition in Moscow. The girls arrive on the 16th, James on the 19th.

With love from us both, Iain

c/o The FCO etc Thursday 4 December 1975

Dear Dorothy,

In between bags, too late for Wednesday and ready for an early closing Friday, tomorrow being the Day of the Constitution and a public holiday. I write quickly before going to represent the Embassy at the Thai National Day. Iain and the Ambassador are going to make a farewell call on the President of the Soviet Union, Podgorny, and will not be there. Then there is a cocktail at the residence for the Ambassador to say goodbye to all the staff. The Garveys leave on Saturday which will be very sad for us but we won't have much time to think about it as we have visitors arriving immediately afterwards.

The following week all the children arrive and then it's Christmas. We are giving all the Embassy Christmas parties (four) and two are for over 150 people. Fortunately I have a lot of help but it entails much organising.

No more time but love from us both, Jeanne

24. Iain opening the Turner Exhibition at the Pushkin Museum in Moscow, December 1975.

c/o the FCO etc 29 December 1975

Dear Anne,

I'm sorry I didn't get round to writing before Christmas. Things were rather hectic. I thought I was going to get tolerably well through the four weeks of Garvey departure, Turner opening, attendant guests and entertainment; the children's arrival and Christmas week, and probably would have done if I hadn't missed one whole night's sleep when the children arrived at 5 a.m. in the morning and then coming down with a terrible cold which they brought with them, on Christmas Eve. So things got a bit dazed by the time we got to the Christmas Day meal for 14 and the Boxing Day Buffet for 150. It was bad luck that Alex and Liz were delayed in what turned out to be atrocious conditions at Heathrow. But they arrived safely and James was only half an hour late on the Friday.

A very happy New Year to you both, Jeanne

c/o the FCO etc. 7 January 1976

Dear Dorothy

I raise my head from the Christmas and New Year festivities and before greeting the new Ambassador on Friday, to catch today's bag. We have had a very happy family time together and I shall hate saying goodbye to them all on Sunday. James's friend Paul's visit has been a great success and four is obviously a better number than three in a family.

This week is very cold, bright and dry like the Moscow I remember with a temperature of -20 C. James seems more relaxed. The beard suits him. Iain has not said a word. Paul has one too and when I took them to the Tolstoy museum the cloakroom lady asked me if they were poets. 'Only young men who are poets', she said, 'have beards in the Soviet Union'. Alex is much happier and more cooperative now she is at Bedales and Liz is her usual cheerful self. So – I wish they could stay.

They have all been busy too – going to German, American, Irish and Norwegian parties, the theatre and the opera, and skiing once with the daughter of one of my Russian colleagues at the university. Alex helped to entertain a delegation of boys from Bradford Grammar School and Liz took some younger children to represent the Embassy at the Kremlin New Year Party.

Lots of love from us all, Jeanne

c/o the FCO etc. 16 March 1976

Dear Dorothy,

We left on Thursday evening for a marathon train journey from Moscow to Riga (Latvia) and Tallinn (Estonia) and back to Moscow, spending three nights in a train and one in a hotel. We are not allowed to visit the Baltic Republics officially because we do not recognise them as being part of the Soviet Union. But we were allowed to go on an unofficial visit, making only calls on cultural institutions and not government or party ones. Riga and Tallinn are two old, once walled cities dating back from the 12th and 13th centuries. Riga has very few old buildings left but Tallinn has many in varying stages of decay or restoration and a fairly large section of the town walls left. It was all strikingly different from Moscow in style of architecture, the features of the people and language. Very little Russian is spoken and particularly in Estonia, they do not like to speak Russian but prefer German or English. With usual 'Iain' thoroughness we walked for many hours visiting the sights. The weather was mostly bright with occasional snow flurries, but not much below zero most of the time. Fortunately, unlike Moscow, there were the occasional coffee shops where we could stop for a hot drink and something to eat.

Now we look forward a week on Friday to the girls' coming out. James does not come this time as he has only two weeks holiday.

Much love from us both, Jeanne

c/o the FCO etc. 15, April 1976

Dear Dorothy,

Not much time this week for letter writing as the girls have been here, I have had my teaching and the maid has been off sick with a bad attack of flu.

Tonight we are going on the night train to Leningrad with the girls, staying two nights and coming back on Sunday night. Let's hope the weather stays as it has been for the last few days. Spring arrived suddenly and the pile of dirty snow in the garden is rapidly melting and little shoots are appearing. We have been to a skating show, demonstration of the world champion skiers; also to a Russian folk-dance programme, the circus, an organ recital by James Dalton and a ballet at the Bolshoi. Alex has quite a lot of work and Liz has been cooking and sewing a bit. We have also entertained all the Embassy teenagers.

A happy Easter holiday and much love from us all, Jeanne

British Embassy, Moscow, 30 June 1976

Dear M and Anne,

I am sorry we have not written more frequently in the last few weeks. Did you get a postcard from Tbilisi, Georgia? Jeanne and I returned from our Caucasian journey on Saturday. We went on from Tbilisi to spend three days in Baku, the oil capital of the Republic of Azerbaijan and third largest city of the Soviet Union. On Sunday last we had fresh sturgeon shashlik for lunch and were bathing in the Caspian, on the northern sandy shore of the Apsheron peninsular, if you want to pinpoint the area on the atlas. In fact due to a shortage of roads along the seashore and Jeanne's insistence that we wanted to go down to the sea, we were driven by a mad Azerbaijani driver across the sands in a Russian Volga car, and when there were obstacles such as breakwaters he simply drove into the sea and round them – 'a Volga in the Caspian'! The driver and the young third secretary from the Azerbaijani Ministry of Foreign Affairs seemed very happy to indulge our wish to do something less informal for the Sunday afternoon. Hence the visit to the beach fish café and the swim, not so easy to achieve usually on official visits.

We returned to Moscow to hear that what I had indicated in the postcard sent just before our departure for the south had been confirmed – that I have been appointed to a job in the Office in London – Assistant Secretary concerned with European affairs (not a promotion but a post of great interest) and that they wish me to start very soon there. The date is still the subject of exchanges with London. I was at first asked to be at my new desk on August 2. But I cannot leave here before August 16 and I have insisted that I want some leave after that rather than later in the year. This is quite unexpected. Less than 3 weeks ago I had been assured that we should be returning to Moscow after leave and, on the basis of what I had been told earlier in the year that my next post would almost certainly be abroad. We are pleased to be coming back to London. But the timing and the lack of notice create many problems.

We have decided that Jeanne should leave as originally planned to take over Cholmeley Park from the Flathmans, our tenants, and to see the girls out of school. So she leaves Moscow for good on Saturday

July 10. The Flathmans leave for America the following day. She will stay the night of the 10th at Elaine's (with Elizabeth). Elaine is now staying with us in Moscow and leaves for London with her package tour this Saturday the 3rd July. We also met up with her for a Georgian supper in Tbilisi last Tuesday evening, with her friend Olive and Mr Rukhadze, the official who accompanied us during our stay, and his wife.

My plans after August 16 are at the moment in the air. I must wait to hear whether the office accepts that I can take leave immediately after my return.

Glad to hear that the garden is flourishing. So was ours at Vakhtangova, but it is now full of *pukh* (fluff) from the poplar trees.

Love Iain

9

DEMOCRACY IN ATHENS 1978–82

This was the significant posting, the first for Iain as ambassador. It came after two years as Assistant under Secretary for European Affairs in the office in London, a prestigious post which he had enjoyed, although in some ways he missed the back up of Embassy life. Only a year after our return from Moscow he was offered the Embassy in Belgrade but it seemed much too soon to move again. At that time Greece turned out to be the more interesting post.

Our only experience of postings in Europe was the two in Moscow and one in Belgrade. It was a strange but pleasant sensation to find ourselves en poste in a European country where we were free to move around as we liked, to be treated as friends (in fact often to be overwhelmed by Greek hospitality) and not to be under any kind of suspicion or political supervision. Iain of course was very happy to be given his own embassy as a major promotion in his career. The job of head of mission is a responsible and demanding one, work wise, and the ambassador is rarely completely free as long as he is in the country of his posting. He is constantly in public view and it is not easy to get used to the loss of independence and the *goldfish bowl* atmosphere. For the ambassador the social activities are largely an extension of the work of the Embassy and often an easier way of making necessary contacts. It was often difficult to get time to ourselves.

For me too life was to be more restricted as the wife of an ambassador. There was little chance of working but I spent the first year taking the Royal Society of Arts course on teaching English as a foreign language (TEFL) at the British Council, and afterwards teaching once a week at a home for girls with learning and behavioural problems.

We arrived at a time when Greece was about to be accepted for membership of the European Economic Community (EEC), when she was, so to speak, to return to being part of Europe. As Richard Clogg puts it, entry into the EEC 'symbolises the healing of a breach with western Europe that began with the Great Schism in the eleventh century'. This was taking place after 'Four hundred years, and more, of Ottoman rule and the legacy of Orthodox Christianity had contributed to the formation of distinctive values and attitudes and these in turn had helped to shape the country's political attitude'.[1] It was an exciting moment for Greece as it was for us, facing a new and different experience.

After years of fighting for independence and stability in the 19th century, two world wars followed by a civil war in the first half of the 20th, more struggles and a military dictatorship in the 1960s and 1970s, Greece was at last beginning to find some stability and democracy. The Prime Minister, Constantine Karamanlis had emerged, like a *'deus ex machina* as the Colonels' dictatorship disintegrated under the burden of its own incompetence in July 1974, as the one politician capable not only of returning the military to the barracks but of ensuring that it stayed there'.[2] He had still many problems; Greece's difficulties with Turkey over Cyprus and the Aegean,[3] the question of Greece's relationship with NATO and the hostility in the country to the presence of the American bases were among the most outstanding.

Karamanlis was to lead a Greece more united than for centuries and he and his supporters felt that entry into the EEC would help to support the republic's 'newly established democratic institutions'; as well as helping to improve the economy of the nation. When signing the Treaty of Accession in May 1979 he said 'As of today Greece irrevocably accepts this historic challenge and her European destiny while conserving her identity.'[4] The 1974 referendum on the monarchy had found in favour of a republic by 69% to 31% and in 1975 the new Constitution was formed giving great powers to the then President, Constantine Tsatsos, although he never had to use them. As part of the democratisation of the country the Greek Communist Party, the KKE, was legalised. Karamanlis' new right-wing party, Nea Demokratia (New Democracy) was formed. In the 1974 elections they won 54% of the vote and 219 seats in parliament. The Panhellenic Socialist

Movement (PASOK) led by Andreas Papandreou, received nearly 14% of the votes. His party expressed strong anti-American, anti-Turkish and anti-western sentiments. Before he came to power in 1981 Papandreou threatened that if he won the election he would take Greece out of both the EEC and NATO. His position after he won became gradually more moderate.

In Athens there did not seem to be much acceptance of these democratic changes among the, largely right-wing, company whom we met in the first months. Many people, especially wives, expressed amazement at the thought that we had actually lived for some time in the Soviet Union in recent years and had survived unscathed. Our Social Secretary who had been with the Embassy for many years was horrified when asked to send invitations to the Queen's Birthday Party (the annual British national day celebration) to the leaders of the Socialist and Communist parties in Greece and I often wondered whether she actually sent them. However, PASOK was to be successful in the parliamentary elections in 1981 and the succession took place smoothly and peacefully.

* * *

There are not many letters home from Athens. My mother-in-law died in 1980 soon after a visit to us in Athens when sadly, she was already ill. I rely mostly on a diary for events of the years in Greece and the continued story of the family, now all either at university or final years of school and only with us in Athens in the holidays, coming and going alone, with each other or with many of their friends. Greece being a very popular place for holidays, in the summer months particularly, we were rarely without visits from friends or family, and/or official visitors – ministers, senior military officers, official business contacts, artists, musicians, minor and sometimes even senior members of the royal family. The residence, bought in the 1930s from the widow of the former Prime Minister, Eleftheros Venizelos, is large with many guest rooms, big areas downstairs for entertaining and a large garden. They were all being used fairly constantly. I was soon to realise that besides a home I was virtually running a hotel and restaurant. And I inherited a large staff, of which some were English, some Greek and some Asian, and several of whom had worked in the Embassy for 20 or more years and were so entrenched in their ways it was difficult to get them to do anything differently. My diary begins with our departure which was neither smooth nor peaceful.

* * *

Thursday 11 May 1978

Due to bad traffic we were late reaching the airport and we arrived panting and breathless on the aircraft. An early lunch (Greek time being 2 hours ahead of UK) made up for missed breakfast. Also there was time to read about the Greek cabinet reshuffle, announced that very day. The new Foreign Minister was Rallis and Mitsotakis the Minister of Coordination.

We were met by cameramen and television crews; Iain had to make a speech. We rode back in the dark green Rolls to a tour of the residence with Mr Reg Boyes (not to be confused with Reg Voyce, the chauffeur; they were known as Boyes the butler and Voyce the vehicle). After a short rest we were taken by the Everards and Oliver (senior political officer and number two at the Embassy) and Julia Miles to eat in a typically Greek taverna.

Friday 19 May

We were thrown immediately into the deep end, the commemoration ceremonies of the 1941 battle of Crete, a defeat for the Allied forces although the Germans also suffered enormous losses. It involved two days of non-stop ceremonies, marching into gatherings on hillsides, in churches or military cemeteries, music playing and flags waving, and then together with other guests of honour leading everyone out again, national anthems playing. The first day there was a religious and civil ceremony up in the hills to honour the dead of the military academy and then a parachute jump display on the airfield so hotly contested during the war and finally captured by the Germans who were then able to force the Allied troops off the island; in the afternoon more ceremonies, one at the Souda Bay War Graves Cemetery, the most attractive and serene of them all. Dinner was at the Officers' Club with Mitsotakis and Venizelos (grandson of the former Prime Minister) and other celebrities.

Sunday 21 May

It began with a Te Deum in the Hania Cathedral and then up into a mountain village for another service at the local War Memorial, this time together with the Australian and New Zealand veterans, including a Maori who had led a bayonet charge in the area during the war. After the German victory the veterans had been hidden by the villagers until they could reach the south coast where many were rescued by the British Navy. Some had not seen their rescuers for 38 years but ever since had helped the villages with money for children's playgrounds and schools. The evening was taken up by a long and protracted 'classical pop' concert given by the Greek composer Marcopolos and his orchestra which lasted from 9 until nearly midnight – a heavy session of excruciatingly loud music on an icy windswept football stadium sitting on hard and back breaking chairs.

Monday 22 May

This was the most eventful day; the day the party was to walk the Samaria Gorge, a 16 kilometre downhill hike from the mountain plateau town of Omalos to the sea. Armed with local walking sticks and with the men, defence and naval attachés, carrying heavy packs of supplies we set off. Iain came only as far as the mountain as he had been summoned to see Mr Karamanlis early on Tuesday morning and had to return to Athens. The walk was hard and the going sometimes rough. The scenery varied from steep cliffs enclosing a narrow defile to a wide valley with rocks and stones and a full, winding but fast flowing river which we had to wade through several times up to our knees in icy cold water. It was surprising to come out into near civilisation in Aghia Roumeli at the entrance to the gorge and meet some of our fellow walkers all waiting for the next ferry to take us back to Hora Sphakion. There was the arrogant young German in smart climbing boots springing from rock to rock, the tired French girl telling her boyfriend, 'Je ne peux plus marcher pieds nus'. She was still with him.

3 June

Our first official visitor was Gerald Kaufman, the Minister of State for Industry. He had expressed a wish to visit Olympia so Iain and I, the Minister and his private secretary left in the Rolls and the Humber. Olympia was the home of the main sanctuary of Zeus in Greece and also of the original Olympic games. It is situated in beautiful countryside between the rivers Alphaios and Kladeos, in a remote corner of Greece in the western Peloponnese. The site was associated with the cult of Pelops, the mysterious hero who gave his name to the area. The highlights are the temple of Zeus, the Stadium and the Museum. Most of the statuary had been taken there for repairs including Pelops, with the piece missing from his shoulder, eaten by the absent minded Demeter, when he was served up at a feast.[5]

25. Iain in ambassadorial uniform at an investiture in the British Embassy, Athens.

***

British Embassy Athens Thursday 31 August 1978

Dear Dorothy,

Thank you for your letter. I'm glad to hear you are back safely in Cults and managing to get your exhibits organised.

We have had our usual flow of visitors. James arrived last week with his friend Rupert. Liz's friend, Tim, has been with us since Saturday and I shall give this letter to him to post in the UK. He nearly set fire to the house in Saronis on Saturday night by dropping his jeans on to a mosquito coil on the floor. Fortunately James was in the same room, smelt smoke and threw the jeans out of the window, where they burst into flames.

With Liz and her friend Marian, Alex and I drove to Delphi last week. The archaeological site, which is high up in the foothills of Mt. Parnassus, is packed with tourists in summer so we started early in the morning before all the coaches arrived. On the way we saw the monastery of Ossias Lukas with its gold mosaics and frescoes. This weekend official visitors keep us in Athens until Saturday when we hope to have the rest of the weekend in Saronis.

Keep well, love from us all, Jeanne

c/o The FCO (Athens), London SW1A 2AH,
Monday 2 October 1978

Dear Dorothy,

I'm sorry not to have written for some time. I have been distracted by the comings and goings. Liz went back two weeks ago, in fact nearly three and so far there has been no word. James went last Monday and Alex leaves tonight. So finally we are on our own, but only for one morning as Anne and Elaine arrive on Tuesday afternoon. We had a second visitation from the Menuhins at the weekend; I say visitation rather than a visit as she is very imperious. He is mild and gentle and seems to do what she says. In fact she runs his life in the most spectacular way, but always the way he wants it. He likes living in Highgate so they continue to live there but she complains all the time.

Love from us all, Jeanne

Thursday 19 October

Our next official representative occasion outside Athens was the 151st celebration of the battle of Navarino. When I made the mistake of saying to Sir Steven Runciman, the eminent Byzantinologist and historian, that I thought it was something like the celebration of Orange Day, he said rather scathingly that that was 'an amoral and unhistorical attitude'. However, it is celebrated more as a symbol of Greek independence than as the defeat of the Turkish Navy.

The road ran through Argos, Tripolis, and Megalopolis; then down nearly to Kalamata and across to Pilos, through lush green countryside to the Bay of Navarino, where 4 Greek warships were at anchor for the occasion. An afternoon's boat trip took us to visit the memorials of French and Russian sailors on Sphacteria and the English on the small island in the centre of the harbour. Simple and thankfully short ceremonies took place at all three.

The next day started with a Te Deum in a cool church on the hill inside the walls of the castle. At the lunch afterwards Iain made a short speech in which he cleverly suggested that the occasion should also be a commemoration for the defeated, and one of international cooperation.

The following day we set off for the Mani to lunch with Joan and Paddy Leigh Fermor. The house is beautiful and the situation quite extraordinary. Behind are the sharp crags of the Taigetus and below the house the sea laps at the rocks and shines in the sunlight. Steps give access to a minute beach protected by rocks on either side so that, as Mrs L.F. said, no one can reach it except by the house or from the sea. 'Not a house in sight, nothing but two rocky headlands, an island a quarter of a mile out to sea with a ruined chapel, and a vast expanse of glittering water, over which you see the sun setting till its last gasp, Homer's Greece in fact.'[6]

After lunch we followed an unknown road around the upper Mani along the coast on the edge of the Taigetus until we reached Mistra in darkness and rain. There is not really a modern town of Mistra, only a collection of houses lying at the base of the hill. Old Mistra, built between the 13th and 15th centuries climbs up the hill in stages – urban dwelling houses, then monasteries and churches, to palaces of awesome size and shape and finally to the Frankish castle at the top. It took us over 4 hours to reach the top, come down again and to make our last visit, to the Peribleptos Church with the cleanest and finest frescoes of all.

Tuesday 24 October

Yet another conference under the auspices of the Council of Europe, this time on Culture. We have the Minister for the Arts, Lord Donaldson, who arrived last night, staying with us. I sat next to Mr Averoff (Minister of Defence) at dinner given by President and Mrs Tsatsos. We discussed détente and SALT and Greece's entry into the EEC. But he was most interesting about his own experiences and the books he had written and was writing. He had written a play about the Trojan War, including Nestor whose palace we visited at Pilos.

Sunday 29 October

A great reunion with Jim and Barbara Barker; he is the new Canadian Ambassador in Athens whom we had not met since Moscow 25 years ago.

All the talk among diplomats this week in Athens was of Paulo Barbosa, the handsome young Portuguese 1st Secretary who mysteriously went missing during a fishing trip in his boat. There has been no sign of him or his two companions, and aircraft from the Greek Navy, the American Base and the helicopter from the Ark Royal were searching for them. Suddenly we heard that Paulo was found on Anti-Kythera, in between Kythera and Crete. The boat had drifted for four days, during which time they were without food and water, obviously vastly unprepared for sudden bad weather. Finally they abandoned the boat and swam for shore. Barbosa made it but his friends perished.

Thursday 14 December

The Christmas season is now in full swing. Today was Mrs Tsatsos' end of year party which included ambassadresses, wives of ministers, under secretaries' wives, you name it. I said goodbye and wished her a happy Christmas and wondered how she must be feeling about the recent scandal over the extracts from her husband's love letters appearing in the Daily Telegraph. There have even been suggestions that he would have to resign, possibly in favour of Karamanlis.

Wednesday 20 December

It is lovely that the girls have arrived, the best thing to happen for weeks. But everything is becoming rather a strain and I am tired from sleeping badly for some weeks. Alex and Liz are being very helpful with all the Christmas preparations, decorating and organising the children's party. Today I left early for the Korydalos women's jail to visit the English girl, Denise Ashe, sentenced to 3 years for possession of heroin. (In England they say she would have got off with a caution.) The place was not horrific just bleak and bare and she never stopped talking so my worry about what to say was quite unnecessary.

The Embassy staff party was said by everyone to have been a great success. We had songs and carols led by the choir and dramatic readings from The Christmas Carol.

Saturday 23 December

The piles of Christmas cards and large hampers of bottles and diaries etc continue to flow embarrassingly into the house but otherwise it is fairly quiet. We had lunch at Rafina, opposite the port in a fish restaurant and then drove across country to Paiania getting hopelessly lost trying to find the Vorres Museum and house. Sunday was a quiet day apart from the service of nine lessons in the English Church, presided over by the Reverend Peake. In the evening Katya Furse (daughter of our friend the charismatic Elizabeth Furse), arrived after 3 months on a kibbutz in Israel.

Christmas Day was fine and sunny so I took everyone on my favourite walk above the Kesariani Monastery on Hymettus. We had a glass of champagne with the staff who came in to cook our dinner. In the afternoon I had a tremendous 2 hour siesta no doubt due to the large meal and wine and my new addiction, the Marie Brizzard Pear Liqueur, found in one of those embarrassing hampers! Just as well as we played racing demons on the floor until 1 a.m.

Thursday 28 December

The girls and I took an 'Express' boat to the island of Aegina. The temple with its fine view of Aghia Marina on one side and the Saronic Gulf on the other was deserted. It has an impressive array of columns within columns but has lost all its statuary to the Museum in Munich. The Monastery of Paleohoria sprawls up the hillside 'like a miniature Mistra' with some 30 small churches scattered over it in various stages of decay or restoration. An especially stunning sunset saw us off the island on the last but one ferry boat, the sea dyed crimson and on fire before us.

Friday 5–8 January 1979

In spite of much opposition by the family we managed a visit to Rhodes. The old mediaeval town was founded in the 12th and 13th centuries by the Knights of St John, restored by the Italians in the early 20th century, having suffered invasions by Byzantines and Turks. All within the walls belongs to one or other of these cultures, the centre being mostly influenced by the Knights, the outskirts by Turks or Jews – a mixture of Italianate palaces, mosques, synagogues and small red-roofed Greek houses. The narrow streets are protected against earthquakes by stone arches and are paved with black and white pebbles sometimes set in intricate patterns. On two sides the walled town is surrounded by the sea, by the small Mandraki Harbour and the larger commercial harbour.

We arrived at the Mandraki Harbour just in time for the priests' procession, the blessing of the water and throwing the cross into the sea. Several shivering young men waited on a boat to jump in to rescue it. Afterwards we visited the Church of St John the Evangelist and the graveyard of the Mosque of Murat Reis, near where Lawrence Durrell lived in a house off the courtyard after the war. Later the girls and I left for the ancient site with the Temple of Apollo, stadium and theatre, all much restored by the Italians. (The Italians occupied the Dodecanese islands from about 1912 until the end of the 2nd world war.) Unpleasant experiences with what Alex called 'silly wankers' in the bushes led us to leave the area rather suddenly and return for restorative coffee in the 'New Market' opposite the Mandraki. It was a new experience for me walking round with two young girls and being constantly interrupted by 'Hello baby', 'Are you English?', 'I love you…', 'Kiss me…' etc. I began to have a sneaking sympathy for the flag tramplers in Salonika!

We were collected by the Honorary Vice Consul who took us to Lindos. It appears suddenly over the brow of the hill, tucked comfortably into the hillside along the bay, completely sheltered by a natural rocky harbour, unused except for very small fishing boats. Further along, past the sheer 400 ft wall of rock on which the Acropolis stands is the tiny harbour of St. Paul, where the disciple is supposed to have entered during a terrible storm when the rock parted to make way for his boat.

The Acropolis is a surprise. You can see nothing as you wind up the steps, past the mediaeval castle and the remains of the Byzantine church. The best part is the view on all sides down to the sparkling blue sea, down below the wall of rock to the beach on one side and the almost circular St Paul's Harbour on the other.

There was time only for a quick visit to the museum to see the 'jujube' marine Venus, as Lawrence Durrell calls her and Aphrodite drying her hair before all going to see the Mayor. We were loaded with gifts – a white shiny replica of Aphrodite, key rings and badges of the Sun God, prints and literature and plates. One last look at the harbour and the sea still crashing outside the hotel, a last rush to the airport and home to Athens. We had seen Rhodes without the 40,000 tourists of the summer season.

Thursday 18 January

At the Tsatsos dinner I was in a strategic position between the P.M. and the Defence Minister (Karamanlis and Averoff). I forgot about Karamanlis being deaf, presumably why he seemed not to understand much better in French than in English. However we managed to discuss the week's parliamentary debates – four hours of speeches and counter speeches sometimes with interruptions by Papandreou and others; his plans for the future, the introduction of a prices and incomes policy; the EEC. 'Parliament is much quieter than it used to be before I came back', he said, 'They would have been at each other with pistols then!'

After dinner I was taken to sit on the sofa by the fire with Mrs Tsatsos, where we talked about poetry and how to translate it and her book about her brother, the poet Seferis, Mon Ami Georges.

1–3 February 1979 – official visit to Salonika

The big church of Aghia Sofia was supported by pit props since being damaged in last year's earthquake. Lunch was with the Minister for Northern Greece, followed by a visit to the American Farm School to present Ford tractors handed over by Iain and Paul Condelis, head of Ford in Greece. The farm is trying to drop the 'American' and become a Greek centre for training, especially to help the needs of the small farmer.

The most interesting place we visited on this trip was the cave of Petralona where Professor Poulamiós claims to have found bones of a Paleolithic 500–600,000 year-old man give or take 50,000 years or so, he said. The anthropologist professor has a strange background. He lived in New York, and in Moscow for 16 years and his wife is a gynaecologist who works in Athens and 'supports the excavations'. He took us to the local pub and gave us tsipuro *(a strong Greek liqueur made from distilled grape stems) which we drank on an empty stomach so that we all fell asleep in the car until the next stop. I suppose the climax was the visit to the tourist and agricultural complex of the ship owner, John Carras. The two massive 1000 bed hotels, marina and fake village were in fact a disaster, but the vineyards and the Carras wine have become well known. Although he was not there we spent the night at his house, with the tremendous view of the coastline of Sidonia, the first finger of the Khalkidiki.*

Friday 23 March

Andreas Papandreou, an old friend of George Richardson from Berkeley, California in the 1960s and currently leader of the opposition socialist party, PASOK, came to lunch. He was pleasant, bright and intelligent and made perhaps a better impression socially than Karamanlis. His wife was more aggressive, currently engaged in organising, with some difficulty, a conference of East Mediterranean women's organisations.

13-15 April

To Nafpaktos with Alex and Liz for the ceremony of the sortie of the garrison *in Messalonghi, consisting of a slow march from the port to the cathedral to deliver the holy painting of the 'Exodus', and laying a wreath on Byron's place of death. After a lunch at the hotel we walked in the 'high' town of Nafpaktos, along the fortress walls and in the narrow streets, followed discreetly by Iain's 'guard', imposed since the death last month of Airey Neave in London and Richard Sykes, shot outside his Embassy in The Hague.*

On Monday we picked up the Cortina at Patras and took the ferry to Cephalonia. We were to present books to the Museum of Argostoli from the Anglo Hellenic League – on early Italian costume, the great interest of the curator of the museum, Mrs Helen Cosmetatos. She is a formidable lady, educated in England, very anglophile, who later became a friend to our son, James, when he was doing his research on the turtle beaches of Cephalonia. On the last day we attended the Good Friday service at the cathedral, followed by the stages of the cross march through the town and being liberally sprinkled with holy water. Finally we took the ferry back to Patras and Athens.

Sunday 29 April

Continuing our search for a peaceful summer retreat we at last managed to go to Karystos, on the island of Evia, to see a house recommended by one of the Athens agents. After much difficulty we found the village of Aetos and the house in a delightful situation, on the slopes of Mt Ochi, looking down on the sea. We were only put off by the cats (mother had given birth to several kittens in the bathroom cupboard), and the distance from Athens. The next day I had to see Alex off at the airport and came back feeling battered and even more aware of another 'limb' gone and awful emptiness. My parents arrived on the evening flight from London the next day and so began the long hot summer of continuous visitors.

* * *

My parents were with us from 1st until 17th May, which was a very happy time for me even though we had several other people there at the same time, the Squires again, Katya Furse and friend Patty and James; and I was taking the practical teaching exams. We took them to Greek tavernas; to the Agora with Hector Catling, the Head of the British School of Archaeology, on a wives' outing when my father rather stole the thunder by asking the best questions; to the pre-election party when Mrs Thatcher was victorious and impressively self-controlled about it; he argued with Katya about kibbutz life and sometimes Iain and I had to leave them to attend official functions. But they were determined to enjoy themselves, loving the luxury of the residence and being looked after. D was marvellous with M who relies on him for everything now, including where she's left her book or put her glasses.

* * *

Friday 18 May

We caught the evening plane for Hania and this year's commemoration of the battle of Crete. The first two days were a repeat of last year but no Cretan runner at the Galata ceremony, fewer veterans and a new less charismatic Nomarch and wife. Iain walked the gorge this year, not I.

After the weekend we set out on a tour of archaeological sites in Crete. Phaestos, my first Minoan site, is impressive, particularly because of its situation, high over the Mesara plain; built like Knossos on a rock but unrestored and scenically more natural. It has great wide palace courtyards, surrounded by rooms for storage and temples for worship and probably places for the 'bull games'. Mary Renault's The King Must Die *helped to paint the picture of Minoan Palace life.*

From there to Mátala, a resort on the south coast whose caves, until last year, were inhabited by hippies who caused a big scandal because of the filth they left. It seemed to have been cleaned up but the beach, lined by tavernas and small hotels, had a stifling feeling about it. Is Crete such a wonderful place for sea and swimming holidays? Beaches are polluted by tar, covered by tourists and maltreated by hippies…

Thursday 24 May

The day was devoted to culture; an hour in the Heraklion museum dodging the large guided tours in order to see the pots from the neighbouring sites, strangely modern designs on the ones from Phaestos, more classical and traditional on others. From there we went to Knossos and the Taverna, *the small house where the British School has its centre. I enjoyed the visit much more than I had imagined. The restoration is discreet and the general appearance helpful for understanding other 'unrestored' sites. It is not over restored in the manner of the heavy walls round the temples at Lindos. Lunch at the* Taverna *followed and a visit to the museum, the 'unexplored manor' and finally the Villa Ariadne, Sir Arthur Evans' home, donated to the Greeks some 20 years ago.*

Monday 28 May

Lord Carrington arrived for the signing of the Act of Accession of Greece into the EEC. It was celebrated with much pomp and ceremony (Giscard d'Estaing as the star) at the Zappion Palace. Dinner was followed by a massive reception in the garden of the palace. Karamanlis invited Carrington and Iain to sit with him and Molyviatis on the raised area of the summer house for nearly an hour, apparently discussing Turkey and Cyprus and NATO in this stage-like setting. So much for Lord Carrington's desire to go home early. He looked as though he didn't know what had hit him, explaining that since he had been appointed Foreign Secretary his activities had been non stop, including a royal visit.

Finally the 6 June dawned and the first written exam. My friend, Nancy Lubin arrived on her way home from a year in Tashkent, Iain left for his Heads of Mission conference in London. Nancy told me extraordinary stories about Uzbekistan and we planned our trip to Israel to meet her parents the next day. We left on Thursday evening a few hours after the last exam.

Saturday 4 August

Due to the now intense heat during the day we left very early en famille for Epidavrous, stopping off to see the archaeological site at Mycenae. Again I was struck by the immensity and the imposing situation where in contrast the detail seems insignificant. Epidavrous did not seem as peaceful as last year but it was still wonderful in the packed theatre for Prometheus Bound *or under the pines on the edge of the main temples of Aesclepius etc. Prometheus was played by Menottis, the well known, now not so young, Greek actor, which must have been a most exacting role, for nearly two hours in his crucifix like position on a wooden platform. Poor Karin, my twelve year old niece, found it exhausting and I too found it heavy. Perhaps I was not in the mood for Greek tragedy?*

* * *

In between the official functions, and sometimes with our visitors, we took refuge at the house on Evia, where we were enjoying the empty beaches, with usually nothing more than goats, sheep and donkeys for company. By the middle of September most of the guests and the family had gone and Iain and I left for a tour of Tuscany.

Friday 26 October

'The tug is gentle', was the strange sounding message being relayed by the Captain of Ajax to the Captain of Scylla, following us into Patras Harbour on a wet, cold, windy day. Strange to me anyway, who had never been on a naval vessel when moving before. And I had no desire to do so when we drove into Corinth about 9 o'clock that morning and saw the rain falling, the wind and the waves out at sea and imagined the uncomfortable transfer from the coastguard vessel bobbing up and down in the harbour. I waited hopefully for someone to suggest that I continue by car but no one did. I was too

cowardly to suggest it. So I found myself being taken across the sea to the frigate Ajax, stumbling in the rain and wind off the boat and up the gangway to the ship. At least I made it – I hadn't actually slipped and fallen in the sea or had to be hauled up by sailors. I was on board and there was a warm welcome from the Captain of the frigate squadron.

This was the first naval visit to Patras for many years and it was suggested that the Ambassador should make an official visit at the same time and that he should arrive in one of the vessels. We were invited onto the bridge to watch the passage through the very narrow Corinth Canal. A tug kept the frigate on course and a Greek pilot gave instructions. Once out of the canal we were exposed to the full force of the elements. The final manoeuvre into Patras Harbour caused concern to the Captain and officers but was carried out without incident. The frigates are long, the wind was very strong and the entrance to the harbour fairly narrow.

8–9 December (my 52nd birthday)

Iain and I had a weekend in Nauplion, stopping off at Nemea, an attractive small site in the plain between Corinth and Argos, source of a good Greek red wine and also where Hercules killed the lion according to legend.

There then began the run up to Christmas with all the attendant functions, staff parties, visitors, family arriving with some of their friends. I was not well with some kind of virus but I managed my bi-annual visit to the women's jail. Denise was still there looking paler and not too well physically but calmer and more serene mentally. She hopes to be out soon.

Christmas day 1979 – with all the family and their various friends and two Greek loners, Marina Dimitropoulou and Ion Vorres, constituted a mixed bag but we managed to break the ice with some of Alex's 'psychological' guessing games.

On 4 January 1980 we used them again during a buffet supper party for Alex (to be 21 on the 29th) of mixed age groups, and with dancing in the 'Venizelos Library' (now refurbished) in the basement. After the usual family 'agro' about how to organise it everything went well.

Friday 18 January

Lunch with Marina Dimitropoulou and another Greek friend who left early but I was kept until 4.30 being told about her love life, the romantic story of her 21 year affaire with 'the golfer'. It started when she was 18 and she met him in France when he was Prime Minister of Greece for the first time and still married. It continued in Paris during his 1963–74 exile. In 1974 they planned to be married. She was in Greece waiting to fly to join him in Paris when the coup occurred and the colonels were overthrown. All flights in and out of Athens were cancelled. The Greeks decided they must have Karamanlis as leader and sought him out in France. Giscard d'Estaing loaned him a private plane to fly back to Athens.

There were confused and breathless descriptions of his falling in love with her, her eventual love and admiration for him which had led her to be faithful to him for so long, someone she sees only once or twice a week, or on holiday. A bunch of photos of her, mostly before 1974 and the extra 10 kilos, showed him looking relaxed and handsome, in a way one does not imagine now, seeing him in the rather stern and austere political profile. Since 1974 he has been married to politics. I imagine he always was.

Wednesday 20 February

Dinner at the Vardinoyannis flat opposite us in Loukianou. There was much talk at table of the now all-absorbing subject of Karamanlis' future. Vardinoyannis maintained that K had told him recently he was 50% for retirement, 25% for remaining head of New Democracy and 25% for the Presidency. It is thought he will make a statement in mid-March. The elections for the Presidency are in May. No one thinks he will allow himself to retire.

Tuesday 26th February

I was told at a party at the Barkers that 'all is organised'. Mr Karamanlis will become president; he will appoint Papaconstantinou, the deputy PM, as Prime Minister with two deputies, Averoff and Rallis, which will give time to decide which will take over. K will become president in the third ballot; he will not stand in the first two when someone who cannot win will be put up. Can this all be right?

British Embassy, Athens, Sunday 9 March 1980

Dear M,

I shall be at the Olympic terminal to meet you on the 28th and shall arrange that you do not have to wait for your luggage. Harold Macmillan (and also Simone Weil, President of the European Parliament) is coming to Athens to receive prizes from the Onassis Foundation that weekend for his sponsorship of the 'Save the Acropolis' Fund. Macmillan will also be on the flight, accompanied by his grandson, Adam Macmillan. They will be entertained and looked after by the Onassis Foundation, but he has expressed a wish to spend one night in the Embassy, which he knew well during and after the war, and will stay with us one night.

Love from Iain and Jeanne

12–16 March – 'familiarisation' visit to Cyprus

We were allowed one official visit to Cyprus and one to Turkey during our tour of duty. My general impressions of Cyprus were of great beauty in the coastal and mountain areas, particularly Episkopi and the Kurium site, some of which we visited by small military helicopter, a new experience for me; and the unspoilt area around Kyrenia in the north. We didn't see the tourist resorts or the refugee camps. Nicosia was rather a dull town, like suburban England with Mediterranean vegetation. As for the political situation there seemed to be lots of ideas but no practical proposals for settlement. The two sides poised opposite each other gave an immensely hostile appearance, with ramshackle emplacements made of oil drums and sand bags, the sad and the tragic side by side with the absurd. But how can one get anywhere with a political solution when the military situation still exists? There seems no likelihood of a solution for a long time.

Saturday 28 April

A full Macmillan/Weil day with prize giving in the morning and a very long speech by Madame Weil, followed by a short, off the cuff speech by M about the glories of Greece, European democracy, war and saving the world. Not bad for 86. This was followed by lunch at the Grande Bretagne. Photographers followed everywhere. I sat next to

Macmillan and Ambassador Folin of France. Christina Onassis was on the other side. She seemed a rather sad person, having just got rid of the Russian Kausov, husband number 3, and given him a ship or two in compensation. Asked by Macmillan what she did, she said she lived in Switzerland and skied a lot and sometimes did a little work. He asked me later if she was a student. She seemed quite naïve about international affairs but curious when I said I had been in Moscow for

26. Jeanne with Harold Macmillan at the Embassy during his visit to receive prizes from the Onassis Foundation for his sponsorship of the 'Save the Acropolis' Fund, April 1980.

two years. At the President's evening reception as we walked up the stairs with her she said that it was the first time she had been to the Palace. The press referred to it as her 'first official appearance in Greece'. The celebrations continued with a lunch given by Rallis and a dinner at the Embassy for Harold Macmillan, with the Averoffs, Kanellopoulos, whom M was delighted to see again, Paddy Leigh Fermor and others. In between I was looking after Anne and Dorothy and taking them to see the sights. D said she could walk up the steps to the Acropolis if Macmillan could (they are of the same age). He has a fine memory and tells good stories of his early life and about Greek history and mythology.

We spent the Easter week at one of the houses in the group where Philip Sherrard, the poet and translator of Seferis, lives, at Katounia, near Limni in northern Evia; this was a suggestion from Barbara Noel Baker, when she heard we were looking for a house to rent for Easter. The house is one of those originally used by the former officials of the bauxite mines before they closed down, and now lived in by members of the Sherrard family and their friends.

Sunday 4 May

Back to Athens after a very short visit to London to take over the house from the tenants and to attend the presentation of James' M.Sc. at Southampton University. A week of the London Chamber of Commerce awaited me, with the Lords Jellicoe, Shackleton and Llewellyn Davies, and Sir Peter Parker of British Rail. But the real highlight of the week was the political events in Athens. Karamanlis won the third ballot by 18 votes and is to be President. Surprisingly Rallis, and not Averoff whom most people expected, became Prime Minister. By Saturday noon we had the names of the Cabinet. The main changes were Mitsotakis to the Foreign Ministry, Boutos to Coordination and Everts to Finance. Everything at the moment is calm and quiet but Tsaldaris, at a lunch on Tuesday for William Rees Mogg of The Times talked darkly of 'a crisis situation' and said that after the summer there would be much opposition.

Friday 23 May

Departure for Hania, Crete, was held up for an hour at the airport by the British MPs who arrived late from the UK and lost some *of their luggage. This caused a late arrival too at the Mitsotakis house above Souda Bay with the Richardsons (Bank of England). We were absorbed into this slightly feudal atmosphere of hangers on, petitioners bearing gifts etc. at the house. The sirocco-like south wind blew throughout the weekend, cancelling the parachute drop, covering everyone in red dust and making it difficult to sleep.*

Sunday 1 June

The week was spent in close telephonic link every evening with Anne and bulletins on the progress of Dorothy after her emergency operation to relieve a leaking tumour. Iain left for Wales on Thursday to spend some time with his mother, leaving me with the Menuhins on their usual night stop and a seemingly dry and 'devoted to commerce' Tebbit. He could, I found, be moved to humour when I suggested frivolously that he might end up with nothing but a violin if his luggage got confused with the Menuhins.

* * *

9 September 1980

We returned from the UK via Igouminitsa on the ferry from Ancona with two days leave left to visit Meteora, arriving just in time to see two of the monasteries, Aghia Trias and the Great Meteoron in the evening. They are more impressive in their situation than for their interiors, perched on the top of rock formations. Formerly approached by jointed ladders, nets or boxes, now access is by foot bridge or steep paved paths, up and down the rocky cliffs. We drove on through rolling countryside and orchards of apples and peaches to Salonika, to attend the opening session of the European Community Symposium at the Salonika Fair. Dinner was at the Minister for Northern Greece's grand residence along the coast. He, Martis, made an after dinner speech full of fiery Macedonian patriotism, calling those inhabitants of the People's Republic of Macedonia 'no more Macedonian than I am Chinese'. We arrived back in Athens on the 13th and spent the weekend sorting our mail and preparing for Mrs Thatcher's visit, and also preparing lists of the jewellery stolen in the burglary the day before leaving London.

Tuesday 22nd September

Mrs Thatcher was greeted at the airport by Rallis, Boutos, Averoff, Heads of the Armed Forces, Guards' Band, etc. etc. She made her speech and was whisked away with motorcycle escort to the Maximos residence in Herod Atticus. All her party and Iain disappeared upstairs. She made a quick visit to the residence for a briefing with members of the Embassy before going off to see Rallis.

The visit was to an unfortunate degree overshadowed by the discussions on the supply of the Coal Fired Power Stations, 'promised' by Mitsotakis to English firms under the Memorandum of Understanding signed in London last February. Now it seemed the Greek Government was trying to back out, particularly Boutos, Minister of Coordination who wanted it put out to international tender. Meanwhile the Coal Board was being pushed to reduce the terms so that the Greeks would finally accept them. It seemed unlikely that the agreement would be signed during the PM's stay in Athens, if ever. But the Embassy and various members of the NCB and Dept. of Trade and Industry, who had flown in too, continued to be involved in the issue.

Wednesday 23 September

Mr Thatcher was taken off to visit aircraft maintenance factories. But the next day I took him to visit St. Catherine's School where he did his consort role extremely well, greatly pleasing all the children and teachers. Then we saw them off to Belgrade. The historic first visit of a PM for 22 years, since Macmillan in 1958, was over. It had been marred by the Coal Fired Power Stations issue and had not enough other political meat to leave a positive impression. Neither side had much weight to throw on east/west relations and they seemed to have been discussed only at a superficial level. The right noises had been made about the entry of Greece into the Community and full return to NATO, but the former was already settled and the latter under super secret negotiations.[7] There were no large trade credits on offer as there had been in Moscow in 1975, nor an ageing and mysterious leader to appear out of hiding for the visit. The left made much publicity of Mrs T's NATO urgings and the right over her visit to 'Macedonia'.

11-13 October

Visit of John Nott, Secretary of State for Trade, with John Paleocrassas standing in as host in place of Boutos who resigned suddenly yesterday for reasons of ill health. P. gave a dinner for Nott on 12th after a large 'commercial' reception here. There is still no decision on the CFPS although the Minister has seen everyone involved.

16–21 October

Visit to Salonika for Iain to attend and speak at the Anglo Hellenic Chamber of Commerce lunch, visit the British Council office, meet some local academics, visit Kavala and the Honorary Vice Consul there and the two Prinos off shore oil rigs. Fortunately this did not include being hoisted up in the 'crew basket' as were two German photographers seeking publicity for the German companies involved in the oil drilling. The manager of the plant, an American Greek of Cypriot origin with many years experience in the Gulf, took a very pragmatic view of the Iran/Iraq war. 'A controlled war', he said, 'could only be good for the west as, when all those installations had been damaged, there would be work and employment for many people in repairing and replacing them.'

For light relief we visited the Roman archaeological site at Philippi, near Kavala and after Prinos had a day on the beautiful island of Thassos.

Saturday 8 November

We went with Air Vice Marshal Howe of Southern Command to the 50th Anniversary of the Hellenic Air Force where they played a piece of music composed and conducted by Hatzitakis – words taken from a dead pilot's diary and some contributed by Minister of Defence Averoff. The reception afterwards was a dreary affair in the Icarus restaurant with tired canapés and a colossal birthday cake which vanished in a flash.

11–17 November

Visit of Terence and Rosemary Garvey to Athens. Iain managed to get away for the weekend tour of the Peloponnese, including Corinth, Mycenae (seen in magnificent autumn warmth and sunlight without the hundreds of tourists), Epidavrous, Methana and through the mountains and valleys to the isthmus at Kalloni and home via Aegina. I'd never known better light, temperature and out-of-season peace as on this weekend.

The march to celebrate the Polytechnic students rising of 1974 against the Junta went badly wrong, with police using tear gas and truncheons and rioters smashing windows and seizing hotel furniture to make blazing barricades across the streets.

1 December

Lord Napier arrived with Inspector Harding to discuss Princess Margaret's programme which we went through blow by blow until one in the morning. Her likes, dislikes, needs and wants were discussed at great length – not to be too tired, but does not like to go to bed; doesn't like to be cold, nor too hot; not too long at any one function but needs to be entertained. It seems as though it will be difficult to get it right. We managed, however, to persuade the Lord that Loutraki water could replace Malvern. We also tried το περιβολι τον ουρανου (The Garden of Heaven) as a night club for HRH but it was much too noisy. Pity because the music is interesting.

Thursday 18 December

We had a staff party with 20 from the Archaeological School as well this year. Slowish start but successful once it got going and especially after the singing of carols by the St. Catherine's choir, standing on the stairs in their red blazers. Iain was called to see the PM for a final 'No'

27. HRH Princess Margaret driving with Iain to the opening of the Turner Exhibition in Athens, 7 January 1981.

to the power stations contract and missed all the singing. This final negative was all the sadder after 6 months of negotiations, hard work and money spent on the British attempt to satisfy the Greeks for the £150 million contract.

Friday 26–29 December

This year's Christmas weekend trip was to the island of Mytilene, arranged largely and with great kindness by Greek friends in a house in Molyvos. Lesbos (or Mytilene) is the island of the olive and picking was in full swing. Ladies in brightly coloured knickerbockers crouched under the trees to harvest the olives lying in the nets, some of which were dark and sombre and some white like bridal veils. The next day we were to see the factory in the mountains above the town, with the remains of the crushed fruit pouring out of the funnels like a stream of brown earth.

Later in the day we went to the Teriade Museum in Mantamados to see the paintings of the naïve artist Theophilus and the volumes of French modern art, bound and ordered by the art publisher, Teriade. They were by Picasso, Matisse, Chagall and others in the 1970s and given to the museum. The prints, lithographs and copies, produced in volumes of restricted publication with texts by the artists were a strange collection to find in an olive grove in Mytilene. Theophilus, originally a house painter, was encouraged by Teriade, who supplied him with materials and money. His pictures are now worth millions but he died in poverty. It was an interesting visit though the weather was mostly cold and wet.

Back to Athens in a plane full of soldiers going on leave from the border posts on the island. There was a big camp outside Molyvos and small fortified gun emplacements and long areas of 'mined' beach and coast land constituted the barrage.

Tuesday 6 January–Friday 9 January 1981 – Visit of HRH Princess Margaret to Athens

I was so busy watching her come off the plane that I almost forgot to curtsey. We were immediately swamped by photographers and it was impossible to introduce members of the staff as planned. Rosemary Garvey was right about Princess Margaret's being intelligent but not quite knowing whether she wants to be a personality in her own right or just the Queen's sister. One thing was sure she was a lot less demanding than her secretary. Ten to fifteen minutes with the press, who she said asked rather silly questions, was followed by dinner for those who were involved with the Turner Exhibition which she had come to open at Iain's request.

The next day's snow, heavy rain and sleet caused all the arrangements to run far behind and the planned visit to the school to be very rushed. But the opening of the exhibition went beautifully and was well organised. The Prime Minister made a nice speech and President Karamanlis met her at the entrance under an umbrella in pouring rain, a rather touching scene. The reception afterwards at the Embassy seemed a success too and the right people were all brought up to talk to her as planned. Afterwards we had dinner at the Mirtiá *(Myrtle) restaurant where the food was good and the guitarists played and sang to our table just enough. That night she stayed up late after the party and regaled us with stories about her family and 'Freddie' (aka Queen Frederica).*

The helicopter trip to Epidavrous and Nauplion had to be cancelled because of the dreadful weather. Instead we organised a 'shopping trip' for the morning, to visit a leather shop and then the two famous Greek jewellers, Zolotas and Lalaounis; the afternoon at the Benaki. The highlight of the visit, the PM's dinner, was that evening. Afterwards we sat round the fire again at home and talked about Greek politics and the world situation. Next day we saw HRH off on her plane home, with some relief but generally happy memories. The visit had been a success, the Greeks were pleased that she had come, and she had given the Turner Exhibition excellent publicity.

Monday, 9 February

This week Queen Frederica died in Madrid and on Sunday 20 people were killed in a stampede at a football match between Athens and Salonika. 'We are barbarians', said one distinguished Greek guest at a dinner party. King Constantine has asked the Greek government to allow him to bring his mother back to the Royal chapel at Tatoi, outside Athens, for burial; there was much opposition from the Communists, Papandreou and all the Centre Parties. The area around Tatoi has been cordoned off but the streets in Kolonaki are scattered with leaflets urging 'All to come to Tatoi'. The funeral was to be attended by many visiting royalty, including the King and Queen of Spain, a daughter of Frederica, ex-King Constantine, Queen Anne Marie and all the family, the Dutch and Danish royal families and Prince Philip.

Iain went to Tatoi at noon to meet Philip, flying in in his small Anson. Vast quantities of people got through the woods into the grounds at Tatoi and Iain and David Dain were crushed against trees and members of European royal families as they tried to accompany Philip to the chapel. It was pretty much of a shambles as over 1000 people shouted for the King, who finally had to speak through a megaphone to ask for quiet so that the ceremony could begin. But there were no serious clashes between monarchists and anti-monarchists and it all seemed to have been handled fairly well.

Tuesday 24 February

About 11 p.m. there was a very severe earth tremor. The door to the study opened, windows rattled and the whole house began to shake. By the time we had rushed down the stairs and were underneath them it had stopped shaking. People were gathering in the streets and there were excited voices outside. Iain began to phone people. Everything was all right at the Chancery except they had no light. Our lights were still on but the chandeliers in the hall were swinging back and forth. I heard English voices outside and found two members of the Embassy who had left their fifth floor flat in terror.

Tremors continued throughout the night and the next day. Athens was deserted, shops were closed and there were rumours that there was more to come. The aftermath of the earthquake, whose epicentre had been near Corinth, lasted for days as people refused to go home and camped in the parks, only going back to their houses to eat and wash. In Athens damage was restricted to cracks in walls but nearer the epicentre many villagers' homes were destroyed.

Friday 27 February

A weekend away was abandoned because Iain had to stay to deal with negotiations over yet another half promised contract, this time for the Salonika railway. However it was fortunate that we had not gone as we were there for the unexpected arrival of the three Anglican missionaries held for eight months in Iran and released a few days before, who stayed in the residence on their way home. They were fine people, a surgeon and ordained Anglican priest and his wife, Mr and Mrs Cameron, and the Secretary to the Anglican Bishop, Miss Wadell, who had been shot in May, and after recovering, imprisoned. The Camerons were arrested one day in July, whilst visiting Teheran from Yazd, where they had their clinic and church. All had been charged with spying. The Archbishop of Canterbury's foreign affaires advisor, Terry Waite had been negotiating their release for several months. Modest and unassuming people, they insisted that they had not been ill treated; only kept locked up.

Saturday 11 to Monday 20 April

We had finally accepted the family's long standing invitation to visit the Averoff foundation in Metsovo, to be combined with a visit to Corfu to present the Mantles and Insignia of the order of St Michael and St George to the museum. The guest house in Metsovo where we were to stay is a restored wooden building in typical Epirote style, the lower half housing the museum of life in Metsovo since the beginning of the Ottoman invasion.

In the following days we visited Ioanina, the lake and the archaeological site at Dodoni, the home of the oracle; the area of the Zagoria with its attractive villages built of grey stone with the same brownish grey roofs, now mostly deserted by the former Greek merchants and the Sarakatsani shepherds, who once inhabited them. After a quick look at the Vikos gorge we left for Igouminitsa and the ferry for Corfu.

Iain visited the Consulate, the Mayor and the Nomarch and only by late afternoon we reached the house on the sea where we were to stay. The next day Iain presented the Mantles and Insignia and made a short speech in the presence of local dignitaries. We visited Paleocastritsa, which seemed cold and unattractive under an overcast sky with crowds of English Easter package tours. On the higher road we found sunshine again and stopped to watch the olive pressing, more primitive than on Mytilene, pressing the fruit with mats.

Tuesday 5 May

There is much trouble in Ireland over the death of Bobby Sands. Tight security measures are in force at all posts and Iain is not supposed to go out unprotected.

I had now to take the Lower Foreign Office Greek exam, which I had unfortunately signed up for in November, but I was not at all ready and too much was happening. We had to be locked and barred against the twice daily demonstrations over Bobby Sands. The oral came in the middle of the second demo which made it difficult to get into

Chancery for the exam. It was also difficult to concentrate between lunches and receptions for the Conference being attended by the Under Secretary for Trade Tebbit. They finally departed after a morning spent by him at the Scaramanga shipyards whilst Mrs T was being taken by me, with Anne and Liz, to the small but delightful site of Rhamnous. On the way the alarm on the Rolls went off and we screeched and flashed along the road until the Greek driver who took over from Reg Voyce managed to stop it by pulling large chunks of car from under the front wheel. No one had taken much notice.

Thursday 21 May

Lord and Lady Caccia arrived to take part in the Crete activities, this year being the 40th anniversary of the battle. An official dinner was given for them together with the Averoffs, Dilys Powell, and others who were attending this year's extended ceremonies. Averoff told us that the talks on the American bases would have to be finished before parliament rises in July and that they were waiting for 'some replies'.

The Olympic strike threatened to leave us without transport to Hania so we were all given seats in Averoff's plane which took off from Tatoi in the evening of the 22nd. The ceremonies seemed never ending as we toiled round with over 100 veterans, three Ministers of Defence and Mitsotakis, Scottish pipers, Australian buglers and Greek military bands. It was tiring, interesting and at times particularly moving, as in Galetas, which was in the centre of the battle, and Souda Bay where the Australians broke into singing God Save the Queen *as the anthems were played. A significant difference was the presence of the German Delegation for the first time. I wondered about the advisability of this, thinking of the fierce Cretans whose men folk and even whole villages had been massacred. Thanks perhaps to the German Ambassador's own personality all went well. His first wreath was laid in silence and finally his last to a round of applause. There was lunch given by Costas and Marika Mitsotakis at the Panoroma Hotel and in the evening a massive reception given by them. It became obvious that this was not only about the Battle of Crete but also about the elections now not far away; and also about the rivalry between the two Greek Ministers, Averoff and Mitsotakis.*

Sunday 25 May

After the Te Deum and three more wreath layings there was lunch at the Officers' Club given by Averoff, who scored heavily with an excellent

276

speech about peace and allies all helping each other, including references to NATO. Then we boarded Averoff's plane again for Heraklion to join a street party in the middle of the town, organised by the PASOK mayor.

Monday 26 May

The party set off for Mount Ida and the village of Anoghia to meet Paddy Leigh Fermor's resistance friends for a lunch in the mountains and to hear stories of how the men folk were shot and the village burned in reprisal for the acts of sabotage perpetrated by the SOE fighters. We collected the mayor and Dilys Powell in the Rolls and took it up the rough road to Psiloriti near the Cave of Zeus. Here the air was fresh and crisp, and together with the veterans of the underground resistance, we sipped raki and ate local cheese outside and then went inside for crisp hot lamb and more local wine; all this accompanied by playing of the lyre (lira) and singing by Paddy and his companions.

The climax was the 'simple taverna party' in the evening outside town for the veterans. It was given by Kefaloyannis, the large, burly moustachioed Cretan who was at the lunch in the mountains and whom I had taken to be a shepherd and not a hotel owner, in his 600 bed hotel. Twenty to thirty of us were wined and dined, given champagne, serenaded by the hotel singers (more Filaden, Filaden), watched dancing and plate throwing and finally our host firing bullets through his hotel windows. I was told the story of how Kefaloyannis had abducted a young Cretan girl in the 1950s, the daughter of a Venizelos supporter and therefore a declared enemy, as K was a Royalist. When the island had been brought to the brink of civil war over it he came down from the mountains and went to prison. Later they were married.

13–16 June

A last minute and unplanned visit to Mykonos on a madly overcrowded ferry. We stayed in a hotel outside the town where the wind howled through the open corridors and the beaches were populated mostly by transvestites or nudists. But we have now seen the 'maze of whitewash', as Durrell calls it, the box-like white houses, the picturesque windmills and the hundreds of tourist shops. It was perhaps all worth it for the beauty and peacefulness of Delos, the island with a large archaeological site which you can visit from Mykonos but where no one is allowed to stay overnight.

The talk now is all about the American bases in Greece. Protracted negotiations continue between the Greeks and the Americans but an agreement seems unlikely now before parliament goes into recess at the end of June. Did the Greek government decide it had a better chance of winning the elections without an agreement?[8]

Sat/Sun 20–21st June

June became the usual mixture of 'end of term activities', oppressive heat in town with occasional getaways to Aetos, Evia where we rented the house again for the summer. I only heard when Alex came out to join us of the death of Reg Voyce after a relapse following his operation to relieve a blocked intestine. It was a great shock and sadness to lose this long standing driver and friend of the Embassy and we returned to Athens for the funeral.

In August we packed up the house at Aetos during a furious meltemi wind which closed down all the ferries and brought fires and destruction to many houses in the outskirts of Athens; and after a week's preparations went on leave to the UK. We returned in September to still extreme heat, very oppressive after wet Wales.

* * *

Thursday 15 October

The green/yellow PASOK rally was watched from the Information Section office on the 5th floor overlooking Syntagma; it had a festival like atmosphere, great enthusiasm, shouting slogans 'Ολο για την αλλαγη' (all for change), cheering, balloons, fireworks and of course Andreas. The next day it was all repeated in blue with less people, more noise and a less charismatic Rallis for the New Democracy Party.

The elections came on the 18th with an election TV supper for 20 as the results came out. After less than an hour there was no doubt of the PASOK landslide victory. Hooting horns all night.

Monday 19th

All is quiet. Still Zeus has not sent a thunderbolt. The earth shaker Poseidon has not sent a storm. In fact the fine weather lasts, today the sky was blue, not a drop of rain or even pollution. When will the change come? Where will it start? How will it manifest itself? Where will all those sophisticated English and French speaking Greeks go? To dinners with foreign diplomats? A first socialist government in Greece.

Wednesday 21st

New ministers were announced – Haralambopoulos to be Minister of Foreign Affairs, Simitis to Agriculture, the rest I do not know (except Mercouri who has Culture).

Not much has happened so far. Abolition of film censorship was announced (except for obscenity). Mercouri announced no more loans of antiquities to Greek Embassies abroad. Peponis, Minister of Industry, warned the cement industry of early 'socialisation'. The government is considering the introduction of civil marriage and abolition of legal penalties for adultery.

Papandreou gave interviews to the ABC and the BBC. On the first he reiterated the usual story about Greece not being protected against Turkey by NATO. On the contrary they provided arms to an enemy, or someone who lays claims to Greek territory. Even so he will not take Greece out of NATO nor ask the Americans to remove bases without negotiations and not before March.

Cyprus has been in the news; another initiative, this time from the UN through Gobbi, the UN representative in Nicosia. Papandreou has promised a tough line on Cyprus and Turkey and threatened to return to the policy of demanding withdrawal of all Turkish troops before any new negotiations can begin. On the 27th he made a statement during a Cypriot TV and Radio interview to the effect that he was considering that an international conference, as suggested by the Soviet Union, should be set up to consider the Cyprus case.

Iain's comments were that Papandreou had probably scuppered the Gobbi initiative just when it looked as though there was a chance of success. Lazarides, the Cypriot socialist leader and the agent of the PLO in Cyprus, and Papandreou have announced the establishment of an official diplomatic representative in Athens of the PLO, equal with the Israeli representation; this could mean a possible tie up between Cyprus and PASOK government policy and the new Greek government's closer links with Arab States, e.g. the PLO.

Saturday 31 October to Sunday 1 November

As Britain is at present chairing the EEC there followed a 'weekend of Sinai' and the problems of the peacekeeping force, to be set up after the final withdrawal by the Israelis. Two days were spent trying to get the Greeks to agree to the wording of a statement about the participation of the 4 – France, Holland, UK and Italy – but no agreement was reached. Then on Sunday 15 November after a wet Remembrance Service at Phaleron we had lunch afterwards at the Psaroulas Restaurant where we met Papandreou, whom Iain had been trying to lobby again in the last few days in an attempt at agreement on the statement on Sinai. (It all revolved around the fact that the 4 countries involved in the peacemaking, plus, and particularly, Greece, did not want to exclude the second part of the arrangement set out at the Venice meeting – the eventual autonomy of the Palestinians. Israel cannot accept any reference to this. Much later a statement was agreed which was so anodyne as to be more or less meaningless.)

Much publicity appeared over 'the kiss', a press photographer having caught Iain in 'a warm embrace' with Melina Mercouri at a reception, Iain all the while expostulating that 'she had kissed everyone'.

Thursday 3 December

Dinner with the Vardinoyannis was the usual Kolonaki mixture but without any members of the new government, except Beis, the Mayor. Paul Vardinoyannis lost his seat in the elections and is now living a delightfully 'free' existence which he swears he is enjoying enormously; he says he is a great friend of Andreas who 'is more right wing than Karamanlis'. Andreas is all right, PASOK perhaps not so good. Rallis is to resign as leader of New Democracy.

Our plans to spend Christmas on the island of Spetses were thwarted by the weather which prevented boats leaving so we put everything in the car and took off for the Gannymede hotel in Galaxidion (near Delphi) run by the two Australians, Bill and Bruno and where we had stayed the year before. We drove up to the snow level, walked in the Galaxidion area and visited the site at Delphi which James had not seen – a pleasant, peaceful, family occasion.

Thursday 31 December

The English papers published the New Year's Honours list with Iain's KCMG. He had told the children the day before. Alex had overheard my telling my father in London, Liz said 'about time too', and James said it was all nonsense! Patrick Fairweather made a very nice speech during the party. I am very glad for Iain that he has his K. Liz was right – it was a long time coming, but perhaps that makes it look even more as though he has really earned it, which he certainly has.

Monday 11 January 1982

Iain and I had lunch alone for first time for weeks, accompanied by a big pile of Iain's 'fan mail' which arrived in the bag. General themes were that 'it does not come with the rations' nowadays; much deserved for all his hard work; one honour in which the wife, deservedly, participates...

Sunday 31 January

Drinks for our party on the opening night of Ballet Rambert; our departure was delayed by Melina's late arrival. When we got to the theatre Melina was furious because there was no photographer present, 'when she and the British Ambassador attend the première of the Ballet Rambert, together with the Cypriot Ambassador and the Minister of Finance'. *By the second interval the TV had turned up and we all appeared back stage to be photographed with the scantily dressed 'sauvages' of the last ballet.*

Thursday 25 February to Saturday 13 March – *familiarisation visit to northern Greece and Turkey – Kavala, the consulate in Istanbul, the Embassy in Ankara, and a tour of the archaeological sites in western Turkey where we found much evidence of Euboean cipollino at Pergamon and Ephesus.*

Saturday 20 March

With house guests Natasha and Peter Squires we drove to the Peloponnese – Corinth, Argos, Tripolis, Megalopolis, Andritsaina and Vassae. Warm sunshine changed to cold wind and an icy picnic at Vassae, vast, grey and scaffolded with traces of snow around. Across a doubtful road which brought us to Olympia at dusk for dinner and a night's rest at the hotel where we had stayed in 1978. The new museum is now open and the statuary from the pediments arranged along the walls. The Lapids and satyrs are particularly good and the museum is carefully hidden in the trees. Several columns of cipollino marble (quarried in the Karystia area of Evia) were found in the Nymphaeum and traces of six others. We also found pieces in the Roman baths at Argos the day before and in Corinth. My search for it at Roman sites is becoming very rewarding.

Friday 2 April

We were invited to the American Embassy to meet their defence college students. The Stearns were cheerful and unflappable after a bomb had been thrown over the garden wall, exploded and smashed their windows 2 nights before.

Friday 10 April – Easter weekend (English)

We all flew to Samos to stay with the Wards (Consul in Salonika) in their house on the far side of the bay of Samos. It is situated on a steep hillside overlooking the sea in an olive grove with terraces below. It was a pleasant, relaxed weekend, walking, sleeping and eating, with one official visit to the Honorary Consul. Samos is different yet again from the other islands, softer than Chios and similar to Skiathos or Thassos in its greenery and meadows round the coast and houses scattered among the trees.

Tuesday 13 April

Plunged back into the social world we gave probably our last dinner party – for the Speaker and Mrs Alevras, Amalia Fleming (widow of Dr Fleming of penicillin fame and PASOK MP), the Karapanayotis from To Vima, Italians and Yugoslavs. The Deputy Minister of Defence and Mrs Petros did not turn up at the last minute but the evening passed off well. The Alevras are charming, the Karapanayottis very full of life and Lady Fleming much less aggressive than when in opposition.

We are now starting the run up to our departure from Greece, the clearing out period before packing. But there was to be one last weekend away for Greek Easter, invited by Marina to stay with her in Delphi. We left on the Friday via Osias Lukas and arrived in time for the Epitaphios *service when the bier and sepulchres are carried from the churches to meet in the main square at Galaxidion.*

Friday 30 April to Sunday 2 May

I spent the weekend in Santorini by myself as Iain could not leave because of the Falklands crisis and I wanted to see it before I left Greece. Santorini is a kind of Mykonos with a wind and white houses of similar shape and architectural design and no trees. But the wind does not howl and the town is not fashionable, still quiet and casual at least in April though probably less so when the cruise ships come into the harbour and take all the tourists up the steep steps on mule back.

On Saturday I made an excursion up to Mesa Vouno and ancient Thira on a mule. A widely scattered site where temples to the Egyptian gods, Isis, Osiris and Anubis jostle with those of Apollo and Dionysos, where Mycenean type architecture keeps company with Roman baths and cisterns. On Sunday out to the Minoan site excavated by Doctor Marinatos to see mostly ceramics from there and statuary from Ancient Thira.

It is difficult to get Iain out of the office because of the flow of telegrams from London asking for explanations to be made to the Greeks on the latest Falkland moves. It is now 3–4 weeks since the task force set out for the South Atlantic. Greeks, who are very sensitive on issues of military juntas and offshore islands, have given unstinted support. 'And we shall continue to support you' as Andreas Papandreou said at lunch on Friday, 'You can tell Mrs Thatcher that we shall support you, although we do not agree on all issues.' The Papandreous came quietly to lunch instead of an official farewell call.

Saturday 8 May

I managed to get Iain away in time to arrive by 2 o'clock at the Perivoli Tripou (Tripou Farm) just outside Corinth (Greek farmer married to an English wife from North London). The gipsy orchestra was still playing and Morris dancers were still dancing but the lamb on the spit was finished. Maria Tripou and David Marinos were married in an Orthodox ceremony outside the small chapel of St Nicholas in the spring sunshine with the scent of the orange blossom on the trees. Later there was a reception in the barn and dancing to Greek music.

There followed a string of 'lasts', last tennis with our ladies' group, last sale of work, last goodbyes at the Roumanian doyen of the diplomatic corps, last reception at the residence to say goodbye, when for the first time I never left the receiving line; it seemed as though they all filed in and then filed out again but I suppose there was a party going on, a sort of mini QBP.

Thursday 13 May

The last packing and finding somewhere to put all the presents – it has been like Christmas since Tuesday: golden goblets, bronze ashtrays, silver sun discs and books on Greek art and 6–7 pieces of embroidery. Last *week I phoned Professor Chapman to ask whether his house on Evia would be available in the summer for our successors. He told me he had decided to sell it by the end of the year. So today we had a session with the Embassy lawyer about the financial problems of buying property in Greece, tax and so on. He offered to act for us and we agreed that he should go ahead and make some enquiries.*

A last taverna evening with Toni and Monty Stearns and Mario and Inci Modiano after goodbye drinks for the Embassy when they presented us with the carved olive wood octopus by Colin Miller.

Monday 17th

The day dawned fine and sunny. We pushed the last things into bulging suitcases, paid the last bills, handed over the 25 thank you letters. Iain went into the office to sign off his 'valedictory' despatch while I supervised the packing of the car. We took photos of all the residence staff and got into the car to drive to Patras. Four years and 6 days after our arrival we left Athens.

10

THREE FUNERALS, MOSCOW 1982–85

'It was announced by the Foreign and Commonwealth Office on 3 June that Sir Iain Johnstone Macbeth Sutherland, who has been Ambassador in Athens for the past four years, is to succeed Sir Curtis Keeble as British Ambassador in Moscow. Sir Iain left Athens on 17 May and will be taking up his new appointment in the autumn.'

It seemed inevitable that Iain should go back to Moscow as ambassador after his long experience of the country. It was his last post (members of the diplomatic service retire at 60) and one of the most senior posts in the service. It was not going to be easy, and perhaps somewhere like New Delhi, which might have been on the cards at that time, with hindsight would have been less demanding. But we went back to Moscow for the third time.

Back also to Brezhnev, now in his last few weeks as leader, a very sick man, as we now know, with a pacemaker and needing constant nursing care. The country was facing 'four consecutive years of falling agricultural output. Abroad the Soviet Union faced a costly and unwinnable war in Afghanistan and unrest in Poland, while relations with the United States were at their lowest point in a generation. Relations with China were no better.'[1]

Each time we went back to Moscow we hoped that life would be easier, for us and for the Soviet population; that the economic situation would be better, food would be more easily and readily available and there would be more choice; that life would be more relaxed; but there were always the same difficulties, the same suspicion and surveillance. Excuses could be made in the 1950s for the continuing lack of consumer goods – they were still suffering from the effects of the war – even for the 1970s; but if the Soviet system was to succeed it should have happened by now.

The three years in Moscow in the 1980s turned out to be very difficult ones. Apart from the economic hardships, the country was suffering from their elderly and ailing elite, who were unable or unwilling to do anything about it or to retire in favour of a younger leadership. While we were there one after another of these old men died and another was appointed. East–west relationships had become more difficult since the Russian attack on Afghanistan in 1979 and the subsequent sanctions imposed by the US and other western nations. The UK had followed the so-called 'Afghan guidelines' to the letter so that in the last three years all but the most basic of cultural, scientific and social contacts had been lost. Although the guidelines were now to be abandoned it took months of weary negotiating to try to get back to the pre-1979 position.

At that time we were not to know the whole extent of the country's problems and certainly no one would have guessed then that in less than nine years the Soviet Union would have fallen. It was only just before we left that some Russians were starting to talk openly about 'serious problems'. One Russian friend, the poet Evtushenko, had said in conversation that he thought that the Soviet Empire would fall eventually, perhaps in 50 to 100 years time…

* * *

16 September 1982

We left Heathrow for Moscow. Incredibly we managed more or less to repeat the performance of 4 years ago when we left for Athens, to leave at the worst time of day – the early morning rush hour – and to be caught in the same appalling traffic jams all the way to the M4.

The arrival was very different from Athens; no cameras, no TV, no speeches of welcome; only two fairly insignificant members of the Russian protocol department awaited us as we made our way through the new arrivals area (a new airport had been built by the Germans since the 1970s and was still shiny new) to the VIP lounge. There was a row of members of the Embassy there to greet us and an enthusiastically warm welcome from the European Community. Another friend was waiting for us outside, the driver, Leonid. He too had first come to the Embassy 30 years ago like us and we knew him since the days when we were very junior members; then there was the cold shock of the grey day and the grey Moscow streets. Only the slightly golden trees with their autumn leaves softened the Russian scene.

We drove into town along Gorky Street and finally to the Naberezhnaia (Embankment), still then called after Maurice Thorez, and the Embassy with its imposing situation on the banks of the Moscow River and with its magnificent view of the Kremlin opposite. The building was full of the ghosts of former ambassadors and ambassadresses we had known. It would take a long time to lay them all and implant our own personality on the building. The domestic staff was nearly all unchanged, only a little older, but I was soon to be told that three were to leave, one by her own choice and two at the order of the UPDK.

Friday 17 September

The Bereska Gastronom (the special food shop for diplomats) has not changed in the last six years. We drove back through Gorky Street again, through Marks and Engels Square, the old familiar places. Up the Sretenka and out to lunch with the Irish, a European lunch and more welcome from our European colleagues, some of whom I now recognise – the Dutch, van Aght, with a Canadian wife, the Italian with a Czech wife, and Metaxas, one of the few Greek ambassadors not to be moved since Papandreou took office.

The list of things to be done in the residence is going to be never ending. Such is the nature of the mansion of the ex-sugar merchant, Kharitonenko, built in 1893, the interior designed by the architect, Shekhtel, to combine an eclectic mix of styles in its construction. As a result we have Gothic, Empire, Italian baroque, Scottish baronial, all side by side; and all of it separated from its source of food, the basement kitchen, by 63 stone steps; this is the only access to the kitchen, divided as it is from the residence on the first and second floors, by the Chancery and all the office buildings on the ground floor.

Tuesday 21 September

The heavy luggage was delivered (120 cases from Athens and 20 from London) on the day of our party to meet the whole of the Embassy staff. Then Iain left for Kishinev, Moldavia with the Trade Delegation and Minister Rifkind, our first official visitor, and I struggled with preparations for their return, shopping with the cook, talking to the rest of the staff and interviewing prospective new ones. The delegation came bouncing back from Kishinev with the head of the Russian delegation, Brezhnev junior, suffering from some illness or acute form of alcoholism. There were visits to the ballet to see a new addition to the repertoire called The Indian Poem, *a mixture of oriental style and classical dancing which did not mix well; visits to a stud farm where we were given a troika ride, several very exhilarating circuits round the ring, which would have been even better riding in the woods or pulling a sleigh through the snow; then came the lunch for 50 which we had been planning for a week.*

Friday 1 October

Credentials were presented to the Georgian Deputy President on duty for receiving ambassadors, and Iain returned with his Embassy party, the Minister, Alan Brooke Turner, Head of Chancery, Christopher Meyer, Attachés, first secretaries and Commercial Counsellor David Beattie. With them came Nikiforov, still as urbane and in his job as head of Protocol Department after 6 years; Suslov and Semeonov from the 1st European Department of the Ministry of Foreign Affairs, also 'old friends' from the 1970s. Champagne was drunk and toasts given once again.

But the day was not over. There was another delegation in town, the Edinburgh Group, with General Carver, former Joint Chief of Staff, whom we had known in Indonesia, Nigel Calder and John Erickson; they meet regularly to discuss the problems of nuclear armament and international tension. With them came to supper, again at round tables in the dining room, some of their Russian colleagues at the talks, Dr Yanaev engineer/historian/philosopher; Mr and Mrs Alexandrov, he a member of the Central Committee of the CPSU, with an interesting line on the problems of dealing with unstable western governments which never last more than 4–5 years. He did admit that there could be problems with one-party governments too, even such things as internal struggles for power, but he did not throw any light on present possibilities in the Kremlin.

Thursday 14 October

I made my first visit to the MGU (Moscow State University) since 1976. The Head of the English department whom we knew well from the

1970s, Olga Sergeevna Akhmanova, had invited us to her dacha previously and seemed to be delighted to see us; no sign of the previous rift with the Embassy presumably now healed. At the university I was introduced to her new programme of teaching, the rhetorical style to be achieved by everyone, the sort to be used at any international conference. The cult of personality is stronger than ever.

Friday 15 October

An unfortunate day for the Sutherland family. The residence cook of 31 years is due to leave. While I was at my Russian lesson Alex had phoned to say she had an accident on her bicycle. Thankfully although the bike is a write off she is only bruised and shaken. Later in the evening Konstantin, number two driver, phoned from Leningrad to say that he had crashed the Cortina which he was bringing from Helsinki. He was all right but the car is a write off too. I was furious and frustrated that I could not have my own car, knowing as I did that Konstantin's driving was well known to be fast and dangerous. When not working at the Embassy he is a stunt rider of motorcycles on ice, which is no excuse for trying to drive a Cortina into a road block and making it look like Concorde.

Friday 22 October

On the advice of the wife of our Indian colleague who is a teacher of Russian and former Nehru interpreter, and who knows everyone in the artistic, cultural world, we went to see The Three Sisters *at the Taganka Theatre. It was full of shouting, screaming, and brass bands on stage, clattering of metal décor, very tiring and noisy, more Lyubimov (the new director) than Chekhov. I am told that Lyubimov has imprinted his personality on all the productions at the theatre and that there has been a complete revolution in theatre production; that there are no longer any of the more gentle old style productions of the classics, even at the MXAT, the Arts Theatre. It is the English who now cherish the image of the old style Chekhov plays, the birch trees, the falling leaves and the sad sentimental style.*

This is part of the changes which have taken place since the 1970s, the more modern and experimental atmosphere. This does not mean that it is any easier to socialise with Russians. We still cannot meet politicians or members of the party freely, but those who are involved in commerce with the west are now allowed to meet us, as are artists, musicians, film and theatre directors and most members of the literary and artistic world. At the same time there is a greater knowledge and acceptance of the west, pop music records are on sale, and foreign language books, imported clothes and shoes. The west is no longer hidden or ignored (it is too accessible now to the locals); what is useful or considered harmless is accepted, openly, but only what is sanctioned officially.

Unfortunately corruption is rife. The clumsy bureaucratic organisation has become so creaky that to get things done you have to circumvent it. So if you need something you offer the person who can supply it something that he or she wants. Instead of paying a private doctor as you might in the UK you bribe one of the state doctors (there being no others) or make an arrangement to 'provide something he or she needs and you can supply in return'.

Monday 25 October

Academician Skriabin was very charming; he works at the Biological Institute in Moscow and has a laboratory in Pushchino where there are 8 institutes, schools and hospitals – a whole town. He has promised to invite us.

I am enjoying my visits to the MGU in spite of the new restrictions. I am not allowed actually to conduct a class myself, but I can talk quite freely (it seems) with the students and they can ask questions; (not quite sure about political questions yet).

I am more impressed than I thought by Olga Sergeevna's methods and results and quite intrigued to watch. I enjoy the contact with the teachers and students and taking part in the lessons. It is stimulating to get away from the Embassy and they protest so fulsomely that I am useful that I almost believe them.

Sunday 7 November – Anniversary of the Russian Revolution

In spite of snow and an icy wind it was a fine bright day. The European Community's boycotting of the military parade saved us a cold morning. How do all those old men from the Politburo survive, standing for hours watching the parade go past? A reception at the Kremlin in the Palace of Congresses followed with several thousand guests and all the Politburo and government. Rooms of tables were piled with food in typical Russian style with two set aside for foreign diplomats and members of the Ministry of Foreign Affairs. We were *presented to Brezhnev who seemed by this time not to be noticing anything and had difficulty focusing on anyone. Gromyko (still Minister of Foreign Affairs) claimed to recognise us and promised Iain to see him in 10 days or so. I later found Mrs Gromyko who at 72 seemed little changed and still as warm and friendly. We talked with the ex-ambassador from London and Mrs Smirnovsky, Nikoforovs, Arkhipovs, Arbatov, Adamshyn and others. This is the one opportunity of the year to meet some of the party and government. There was no sign of Mrs Brezhnev whom I last saw in 1975 at the time of the Wilson/Callaghan visit.*

Monday 8 November

A bank holiday so we made a visit to Kolomenskoe, looking out over the residential developments of Moscow built in the last 20 years, miles of identical apartment blocks which enclose in the small area of woods and meadowland, the churches of the Ascension (1532) and the Kazan Church (1660). In the evening we saw the revival of the ballet by Shostakovich, The Golden Age. *To the local audiences it is meant to represent the contrast between the decadent dying world of the 1920s, as personified by the Golden Age restaurant run by the NEP (New Economic Policy), where there is drinking and dancing in western 1920s style, and the new emerging world of youth and enthusiasm; 'between the world receding into darkness and the world striving towards brightness and light, the world of great emotion and poetry' to quote the review article by Nikolai Elyash in Izvestiya of Saturday 6th.*

Thursday 11 November

My concern for the elderly at last Sunday's parade was not misplaced. Brezhnev's death was announced at 11 a.m. this morning although he died at 8.30 a.m. the previous day. The TV played solemn music all day interspersed with news bulletins devoted to obituaries of Leonid Ilych. Among the Russian staff and on the street there appeared no emotion and little excitement. It was as though nothing had happened. Twenty nine years ago last March when Stalin died our cook wept as did many people throughout the country. There seemed no emotion left for the unhappy man who had appeared recently merely programmed to perform his role and protect their positions and power.

Saturday 13 November

We heard late on Monday that Secretary of State Pym would come to the funeral, as well as Michael Foot and David Steel from the opposition parties. The centre of the town is closed. Militia stand across the streets at junctions of the main arteries. The Rolls was allowed through to the gastronom *to buy supplies for Monday. They are not risking a repeat of what happened after Stalin died. Gorky Street was closed to everything as the long trailing queue to view Brezhnev's body lying in state wound up from the side entrance to the Hall of Columns in the Trade Union building. Diplomats were invited to attend this morning but wives were not allowed. So I can only rely on Iain's description of Brezhnev propped up as though in a hospital bed, surrounded by wreaths and flowers, his medals laid out beside him. There was an orchestra (was it the same Borodin Quartet that played at Stalin's funeral?) and a long queue winding up the staircase but diplomats were led across it and straight into the presence. Only two members of the Embassy were allowed to accompany Iain. How different from the jolly party which filed past Stalin 29 years ago when some were so distracted by the music, the flowers and the people that they never saw Josip Vissarionivich lying on his bier.*

For eighteen years B has been in power, as General Secretary of the CPSU since he ousted Khrushchev in 1964, first as a member of a collective with Kosygin and Podgorny and gradually taking over power until, in 1977 he became President of the Supreme Soviet as well. He has seen détente, *the build up of nuclear forces to parity with the US; the decline of the Soviet economy until now when there are serious food shortages and agricultural problems; the meetings with Nixon in the 1970s and Poland's military rule. As Soviet rulers are not elected but selected by the Politburo they stay until the end. There is no dignified exit except death.*

Yesterday the Central Committee announced the appointment of Andropov, the ex-KGB chief, as the new General Secretary. So far they have not announced the name of the new President but it is likely to be someone else at this stage, until and if one central figure gains power. This has been the policy in the past. Stalin shared power in the 1920s, after the death of Lenin, with Kamenev, Zinoviev and Trotsky, Khrushchev with Voroshilov and Bulganin until assuming full power in 1956, and Brezhnev ruled with Kosygin as Prime Minister and Podgorny as President of the Supreme Soviet until he took over when Podgorny died in 1977.

Sunday 14 November

Secretary of State Pym did not arrive at Sheremetevo airport until 10.30 p.m. and then disappeared to various meetings until 2 a.m. He and Iain had to leave next morning at 8.30 to lay wreaths from the Queen and the British government in the Hall of Columns. They had to be with the rest of the party in Red Square by 11. The advantage of not being at the funeral was seeing the whole story on television. There was a deathly silence in Red Square as the first pictures were shown of the crowds of people carefully selected as spectators. Occasional glimpses could be seen of official visitors who had assembled from all over the world. Foot was easily recognisable with his white hair; also Indira Gandhi and Yasser Arafat. But somewhere behind were representatives of most of the countries of the world. Mrs Marcos represented the Philippines, the Indonesians had a party of 17 or 18, Fidel Castro was there as were all the socialist leaders naturally; Foreign Minister Hua from China, Trudeau from Canada, Vice President Bush and Shultz from the USA, Papandreou from Greece, Palme from Sweden, Dutch and Danish Foreign Ministers and de Lorca, the caretaker Foreign Minister from Spain. The biggest gathering of world leaders ever known in the USSR was how one newspaper described it. The event had become far more than poor Brezhnev's last journey to Red Square. There was barely time for that squeezed in between the meetings with Andropov, Gromyko or Tikhonov (Prime Minister), which took place after the funeral. Advice poured in from the western press. This was a time to develop a closer relationship with the SU, to take advantage of the change of leadership, said some; others warned against being rushed into giving anything away at a time of change, that it was a time for even greater caution and restraint.

The funeral over, the foreign representatives were invited to the St George's Hall in the Kremlin where they were to file past a line of Soviet leaders drawn up to greet them, led by Andropov. Meanwhile the backup troops and I sat down to lunch, fondly believing that either they would be given a buffet at the Kremlin or that our lunch would be finished long before Iain, Pym, Foot and Steel could return. They arrived just as we reached our boeuf stroganov *and from 13 we became 17 and all began to move up the table and jump around like a scene from Alice in Wonderland.*

At 6.30 they left once again for Sheremetevo and home.

Tuesday 16 November

Our pre-arranged house guest, on her way home from Tokyo, arrived an hour after the official guests left. I took her a walk from the National Hotel to Red Square, attaching ourselves in a drizzle of cold rain to the queue for the Mausoleum, and managed to make our way down the steps and file silently and reverently, with all coat buttons fastened and no hands in our pockets, past the body of Lenin (if it is still Lenin). I thought he looked a shade waxier than the last time I had seen him in the 1970s. I remembered the twin-bedded effect when Stalin was also for a short time lying in the Mausoleum, from his death in 1953 until his fall from grace in 1956. He was later removed and buried in the same row of graves as Brezhnev yesterday.

The week passed in digesting the events of the last few days and in unending speculation on the future of east–west relations, the direction to be taken by the new leadership and relations between the USSR and China.

Thursday 2 December

I was much amused and surprised by the presentation by the first year students who gave excerpts from Chaucer, skits on their lectures, songs, sketches from The Importance of Being Earnest, *take-offs of their teachers – all very funny and well done and so refreshing to know that it could be done by Soviet students who have, presumably to comply with the tenets of Marxist-Leninist behaviour and whose teachers had just attended a party meeting calling for greater discipline and prompt attendance at lectures.*

Thursday 23 December

I arrived back from London a few hours before the start of the Embassy Christmas party. Over a hundred came, ate, drank and watched the apparently traditional 'cabaret'. It included take-offs of Chancery, Registry and of course, the Ambassador (the latter mostly a clever monologue by Christopher Meyer). There was also an excerpt from Swan Lake, *given by the attachés in long johns and tutus.*

Friday 24 December

A late service in the Embassy at 11.30 conducted by Alphonz Lamprecht, the American Anglican chaplain, and Archimandrite Niphon of Antioch, who took part in the serving of communion, Orthodox and Anglican celebrating communion together. Greek Orthodox do not allow Anglicans to share their Communion but Niphon is a law unto himself; trained in the American University, Cairo, and Zagorsk Seminary, Lebanese by nationality, he officiates at his two churches in Moscow.

Christmas Lunch was for 11, with some single members of the Embassy, the students and family. A wet walk through Red Square afterwards; the first non-white Christmas I have ever known in Moscow. What is happening to the winter?

New Year's Eve was spent with the Hartmans dancing to their jazz band.

Wednesday 5 January 1983

Peter Donohoe, the brilliant young Tchaikovsky prize-winning English pianist gave a magnificent concert in the residence, playing Prokofiev, Stravinsky and Rachmaminov. Petrushka was very loud in the front row of the ballroom. Many Russian musical personnages came, including Richter, who they say does not often go out.

Friday 10 February

The Pattersons arrived from Ulan Bator to stay for 4 days. On Saturday evening we took them to the opera, Eugene Onegin. Tatiana was too big and mature but the ball scenes magnificent and the music good. On Sunday I took them to the Zvenigorod Monastery in the snow and cold. It is much restored since a last visit there in 1975.

By the evening I was really too tired for The Master and Margarita at the Taganka Theatre and I had not had time to re-read it. (This is Bulgakov's masterpiece written on three planes, the trial of Christ, the goings on with the devils in Moscow and the love story.) I liked the scenes with Pontius Pilate which were quieter and easier to understand; as were the ones in the psychological hospital. The tricks of the three devils' associates were more complicated, as was the Master part. Margarita did not fly off at the end but she did swing naked from a clock/swing on the stage half way through.

Friday 18 February

At last the day of our visit to Pushchino dawned, and with it a fine sunny day along the 100 kms of the Simferopol Highway. It all looked as *Mother Russia is meant to in midwinter, white birch barks against the snow and heavy snow laden pines. The men went to see the Microbiological Centre (the main centre in the SU) and I went to see the school. Its only claim to being special is that it carried out any experiments in secondary education the Ministry of Education cared to send it, including having an 11th grade, achieved by starting at 6 instead of the customary 7.*

We went from there to the Palace of Weddings to stand before the altar like construction and to meet the extraordinarily young 'marriage person'. She carried out about 100 ceremonies a year. How many divorces? The national average was one in five but theirs seemed lower. And so to lunch, this time Scriabin being the tamadan *(toastmaster). We were all toasted, together and separately, women, men, women (as superior beings but not as leaders). And we all had to make speeches in Russian.*

Monday 10 March

The programme of the official visit to Leningrad turned out to be very thin, consisting mostly of meals and visits to museums. The only serious interview was with the mayor, Zaikov, at the gorispolkom, *who produced a long list of the city's achievements. Another 'peace' speech degenerated into a rather heated argument. Iain repeated his remarks of the day before about the American disarmament proposals but the mayor would not be side tracked from his anti-Reagan, anti-American line. And the Russian who was supposed to translate replies could not or would not do it properly. We did a tour of the city ourselves, to St Isaacs, the bronze horseman, and out to Smolny in the bright sunshine and blue sky. The city was beautiful with its pastel blues, pinks and yellows, the frozen Neva and the canals.*

We then drove with Leonid to Helsinki. The difference between the two sides of the frontier is very marked. Immediately after reaching Finland there is a simple but smart coffee shop with bright paint and clean tables, selling good coffee and cakes. If the Finns can do it why not the Russians?

Helsinki is small and unpretentious but with its own charm and some attractive 19th century buildings. We walked across the frozen Baltic to an island turned museum of old wooden Finnish architecture and a visit to the Sibelius Monument made of steel tubes. There were Finns on skis, on foot, pulling their children on sledges, all looking relaxed and prosperous.

Wednesday 16 March

After some weeks absence I attended the 4th year poetry class again at MGU. After the class Olga Sergeevna told me that the university had decided they could no longer allow British diplomats' wives to teach at the university. I could continue only with the teachers' in-course training and perhaps sometimes with postgraduate students. I went back with Irina (one of the teachers I have known since the 1970s) to her communal flat, where they still live behind Telegrafny Pereulok, for lunch with her and her mother, a gentle frail lady who attends Niphon's church regularly and was delighted to learn that I knew him.

Friday 25 March

The CBI (Confederation of British Industry) was holding its Round Table Conference with the Russians on economic and scientific affairs in the Tourist Centre in the ancient city of Suzdal. Those of us not taking part in the discussions were given the full Suzdal tour – the Kremlin with the Church of the Nativity, the Yefimovsky Monastery has its red brick fortifications and the Cathedral of the Transfiguration, its domes and half columns of Suzdal 12th–13th century style. After lunch it was the turn of the Pokrovsky Monastery (Intercession), formerly a convent for nuns and where various female members of aristocratic families who were unwanted were imprisoned. Eudoxia, the first wife of Peter the Great was one of them. The convent area is now filled with wooden chalet-houses for tourists and the refectory church has become a restaurant. The town has been developed as a tourist centre for the whole area of the Golden Circle, as they now call the collection of ancient cities of northern Russia.

There are a total of 50 churches in the town which was made into his capital by Yuri Dolgoruky (founder of Moscow) in the 13th century, but his son, Andrei Bogolubsky did not like it and moved to Vladimir, which became the larger and more important capital. Suzdal remained the ecclesiastical centre. Being totally devoid of industry it has remained an unspoilt village and therefore an easy place to convert into an architectural and tourist centre – of restored churches, and now hotels and restaurants.

Sunday 27 March

In Vladimir it was a warm sunny day and the two cathedrals on the outskirts of town, St Demetrius and the Uspensky cathedral *were looking fine, although the countryside was drab in its half melted snow and brown bare earth. St Demitrius is the unique example of carved white stone architecture, its outside walls being covered with fantastic creatures, trees and human figures. A special feature are the frieze of lions, with shining and beaming faces and upturned tails in the form of flowers. The Uspensky, the model for the Assumption Cathedral in Moscow, is famous for its Rublev frescoes but there was a service and the old ladies muttered at us as we walked about at the back, trying to peer through the darkness without disturbing them and finally we gave up and left.*

The Conference ended this evening with everyone walking down the corridors muttering how interesting and useful it had been. What had been achieved? It was difficult to assess.

Sunday 3 April

This weekend visits to the Vavilova market to buy wooden Easter eggs made by the villagers and brought to Moscow every year at Easter for sale; also to Leninski Gorki, the last home of Lenin, where he died in 1924, formerly an estate of the Morozov family, with a pleasant classical Russian style building in large grounds surrounded by birch woods. The house walls are covered in memorabilia; you see his bedroom, his study and the bed behind the screen where his wife Krupskaia watched over him; finally the room where he was laid out after he died with death mask, chandelier, draped in black, black bordered photographs etc., a kind of permanent death room. Would the world have been different if he had not died in 1924 but lived until the 1940s or 1950s?

Monday 18 April

We gave a reception for 200, including 50 Russians but only 10 came. Another tit-for-tat expulsion occurred from the Soviet Embassy in London. All the London Symphony Chorus came, plus their hangers on. The director/conductor turned out to be Richard Hickox, brother of a friend I worked with at the Polytechnic of North London. The chorus had been invited to sing with the Soviet State Orchestra by Svetlanov, who had conducted with them in the UK and invited them because 'no one here could sing Dream of Gerontius'.

Saturday 4 June

The weekend visit to Kostroma had to be postponed as I was too ill to go, with a high temperature by the evening. This was the first of a series of sudden mysterious illnesses which pursued me during the three years in Moscow – colds, chest infections with long lingering coughs, anaemia, headaches, stomach upsets, and hepatitis. Iain, who led a very unhealthy life, smoked, ate large heavy meals late at night and did not take much exercise, was, strangely, rarely ill during this time, or at least did not admit to it.

Wednesday 15 June

The day of the Queen's Birthday reception so no time to relapse; flowers to buy, hair to be done at the International Hotel as our hairdresser had been removed, this of all weeks, ostensibly because of ill health; but she is to go and work for a Japanese journalist. Rain poured down at 5 p.m. so the 3 o'clock decision to have the party inside was justified. About 480 came but it was never too crowded and there seemed always to be someone to pass food and drinks. The Russian attendance was better than expected. There would have been room for the entire Embassy whom we had thought we had to ration. Pity.

Tuesday 21 June

Another week of illness until a final essential rally for the arrival of Sir John King of British Airways, Babcock International and various other firms; he is Mrs T's favourite businessman, Iain told me. He seemed more credible in the role of huntsman, fisherman and country squire. The lunch was very difficult to organise with such a disparate guest list – the Kings, their friends the Parker Bowles, de Rosas of Fata (Italian business connections who spoke only Italian), and Mr Timofeev, Minister of Civil Aviation, who spoke only Russian. Sir John King and Timofeev however seemed to get on together once it was established that they were both interested in fishing and salmon breeding and at lunch Mr T told us all about the habits of the Amur salmon.

By the weekend I was feeling better, now being dosed with iron pills for anaemia, and there was talk of a visit to Yasnaia Polyana but all was abandoned, swamped under the pile of papers in the 'box'. Living as we do right over the shop it was too easy for Iain to work in the evenings and over the weekend.

Monday 27 June

Saw the play, Dom Na Naberezhnoi (The House on the Embankment), *adapted by Lyubimov from the novel by Trifonov. There were more Lyubimov tricks, banging on doors and walls, throwing water about, a very dark and dismal view of life in the 1930s and war years in the big apartment block for privileged party members and others, situated near us. A young man was trying to climb the social and academic ladder without any real merit and without writing his thesis, through his contacts with a war-wounded philosophy professor and his young daughter who is in love with the young man. We discussed it at Ekaterinovka with Olga Sergeevna and others the next day. Natasha thought the play much too dark and miserable. She had lived there until her marriage and they had such a happy life with so many young people and children, all very positive. And all the old Bolsheviks lived there. O. Sergeevna did not like dark and negative literature and anyway she never reads modern literature. She could not stand the people in* Doctor Zivago *who complained all the time because of the things they could not get. I defended it as an authentic picture of the times, a period of great confusion and chaos but she could not agree.*

Friday 1 July

In the evening we drove to Rostov Veliki to stay in the hotel 'Rostov'. We last saw Rostov in the snow of winter 1975 when the lake was frozen. Now children picnicked on the banks, women were scrubbing their clothes and men fishing. We visited the churches restored since the amazing whirlwind of the 1950s – the Kremlin, along the covered walks as far as the Church of the Resurrection. After lunch we continued to Yaroslavl which we had also last seen on the same visit when all the churches were closed. We were able to see the Church of the prophet Elijah in the main square and the restored 17th century frescoes. It is now a museum with tickets, guides and large groups of Russian tourists gazing at their religious and historic heritage.

On to Kostroma, last visited in the 1950s in very different circumstances, and where we saw the Monastery – Trinity Cathedral and Museum of Religious Objects.

We stopped at Kabikha on the outskirts of Yaroslavl on the way back, the site of a museum where the writer Nekrasov spent his summers; idyllic scenes of Russian rural life, women scything and gathering hay in the garden, looked straight out of Tolstoy. Our final stop on our mini 'golden circle' tour was at the very large but sadly dilapidated monastery at Pereslavl, all crumbling except for the walls.

Saturday 23 July

We left for a weekend at Zavidovo, the 'diplomatic' resort with hotel and dachas in the woods where the Volga joins the Shoshka River. Walked along the banks watching the ducks, herons, swifts and other birds. The fields were bright with wild flowers and frogs popping up every few yards. Back at the hotel Iain was overcome with fierce chest pains and had to be put to bed and given bouillon and toast. He recovered by the morning but the weather changed to pouring rain and we decided to go home, Iain driving the new Sierra, bought from Stockmans and still with Finnish number plates. A militiaman on the way back stopped us and asked where our old car, that nice Rolls, was.

Friday 5 to Wednesday 10 August

As this was to be Iain's first official visit outside the main part of the RSFSR he decided to go somewhere not visited regularly by western diplomats. The autonomous republics of Dagestan and Chechen Ingushetia could not be less like the central areas of the Russian Federal Republic. They are mountainous areas rising to over 4000 metres. In Dagestan there are 33 nationalities, each with their own languages although only four or five are regularly used. The local tribes lived in the valleys divided by high mountains, with no lateral access and grew up speaking their own languages. There is a story about God travelling over the Northern Caucasus, distributing languages. His bag broke and all that was left fell into the small area between the Black Sea and the Caspian.

The languages were not written down before the revolution, or perhaps only in Arabic in later years, and most people were illiterate. According to the rector of the University of Mahachkala, capital of Dagestan, lectures were given now in the four main languages, Avar, Dargin, Kumukh and Lesgian. We did not hear these languages much in Mahachkala although the nationalities were well represented among the officials whom we met. The common language was Russian. In Derbent the position was different, especially in and around the mosque. But everyone could speak Russian, sometimes with a heavy local accent.

In the Autonomous Republic of Chechen Ingushetia (now divided into the troubled Chechnya and Ingushetia) there are two basic languages, Chechen and Ingush which are mutually intelligible. Our companion, Magomedov, often spoke Chechen both in town and outside.

We were treated rather like senior party members and in Grozny we stayed at the government/party guest house in great splendour. There as in Mahachkala we were always accompanied by one official and an interpreter (never left on our own) and we travelled with a police escort in front to clear the roads, with loud speaker, much to my embarrassment.

Friday 19 August

The incident of the bomb. At lunch time the alarm bell rang. Half an hour later I found that a Russian had driven into the Embassy, through the militia on the gate, had been seized, dragged away and beaten up. The small white Moskvitch still stood by the flagstaff. The militia had smashed the glass and dragged him from the car. Later it was taken round to the back of the Embassy and examined, the 'device' was found, removed and set on the lawn. We shall never know what the man intended to do. Blow us up? Take us all hostage until we promised him asylum? Who knows? Perhaps only he.

Tuesday 1 September

Back to school for all Russian children; the first lesson to be 'a lesson of peace'. That night came the news of the shooting down of the Korean 747 jumbo jet over the sea near Sakhalin. An American base in Japan revealed that Soviet planes intercepted the civilian airliner and fired at it; thereafter it disappeared without trace; the rest of the weekend was concerned with the incident. Reagan, emotional and violently anti-Soviet, accused the Russians of murder and massacre. Russians at first silent later accused the US in turn of provocation and did not admit to shooting down plane. Most nations expressed their shock and horror.

I was struggling with a painful abscess on my neck which all available modern medicine had failed to cure. On my last night, after the reception, Nadya the cook offered some homeopathic help in the shape of a baked onion and honey (wrapped round my neck in a residence napkin) which finally started the improvement the morning before we were due to leave and I was pronounced able to travel. We were leaving by train for Odessa and then by boat to Piraeus with a large cargo of things for the house on Evia. Konstantin, never to be outdone, drove us in pouring rain right

A nice touch

Diplomats have their own and various ways of dealing with what are, sometimes euphemistically, known as provocative incidents. The reaction of the British mission in Moscow to the Soviets' handling of a mysterious stranger who drove into the embassy court-yard with a home-made bomb — diplomatically classified as a "small device" — is interesting. It is not clear from the reports whether the stranger intended to blow up the embassy or to seek sanctuary within its walls. At all events he was manhandled off the premises by the Russian police whom he had eluded. A spokesman later disclosed that the British Ambassador had spoken not only to the Soviet authorities about the unauthorised entry but also about the strong-armed methods employed by the Russian police in removing the intruder. Other members of the embassy, apparently, had also shown concern over what they considered the excessive use of force.

The British Ambassador in Moscow is Sir Iain Sutherland, an Aberdeen man. He was educated at Aberdeen Grammar School and Balliol. One trusts that all Grammarians and all Balliol men will consider that Sir Iain's conduct reflects credit on his school and on his college and that it conformed with the highest Foreign Office standards. It was also a tribute to his upbringing, not perhaps so surprising, since both his mother and his father were distinguished artists held in esteem and affection by all who knew them. When one reflects that the man with the small device was not a pedestrian passing through an Alpine village at dusk and holding aloft a banner but a motorist, whose intention might well have been to blow up the embassy, the reaction of Sir Iain and his staff seems all the more civilised and humane.

One wonders what the Muscovites made of the interest shown by the British Embassy in their unofficial visitor's rights. Moscow does not abound in civil rights societies ready, at the drop of a fur hat, to bound into action when a policeman lays so much as a little finger on a suspected pickpocket. The notion that the accused must be treated as innocent until he is proved guilty has not been much favoured by the Kremlin, let alone the belief that even if the accused is found guilty he should be spared rough handling. At a time when parts of the world dispense barbaric penalties it is comforting to know that the dignity of man, even of suspect man, as extolled throughout the ages in Aberdeen Grammar School, still finds its champions within our foreign service.

28. A report from *The Scotsman* on 27 August 1983 of an incident when an intruder drove into the British Embassy, Moscow and was roughly removed by the Soviet Militia.

*on to the platform and we piled our 11 pieces of luggage into
the compartment.*

*Iain was unhappy about leaving in what he called the worst crisis
since 1978. BA and probably other airlines were to cease flying into
Moscow for 60 days as a protest against the shooting down of the
airliner. The Russians more or less admitted to shooting it down but
still argued that it was a spy plane sent by the Americans; some spy
plane with 269 people on board. Reagan still threatens reprisals but
no American airlines fly into the SU anyway since Afghanistan; and
they were not going to cancel the recently signed grain agreement.*

*Politically it has been an interesting year, with Brezhnev's death and
the attempts of Andropov to introduce reforms and improvements
into all fields of labour and industry. His job is unenviable as he is up
against the old school inside the party and government as well as
millions of Russians not inspired by idealism, not accustomed to doing
much more than a quarter of a day's work and not ready to give up
their 'getting round the system'. Throughout the year there has been
the battle for nuclear disarmament, or balance. Offers from Andropov
to withdraw some of their medium range missiles if the Americans do
not introduce Cruise or Pershing missiles into Europe were followed
by assurance that the Russian missiles would not only be removed but
would be destroyed and not turned against the east. At Geneva the
battle continues. But how does one judge when there is complete parity
and how to maintain it even then?*

* * *

Monday 8 November

*The parade and the Kremlin reception; no Andropov at either; lovely
weather, colourful, short parade with Ustinov taking the salute and
Chernenko in place of honour on the Mausoleum; no excuse for
'someone with just a cold' not to be there. At the reception Tikhonov
made the speech, no one was presented to any member of the Politburo.
They ate their food, sat and watched the show and walked out,
obviously scared that someone might ask 'Where is Andropov?' Kidney
trouble, heart trouble, shot in the arm in a family quarrel, dead
perhaps, these are the rumours going around Moscow. As it was the
first time the General Secretary did not attend the parade something
serious must be wrong; or else a coup. But his name was still being
mentioned, his exhortations quoted. No one was taking over the*

leadership; who would? Was Chernenko making a comeback? Would the successor be Romanov from Leningrad, with that and his name against him, or Gorbachev, in his mid fifties?

There is more speculation about Andropov but still no news and he has failed to appear in public in spite of rumours that he would. Much speculation about the Soviet attitude at the INF talks at Geneva. A report from Germany said that the Russians had offered to exclude the British and French deterrents from negotiations on disarmament. This was denied by the SU. Pershing and Cruise missiles have been delivered to the Greenham Common base this week amid the threats of the protesters who say they will stay as long as the missiles are based there.

Friday 18 November

There is still no sign of the promised residence uplift. Admin section refused to bring a dishwasher from Helsinki saying that they did not have authority from London. How can one be expected to entertain hundreds of guests a month in this day and age without a dishwasher.

The British delegation for site negotiations (to arrange compensatory terms for a move from present building, a move which has been on and off since 1951) arrived, including Roger Carrick now in charge of Overseas Estates Department (OED) and Curtis Keeble, our predecessor. I asked Carrick to talk to the wives about the constant delays in the replacement of furnishings in Embassy accommodation, sometimes for a year or more.

Thursday 15 December

I am up late every night reading the novel of the contemporary Siberian writer, Rasputin, about a village under orders to evacuate before it is flooded by the waters of the river Angara to feed the local hydro-electrical station at Bratsk. Rasputin belongs to a group of 'Village Writers' whom we are reading for the Contemporary Soviet Literature Group. It is hard work but rewarding as there is some interesting literature being published at the moment, much more so than the approved literature of the late 1960s and the early 1970s.

Sunday 18 December

The family arrived from London just in time for the Nine Lessons Carol Service; usual ecumenical service went off well with Russian Orthodox and Baptist clergy reading lessons, as well as American Military, women and Iain. Niphon gave a blessing. The International Choir was invited by me to take part as Iain had said they could not give a concert that afternoon. They nearly drowned the front row and the conductor nearly knocked over Niphon; I had the music stand in my chest but otherwise all went well. The usual students arrived to spend Christmas with us, from Voronezh this year, and we were 8 for every meal, with 16 for Christmas day, which ended with a visit to a very complicated 4 hour opera, The Town of Kitezh, at the Bolshoi.

Wednesday 11 January 1984

We attended a special performance at the Bolshoi in honour of the 20th anniversary of the work of the choreographer, Grigorovich. They danced the 1st act of Romeo and Juliet, 2nd act of Spartacus and 3rd act of Golden Age. There was great excitement throughout the theatre, which culminated in a reception on the stage to which we were invited. G was bounced up and down by the dancers and champagne appeared through the floor in an explosion and a puff of smoke. All the former ballerinas were there including Golovkina, the head of the ballet school, doing little turns on the stage.

Tuesday 24 January

Arrival of David Steel and company on an official visit at the invitation of the Russians. I went with Mrs Steel to the Russian Women's Committee where she questioned them about independent women's movements and peace movements, designed to put pressure on the Soviet government, which of course does not happen here. Terence and Rosemary Garvey arrived for a visit on the 26th, the first time since they left in 1975.

Some juggling needed to combine the two sets of guests but we took the Garveys to the Kremlin tour organised for the Steels. There was much sentimental reverence for Lenin, the man, in the tour of his apartments – old news reels and stills in the Kremlin, disembodied voices and favourite music, all a bit over the top; interesting however to be reminded that he lived for two years after having his stroke in 1922, most of the time as leader. I wonder how much he appeared in public compared with our present absent friends. Terence thought that he was not so much of a single leader as now; there were of course Trotsky, Kamenev and Zinoviev, as well, not to mention Stalin, slowly building up his power.

* * *

Monday 13 February

Yuri Andropov died on 9th but as usual it was announced a day later and it was decided that I did not need to come back early. The airport was completely jammed with delegations arriving for the funeral and I had to wait hours for my luggage. I got back to the Embassy just in time to change and see Iain briefly before he left for the airport, and to walk through the rooms and check that all was in order for the visitors. I met Mrs Thatcher at the top of the stairs. She looked thinner and younger than in Athens in 1980 and we had more conversation together this time, before and after her briefing. Dennis Healey came instead of Neil Kinnock who is in the States. David Steel as usual represented the Liberals, but this time also with David Owen as head of the SDP Alliance.

Tuesday 14 February

Valentine's Day and the day of Andropov's funeral. It all seemed very familiar, the same slow music, the slow goose step, the gun

29. Mrs Thatcher received by Chernenko in the Kremlin, after the funeral of Andropov, 14 February 1984. Iain stands next to Mrs Thatcher who is opposite Chernenko.

carriage, the flowers. But it lacked emotion and all seemed rather perfunctory. This time the camera did not show the coffin being lowered into the grave (with a thud as in Brezhnev's funeral). It did show Mrs Andropov who has never appeared before and a son and daughter. After the funeral Chernenko, the new General Secretary received the guests. (He was announced on Monday and we were told in mid-flight.) After lunch and various bilateral meetings and press conferences they all departed for Sheremetovo airport.

It was better organised, by us as well as the Russians this time, but with none of the sense of drama and expectation. The appointment of Chernenko, after all the speculation about Romanov and Gorbachev, was an anti-climax and the return to an old Brezhnev man seemed to lack interest and hope of any change either good or bad, hard line or soft. Nigel Wade, the Daily Telegraph correspondent, seemed to think life would be dull and uneventful. But David Owen, as we talked before the delegation left, was convinced Mrs Thatcher wanted a change in the relationship and this would come about. Healey had a funny story about catching the two alliance leaders with their trousers down in the Military Attaché's office after the funeral – taking off their long johns.

Wednesday 22 February

The Ratfords are back from leave. I hope this will give Iain a bit of a break. But will he take it? The house has been in an uproar with Courtalds all over the place, preparing for the fashion show. They produced a wonderful show with 8 beautiful girls, well rehearsed and presented as great entertainment – music, dancing, lights, real cat-walk atmosphere; a pity so few Russians came and no high ranking ones, after all that work. Zaitsev, the Russian designer, came in time for the last scene. There was a distinct sense of anti-climax as they came to take down the catwalk and remove all those racks of clothes. The sense of let down was worse because we were meant to be in Central Asia and to have left for Uzbekistan and Turkmenistan on Thursday. It was not convenient for us to go this week we were told by 2nd European Department. But was it really the earth tremors or the elections (surely they are a forgone conclusion) or did they just not want us to go travelling then, or not at all...?

THREE FUNERALS

Monday 27 February

We left in the car with Konstantin for a short tour of northern Russia, in bright snowy weather with a temperature of -13° C in Yaroslavl, where we stayed one night before going on to Vologda. Churches both in Yaroslavl and Vologda were mostly closed, either for the winter or for restoration. No way could we get to see the frescoes in the Cathedral of St Sophia even though we invoked the help of the Deputy Chairman of the Vologda town council. A protracted tour, escorted by a well informed graduate of the Institute of Pedagogical Studies, of the Kremlin buildings, meant that we arrived too late in the near dark at the Prilutsky Monastery. But they opened the craft museum for us and we returned for a quick look in daylight the next day. It was cold and fine and the Monastery was very impressive with its towers and fortifications and the Church of the Cathedral of the Origin of the True Life Giving Cross, a severe square stone building in monumental style.

The road to Kirillov was more icy and difficult. We turned off the main road to see the Therapontos Monastery. The village seemed deserted at first with its brightly painted wooden houses and domes and walls of the monastery, standing out against the white snow and blue sky. Then a horse drawn sledge appeared and a tractor pulling wood and a young girl, another student from the Vologda Institute who offered to show us round. She showed us the churches but again the cathedral was shut and we were only allowed to peer through the scaffolding to look at the frescoes by Dionysus and his school.

Monday 5 March

We left for our postponed tour of Central Asia. Neither of us had been there since the 1950s and I especially wanted to see the beauties of the Fergana valley in spring. We were combining official visiting with sightseeing. In Turkmenistan, where we had never been before, we visited the Head of the Academy of Sciences who explained how they were solving the water problems of the republic with the opening of the Karakum Canal, which enables them to grow cotton; he discussed too other plans for irrigation including the contentious diversion of the Siberian rivers, the Ob and the Irtysh.

In the space of two days we saw the extensive 2nd–1st century BC Parthian site of Nissa; were taken on a boat trip on the Karakum Canal; visited a large state farm, the ancient city of Merv with the 12th century Mausoleum of the last Seldzhuk Dynasty Sultan, Sanjar; the 6th–4th century BC town of Gyaur-Kala and Erk-kala, spent 10 minutes at a gas fired electric power station and were finally put on a train – the train which existed in the Moscow time-table but which had been denied to us as foreign diplomats and then said not to exist. Geoffrey Murrell, who with his wife Kathy came with us on the journey, thought perhaps they had laid it on just for us.

The train arrived punctually at 3.30 a.m. at the wayside station of Kagan, 10 kilometres from Bukhara, our next stop. When Fitzroy Maclean made this journey in the 1930s he had walked to Buhkara. As we had a lot of luggage and it was by this time pouring with rain we were glad to be met with two cars. Next morning we toured the town in cold bright sunlight. Most of the buildings of interest are of the 16th and 17th centuries which were the period when Bukhara flourished. But most have been restored in the 20th century, rebuilt is a better word. Since my visit in 1953 the town has been almost completely rebuilt and cleared up. Romantic ruins have been restored and the Minaret (Tower of Death) rises from a tidy courtyard not a heap of earth. The small, scruffy hotel I could no longer find. The new tourist hotel is on the other side of the town away from the old narrow streets, lined by brick and mud houses, with no windows looking out on to the street, and chaikanas (tea shops) at every corner. I walked through the small streets to the charming Chor Minor Mosque with 4 minarets, to linger by the Labi Khauz reservoir. They said they would not knock down the old town (as they have knocked down most of the old walls) but who knows what they will do in the interest of tourism and progress, even destroy the very things which tourists come to see.

Friday 9 March

At Samarkand we found snow on the Gur Emir Mausoleum of Tamburlane and the inside gilded and restored. The Registan has been paved, the people and untidy market cleared away, and it was naked and cold except for a few groups of shivering tourists. Registan means a square (stan) covered with sand (reg). The square is paved and the three medresses restored. Ulug Beg, Shir Dor, tili Kari, Shaki Zinda, the group of mausoleums, is built round the tomb of Kusum ibn Abbas, Mohammed's nephew who, according to legend, was killed at prayer and so never died, but took up his head and descended to the basement where he lives for ever; hence the name Shaki Zinda, the living king. There are beautiful tiles in many of the mausoleums but most beautiful of all in his, a lovely place to be buried. Samarkand had grown but it *was never the charming dusty oasis of Bukhara and so the shock of restoration is not so great.*

Our guide agreed to take us to the Bibi Khanum Mosque, although it was under repair having some 17 million roubles spent on its restoration, partly paid for by UNESCO. What will be the fate of the new architect? The original one whom legend says built it during the Indian campaigns of Tamburlane, on the instructions of his favourite wife, Bibi Khanum, met a tragic fate. He fell in love with Bibi Khanum and insisted that she should give him one kiss if she wanted the mosque finished in time for T's return. She resists for some time but finally gives in. Such is the fire of his passion that the skin on her face shows a burn mark. T returns, delighted with the mosque, rushes off to thank B K, sees the mark, realises what has happened, the architect is condemned to death and B K thrown from her own minaret. After this women had to wear veils so that men should not see their faces. But there are practically no veils in Central Asia now.

Saturday 10 March

We set off by car for Kokand complete with police escort; not a very exciting drive through flat and mostly treeless land except for mulberry hedges where the silk worms are reared; still the brown earth and late spring due to the cold February weather. We caught sight of Leninabad, the capital as we drove through a corner of Tadzhikistan, the first foreigners to make this journey by car, and were met in Kokand by a large delegation of people from Intourist (Fergana), and town authorities, headed by the manager of Fergana Intourist, Rakhim Yusupovich Isakov.

The next day we saw the sights of Kokand, accompanied everywhere by Isakov whom we christened 'the godfather' because he seemed to run everything. Another straight road took us to Fergana 100 kms away. After lunch we visited the museum dedicated to the first President of Uzbekistan, were shown a film of him helping to dig the Fergana canal, constructed in 45 days by 160,000 workers. The area is supplied with water by the Syr Darya and its tributaries, and irrigation has made it one of the most fertile regions in the SU. Unfortunately we had to imagine all this as the famous Fergana valley was not the green and flourishing place I had dreamed of seeing. It was still just brown. But it produces half the cotton grown in Uzbekistan and the silk worm cocoons; also melons, pomegranates and grapes.

Monday 12 March

Tashkent had been rebuilt since the 1964 earthquake and is almost a new town. There are vast buildings and wide squares, high rise blocks of flats, a metro, and a big new concert theatre. Tashkent is now a big centre of culture, commerce and tourism.

There was more talk at the Academy of Sciences about rivers and their courses, deserts, crops, cotton, culture and excavation; and discussions about the serious architectural problems of building in a seismic zone after the earthquake. The old houses in the 'old' section of the town are to be removed. They say it is not possible to conserve any part as the clay disintegrates. During the afternoon visit we found that there was more left than I had expected – a maze of small streets with mud houses in poor condition. The large market has been removed to 'somewhere more convenient'. There is a mosque and a medresse and further into town the large Kukeldash Medresse, now restored with tile decorations. An evening at the Zarafshan Restaurant with belly dancers and a daring attempt at a night club cabaret was the climax of our stay.

C. Asia is no longer virtually cut off from the rest of the country by its deserts as it was in the 1950s. Some of the deserts have been watered by extensive irrigation. The people live well, we were told many times. They do not want to leave their republics. With the great increase in production of cotton, specifically, they have become rich, and to a certain extent independent. Tashkent, Samarkand and Bukhara are now big tourist centres.

By 2006 these changes have been magnified considerably. In 1984 who would have thought that in the 21st century Uzbekistan would become home to an American military base and an oil rich country exporting to the west?

Friday 20 April

An Easter weekend at Pskov with Bianca and Karl Fritschi from the Swiss Embassy; we spent the day seeing the Kremlin and the local churches, and after lunch went to Izborsk to see the fortresses and to Pechory where the monastery was closed in preparation for evening Easter mass; attended the midnight service in the more modern, 19th century, cathedral of Archangel Michael, conducted by the Abbot Gabriel. The church was very full but it lacked spontaneity and excitement at midnight. It was better in the *smaller Pokrovsky church where the congregation was taking part in the singing.*

* * *

19th May

We returned from three weeks leave for a busy summer programme which started with the visit by the Channons (Paul Channon, Minister of Trade) for the meetings of the joint commission on trade. On 23rd the party was taken on a visit to Kiev hosted by the Deputy Minister of Foreign Trade. We had a heavy programme of sightseeing, including the war memorial where we were constantly told how the Soviet army liberated Europe with never a mention of the allies. The Pechorskaia Lavra was cleaned up; even the caves had stone flagged floors and electric lights. Gone were the dirt floors, candles and grease covered, much kissed coffins of the monks who were buried alive in the caves. Lunch was given by the Ukrainian Minister of Trade and afterwards we were taken on a cruise along the Dnieper with more food and champagne and a group of Ukrainian singers; all too soon back to shore for a quick visit to the exhibition 'Britain Today'.

No sooner had the Channons left than the Pattersons arrived from Ulan Bator for a break from their very restricted life. At the same time the Turners (Richard, former naval attaché in the 1970s, and Italian wife Mima) arrived as our guests. I juggled official duties, university visits and entertainment for our various guests. The Turners were replaced by the Richardsons, George and Isobel from Oxford. I took them to Peredelkino to see the Pasternak dacha and visit the Yevtushenkos in thunder and lightning and pouring rain; a very damp pilgrimage to the Pasternak grave. The summer season was becoming almost as bad as Athens, but without the heat.

Saturday 16 June

The text of Iain's 'British National Day' TV broadcast was rejected and he refused to negotiate further. The section about free movement of peoples was pronounced demagogic and the bit about welcoming the SU as an ally after 2 years of fighting the Fascists was unacceptable as I had imagined it would be. Was he perhaps a shade relieved to be off the hook?

Tuesday 26 June

Told by the doctor what I had already guessed, that I had hepatitis. It was a relief to be able to stop trying to feel all right and to obey instructions to relax and rest.

In view of the imminent visit by Secretary of State and Lady Howe telegrams were sent to London. The visit was to go ahead as planned, staying at the residence. Ulla Ratford would accompany Lady Howe on her visits and I would do only the minimum. I spent the week sleeping and reading and talking to my visiting friend Nancy Lubin from Washington when she came in and out from her meetings on medicine in space, etc.

Saturday 30 June

At the weekend the Russians suddenly came up with a new offer of talks on anti-satellite weapons (yet another acronym ASAT). The offer was immediately accepted by the Americans who said they would agree to ASAT but would like also to talk about missiles in general, i.e. back to the bargaining table. The Russians chose to interpret this as 'pre-conditions' and as Sir Geoffrey Howe put it, refused to take yes for an answer. The usual anti-American propaganda was stepped up to accuse them of not properly responding to the latest offer. All this to some extent took the wind out of the sails of the Howe visit. Gromyko railed in an unpleasant way during his speech at the lunch at the Guest House. Sir Geoffrey's was a dignified but firm response.

Monday 2 July

The lunch was friendlier personally than officially. Lidya Dimitrovna, (Mrs Gromyko) was still the same, adding her own idiosyncratic remarks. Gromyko to her, 'When I told Lady Howe I did not smoke, she said I was a good person. I said she should tell you that.' Mrs Gromyko to him, 'Perhaps you would be better if you smoked.'

The next day there were more talks for Sir Geoffrey with Gromyko. Lady H went to the Women's Committee where they had a rather formal session with Tereshkova and never got down to the nitty gritty of women's problems. Lady H, an ex-President of the Equal Opportunities Commission, is well informed and interested in employment for women and other questions. A lunch at the residence was followed by a session *for Sir G with Chernenko, a press conference and two interviews for the BBC TV and radio.*

Wednesday 18 July

The team negotiating sites for the Moscow and London embassies are back again – Curtis Keeble, Carrick and Bertram the architect; much joking at lunch with Carrick, Sapukhin and Christopher, about when the new embassy would be ready; by next century (give or take a decade or two) – 'hope they would not have moved the capital when we had just got it finished, back to Leningrad perhaps', I suggested; 'or Kiev', suggested Mr S enjoying the joke immensely; 'FO get it wrong again' quoted Christopher. 'Poor intelligence', I added, 'and the Russians knew all the time.' Mr S convulsed with laughter.

Away from 23 July to 3 October – Moscow-Irkutsk-Baikal-Ulan Bator-Peking-Hong Kong-London-France-Switzerland-Italy-Greece (Aetos)-Odessa-Moscow – a fascinating but exhausting marathon.

* * *

Wednesday 3 October 1984

Back to Moscow by air from Odessa leaving Leonid to drive the new Sierra back. They had actually finished the building work in the residence; finally there were proper guest loos behind the pantry area – clean, tidy, and a bit clinical but at least hygienic. And the whole area was cleaned up, with new floor and odd bits of furniture removed. Will everything really be finished before we leave?

Thursday 25 October

I now know what a jam session is. Kenny Ball and his jazzmen came to play at the residence and the 3 Russian bands, who were invited to hear them, all brought their instruments (unasked) and began to play. They played in turns after the concert and then played all together with Kenny joining in too; an extraordinary evening with several unexpected Russians very excited by the music, rocking and tapping and finally dancing, led by Donna Hartman.

Friday 26 October

A rushed departure for an official visit to Georgia which by chance coincided with the Tbilisi Autumn Festival, taking place on the last Sunday of October, the Tbilisoba. After two days of meetings and discussions with the local authorities and visits to theatres and restaurants, we were taken to the parks where each region had its celebrations, singing, dancing and stalls selling Georgian food and trinkets. At the entrance gates we came face to face with Shevarnadze, the 1st secretary of the Georgian Communist Party (later Foreign Minister under Gorbachev) so that Iain was able to have a short unscheduled conversation with him, which they had not been able to put into his programme. We left in the afternoon for Telavi in Kakhetia, where we visited the Tsinandali vineyards and vodka plants, where vodka ran out of the taps in the walls; then to the Shuamta Monastery, a group of buildings dating from the 5th to 16th century with good frescoes.

Hospitality was almost overwhelming and involved the usual gargantuan feasts of Georgian food and drink, with toasts given by the tamadan (toast master) which Iain and Raymond (Asquith) were obliged to drink do dna (to the bottom). I was excused and at breakfast I also got out of the special morning-after soup, hashi, a greasy tripe soup with a strong garlic sauce, but managed the buffalo milk yoghourt without the caviar and brandy. The last day Iain paid calls on the Deputy Chairman of the Council of Ministers and I went to a school and the Children's Rehabilitation Centre. A visit to Mtskheta, more eating and drinking, music and dancing ended our stay.

Wednesday 31 October

Kathy Murrell arrived from Moscow for our drive to Erevan. Our burly Georgian driver was cheerful and cooperative and we stopped to see the monastery of Gosh and photographed the khatkars standing outside the bare but beautiful churches; on to Haghartsin and more northern Armenian mediaeval churches with their altars on raised platforms ascended by steps rather like a small stage. None of these churches was in use but the burnt out candles showed that they were still visited by the faithful. From Haghartsin we drove through a pass on to Lake Sevan, 6000 feet above sea level. The sky was dramatic with wild black and white clouds blowing across the white-capped peaks of the volcanic mountains. We made one last visit to Tsakhadzor and the Monastery of Kecharis, just as the light was fading and we reached Erevan by 7 p.m.

We left early the next morning without seeing Erevan in daylight. Our objective was to visit Zhenia Evtushenko and his English wife, Jan, in Sukhumi on the Black Sea where they have a house. We were not allowed by the Russians to stay with them but they met us at the airport in their Zhiguli and took us back to breakfast and then to our hotel. They drove us into the hills to visit the 6th century fort of Tibilium with the archaeologist who had excavated it. At an ethnic Armenian restaurant with a wood fire and cauldron of food hanging over it and meat hanging up to smoke above, we had a 'medium feast' of cheese, smoked meat, salad and wine while Zhenia regaled us with funny stories of his visit to Canada for a poetry conference and an elderly drunken American poet who snored and farted throughout the poetry sessions.

On a fine warm day we were driven at great speed across empty river beds, shallow streams and up stony inclines in the unprotesting Zhiguli while its owner quoted newly composed verses. We stopped at a pool heated by a geyser where Zhenia and Kathy splashed about in the water, scalding themselves as they tried to make a comfortable mix with the hot and cold water. We left again over the same route to catch our plane, sadly leaving the warm sunshine for a grey misty Moscow.

Friday 23 November

Although there was some displeasure on the Russians' part that the Kinnocks had stayed at the residence (Iain had felt particularly strongly that they should do this) they came in large numbers to the reception on 26th. Neil Kinnock appeared very mild on most issues but obviously hated every minute of the miners' strike. Glenys protested at one school teacher's rather provocative example of English pronunciation, using 'think, thank, Thatcher'! She stood up to the Deputy Head of the Peace Committee who branded the CND as lackeys of bourgeois imperialists and told them that she would demonstrate against all nuclear weapons, including the SS 20s.

We saw them off at the airport with what Healey called 'the same old mafia' in attendance. No doubt it can be considered a good visit. They were lucky in their timing, coinciding with the announcement of the meeting between Schultz and Gromyko in January. Even if the promise of reducing the nuclear threat is no more than empty rhetoric it could reflect a mood, a softening of the situation, in official terms.

7–17 December

Visit to England, Christmas shopping and seeing my parents and overlapping for 2 days with the visit of the Supreme Soviet delegation headed by Gorbachev, with Iain in attendance. This visit constituted a démarche to get to know the younger members of the Politburo and established the 'can do business with him' policy of the PM. We had an interesting meeting with Gorbachev and Mrs G; she is a Doctor of Philosophy but did not say what she was doing now. He gave an after dinner speech, jokey and without notes. It is not usually like this. Why were they doing it? From Afghanistan and SS 20s and tough US reaction, to trying to bring back 'parity'; from Soviet anger and accusations of escalation to each side climbing down, to a bargaining table, or is it all just hot air? As the Spectator *article by Timothy Garton Ashe says, all this talking means little in real terms of reductions of weapons, as have talks in the past, SALT, START and all the rest; just that talking is better than not talking. It could mean less increase in weaponry. It improves the international situation, the official situation, but it does not do much for human rights or personal relations. I have been told that the foreign affairs department of the university will not allow me to go there any more. This may be due more to the end of the Akhmanova era. She never asked permission for anything, as she has told me many times.*

It was a real, white, cold Christmas with lots of snow, immensely beautiful in the country and even in town. It was announced that Gorbachev was coming back to Moscow a day early but not why. All rumours indicated someone dead and as Judith said, 'He has to be back for the power struggle'. Later it was announced that General Ustinov had died and Gorbachev had told the press at Edinburgh airport. He carried out one part of the Scottish programme and then flew back to Moscow. The delegation flew in and so did Anne, James and Alex.

Monday 24 December

Continues very cold -15°C. In the morning was Ustinov's funeral – usual slow march, but only an urn in a niche in the wall. It was decided that no one should go, not even the Defence Attaché; seemed odd to me.

Friday 29 December

Our weekend at Zavidovo was more beautiful than last year and the food as good if not better. Elizabeth Furse was in great form which made the after dinner hour hilarious. Much colder, five layers not three needed outside but the skiing was very good. We took Anne for a sauna on the last night and left next day for the successful New Year party at the French Club for the young and not so young. Home about 2.30 a.m. but the young home for breakfast at 6.

Time passed imperceptibly during the week before they all had to go back. We talked and walked and did some more sightseeing – Gorky's house, Anne and E Furse on a very chaotic two day visit to Leningrad, Zagorsk, Swan Lake at the Bolshoi; and Peredelkino in two cars in a blizzard, James driving the Sierra. The trees covered in snow looked like ghostly figures. Had tea with Jan and Zhenia and stopped at the church on the way back where vespers for Russian Christmas Eve was just starting.

Wednesday 9 January 1985

A Dutch dinner for the Chinese, sitting next to the Chinese Ambassador Showzheng I asked him how he understood the Chinese interpretation of Marxist-Leninism. He said that China would take the best and fastest path to modernisation and it would be socialist. China would catch up with the west in 60 to 70 years at about the same time as Hong Kong would be released from the undertaking to keep its system going in the present form. So did they hope that by then conditions would be the same both sides of the border? They did not want a poor Hong Kong. It would be no use to them.

Saturday 12 January

Art Hartman came to lunch on his return from Geneva and the 'great talks about talks'. The subject is being treated exhaustively in all forms of media. Most UK papers treat it cautiously; the Spectator *(12/1/85) warns against thinking anything new or different or better is about to happen. 'We got a mouse', said Art. The 'Mouse' is an agreement to hold meetings on arms reduction on 3 levels; strategic, medium range and in space. The Americans refused to agree to stop research on SDI (Star Wars) and the Russians insist that the US space programme is offensive; Gromyko not as on the ball as in the past.*

Saturday 26 January

In the evening we finally managed to see Aitmatov's A day lasts longer than a century; *an excellent performance by Ulyanov as Edigei, who*

319

addresses the audience all the time, 'You see folks...' The cosmic element is portrayed successfully by lights, laser beams and sound, but it appears a much lesser theme than the human factor. The old Kazakh legend is much more moving – the boy whose head is bound by tight hoops until he loses his reason. The motive of manipulation is echoed in the attempt at communication with the people of another planet; and we have the final union of the human and cosmic elements as the four arrive at the ancient burial ground to find it is fenced in, having become part of the space programme and a forbidden area. There is much very obvious criticism of the ills of the Soviet system in the arrest and death of the schoolmaster, the loss of Kazangap's family in the destruction of the Tatars and the more general criticism of the great powers in their manipulation of space.

Friday 1 February

An interesting lunch with the ladies from the Shekhtel Museum. (Shekhtel was the interior designer of the Embassy residence.) They maintained that the house was all Shekhtel, and they destroyed various misconceptions about the house and its history. It is typical Shekhtel style with the heavy carving in the smaller rooms and white and gold in the grand room, as in the Morozov house, used by the MFA. There was a house here before the 1890s. Kharitonenko must have rebuilt it or changed it, not built it.

Friday 3rd–5 February

Iain's official trip to Siberia was nearly postponed because of a scare about Chernenko but we arrived in Novosibirsk in the evening after a peaceful sunny journey above the clouds and the snow. An early supper followed by a visit to the opera to see Traviata.
    The next day we drove to the Akademgorodok *(university town) outside Novosibirsk, past villages of wooden houses; first to the special school for mathematics and science, founded in 1963 by Academician Lavrentiev, the then head of the Siberian branch of the Academy of Pedagogical Sciences. It was the first of these schools to be set up in the SU. I was particularly interested because the special schools had been the subject of my MA thesis in 1976. We were taken round by the director, Bogachev, who explained how the pupils were chosen by 'olympiads', exams taken by thousands of school children, from the ages of 14–16... The aim of the school is to build up a cadre of*

specialists, to prepare children for higher education and to develop their scientific interests.[2]

There followed a leap round the Museum of Geology and Physics, visit to the President of the Siberian Branch of the Academy of Sciences, Koptyug; after lunch to the Institute of Economics (director Granberg) where talk centred on the problems of the development of Western Siberia, the general feeling at this time being that it should not be opened to foreigners. We met Zaslavskaia, the social scientist who was about to leave for a conference in Brighton, very realistic about the problems of attracting labour. Thence to the computer centre and finally, an addition to the programme, to the Institute of Nuclear Physics, the most incomprehensible for me but where the people were the friendliest; their main aim, they said, was to develop the use of nuclear power to take the place of other fuels. Lastly we were shown a tokamak experiment, involving a collision of synchrotons and neutrons.[3]

The next day was spent in Novosibirsk visiting the deputy chairman of the oblast executive committee where talk was again about the economy and education; from there to the special English School where most of the parents seemed to be electronic engineers or geo-physicists, and those pupils who did not want to be English teachers wanted to be scientists. The second, smaller Akademgorodok was an agricultural institute set up 15 years ago to solve the problems of feeding the community – a difficult job given that there are only 110 days a year free of frost. Winter rye and spring wheat are grown (they have not yet found a type of wheat strong enough to winter over); Hereford cattle are raised ('their kind'). We had little time to see the town before dark but the local supermarket had the usual row of preserves and household equipment, plus a few eggs and jars of jam. Everyone who works in the Akademgorodok receives special rations. We left Novosibirsk at 2.30 a.m. to travel to Ufa, the capital of the Bashkir autonomous republic (now Bashkortostan). In Ufa at four in the morning we were met by the Minister of Forestry and Tatiana, a teacher of English. At the hotel Rossiya we were given a 3 roomed suite and served caviar, tea and Bashkir sweetmeats and then left to rest until 11 in the morning.

Wednesday 6 February

We were taken out of town to inspect the site of the proposed petrochemical plant to be tendered for by British firms, an area surrounded by graceful woods which were to be uprooted, fields covered in snow and a village of wooden houses to be destroyed to build the plant. Even Abdullov, of the Minister of Forestry, was mildly saddened at the sacrifice of some of his trees. But they had looked everywhere and there was nowhere else in the area. Blagoveshchensk it had to be. They hoped we would come back to open the plant.

Monday 25 February

Showed the film Champions *to a mixed diplomatic and Russian audience – the story of the jockey who fights cancer to survive and win the Grand National; one scientist, a veterinary expert came; no one from the Oncological Institute. One lady apparently fainted. The next day I saw Paul Kamill, the Embassy doctor, about my lump. He thinks it not likely to be serious but I should go back before the end of the month. He would arrange an appointment at the Marsden. I could go ahead with the two weeks leave in Greece which had already been booked.*

Tuesday 12 March

Returned four days early from Greece for the funeral of Chernenko who died on 10th. His death was announced on Monday morning in Moscow and we heard the news on the radio in Aetos at lunch time; very hasty packing up, departure and drive to Eretria where we caught the last ferry to Oropos and reached Athens about 11 p.m. Malev airlines took us to Budapest at 4.30 a.m. and Aeroflot to Moscow got us back by 4 p.m. with just time to look round the house and find all ready. The Chancery and the residence staff knew the routine by now and had gone into 'funeral' mode. Mrs Thatcher, Geoffrey Howe, Kinnock, Steel and Owen arrived about 11 p.m.

Wednesday 13 March

Usual day of constant coffee, tea, drinks and food, starting with breakfast and laying a wreath at the Hall of Columns; funeral at 12, an hour later than usual. It seemed very perfunctory to us, the fourth state funeral since our arrival, including Ustinov on Christmas Eve. Gorbachev had been immediately appointed head of the funeral committee on Monday and General Secretary of the Communist Party of the Soviet Union by Tuesday; at last someone who may not die the next year. He gave the oration which was short and crisp, not aggressive or sentimental.

Lunch at 2.30 with the Conservatives at Iain's end and the opposition my end. Mrs Thatcher saw Mrs Ghandi, Shultz, and others during the morning and afternoon. There were always little huddles of people in different rooms. In the evening she dressed in her black chiffon to see Gorbachev followed by a press conference. She still likes him and 'thinks she can do business with him'; but he is wrong, she told him, about a nuclear freeze; it would merely freeze the imbalance. They had all left by 10 p.m.

Saturday 13 April, Orthodox Easter

Susan Harley and her son Robert arrived in the evening and we took them immediately to the midnight mass at the church of Our Lady of all Sorrows in the Bolshaia Ordinka. There was a great crush of people at midnight and we only just managed to get out with our candles.

Wednesday 8 May

After weeks of telegramming back and forth and discussing with the EEC colleagues – a decision was made. Iain is to attend all the celebrations for the 40th Anniversary of the Glorious Victory in the Patriotic War, the meeting, the wreath laying, the parade and the reception. Gorbachev read a long, rapid speech, giving meagre tributes to the Western Allies' activities during the war ('oh yes there was the second front but it was a bit late'). We did not stay for the second part – another eight speeches and a concert but went back to prepare for supper with Denis Healey and the two British Legion representatives. Denis was plugging a hard labour line, did not think G's speech was grudging, what did we expect if we did not send any proper representative? At least Mrs Thatcher could have sent Rifkind; and any way we could not have won the war without them and they probably could have won it without us; all good cheery banter.

The next day was the great day itself, the 40th Anniversary Parade and my first ever official attendance at a parade in Red Square. It was not very impressive but fairly gruesome; I do not like the goose stepping and all those missiles look not very new but very nasty. The reception was at 2 p.m. afterwards after a big traffic jam at the Kremlin entrance; completely out of hand with cars converging from 5 different directions; finally we arrived at the end of a speech which was apparently much friendlier than the day before. In the receiving line Gorbachev talked to Iain for 5 minutes while the line waited

*behind and the rest of the Politburo stood waiting too. He said that
we had had some problems but they were over now. Iain mentioned
his departure and hoped that he would see G before he left.*

Sunday 12 to Friday 15 May

*Iain made his official farewell visit to Leningrad. We were much better
received than on the last visit, managed to see the rector of the university
and all the English students and teachers there, were given a grand tour
of the Hermitage, taken to the Piskarevsky Cemetery where the victims of
the 1941–44 blockade were buried in 10 sets of mass graves containing
3000–4000 people. It is the most moving of all the war cemeteries and
memorials, with photographs of life during the blockade, featuring the
small piece of bread which was the daily ration, during the collection
of which many people collapsed and died in the street from hunger.*

*Iain called on Secretary, Zaikov, and I was taken to the Smolny
apartments, the former school for daughters of the nobility where Lenin
proclaimed the first Soviet state in 1918. At Iain's special request we
were allowed to visit the palace of Gatchina, given to Orlov, Catherine's
favourite, by her, afterwards lived in by her son Paul and becoming
in the 18th and 19th centuries the Tsar's summer residence. Before
returning to Moscow we made a short last visit to Novgorod, which I
had not seen since 1954. The cathedral of St. Sophia was looking as
splendid as ever.*

Friday 31 May

*Kathy Murrell and I left to drive to Uglich, having been given permission
only the afternoon before. No one stopped us at any time but they
probably did not know where we were as we took a wrong turning after
Yaroslavl and travelled on a very bad road, eventually arriving covered
in dust at 6 in the evening. The town was still small and peaceful like
Kostroma in the 1950s and we spent the next day wandering round
visiting the three main monasteries and the Kremlin. In the Church of St
Dimitri in the Blood, Boris Godunov's son reputedly had his throat cut,
possibly by his father although some sources suggest it was an accident.*

Wednesday 5 June

*Liz and a friend arrived on the evening plane to spend some of the last
days with us. From now on everything was a lead up to our departure*

and the days were filled with farewells and last meetings, of the literary group, of the Embassy wives, of Olga Sergeevna's dacha sessions, tennis games and last Russian lesson with Elena. Everyone discusses the new Gorbachev alcohol laws. O.S. thinks he must be very brave and courageous but her son finds it very difficult now to entertain visiting scientists without vodka and caviar. Irina thinks it is too late and should have been done 20 years ago. Nikiforov said it would repay the lost revenue in fewer working days lost in industry. I wonder. Lenin had a dry period in the 1920s and ended up withdrawing it and introducing NEP.

Farewell dinners with the Indians (a fairly sombre affair) with the French (a gourmet affair with great taste and elegance, and warmth too), lunch with Niphon (a large buffet very well organised as usual and a present of a St George icon), dinner with the Stevens where Mikoyan's son, Sergo, told me that there needed to be big changes or there would be a catastrophe – or nearly he corrected himself. Farewell lunch with the Yugoslavs and more speeches. Iain is doing very well with the speeches. The Foreign Office lunch was given by Ryzhov, a Deputy Minster of Foreign Affairs, instead of the traditional lunch by Gromyko, for which there was no explanation. I wondered afterwards if this was something to do with Gordievsky who must have been escaping the SU at this time, as we knew later. Iain felt it a serious snub. But he was allowed to make his TV broadcast.

Wednesday 12 June

The last QBP; too wet for the garden again although it did not actually rain until most people had gone at 8 o'clock. I spent the time saying goodbye to many people; so much more final here as it is more difficult to be sure of seeing them again. The next day the packers arrived early and the house was torn apart. They worked faster than I have ever known and would have finished by the late evening but we sent them away at 5 and told them to come back the next day to finish and take things away; just as well as we found 15 more pictures and other objects.

Saturday 15 June

The 60th birthday and we are still here. Iain must be one of the few to have stayed en poste after turning 60. It was too wet for a picnic party at Peredelkino so we had it by the fire in the Australian Embassy, a quiet group eating 'Commonwealth' chicken. Now we have to pack the suitcases. Sunday was at last a fine day and I had breakfast with the girls returning from Leningrad before all going to a picnic at the American dacha in our honour. We played tennis and had a delicious barbecued lunch, the French, the Germans, the Hartmans, we four, the American's Italian cook and family and the drivers.

In the evening we were invited to the 'dark bar' near Taganka by Judith, Lesley and George Edgar; had drinks and zakuski and watched the guests and the cock and hen who live in the light fixtures and sometimes alight on the guests. Back to the house for the birthday cake and its 60 candles and red Moldavian champagne on the terrace opposite the Kremlin.

Monday 13 June

This is the final stage. The car is to be packed ready by early Tuesday morning for Leonid to drive to Helsinki. This is called driving home to England but we are going by train to Helsinki and Leonid is to have his last trip to Finland before retiring at the same time as us. He is to meet us at Viborg station at 8 a.m. on Wednesday morning. This suits us all. Pre-lunch time drinks with the residence staff. The girls leave for the airport with Konstantin. In the evening was a dacha party given by the Embassy with a magnificent display of food and drink. There was a warm and friendly atmosphere and a chance to talk to everyone from the Embassy and the British community. Two exquisite miniature palekh boxes were given to Iain from the staff and one for me. We finished packing the car about 3.30 a.m. I am not sure where the last pieces will go but there is still the roof.

Tuesday 18 June

The final day was spent packing up presents for the residence staff and saying goodbye; lots of tears. The last presents bought, the last pictures taken and the last bits and pieces stuffed into the eight small pieces for the train.

After the wet day the evening was fine and the sun shone. As we left the Embassy the mist was rising over the Kremlin and the towers blurred in grey light as we drove over the Kuznetsky Most. Then the last view of the three stations, Shekhtel's Yarosklavsky, the elaborate Kazan and the more classical traditional Leningrad station where I first arrived 33 years ago.

As the train moved out of the station high buildings rose where once the countryside had extended in that wide limitless way of Russian horizons. Nearly half the Embassy had been at the station and nearly all the European Community. The large imposing VIP room was full.

Champagne flowed and Franz van Agt made a speech – a last speech about leaving in the traditional way on the chuff, chuff, train. Then climax – time to go. Donald started to pipe and piped us all the way to Wagon 10. All our friends surged after us down the station. Was it more splendid or ridiculous? One Russian raised his hands above his head in approval. Others looked on in surprise. I was saddened and touched by all the outstretched hands, faces raised to kiss. Then the emotion was broken by Guy de Muyser 'I refuse to look as though this was a funeral!'

This was the final departure – out into a steamy misty night on the 'Tolstoy' train – an Anna Karenina touch – Yasnaia Polyana on the curtains.

30. Final departure from Moscow in June 1985. Jeanne and Iain seen through the window of the train leaving Leningrad station, Franz van Agt, Netherlands Ambassador on the left.

EPILOGUE

Lord Brimelow writes: Your obituary of Sir Iain Sutherland gave the facts of his career. May I be allowed to add something about the man?

A career centred on countries under communist rule calls for special qualities. It calls for a sense of service, willingness to be posted more than once to a capital where the political climate may at times be acutely uncongenial, discretion, careful behaviour, cheerfulness, patience, the skills needed to interpret communist jargon, and the ability cautiously to evaluate the signs of change. It requires the ability to put up with frustration, since communist regimes are at pains to protect themselves against foreign influences. And it demands equanimity, given that years of diplomatic effort and patient promotion of trade may at any time be undone by outside events, such as a large-scale expulsion of spies, or the invasion of Afghanistan. It helps if the diplomat and his wife take an interest in the history, the culture and the people of the country to which they are assigned and make it their task to develop personal relations, within the limits of what is permitted, with such of its inhabitants as are less affected than bureaucrats by the ups and downs of inter-governmental relations. These qualities Iain and Jeanne Sutherland had in high degree.

Iain Sutherland was a man of reserved and sober judgement, and it took time to know him well. Both his parents had been distinguished Scottish painters, and when the family went on holiday, each child took a sketchbook. Iain was a rapid and amusing sketcher and when I first saw some of his drawings thirty-five years ago I thought he would have made an admirable illustrator of children's books. But having learnt young that drawing and painting were to be taken seriously, he did little in this field. He none the less took a scholarly interest in the art and

328

architecture of all the countries in which he worked, and it was because he had the eye of an artist that he so enjoyed his time in Indonesia.

He found pleasure in the vivacity of the Cubans at the beginning of Castro's regime – so much so that he was looking forward to revisiting Cuba in the retirement he was destined not to have. He delighted in the freedom and vigour of intellectual life at Harvard and in the frankness of relations with the Department of State in Washington. He liked those aspects of life in Yugoslavia which showed less constraint than life in the Soviet Union. It was however in Greece that he and Jeanne found it easiest to make the close personal friendships which underpin the best diplomacy. The messages that have come from Greece since Iain's sudden and early death have been many and most touching.

He found Moscow his most interesting and challenging post. When he was posted as Ambassador there, at a time of tension in Anglo-Soviet relations, he determined to retain and develop every permitted contact. He and his wife found that they were able to renew and build on personal relationships which they had first made in the easier conditions of the '70s. In that way, they succeeded, in spite of the strains in official relations, in expanding contacts in the world of letters and the arts, and Iain was glad to be able, before he left Moscow, to negotiate a new agreement on cultural exchanges.

In addition he and his wife travelled widely in remote parts of the Soviet Union, finding them full of interest and encountering much friendship among the people they met there.

Despite all the years he lived abroad, he kept close links with Scotland, and when he left Moscow it gave him much pleasure that the University of Aberdeen conferred upon him the honorary degree of LLD, as it had on his father before him.

Published in *The Times*, 10 July, 1986

NOTES

CHAPTER 1

1 Leonard Schapiro, *The Communist Party of the Soviet Union*, University Paperbacks, Methuen & Co Ltd, 1963, p. 519.
2 National Archives, FO 371/94804 NS 105/6 N of 19 January 1950, letter from Sally Leyland describing first impressions of Moscow.
3 FO 371 94908 NS 1632/1 of 4 January 1951, despatch from Sir David Kelly, British Ambassador.
4 Geoffrey Hosking, *A History of the Soviet Union*, Fontana Paperbacks and William Collins, London, 1985, pp.313–14.
5 Adam B. Ulam, *Stalin, the Man and His Era*, The Viking Press, New York, 1973 p.705.
6 Ulam, p.725.
7 Hosking, p.312.
8 Schapiro, pp.520–21.
9 Ministry of State Security.
10 NA, NS 10385/1 of 9 April 1952, from British Embassy, Moscow to Foreign Office. The interview granted by Stalin to the Indian Ambassador, but not to departing Western Ambassadors in Moscow, was thought to be granted because the Russians wished to impress eastern bloc delegates to the Moscow Economic Conference taking place at the same time.
11 Also NA, NS 1026/17 for Stalin's interview with M. Louis Joxe, the French Ambassador.

CHAPTER 2

1 George F. Kennan, *At a Century's Ending, Reflections 1982–95*, W.W. Norton & Co. New York and London, 1996, p. 40.
2 National Archives, FO 370 100819 NS 10262 letter from Embassy to the Foreign Office, 7 October 1952.

3 George F. Kennan, *At a Century's Ending, Reflections 1982–95*, W.W. Norton & Co. New York and London, 1996, p.41.
4 National Archives, F 370 199823 NS 10110/1, interim note prepared by Research Department of 22 August 1952.
5 NA, FO 370 100816 NS 10914/8 212, despatch of 24 October 1952.
6 NA, FO 370 100926 NS 1963/2 of 31 October 1952.
7 NA, FO 100926 NS 1963/4 telegram No. 612 from Moscow dated 7 November 1952.
8 NA, FO 106510 NS 1015/39 of 16 July 1953, Principal Events in Soviet Affairs January–June 1953.
9 G. Hosking, *A History of the Soviet Union*, Fontana Paperbacks and William Collins, London, 1985, pp.315–16.
10 NA, FO 371 106516 NS/10110/52 of 9 March 1953, from British Ambassador to Foreign Office.
11 NA ditto.
12 NA, FO 371 106517 NS 10111/2 of 7 March 1953, details of appointments made after Stalin's death.
13 NA, FO 371 106517 NS 10111/5 of 13 March 1953, despatch from Sir Alvary, analysis of changes.
14 NA, FO 371 106517 NS 10111/6 telegram No. 152 of 21 March 1953.
15 Leonard Schapiro, *The Communist Party of the Soviet Union*, Methuen & Co Ltd in association with Eyre and Spottiswoode, London, p.559.
16 NA, FO 371 106518 NS 10111/24, telegram No. 506 of 10 July 1953.
17 NA, FO 371 106518 NS 10111/32, despatch from Sir Alvary of 16 July 1953.
18 NA, FO 371 106518 NS 10111/38 of 12 July 1953, letter from Sir Alvary to Paul Mason of Foreign Office.
19 Schapiro, p.560.
20 Hosking, p.316.
21 In February a communiqué in the Soviet Press on the visit of British businessmen to Moscow detailed contracts for 192 million roubles and further Soviet orders for 550 million. NS 1013/9 of 17 February 1954.
22 NA, FO 371 111669 NS 1013/1 from British Ambassador, Sir William Hayter, of 31 January 1954.
23 NA, FO 371 111669 NS1013/3 from Sir William Hayter of 13 January, 1954.
24 NA, FO 371 111669 NS 1013/2 of 6 January 1954.
25 NS 1013/12 of 5 March 1954.
26 NS 1013/17 of 14 March 1954.
27 NS 1013/19 of 29 April 1954.
28 NS 1013/36 of 12 August 1954.

CHAPTER 3

1 G. Hosking, *A History of the Soviet Union*, Fontana and Collins, London, 1985, pp.321–25.
2 Dushko Doder, *The Yugoslavs*, Allen & Unwin, London, 1978, pp.18–19.

3 National Archives, FO 371-124167, RY1011/1 of 20 January 1956, Annual Report from H M Ambassador, Sir Frank Roberts.
4 National Archives ditto.
5 Isabel Emslie (Lady Hutton) worked in Scottish women's hospital units set up by Elsie Inglis, in Macedonia and Serbia. She received many awards and published various medical books as well as an account of her war experiences. When she died in 1960 she was Emeritus Consultant Psychiatrist to the British Hospital for Mental and Nervous diseases.
6 National Archives FO 371-124270, RY1015/34, 2 June 1956.
7 RY1015/43 of 13 August 1956.
8 RY1015/51 of 20 October 1956.
9 FO 371-124269 RY1015/13, telegram of 22 March 1956.
10 RY1015/19 of 9 April 1956.
11 RY1015/55 of 19 November 1956.
12 FO 371-130486, RY1051/1 of 7 January, 1957.
13 FO 371-130488, RY1015/3 of 18 January, 1957.
14 Bridge over the Don on the outskirts of Aberdeen.
15 Phyllis Auty, *Tito, A Biography*, Penguin Books, London, 1970, p.299, Note 21.
16 RY1915/7 of 28 January 1958 and FO 371-145107, RY1011/1 of 29 January.
17 FO 371-153394, RY 1015/2 of 12 January 1960.

CHAPTER 4

1 Luis Somoza of Nicaragua to Nicholas Woolaston, quoted in Hugh Thomas, *Cuba – or the Pursuit of Freedom*, Eyre and Spottiswoode Ltd., London, 1971, p.1091.
2 H. Johnson, *The Bay of Pigs*, Dell Publishing Co., Inc., New York, 1964, p.19.
3 Wayne Smith, *The Closest of Enemies*, W.W. Norton & Co., New York and London, 1987, quoted by M. Bromley, The US Government's Rejection of the Cuban Revolution, unpublished thesis.
4 H.L. Matthews, *The Cuban Story*, George Brazilier, 1961, pp.92–93 and p.246.
5 This was the explosion on board the French ship, the *Coubre*, which was bringing war material from Belgium, in which 75 Cuban dockers were killed and 200 injured. Castro blamed the US but had no proof.
6 There were never enough translators in the Embassy to cover the translation of all of Castro's long speeches. Lois Clark and I, who happened to be Spanish speakers, spent a lot of time translating them.
7 H.L. Matthews, pp.233–34.
8 H.L. Matthews, p.248.
9 Hugh Thomas, p.1234.
10 National Archives, FO 371/139402, 1959, AK/1015/120 of 24 July 1959.
11 Hugh Thomas, p.1208.
12 Hugh Thomas, p.1227.

13 National Archives, FO 371/139402, 1959, AK/1015/135 of 31 July, 1959, from Fordham.
14 Theodore Draper, *Castro's Revolution – Myths and Realities*, Praeger, New York, 1962, p.61.
15 Hugh Thomas, pp.1265–1271.
16 Hugh Thomas, p.1291.
17 National Archives, FO/371/148289, Ambassador Fordham in AK1462/1 of 6 July 1960 to Foreign Office.
18 Theodore Draper, p.80.
19 Hugh Thomas, pp.1301–1310.
20 Theodore Draper, pp.92–101.
21 Hugh Thomas, pp.1323–1330.
22 Hugh Thomas, pp.1314–1352.
23 'Every child, every Indian, every black, every woman…'
24 H.L. Matthews, pp.253 and 259.
25 FO 371 156159, AK 1021, from Iain Sutherland to Robin Edmonds, American Department, FO, 10 May 1961.
26 Hugh Thomas, pp.1355–1371.
27 National Archives, FO 371 156156, AK 1011/1 of 3 July 1961, initialled by IJMS.
28 National Archives, FO 371 156153, AK 1015/281, Castro's speech of 3 December 1961. The events referred to were presumably connected with the large scale expropriation of foreign firms.
29 National Archives, FO 371 162308, AK 1011/1 of 22 January 1962.

CHAPTER 5

1 J.F. Kennedy's acceptance address for the nomination as President of the USA, quoted in T.C. Sorensen, *Kennedy*, Hodder & Stoughton, London, 1965, p.167.
2 National Archives, FCO 371/162579, AU 1015/5 of 28 January 1962.
3 Hugh Thomas, *Cuba – or the Pursuit of Freedom*, Eyre & Spottiswoode Ltd., London, 1971, pp.1396–1400.
4 Hugh Thomas, pp.1403–1415.
5 FO 371/162581 - AU1015/36 of 12 August 1962.
6 FO 371/168405 - AU1011/1 Despatch No 1 from Sir David Ormsby Gore to Lord Home, extract from the Annual Review of 1962.
7 FO 371/162643 - AU1833/2 of 2 November 1962.
8 Sorensen, *Kennedy*, p.470.
9 Sorensen, *Kennedy*, pp.493–504.
10 Sorensen, *Kennedy*, p.503.
11 FO 371/168407 - AU10114/38 of 1.12.63.
12 FO 371/168406 - AU 10114/21, letter from British Ambassador in Madrid to Dodson at Foreign Office.
13 Sorensen, *Kennedy*, p.756.

14 Anthony Summers and Robyn Swan, *Sinatra, the Life*, Doubleday, 2005.
15 FO 371/174261, AU1011/1 of 2 January 1964, Sir David Ormsby Gore to Secretary of State Butler.
16 www.course-notes.org/biographies/lyndonbjohnson.htm
17 FO 371/1742272.
18 FO 371/179557 of 4 January 1965 - Annual Review for 1964.
19 FO 371/179558/AU1015/2 of 8 January 1965.
20 FO 371/179558 - AU1015/8 of 15 March.
21 FO 371/184995 - AU 1011/1 of 18 February 1966.

CHAPTER 6

1 *The Times Concise Atlas of the World*, Times Books, London, 2000. p.56.
2 L.H. Palmier, *Indonesia*, Thames and Hudson, London, 1965, p.13.
3 L.H. Palmier, p.27.
4 L.H. Palmier, pp.73–112.
5 Sukarno, *The New Encyclopaedia Britannica*, Chicago, 1987, p.361.
6 *The New Encyclopaedia Britannica*, p.361.
7 Peter Polomka, *Indonesia since Sukarno*, Penguin Books Ltd., England, 1971, p.21.
8 National Archives FCO 15 - 154 DH 1/1 of 5 January 1968 Annual Revue 1967.
9 FCO 15/170 DH/16 of 2 January, 1968 from Iain Sutherland to Donald Murray, head of South East Asia Department.
10 FCO 15/172 DH/20 of 15 March 1968 from Ambassador to Secretary of State, George Brown.
11 Peter Polomka, *Indonesia since Sukarno*, p.114–115 Note (1).
12 FCO 24/446 letters from Alan Mason to David Le Breton in the South West Pacific Department in March 1969.
13 FCO 24/445 1/16 of 19 August, Iain's covering letter to Suharto's 'Address of State'.
14 Peter Polomka, pp. 192–94.
15 The Soames affair concerned the suggestion by de Gaulle in 1969 to the British Ambassador in France of the possibility of France allying with the UK to create a free trade area. Prime Minister Harold Wilson leaked de Gaulle's proposals to Germany, provoking loud cries of betrayal by the French. De Gaulle resigned some months after and in 1971 the UK joined the Common Market.

CHAPTER 7

1 Paul Johnson, *A History of The American People*, Weidenfeld & Nicholson, pp.731–32.
2 Paul Johnson, pp.743–45.

3 *National Encyclopedia*, p.732.
4 This version of events was in 2007 said to be untrue and it has been admitted that the cause of the war was a 'pre-emptive strike' by Israel, although not many people knew at the time.
5 Obituary of Rose Mary Woods, personal secretary to President Nixon. *The Times*, 25 January, 2005.
6 The Attorney General, Elliot Richardson resigned rather than accede to the President's request to dismiss the special Watergate prosecutor, Archibald Cox, to prevent further damaging revelations in the case. Deputy Attorney General Ruckhaus resigned for the same reason and Cox was finally dismissed by the third in line in the Justice department. Cox's successor, Jaworski, was said to be 'implacable in pursuit of the facts'. (FCO 82/420 AMV1/7 from the British Ambassador, Sir Peter Ramsbotham's marathon despatch, The Fall of a President, 1 October 1974.)
7 National Archives REM 15/1992 25 October 1973 letter from the British Ambassador Lord Cromer to Sir Alec Douglas-Home.

CHAPTER 8

1 William Thompson, *The Soviet Union under Brezhnev*, Pearson Education Ltd. 2003, pp.17–21.
2 *Brezhnev Reconsidered*, ed. Bacon and Sandle, Palgrave Macmillan, London, 2002, p.13.
3 Terence Garvey, *Bones of Contention*, Routledge and Kegan Paul, London and Henley, 1978, p.70.
4 *Brezhnev Reconsidered*, p.91.
5 Terence Garvey, *Bones of Contention*, p.70.

CHAPTER 9

1 *Greece in the 1980s*, ed. Richard Clogg, Macmillan Press Ltd., London and Basingstoke, 1983, p.vii.
2 *Greece in the 1980s*, p.ix.
3 'In ascending order of difficulty, there were three Aegean problems: control of the air space, the extent of territorial waters and rights on the continental shelf under the sea. The last of the three gave rise to the most serious incidents because of the prospect of oil deposits (which were in fact found in commercial quantities close to the indisputably Greek island of Thassos).' C.M. Woodhouse, *Modern Greece, A Short History*, Faber & Faber, London, 1991, p.317.
4 *Greece in the 1980s*, p.41.
5 'When Zeus and other gods were dining at the table of Tantalus, the host proceeded to test the omniscience of the deities. He cut up and cooked his son Pelops. All the gods knew what had happened, and refused to eat. All

that is, except Demeter, who at this time was still distracted by the loss of her daughter; she ate from one of the shoulders, with the result that when Pelops was restored by Zeus to his original shape it was necessary to add a piece of ivory. Tantalus was punished for the crime buy being eternally hungry and thirsty ...'. Michael Senior, *Greece and its Myths, A Travellers' Guide*, Victor Gollancz Ltd., London, 1978, pp.208–9.

6 As described by Paddy Leigh Fermor himself, *In Tearing Haste, Letters Between Deborah Devonshire and Patrick Leigh Fermor*, edited by Charlotte Moseley, John Murray, London, 2008. Caption to photograph opposite p.103.

7 'When Karamanlis reluctantly withdrew Greece from the military side of NATO in 1974, in response to popular feeling that NATO had made Turkey's invasion of Cyprus possible, he never intended the withdrawal to be permanent.' Greece, article in *The Economist*, by Michael Wall, December 16, 1978, pp.645–67. The Greek government was seeking ways to return to the fold, but the problem was complicated by the Aegean question, involving the Greek islands lying off Turkey's shores and the surrounding seas.

8 'Negotiations (over the presence of the American bases in Greece) were begun and suspended several times between 1977 and 1983.' C.M. Woodhouse, *Modern Greece, A Short History*, Faber and Faber, London: Boston, 1991, p.319.

CHAPTER 10

1 W. Thompson, *The Soviet Union under Brezhnev*, Pearson Education Ltd., 2003, p.112.

2 For more details see J.E. Sutherland, *Schooling in the New Russia*, Macmillan Press Ltd., 1999, pp.24–26.

3 The term *tokamak* is a transliteration of the Russian word *mokamak* which comes from the Russian words toroidal'naia kamera v magnitnykh katushkakh (toroidal chamber in magnetic coils). It was invented in the 1950s by Soviet physicists Igor Yevgenievich Tamm and Andrei Sakharov (who were inspired by an original idea of Oleg Lavrientiev).

BIBLIOGRAPHY

Auty, Phyllis, *Tito, A Biography*, 1970

Bromley, M., *The US Government Rejection of the Cuban Revolution*, unpublished thesis, 1999

Clogg, Richard (ed.), *Greece in the 1980s*, 1983

Clogg, Richard, *A Short History of Modern Greece*, 1979

Djilas, Milovan, *The New Class*, 1957

Doder, Dushko, *The Yugoslavs*, 1978

Draper, Theodore, *Castro's Revolution, Myths and Realities*, 1962

Garvey, Terence, *Bones of Contention*, 1978

Hosking, G., *A History of the Soviet Union*, 1985

Johnson, H., *The Bay of Pigs*, 1964

Johnson, Paul, *A History of the American People*, 1997

Kennan, George F., *At a Century's Ending, Reflections 1982–95*, 1996

Matthews, H.L., *The Cuban Story*, 1961

Moseley, Charlotte (ed.), *In Tearing Haste, Letters Between Deborah Devonshire and Patrick Leigh Fermor*, 2008

National Archives, *FO & FCO files*, 1951–73

The New Encyclopaedia Britannica, 1987

Palmier, L.H., *Indonesia*, London, 1965

Polomka, Peter, *Indonesia since Sukarno*, 1971

Schapiro, L., *The Communist Party of the Soviet Union*, 1963

Senior, Michael, *Greece and its Myths, A Travellers' Guide*, 1978

Smith, Wayne, *The Closest of Enemies*, 1987

Sorensen, T.C., *Kennedy*, 1956

Summers, Anthony and Swan, Robin, *Sinatra, the Life*, 2005

Sutherland, J.E., *Schooling in the New Russia, Innovation and Change*, 1999

Thomas, Hugh, *Cuba – or the Pursuit of Freedom*, London, 1971

Thompson, W. *The Soviet Union under Brezhnev*, 2003

The Times Concise Atlas of the World, 2002

Ulam, Adam R., *Stalin, the Man and His Era*, 1973

Woodhouse, C.M., *Modern Greece, A Short History*, 1991

INDEX

INDEX

INDEX